You Can Begin Again:

Hope for the Walking Wounded

By
Alisha Lance

PRESS

You Can Begin Again:
Hope for the Walking Wounded

Contents

To my three children

Remember ye not the former things, neither consider the things of old. Behold, I will do a new thing; now it shall spring forth; shall ye not know it? I will even make a way in the wilderness, and rivers in the desert.

—Isaiah 43:18–19

Acknowledgments

I want to thank and honor the people who have helped me as I have lived the life about which I have written in the pages of this book:

My parents, who taught me many principles of the Bible without knowing it, by their examples of morality and integrity.

My three children, who have filled my life with joy.

My friend, Nora B., who introduced me to Jesus Christ and in turn set me on a course planned by the living God.

I also want to thank the people who assisted me in the preparation of this book:

Dorothy G., my dear friend who encouraged me and with her tape recorder helped me begin the writing of my first draft.

Laurie R., my daughter and sister in Christ, for her constant love and encouragement as well as God's talents in her; and for her willingness to be an honest, discerning sounding board for the writing of my first draft.

Gaye H., my friend and former manager of a city newspaper, whose experience and appreciation for the written word were to my benefit as she critiqued my first draft and enthusiastically encouraged me to persevere to publication.

Glyn B., whose steadfast, sensitive, and loving friendship has been a source of joy, inspiration, and encouragement to me; and for her honest and incisive comments after giving her time to critique my final draft.

Susie C., whose friendship has remained warmly present, and who graciously supported me in the early years to *tell* my story and encouraged me in the latter years to *write* my story; as well as for having generously critiqued my final draft, offering valued observations with her common-sense perspective.

Cara S., for her enduring friendship and faith in this book from day one; for her sense of humor brought to this project; and for her tireless and patient dedication to the typing and retyping from tape recordings, my scribbled writings, and edited pages throughout the process to the completion of my first manuscript draft.

Judy R., who believed in this book and shared my foresight to *see* the reader audience it was meant for and to pray me closer to shaping it into an *instrument* for the Lord to draw them and meet their needs; and for her keen, responsive mind and invaluable, honest, penetrating insights contributed as she assisted me in the editing of my final draft.

My heartfelt gratitude goes out to the aforementioned, but especially to my daughter, Cara, and Judy, who held the vision for this book. Without their constant love, encouragement, and ministry of God's Word to my family and me, I could not have taken on a project of this magnitude.

Finally, I thank my loving, healing Jesus, who by His Spirit miraculously intervened in my life and gave me immeasurably more than I could ever have asked, imagined, or dreamed. To Him, the living God, be all the glory for His works in my life.

-A.L.

A Word from the Author

Never in my wildest imagination would I have believed I would write a book. But then, neither would I have believed I would speak to thousands of people throughout my state and beyond in public forums, on television, and over numerous radio broadcasts. Nevertheless, God opened doors for me to do just that: to tell my story—and now to have written my story. It is not the story of a great woman, but the story of a great God, who proves Himself when challenged and shares Himself when invited in.

The re-creative power of God's redemptive touch can reach His children anywhere—whether they are living in the most ideal or in the most extreme conditions imaginable! This is the central theme of my book, and I am living proof of that truth. I wrote this book to help you comprehend God's unfailing love and sovereign intervention in the lives of His children. I offer you, not an alternative source of help for the conditions in which you live, but what I have come to know as the *ultimate* source of help—Jesus Christ. I promise what God has done for me, He can do for you.

Great numbers of people who have heard my *spoken* story have believed and trusted God for themselves and now tell their own triumphant stories. I pray that while reading my *written* story, you too will be inspired to believe and trust God, so *you can begin again* and tell *your* triumphant story.

I thank my living God, Jesus Christ, for performing His Word in my life and leading me by His Spirit on an exciting love journey through extraordinary experiences, and for the retelling of them in this book. Only some names and descriptions of characters, dates, and locations have been changed to protect privacy. The facts are absolutely true.

- A. L.

Part 1
The Wounding

Prologue

Rude Awakening

It seems like several lifetimes ago since that dreaded January morning in 1985. The past and God's amazing grace are forever with me, and I remember it all.

Moving back in time and space to that morning in the bedroom of my former home, I was alone in my bed. The faint sound of a tree branch softly brushing against the windowpane, gently stirred me. Now I was fully awake. It was just before dawn.

The night-light low on the wall beams a sunburst pattern across the ivory carpet, illuminating a path to the adjoining bathroom, leaving half of the room in shadows. Its soft glow is reflecting in the mirror over the triple-wide dresser against the opposite wall; I see a glint of sparkle in the clear cut-crystal vase with silk flowers and the dim luster of silver frames holding family photographs atop the polished cherry wood surface. Bookshelves line one wall, filled with books I have read and some waiting to be read. The far corner of the draped window-wall is in shadows, but the silk brocade gleams vividly on the lower half of the pale gold lounge chair. The table beside it holds a reading lamp that has an ivory ginger jar base, hand-painted with a delicate oriental design from which only touches of shimmering gold are visible. It is my special corner of the room.

My daughter once said when she sat in this room, the décor made her feel pampered. I was glad I had made the changes after my husband left our home six months before and it had become *my* bedroom. It was still traditional, with its eighteenth-century-style furnishings, but I had created a softer, more feminine look, with a new comforter and matching drapery in a pattern of English roses in muted gold, pink, white, and lavender on an ivory background, and a silk floral arrangement of English roses in the same colors. Throw pillows in luscious shades of pale lavender, blush pink, and cream accessorize the bed. This combination of pastels against ivory carpet and walls did make for a soft, plush-looking but comfy, restful space.

I had to agree; it was, indeed, "girly" and pampering—just what I needed now. It was the only room in the house I had redecorated. Our home was not a mansion, but it was spacious, and I had spent time and thought to make it a comfortable, attractive, and peaceful haven for my family.

I reached over to turn off the alarm before its shrill sound could break the winter morning silence. Slipping into my robe, I walked to the window-wall of glass, drew open the drapery, pulled back the sheer white curtain, and peered out as I did every morning. A misty fog still hung over the ice-covered lake below.

Normally at the break of dawn, from this high, panoramic view illuminated by the moon, our rolling landscape with its many snow-laden trees surrounding the lake reminded me of a peaceful winter scene on a Christmas card. But this early, blustery morning, a harsh wind bent the trees and churned and swirled the freshly fallen night snow. It was anything but peaceful. The sky looked bitter, eerie.

Suitable for today, I thought, with a tinge of sarcasm laced with my own bitterness. It was the norm for me to wake up in a good mood, and usually I felt cheerful and ready to meet the day. But today was different.

This is the dawning of a new day for me, I sighed. Thoughtful for a moment, I took a deep breath and exhaled, groaning in a barely audible whisper, "And a new life, for that matter... a new life I never would have chosen." Unexpectedly, an involuntary shiver startled me.

Dropping the curtain, I grabbed myself, pulling my robe closer to my body in a reflex response, as if to shake off the sudden fear that enveloped me. That same fear had become familiar during the last year, even more so in the last six months, striking from time to time and turning my stomach topsy-turvy whenever I thought about my unknown future—alone.

Moving to the bookshelf, I reached up to the second row and behind Tolstoy's *War and Peace* for my hidden journal and carried it with me back to bed. Turning on the light, I propped my pillows, slid in, quickly pulled up the blanket, and opened my journal to the next blank page.

For years I had kept a personal journal, recording my life events. Only God and my journals really knew my heart. I had been the wife of Alexander Lance most of my life, so most of my life—our life—had been recorded. So much had happened in twenty-six years; there were the good times and the bad times.

Today, I sighed, staring at the blank page, without writing, *I feel desperately insecure… about the days and years to come… my whole life for that matter.* Despite my mild hysteria, I would put this early morning hour to good use. Writing my thoughts and feelings was always, somehow, therapeutic.

Picking up my pen from the nightstand, I began to write, just as I had each day when I found quiet time for myself.

January 15, 1985
D-Day!

Today has to be the worst day of my life! I've been through many difficult things in the past, but nothing has been as difficult to deal with as this. Well, I guess I shouldn't be so quick to declare this. I've experienced some pretty terrifying things in the past. I don't know though. Is facing death worse? This feels like death. It is a kind of death—the death of my marriage, of my family as I've known it. What awaits me this morning will mark the end of my life with Alex (why do I still avoid the "D" word?) and the beginning of the first day of the rest of my life. But I don't feel happy or hopeful about starting a new life today. Instead, I feel sad, emotionally fragile. I still don't understand. Why did he do it? …

A mournful sigh escaped me and I paused, resting my pen between the pages. Inching slightly away from the headboard to straighten my back, I found myself staring absentmindedly into the mirror across the room. Suddenly I was startled by my own image staring back at me. I leaned forward, eyeing my reflection critically. I had held up pretty good for pushing fifty. I was still slender, and my skin, gratefully like my mother's, had been slow to wrinkle—so far.

But no one can hold back time. I could not help seeing changes in my make-up mirror every day. I hoped to age gracefully, like my mother. However, unlike Mom, whose beautiful hair had been black as a raven when she was young, changed naturally to salt and pepper when she was my age, and was now white as snow, my unchanging, dark brown hair came out of a bottle. So much for aging gracefully. That appraisal served to point out other changes that had come with time and the natural progression of my aging as well as the changes that had come to my long-term marriage.

A shiver went through me as simultaneously my image in the mirror caught my attention again. My critical assessment also pointed out, for the umpteenth time, my husband's rejection of me and his having chosen a younger woman for his future. The rejection moved over me like a dark ominous cloud.

I gave Alex the best years of my life. I feel like a prized new car he just had to have—a car he loved to drive and maintain until with a little age, a few slight "dings" appeared on the body to mar its new-looking finish; and maybe an operating glitch under the hood caused it to lose some of its former speed, so it no longer gave him the same thrill it once had. I guess he thought he got as much mileage out of me as he could. And because I was no longer in pristine condition, he traded me in for not just another same model, but a much younger one; a new upgraded model that perhaps had more pizzazz, more speed; that was more fun to drive; and maybe even gave him back that youthful thrill.

Another sad thought occurred to me, whether or not a valid one: *No one is happy about their divorce. No one wants to break up their family, unless they have someone to move on with ... a life waiting for them.*

That thought triggered anger and resentment, mixed with pain, within me, and the pressure of it began intensifying as though a steel band were wrapped around my chest, being pulled tighter and tighter, taking my breath away. I gasped. Firmly grabbing hold of my pen again, I recorded my thoughts and emotions with reckless abandon:

Later this morning the cycle of solid, long-term marriages in my family will be broken by Alex and me. This pain of the last three years has brought me lower than ever. It is deep, wounding, emotional pain in my woman's heart. Right now I feel as war-torn and battle-weary as I did all those years before God rescued me. My emotions are like a yo-yo, going up and down, up and down. This pain does feel the same, but I have to keep reminding myself that I am markedly different from that naïve, idealistic new bride—and radically different from that emotionally insecure, abusively controlled, codependent, hopeless wife I had become after only seven years of marriage...

"There is hope! Always, hope. Because God is with me," I whispered to myself. Actually, I had good reason to be positive despite my painful emotions. My confidence in God and His Scriptures had done so much in me and for me.

Thoughtful now, I reminded myself of how that one experience had been the turning point, the beginning of my new life. It had also been the turning point in my marriage—until three years ago, when, unexpectedly, a turning point in Alex's life had thrust me into what felt like the abyss. With that turning point, this anxious January morning I, also, would be thrust into a new, albeit uninvited, unwanted life—alone.

Heaving a deep sigh, I thought to myself, *Life has a way of changing when we least expect it. My world changed overnight.* But in reality, I knew that was not true. Three years later, my questions were not new, but this morning they were more poignant than ever as I turned the page on my journal to continue:

Did he just wake up one morning three years ago and decide he no longer wanted me, his family, and his Christian life as it was; but rather he wanted a younger woman and a different kind of life? Did the money make him lose his consciousness of God? Was it male midlife crisis? I don't know. All I know now, Lord, is that it hurts so badly. It hurts because I know it didn't have to be this way. I think I would die of a broken heart this morning if not for You, Lord. Still, I confess I do feel frightened at facing the unknown as a single woman in my middle years. I don't know how to walk into my future alone. The children have been there for me to draw from their emotional courage to withstand their father's frenzied behavior throughout our yearlong court hearings. They are here for me today. But I can't expect them to be here to help me make this frightening transition into my future. They're in college preparing for their own futures...

Usually, Michael, Laura, and Steven were up by now getting ready for classes or work, but no alarms, no muffled sounds of music from their clock radios were heard behind their closed doors this morning. They had chosen to stay home today. "We want to be here for you, Mom," they had said.

I am grateful for my caring children and love them so. Yes, I do need their emotional support, especially today; but they also need mine. They're hurting too. All of our lives will be changed in just a few hours from now. Lord, we need Your strength this morning. With You I know we'll get through this together!...

I leaned my head back against the headboard, thinking about that last recorded sentence. It had been more confident.

My pen raced across the page again, telling my journal what my heart knew:

Without question it was You, God, who brought the four of us through these last three traumatic years. I have no regrets about our marriage, because it has blessed me with three fine children. Although imperfect like their parents, I know they have become confident individuals who are sensitive, compassionate, and courageous. No, Lord, regardless of what I know will take place later this morning in that courtroom, I can have no regrets for my twenty-six-year union with Alex.

After I committed my life to You, Jesus, and Alex had too, there was never a doubt that we would be married forever. I know I can't be the first wife, Christian or not, who believed her marriage would last forever, only to learn she was wrong. There are probably Christian women like me out there. I just don't know where they are...

I moaned at the thought but went on recording my feelings on the matter:

Each of those Christian women, wherever they are, probably believed as I, that they and their husbands, their families, would live happily ever after. But I've learned a hard reality lesson: I am not exempt from this kind of trial because I have been a faithful Christian wife and have had a public ministry to women nor because I had a Christian husband and enjoyed a Christian family life for twelve years. Unless both husband and wife are equally committed to their marriage vows, there are no guarantees, Christian or not, for happily ever after. I had no way of knowing three years ago that today I would be writing the last pages of our married life.

Chapter 1

The End from the Beginning

Buzz-z-z-z-z-z-z-z-z!
I gasped, catching my breath, startled by the alarm from Laura's clock radio piercing the early morning silence. Instantly she turned it off. The house was quiet again. Laura and I were the only ones who had to get up early. She wanted to accompany me to the courthouse—and I was grateful. Michael and Steven were sleeping in. They would be here for emotional support when we returned home.

Suddenly I was aware that daylight had been creeping through the wall of glass until it filled my bedroom. Without sunshine, however, it was still dismal, gloomy.

My journal lay open on my lap, the pen resting between pages, marking the place where I had left off on my "D-Day" entry. I read the last line: *"I had no way of knowing three years ago that today I would be writing the last pages of our married life."*

"Sad. So sad," I muttered, taking hold of the pen to write my next thoughts:

There is no more room in my heart for pain. It is full. This new emotional pain of our last three years is not unlike the old pain of our early years that caused me to turn to You, Lord, over and over again—until finally pressing me heart and soul into You. Lord,

You rescued me then, and Your amazing grace has been with me through it all...

"Yes," I whispered under my breath, "God has seen it all—the end from the beginning."

With that, bittersweet memories intruded on my mind, like an uninvited guest—memories of Alex and me when we were deeply in love and on the threshold of marriage, sharing the same hopes, dreams, and expectations for our life together. Tears trickled from the corners of my eyes as I allowed myself to recall how it had all begun.

It was summer 1959, a gentle time in our nation, when love, honor, commitment, and integrity were common virtues among people. It was a time when life was simpler, when marriage and family meant everything, and when young people still believed in the American dream. And so it was with me.

The American dream unfolded for me on that beautiful, sunny blue-skied July morning. I awakened early.

"It's your wedding day, Alisha," I whispered to myself.

I looked wistfully around my room. A bookcase next to my bed held my favorite books, my high school yearbooks, and other memorabilia. I had slept in this room for all of my twenty-three years, sharing it with my sister, Mary, until her marriage. This would be the last time I would call it "my room."

I looked up at my wedding gown, its ivory satin shimmering from where it hung on the closet door. I had designed and sewn every inch of it, and on this wonderful day, its iridescent beads and seed pearls sparkled and danced through the streams of sunlight shining into the room. I hoped Alex, my bridegroom, would like it.

At the thought of Alex, I bounded out of bed. Turning on my bath water full force, I poured perfumed bath crystals into the tub, watching them foam into a mountain of bubbles. Then, rolling up a hand towel to place under my neck, I stepped gingerly into the tub and slid down into the hot, fragrant water. I slipped the rolled towel behind my neck, leaned my back against the cold porcelain, and let my body relax as I inched deeper and deeper into the white froth.

Closing my eyes, I went over my mental to-do list. Everything checked!

"In only two hours, you'll be Mrs. Alexander Lance, you lucky girl," I said aloud.

"Alex," I sighed, as I thought about my good fortune.

There was no question, no apprehension, no fear today about the man I was marrying. I was totally content. The blissful feeling of the soothing water and the luxurious, warm cocoon the bubbles created for me made me feel delightfully pampered.

"I'm lucky." I smiled as I assessed Alex's attributes. He had all the qualities I hoped for in a husband. *He's loving and kind to me. He's thoughtful and caring of me. Oh, there are so many good things about him,* I sighed, as my mind happily settled on the man who would soon be my husband.

Alex was intelligent—sometimes a little too serious, but he also knew how to have fun.

And he's definitely a man given to good hygiene! I thought, with a smile that broke into a giggle. "That's a plus!" I said aloud to myself, thinking about how meticulous Alex was about everything—his person, his clothing, and even his new black Chevy.

"Alex is responsible too," I muttered. Pride filled my heart as I recalled how he had carried a full schedule in college while working nights and then studying into the wee hours of the morning. I knew that had been difficult for him, but I also knew Alex was hardworking and ambitious to achieve his goals.

In addition, Alex was a gentleman. He had a certain, almost enticing, charm about him that attracted people to him immediately, especially when served up with his boyish grin. He was articulate and polished, and had a maturity uncommon to most twenty-six-year-olds.

"He's principled!" I whispered. That was important to me. *Principled* described the other man in my life, my father. How lucky I was to have him too. Dad was a good man—good to his wife and children, and good to others. Alex admired my parents.

The good qualities I saw in Alex were those I had seen displayed in my mother and father, qualities that worked in harmony for their marriage partnership. I had not always been conscious of how their qualities and partnership dictated my criteria for a life mate and my own marriage, but it was always there, deep inside me. Naturally, that was what I wanted for my marriage.

Alex also liked to socialize, despite his usual quiet nature when we were alone. Pondering this, I remembered how he had handled himself with ease during the first large social gathering with my family and relatives, and the several that followed during our engagement period. He liked being with my family. He especially liked their warm hospitality, and he always enjoyed being part of our Sunday dinners. Usually relatives and friends gathered around our table, delighting in Mom's sumptuous, delicious meals—all of us taking pleasure from the easy, open conversation that flowed.

Alex fit perfectly into my family; most importantly, he was the perfect mate for me. I loved him deeply, and I knew he loved me. I was "the love of his life," as he had once written to me in a letter.

I lingered in the tub, reveling in all our hopes and dreams, fantasizing about the wonderful life Alex and I would make for ourselves and the family we would have one day. Thoughts of Alex and his love for me tenderly touched all my senses, like the lofty white foam covering my body and surrounding my shoulders with the smell of rose petals. Inhaling the sweet aroma gave rise to a vision of the bouquet of white roses and lilies of the valley I would carry to meet my groom.

Breathing a rapturous sigh, I stepped from the tub and slipped into my monogrammed white terrycloth robe, the one I had made for my trousseau. I had sewn a matching robe for Alex, along with matching monogrammed white beach towels for our honeymoon on the ocean. Reaching up to my left shoulder, my fingers softly caressed the Old English styled "L" embroidered with black silk thread, the capital letter of the new name I would take in little more than an hour.

Mother came into my bedroom a few minutes later to help me dress. When every button had been fastened, I looked into the mirror at myself, all 105 pounds of me. My dark brown hair was very long, but I had put it up into a French twist for this special day. Mother placed the crownlike wreath of pearl flowers on my head. A very fine, double-layer white nylon net waist-length veil hung from the back of it.

"You look beautiful," Mother said.

"You look beautiful too, Mom," I said proudly, hugging her for the last time as her single daughter.

My parents and I arrived at the church a few minutes early and were greeted by Alex's best man, Jim. Holding the heavy carved oak door wide open so that I and my billowing skirts could sweep through, he smiled at me.

"You look beautiful, Alisha!"

"Thanks, Jim. So do you," I smiled back.

Leaning closer, he whispered, "Are you sure you know what you're doing, marrying Alex?"

What a jokester! "Why do you ask that, Jim?" I laughingly responded, waiting for his pursed lips to curl into a smile. They did not.

"I only want you to be sure about what you're doing," he said somberly. "Alex isn't always the way he seems."

Still thinking he was teasing, I searched his eyes for a twinkle. There was none.

"What do you mean?" I demanded, confused. Before he could answer, the groomsmen were summoned to join Alex and my brother, CJ, in the anteroom.

I was stunned. Troubling thoughts flooded my mind, because Jim's words were not the only unsettling ones I had heard in the last twenty-four hours.

My father had called me aside the previous evening after arriving home from our wedding rehearsal and dinner.

"Alisha," he had said, "if you get to the altar tomorrow and decide you can't go through with it, it's okay."

"What do you mean, Dad?" I had asked, astounded.

"Well, if you can't say I do, just remember that your mother and I won't be embarrassed."

"Dad, is there some reason why you're saying this to me now— the night before my wedding? It's a little late, don't you think? Do you have a problem with me marrying Alex?"

"No," he had answered patiently. "I just wanted you to know how we feel."

And then there was the recurring dream—the nightmare—the one I had been having night after night for the past month. The memory sent chills through me, now:

My arm is securely placed in my father's arm as we walk the long aisle. My eyes are lovingly fixed on my waiting groom, dressed in his spotless white tuxedo. As I near the altar, fear grips me and I stop, frozen in horror. My groom has no face! I can see only an empty black hole. "Oh God, who am I marrying?" I cry frantically.

In my dream, I never made it to the altar.

One night my mother heard me crying, as I always did after waking from that repetitive nightmare. Comforted by her presence, I described the dream.

"It's just wedding jitters!" Mom shrugged. "Don't worry."

Our priest, Father Maloney, told me the same thing a few days later, just two weeks ago, when in desperation I met with him to ask if my dream was a warning from God that I should not marry Alex.

"It's just a dream, nothing more," he said. "Don't worry. Alex loves you very much, and he's a fine young man. He'll make you a good husband. Forget the dream. Just marry Alex and be happy!"

I did not have the dream again after that. I was sure Mother and Father Maloney had been right.

Now... I was not so sure. But the sanctuary was filled. Oblivious to my inner struggle, the members of my wedding party were excitedly placing themselves in line to begin the processional.

If these last-minute disturbing happenings were indeed warnings, I rationalized that they were so veiled I could not know for sure, especially when considering the unchanging, wonderful Alex I had known throughout the year and a half we had been together. With that rationale, I forced back the negative thoughts and emotions and joined my attendants in the processional line. I took a deep breath, giving my father the same confident smile I always used in tough situations. I would wear it now—to the altar.

The processional music began, and I watched my bridesmaids walk gracefully down the long aisle, followed by my sister, Mary, my matron of honor, and her five-year-old son, Tommy, the ring bearer. I squeezed Dad's arm, and we started off in step.

Partway down the aisle, my eyes locked with Alex's. His smile warmed me, and the memory of my frightening dream, Jim's words, and my troubling thoughts vanished. *Alex loves me and I love him. I'm perfectly fine now. I know there's nothing to be afraid of. I see his face—his handsome, familiar face.* I considered Alex's fair, smooth complexion, his fine features, his green eyes edged with thick lashes. His blond hair was perfectly styled, as always, with every hair in place.

Finally I was beside my husband-to-be, who looked at me with loving eyes and flashed his boyish grin. My father carefully lifted my veil to kiss me on the cheek, then smiled at me, gave my arm to Alex, and turned to join my mother.

Taking Alex's strong arm felt good, secure. We stepped up onto the large main altar area. The scent of fresh flowers, the warm soft glow of candlelight, and Father Maloney's words were like background music to the happiness I felt as we exchanged our vows and rings.

"I now pronounce you man and wife."

Alex and I kissed, sealing our marriage. Mary handed me a small floral bouquet as the organist began playing "Ave Maria."

My new husband took my arm, gently leading me down the steps to a small side altar, which held a statue of the mother of Jesus. A black wrought-iron candle rack stood in front of the statue of Mary, illuminated by the vivid votive candles nestled in their ruby, sapphire, and amber-colored glass holders.

Following Catholic tradition, I knelt at the altar to place my special bouquet before the statue of the blessed woman affirmed as the perfect wife and mother. Lingering a moment, I prayed that I, too, would be a good and loving wife to my husband—and one day, a good and loving mother to our children.

Instantly the nightmare resurfaced in my mind, that horrible vision of my groom's empty face. Simultaneously Father Maloney's words blared in my brain, *"Forget the dream. Just marry Alex and be happy!"*

My face and chest beaded up with perspiration. My whole body felt hot. My heart pounded in my ears, drowning out the music.

I began praying again. *Oh God, please take the memory of that dream away. Please bless my marriage. That's all I want, Lord. I want us always to love each other as we do today.*

The song was over; the organ was silent. I tried to get up, but I could not make my body respond. I could hear our guests shifting restlessly in their pews. I flushed with embarrassment. My hands were still clenched and resting on the altar railing, but I was no longer praying for my marriage. I was praying to get up! I knew I had to somehow shake off this emotionally wrenching state I was in.

Taking a deep breath, I deliberately dismissed my paralyzed confusion. I mustered all my strength, rose from my knees, and turned to smile at my prince, who was smiling back at me. The organ music began again and rose to a crescendo as Alex and I walked back down the aisle, smiling at our favorite people right and left.

After Alex and I were sufficiently kissed and hugged by all our guests, we ran down the church steps under a shower of rice. We bounded into Alex's immaculate black Chevy, decorated with our Just Married sign and empty tin cans tied to the back bumper.

Alex kissed me. "I love you, Alisha."

"I love you, too, Alex."

In spite of those terrible, confusing moments at the altar, having dismissed the whole incident, now all was well with my world again. It just had to be.

Ten days later, after a wonderful honeymoon on the ocean, Alex and I pulled happily into the driveway of our new home. Alex carried me across the threshold, and we began our life together on Joyful Road, in one of our city's lower-middle-class areas. That really was the name of the street, and I hoped it was a good omen.

Just two months before our wedding, Alex had accepted a position as an outside sales trainee with a major industrial company. My own position as special assistant to the director of a state association earned me a good salary. Our diligence, controlled spending, and earnest saving afforded us our newlywed home, purchased on a VA loan.

The repossessed government house, situated on a large corner lot, had been an eyesore on the block, but Alex had crammed painting into his hectic schedule just weeks before our wedding. He covered the interior walls in shades of pale aqua, offering a good contrast to the thick brown beams on the vaulted ceilings in the living and dining rooms. The fresh exterior coats of rustic brown paint trimmed with pale aqua transformed the small, contemporary-styled ranch, giving it an attractive individuality amidst similar tract homes in the eight-year-old subdivision.

Alex doctored the large lawn and pruned the wild shrubs that wrapped around the house until they looked healthy and green. I planted perennials and annuals around the yard, neatly edging the side driveway and the sidewalk leading from the street to the aqua front door, with pink and white petunias. Grateful neighbors complimented the improvements.

I sewed curtains and draperies for the windows, and I searched for used furniture in the classifieds to go with the new sofa we purchased and the gift of a new bedroom suite from my parents. I rummaged through secondhand shops to select just the right pictures to hang on our walls. My bargain treasures, combined with our wedding gifts, accessorized our home beautifully.

Alex was proud of my thrifty finds and elegant, low-budget decorating. We shared the same taste and enjoyed working together to transform our three-bedroom house into a home. Our hard work showed, and we were both proud of it. We were content in our commitment to each other and our home. I believe I had a realistic concept of marriage, based upon my parents' stable, happy relationship. With my ideal choice for a life mate, I believed Alex and I were destined to have a long, happy marriage.

A wistful sigh brought me back to the present. Silently I groaned. Life for me had its own way of taking unexpected turns, showing me I was wrong.

I was conscious of the fact that my preoccupation with the past had interrupted the writing of my thoughts about this dreaded morning and even made me forget my morning coffee. Leaving my bed, I hurried downstairs to the kitchen to brew a pot.

Returning to the bedroom with my mug of steaming coffee, I set it in the coaster on the table and turned on the lamp. With one finger, I pulled back the sheer curtain to peek out once more. The sky still looked eerie. I let the curtain fall closed again to keep at bay the winter chill from the wall of glass; then I settled into the pale gold brocade chair in my special corner.

Leaning my head back, I thought, *Oh, to stay right here and escape all the pain of that sad courtroom scene I will face with Alex later this morning.* Sighing at my own wishful thinking, I muttered, "Like it or not, Alisha, you will step into a new season of your life today."

I have always associated the changing times in my life with the changing seasons in nature. Just as the rolling landscape surrounding our home and the lake changes with each new season, so, too, the landscape of my life has changed over the years, both in a natural and spiritual sense, according to the seasons in which I have lived.

At once my thoughts took me back to the *spring* of my life, *my season of childhood,* when I was a fresh-faced young girl just awakening to the world like a rosebud opening to the sun. It was the season of my life when I would try to figure out who I was and how I related to the people, sights, and sounds surrounding me as I blossomed in this family garden landscape.

One of my earliest recollections of my personality as a child is that I was deliberate in my observations of people and happenings around me. I was especially mindful of my own immediate family. Siblings in every family may have different interpretations of life within the same home, depending on the family structure during the years of their own childhood.

I grew up in the 1940s and '50s. Life was slow. Life was simple. When I was old enough to understand what it meant, I knew we were a middle-class family. However, my parents never talked about money. They were unpretentious about who they were and what they owned. If we had been rich, I would not have known; if we had been

34

poor, I would not have known. All I knew was that we were neither rich nor poor. We were comfortable.

Although I had the usual emotional growing pains, nothing extreme or traumatic happened to me or my family. I only remember feeling lonely in my early years. I did not know how I fit into my family. My sister, Mary, eight years my senior, was too old to be my playmate, and to her I was, no doubt, the proverbial pest. My brother, CJ, was four years older, and my being something of a tomboy, I followed him up trees and over fences just to be with him, until he put a stop to his little sister's tagging along after him and his buddies.

When my mother went to work in the mid-'40s, there was a significant change in my home life. I was nine years old when I became a latchkey kid, before the phrase was coined. I always wondered but never knew why my mother went to work—not until many years after she retired when she told me she had worked retail all those years just because she enjoyed it.

During that era, it was rare for a mother to work outside the home. I am sure there were mothers who absolutely had to work, just as I had to at one time; and many mothers today have no choice but to work. But back then, most mothers, at least those of my school friends and my neighborhood playmates, were all stay-at-home moms.

In my young mind, I used to imagine how nice it must have been for my sister and brother because Mother was home each day to greet Mary and CJ throughout their school years. Vividly I recall how I used to be so excited when my teacher acknowledged my good test score or an achievement of any kind and I wished I could run home and delight Mom with my good news. But the house was empty. I missed my mother. Of course, I was not feeling, seeing, or understanding as an adult back then, but as a child.

In addition to coming home to an empty house each day, I felt like I was invisible in my family, lost somewhere in the middle. Perhaps my loneliness was due to the fact that early on it seemed that everyone else in my family was busy doing his or her own thing, and rightfully so. But in my young mind, I used to think there was something wrong with me because it seemed none of them ever had time to read to me, talk to me, listen to me, or answer the questions from my inquisitive young mind.

In fact, I felt there were only two places where anyone cared to talk to me: they were the homes of our neighbors across the street. One was the home of elderly Mrs. Smith, and the other was the home of Joann, the young mother of my playmates. Mrs. Smith was a widow, childless, and a retired schoolteacher, and Joann was a stay-at-home mom. When I was old enough to cross the street, I began visiting Mrs. Smith regularly and sometimes Joann and her kids.

Flashbacks of those happy times warmed my heart on this cold, anxious morning, and I welcomed my memories.

Mrs. Smith would always greet me at her door with a big beaming smile, invite me in, and lay out a treat of cookies or cake and milk for the two of us. She allowed me to express my thoughts. She listened patiently. Most importantly, she was interested. And, she gave me the freedom to be myself.

Just by her words and behavior, that lovely lady taught me so much about kindness, about being sincerely interested in other people and what interests them. She liked my curiosity about people and life and enjoyed sharing her own knowledge and experiences. She seemed delighted with me at those times, as though she took pride in me, as I would imagine she had her star students. Each time I left her house, she told me how much she had enjoyed my company and invited me back again. She might have sensed my loneliness. I do not know. Perhaps, she was lonely too.

My neighbor Joann and her family were Catholic, and her three children, a few years younger than I was, rode a bus to and from Catholic elementary school. Knowing I walked home from public school to an empty house every day, Joann would often call to me from her front porch, inviting me over for a snack and to join her kids in play. Just like Mrs. Smith, she always seemed interested in me.

Later in my teenage years, I spent more time with Joann than with her children, my friends. She was an avid reader. I remember library books—thick as dictionaries—piled high next to her lounge chair. She was always researching something new and interesting. She was interested in history as well as current events, and she was especially interested in people, psychology, and spiritual truths. She shared her newly read discoveries with me. The two of us enjoyed long discussions about the issues of life and current books we were reading. Joann understood me. She was my confidante, the friend with whom I shared my teenage disappointments, experiences, and even my first love.

No one in my family ever knew all the important, in fact, price-less, life lessons and good people skills Mrs. Smith taught me when I was a child and Joann taught me when I was a teenager. They both let me know in one way or another how much they liked me. Mrs. Smith often told me what a pleasant and good little girl she thought I was, and Joann told me I was smart, that I was like an "old soul." I did not have a clue what she meant by an old soul; I only remember that both she and Mrs. Smith made me feel valued as a person.

I was fortunate to have those two intelligent women friends in my life during my formative years. Today they would be called mentors. Their genuine caring, kindness, and good character were important influences to my own character development. From my own experience, I believe children can never have too many good role models in their lives who sincerely love and care about them.

I remember my feeling of loneliness within my family eventually eased when I entered junior high school and got involved in activi-ties. I joined school clubs and made the junior high cheerleading squad. To my surprise, during junior high and into my senior high years, I was voted an officer of several clubs and elected queen to reign over several special events, and a member of the queen's court for the homecoming festivities. I remained a cheerleader throughout senior high and held a part-time job.

Another childhood observation was that it seemed as though my sister and I played second fiddle to my brother. As the only son, he appeared to be favored and obviously was the only one expected to go out into the world and succeed.

My father was a real gentleman. He was tall, slim, good-looking, and had a dignified demeanor. I always thought he carried himself like a noble statesman. He was a man of character, with a strong sense of responsibility and a clear example to my brother of what it would take to make his own way in the world and achieve his goals.

Dad's example rubbed off on me. However, as a young girl, I saw my primary role in life as that of a wife and mother. From my observations of other girls in families I knew, I understood that I was not alone in my perception. Girls growing up in the '40s and '50s generally were not expected to have career aspirations of their own beyond that of wife and mother.

Some girls in my circle of known families did go to college, but for the most part, their degrees were limited to nursing, teaching, or home economics. Others went to business college to prepare for a secretarial position. To my young mind, it seemed that all their options were limited. And all their careers lasted only until they met the man of their dreams and married.

I had my own opinions about limitations placed on girls. Although I could not have stood up to declare them to anybody, still I held fast to them. They kept me from being emotionally bound by a strong sense that I had been born into a man's world.

Nevertheless, I liked being a girl, and I clearly recognized what was expected of me as a woman, based upon observations of my mother. Her virtues and abilities were obvious and easy for me to read, although I was certain I would never be able to do everything as well as she did.

Mom was an excellent homemaker. I admired her many talents; among them were her cooking and especially her baking skills, learned from my grandmother, who had owned and operated a bakery. Mother was creative and enjoyed needlework and sewing. She had a special talent for dressmaking. She could sew any dress pattern, as she often did during those early years for herself, my sister, and me, and the end product would look like it had been professionally tailored. Even after she started working, Mother always kept everything clean, polished, and new-looking in our home.

I was proud of my mother. My father always seemed admiring and proud of her too. Mother was pretty, with fair, beautiful skin, and she was always impeccably groomed. She had a distinguished, elegant look with her own classic style. She had an air of quiet confidence. It appeared, however, that she was unaware of her good looks. I liked her modest demeanor. Mom's nature was noncombative. I never witnessed my mother being aggressive or argumentative. During all the years I lived at home, she never nagged my father. But just because she was easygoing does not mean she was passive. She was assertive when she needed to be. Mom could get any one of us to shape up and do right, with just a look. Mom never spanked me. Dad was the disciplinarian. With Mom it was "the look." When pushed, her correction was short and to the point.

Although reserved, Mother had a lively, fun side too. Mom was simply who she was. She never made a big deal out of the good things she did for her family and others. She was steady, easygoing, and consistent. She made me feel safe, that no matter what situation might come our way, everything would always be all right in our family. When I was young, I liked hearing compliments that I looked like my mother or that I was like her in some way.

Both of my parents were somewhat reserved; it was just their way. Whenever I achieved a goal or received special recognition during my early school years and excitedly shared my happy news with my parents, I noticed it was met without praise or verbal fanfare of any kind. I knew they loved my siblings and me a great deal and showed it in many other ways. Years later Mary and I talked about the fact that it was simply not our parents' natures to speak the words that all children want to hear when they achieve, such as *I'm proud of you*.

They were not touchy-feely people. They did not give big hugs or say I love you or call us endearing "puffy" names. Of course, when their grandchildren came on the family scene, there were lots of hugs for them; and Dad, retired by then, was always there teaching them about life in one way or another.

Accordingly, I learned as a child to live without praise or physical affection. As I grew older, whenever I achieved a goal or received special recognition for any endeavor in school, I usually kept it to myself. My only reward was the gratifying feeling of respect from my peers.

I vividly recall the only time my mother accompanied me to one of my speaking engagements after she had retired from her job. The event was the World Day of Prayer, the day designated to be observed by churches in every major city of the world. In our city, twenty-six different churches participated. Our service, with a reception following, was held in the largest church in the city, which happened to be Catholic, so I knew Mom would be comfortable.

I wondered how she would feel about the hierarchy representing those twenty-six different churches—Catholic monsignors and priests and Protestant bishops and ministers—sitting near the altar listening to her daughter whose name the program listed as the keynote speaker. Moreover, I later wondered what she thought about the swarm of people at the reception afterward, greeting her daughter with accolades and gratitude for her words, which, they said, had "blessed" them.

When I finally asked Mom what she thought about that special event, true to her nature, her only comment was simply, "It was nice." And I only smiled. I realized then that this was the same casual response I had received my entire life.

When it came to my parents' relationship, the perception was formed in my young mind that my mother was an equal partner to my father, as though they shared a "mutual submission." Although I am certain my parents had disagreements just as most married couples do, they did not argue in front of my siblings and me. It was obvious to me that my mother had a spirit of independence that my father was comfortable with; and Mother set an unspoken precedent for my siblings and me: While she was indeed an equal partner, there was only one who was head of our family. Dad was it, and he had the last word.

The husband-and-wife team my parents were showed me a line of authority that worked. That made it okay with me that the husband was head of the family, and one day, my own husband would be head of ours.

Now back in the present, I recognized my memories had pleasantly distracted me, carrying me back to a more pleasurable time and season of my life. I realized that this morning was the first time I had thought about my early years, much less actually examined them, in regard to how they had influenced me. The spring of my life had been so potent with events, feelings, and observations, it is not surprising that collectively they shaped my personality and made for a lively, but comparatively uncomplicated, childhood.

Glancing at the clock, I was aware that little time was left to finish my journaling before I had to shower, dress, and leave for court. Turning to the next page in my journal, I continued to record my feelings:

I do believe You are with me now, Lord, just as You have been with me in every heartbreak and trial of the past...

Pausing, I thought more about that fact. After the Lord had become first in my life, I adopted God's biblical principles for my daily living, which I called "true reality." The power of God and His Word had changed me, changed my personality. Although still idealistic in the sense that I looked for the best in people, I had become a firm realist in my approach to life, its experiences, and in my relationships. More thoughts were coming, and as fast as they filled my mind, my pen was recording them:

Of course, as a realist, I have learned from past difficult experiences that knowing how to deal with them according to God's Word is a far cry from actually walking them out in real time to a successful end. To be honest, sometimes I feel strong about this whole thing; then I can have a sudden attack of weakness and a feeling of desperation. I vacillate back and forth from willful forgiveness for Alex and the "other woman" to resentment and anger toward both of them; and from complete faith in God for my future and confidence in myself to feelings of rejection, self-pity, insecurity, and fear—and as hard as I try, I can't seem to help myself.

Right now I feel full of complex and confusing emotions, so I write them and confess them to You, Lord. You know all about me and my conflicting emotions... You understand. You created me, emotions and all, and you know how to heal me. I must stay focused on reality: things are not what I wish they were... They are what they are. It's all still unbelievable when I think about it.

The painful reality is that Alex has made life-changing choices that have destroyed our marriage and family as we knew it...

By now I felt a big sob sitting on my heart, ready to gush. With sheer will, I managed to hold back the gush, but a hint of tears still blurred my vision as I stared at my writing. I knew I needed to stop here, while there was still time to read a couple of chapters in the Bible before getting ready. Scripture always overcame my negative emotions, fears, and imaginings and brought balanced thinking and peace of mind.

Blinking my eyes until they cleared, I summed up my writing with a prayerful plea:

Dear Lord, please walk with me into that courtroom this morning, into that place of public heartbreak, that place of severing what You have joined together. More later... if I survive this morning!

Chapter 2

Eyes Wide Open

I t was over.
I was again lamenting the life choices made by my husband, as Laura and I stepped through the revolving door of the federal courthouse to brave the frigid morning air. The sky was still burdened with heavy, gray clouds, appropriately gloomy. What felt like an angry wind smacked our faces, whipping us on all sides as we walked. In my mind, it felt like what had happened to our marriage and family. It was as though a raging, evil wind had ripped through our home, rocking it and beating against us relentlessly for three years, until finally it had blown us off course. It was the type of weather I would always associate with Alex.

The silence between us was deafening, like the noisy traffic at our backs, as Laura and I crossed the street to walk over the bridge, then three more blocks to the parking lot. My eyes were burning with tears I prevented from flowing as my mind replayed the last hour of my married life, seeing it again from some distant conscious place:

Laura and I are seated in the crowded courtroom. I am waiting to be called, along with Alex, to approach the judge's bench. I am craning my neck to look at Alex, sitting in the churchlike pew across the room, trying to imagine him before he reached that point from which he had begun to wander from all we had together. Questions burn in me: Has he stopped even once to think about what his choices have done to me?... to our children?... to our family? Is he turning it all over in his mind now, weighing the costs? I quickly turn and aim my eyes to the front of the room, staring but not seeing.

The waiting is almost unbearable.

The anxiety builds. My heart is pounding.

My face feels flushed. My chest is tight. I feel I can hardly breathe.

"I hate this!" I tell myself.

I wait longer. My stomach is somersaulting.

Finally, the two of us, along with several other couples, are summoned. We gather together, forming three lines before the judge as though our moves have been choreographed. The lack of privacy makes me feel shamefully naked. I stand in numb silence. But then, in a split second, I feel strangely insulated, removed, as though I am not a player in this marriage-severing ceremony at all. I am seeing everything through a haze, everything moving in slow motion, words floating over me. Instinctively I know it is over. The judge has given his decree of final severing.

Our marriage, for which I, with God, had fought long and hard, had taken but a few words and only minutes to dissolve. My head reeled with the irony of it all. My mind could not yet surrender to the reality nor to the replay of reality; I was still searching, trying to understand why and how my husband could have let this happen.

If he hadn't been a Christian, I could better understand. But it's unthinkable that Alex ... or any Christian... could have become so blatantly deceptive, so cruel. I know God has been with me through it all, but now I cannot help feeling humiliated, dishonored.

"Oh Laurie," I blurted aloud, breaking the silence that hung between us, "it hurts so much."

"It will be okay, Mom," she answered in a somber tone, nudging my arm in a sympathetic gesture. Laura wanted to reassure me that

I would be all right, but her usually bright eyes were clouded with sadness. She, who was not only my daughter but also my sister in Christ, had stayed close throughout these trying last three years. She had encouraged me with her beaming, praising eyes whenever I made even the smallest step toward emotional recovery from Alex's lies and devious schemes against me. And during these last six months alone, while the four of us had comforted one another, Laura was the one who had kept my sense of humor alive. But inwardly, Laura, along with her brothers, had been living with her own sorrow. I was very aware that I had not been the only one to suffer.

I glanced at my daughter walking by my side. *I'm glad she and the boys are young adults and fully understand the "why and what for" that brought us to that courtroom this morning. Now everything is different for them too. But at least they are old enough to bypass the step where children blame themselves.*

I found myself turning again to really look at Laura, with her long, brown hair blowing in the wind. *It's like looking at myself in a mirror when I was twenty-something, except my hair was darker. She's the same age I was when her father and I married.*

Now as I looked at Laura again, her blowing hair looked like a magazine advertisement for one of those expensive products that make dull hair look silky and gorgeous.

At the same time, I thought about the last three hard years we had gone through, and I wondered how she felt as a young adult, having observed her father's behavior—the treacherous, underhanded things he had been capable of doing to her mother—and how the effects of it all would influence her selection of a life mate.

I know she has goals yet to be met and interesting life experiences ahead before she intends to become a bride. Relatives and friends have always told us we not only look alike but our personalities are so much alike too. I guess that's true. From the time she was a child, she was always full of questions about everything, just as I had been. I wonder if that comes from being an avid reader.

I found my mind wandering back in time again. Like Laura, from early adolescence I had loved to read. Books opened a window of information about life beyond my small corner of the world. My inquisitive mind always wanted to know the meaning and truth about everything, including the things of God.

Having been reared in a Roman Catholic family, I had learned my catechism well, made my first Holy Communion followed by my Confirmation, and faithfully attended Sunday Mass with my family. I liked church; I believed in what I had been taught about God and Jesus Christ, and prayed, believing my prayers were heard. That constant religious influence in my life had given me a sense of unity with my family. Nevertheless, despite that fact, I was conscious of feeling a void within as though something were missing in my life, but I could not figure out why or what it was.

That feeling became less pronounced when I met my first love. He was a fine young man in my class, intelligent and with many abilities and athletic accomplishments. He was from a good family as staunchly Protestant as mine was Catholic. Our personalities, temperaments, values, and attitudes about life meshed perfectly; and we shared the same interests. We were best friends.

During that period, I learned about a young couple I knew well, who were intending to marry, but their breakup had come about because the families were of different religions. That thinking was more common among parents in the 1950s. With that my young mind analyzed the religion issue in our relationship, and despite the fact that each of us was very much liked by the other's parents, I believed neither of our parents would approve an interfaith marriage.

Although back then it was common for many high school sweet-hearts to marry—and I knew couples in our class who were planning to do so after graduation—I was convinced that marriage would be impossible for us. Therefore, something had to be done now, before the two of us would have to face the pain of a forced breakup, should we want to marry. Then our breakup would be even more heart-wrenching to bear. I vacillated back and forth for weeks, not wanting to give up our comfortable, innocent first love, the fun we had together.

Nonetheless, in the beginning of our senior year, I resolved to tell him I wanted to end our relationship. When it came down to sharing my thoughts about this with him, I found I was too embarrassed to tell him that I believed my parents would never permit me to marry a non-Catholic, and so I gave him no explanation. It was painfully hard. Although I did realize it was cruel not to tell him why, in my immaturity I was still afraid, because I did not want him to think my parents were prejudiced against him and his family's religion. He was puzzled, understandably angry; but mostly, he was deeply hurt. Our parting was sad.

The remainder of my senior year should have been happier, but I was pretty miserable. I missed my "best friend." Unfortunately, I did not know how to deal with that kind of loss while seeing him in the school halls on a daily basis. My heart was broken. My study habits, my grades, and my interest in activities waned. I had no interest in dating other guys.

However, homecoming festivities were fast approaching. I turned down a date for the dance, even though I knew that as a member of the queen's court, I needed an escort for the half-time homecoming introduction ceremony as well as for the all-important dance where the crowning took place. I ended up asking my girlfriend's brother, who also was my good friend, to escort me to both events. But I could not help wishing that the arms of the one I loved were holding me, dancing the night away with me at that special, one-time dance.

It would be another thirty years, near the time of our thirty-year high school class reunion, before my first love and I would see or speak with each other again. What had been too painful to remember, we had chosen to forget. However, we did share about our families and how we had spent our lives during those years. I learned he had succeeded to the position of vice president of a large corporation, which did not surprise me. But the best news he shared was that he, too, had become a born-again Christian and was fervently serving God in lay ministry. With great enthusiasm and joy, we shared the details of our individual encounters with Christ and what He had done in us and for us.

Finally, I felt secure enough to confess the reason I had broken off our relationship: that I had prejudged our lives, our futures, and had made a harsh decision because we were of different religions. However, not even that could mar the firm spiritual connection we now felt because of our love for the Lord. We both knew our faith was not in a *religion* but in a *relationship* with the person of Jesus

Christ, and we were able to trust that our lives had taken different paths for a reason.

When we are young, we think we see the big picture. But we do not. We learn academics, but we learn very little about ourselves — except through difficult personal experiences. This breakup taught me a hard reality lesson: do not judge things before their time; or better yet, do not judge, period! Only God knows. It also taught me that I was not a girl who fell in and out of love easily. There was no young love interest after him for a long time. Since that thirtieth reunion, we have not seen each other, but I trust that he, too, is continuing on his spiritual journey. With a faint smile, I breathed a deep sigh and let go of that sweet memory.

Now my mind easily moved on to another teenage memory: my secret dream. Although as a young girl my future role as wife and mother had been clearly defined for me, with a spirit of independence like my mother had, I had another reasonable expectation for my life: my dream of becoming a costume designer.

From the age of fifteen, I had dreamed of studying art and design at a college in New York City after graduation. As I was encouraged by my art instructor, my confidence in my ability grew; and by the time I entered my senior year, I believed, as he did, that I could achieve a career in costume design for theater and movies.

I had already designed and sewn some of my own outfits. Somehow the mechanics of my mind worked in such a way that I could draw a design, measure a perfect pattern from newspaper, cut and sew a fabric, and have a finished garment that looked identical to the design I had sketched.

Although my head was full of plans to become a designer, during the latter part of my senior year, I found myself privately entertaining even deeper questions about God and wondering, *Is there something more?* Also I wondered how the spiritual dimension of one's life fit into the larger scheme of things. My unflagging, inquisitive nature would continue to fan the fire of curiosity about spiritual things. However, the answers to my questions would be hidden from me for the next sixteen years.

My high school graduation was approaching, and with it I would be moving solo into my future. I was aware that my parents expected me to take the same path my sister had taken: attending the local university to receive an education degree. I decided it was time I spoke with them about my own career aspiration to attend art and design school in New York City.

My father was adamantly against it. I tried to explain my desires, ambitions, and plans to work hard to pay my own way through school. I remember his conclusion of the matter: "No. You're not going to New York City! It's not the place for you. You can go to college here—be a teacher, like your sister." End of discussion, if you could call it that.

To say I was disappointed would be an understatement. I felt devastated. When I tried to further reason with him, I heard his last words on the subject, loud and clear.

"No! And that's final!"

I saw red! Angry and with shameless defiance, I haughtily yelled at him through frustrated tears, "I don't want to be a teacher! I want to be a designer! And just remember, you can't stop me forever!"

Mom tried to soften the blow by reminding me that Dad just wanted me to attend the local university because he knew I would be safe there and would continue to live at home. Of course, when Dad had spoken his final no, my anger made me blind and deaf so that I could not see his point and heard nothing else, certainly not what my mother had just told me. I just believed my own plans for my life did not count; that I had to be a teacher—not a designer—in order to meet with his approval.

"You can study art here. You can still be a designer," Mother had softly urged.

She was right about that, but I was still pleading my case.

"Mom, it's not the same! New York is the only place to study theatrical costume design!"

Although I was used to holding in my hurts, at that moment tears welled in my eyes, and I wanted Mom to put her arms around me and soothe my wounded heart and bruised ego. Instead, she did something else I needed; she lovingly embraced me with her words, easing my initial pain.

In the '50s, being a teenager was less difficult for girls than it is today. Although the maturing process was challenging and sometimes risky, there was less temptation to face on a daily basis. Back then it was not cool to smoke or drink, and illegal drugs were unheard of in my circle; but it was cool to remain a virgin until marriage. I was a kid who was conscientious and trying to do it all right; so I could not understand why my dad did not trust me, why he was firmly against my wanting to be a costume designer and studying for it in New York City.

The next day after school, I poured out my heart, including my anger toward Dad, to my neighbor friend Joann. Joann patiently listened with interest and then folded her arms around me. She not only understood my feelings, but being a parent herself, she also understood where my dad was coming from with his decision. Her response brought an emotionally healthy balance for me as she helped me realize that my father did not distrust me, and his intention was not to disappoint or hurt me.

On the contrary, she guessed that, like any other father, my dad was worried about the possible dangers to his naïve Midwest girl living all alone in sophisticated New York City. She encouraged me to let go of my anger toward Dad and to have faith that in time everything would work out for the best. I was not so sure of that. Nevertheless, that day, as so many other times, Joann sincerely listened to me, encouraged me, helped me make a necessary attitude adjustment, and inspired hope in me.

After I cooled off and my ugly anger passed, I chose to believe Joann could be right, even though I did not have a clue about how everything would work out for the best. For me, "the best" would only be nothing short of my dream fulfilled. Anyway, Dad did have the last word—but you already knew he would.

There had been other times during my teen years when my will had clashed with Dad's. I had even been insolent when trying to change his mind so I could get my own way, but I had learned that when he said no, it was final. Consequently, I knew there was no point in trying to further reason with him. I was already on shaky ground. I let it go.

Graduation day in June 1954 arrived, and I was still traveling solo. Dad, assuming the issue was settled and I had gotten New York out of my head, strongly urged me to attend the local Big Ten university from which my sister had graduated. He still wanted me to major in education as she had. But I resisted. By now Mary was teaching high school in a small town northwest of our city. I did not like resisting my dad's advice or feeling the daily underlying friction between us that it had created; but at this point, I felt I was not only trying to hang onto my dream but also fighting to be my own person.

Instead of applying to the university my sister had attended, I immediately enrolled in a small local community college. I worked during the day, having passed the civil service test that landed me a job with the public school administration as secretary to the director of fine arts, and attended school in the evenings. I studied courses in business management. I also studied psychology, a course of great interest to me at that time since I was still trying to grow as a person and figure out what made other people and me tick.

Curiously, I thought I was preparing for one direction for my life, still thinking about design school in New York. However, what I did not know was that all I was studying would be an indispensable asset, indeed preparation, for an altogether different career position yet years away that would prove to be one of the most meaningful experiences of my life.

Now I smiled, recalling that period of time when I began my rite of passage into the *summer* of my life—my *season of blossoming into womanhood*. It was humorous and seriously meaningful, happy and sad, exciting and scary, all at the same time. I was dating again, but there was no special guy, no chance of getting into a serious relationship. However, my summer season gave me a good dose of experiences that could not help but usher me into adulthood.

Exciting things were happening for my brother and sister. CJ was sailing the high seas on his naval aircraft carrier with ports of call on the Mediterranean Sea, visiting cities of Greece and Italy on his military leaves. Mary met the man of her dreams only a short time after embarking on her teaching career and gave it up to marry him. I was proud of her for having worked hard to put herself through college. I was happy for her marriage too. However, I did not want to follow in her footsteps. To my utter surprise during the next year, exciting things also began happening for me.

When I least expected it, I met my second love interest in January 1956. It was instant attraction for both of us. He had an easygoing personality and a great sense of humor. He had been a high achiever in academics and sports at his Catholic high school. We made our special feelings known to each other. Unlike with my first love, each Sunday we were able to attend Mass together.

After he joined the army, we corresponded while he was on military duty in another part of the country. I knew he was determined to go to college and then law school after he mustered out of the service. Knowing him, I had no doubt he would accomplish his goal to become an attorney. Also, I was pretty sure he would not consider marriage before getting his law degree, so I figured we would both be busy for the next several years.

Although there had been no official commitment between us, as far as I was concerned, there could have been no better prospect for a husband. He was a good man. I admired and greatly respected him. One day I hoped to be married and to have a family. A girl romanticizes about such things. But first, I wanted to be a designer.

Then something else exciting and totally unexpected happened to me. Although discussion between my father and me about attending school in New York had abruptly ceased, I learned that conversation about the matter had continued between Mother and him. I was flabbergasted to learn my mother had managed to convince Dad to let me test the waters in New York City when I turned twenty-one.

It was stunning news! Joann had been right. I wondered how in the world Mother had changed Dad's mind. Nonetheless, I was ecstatic! Having been boldly defiant with Dad, for which I was now embarrassed, I thanked him and Mom profusely. I respected my parents. Having their approval for such a weighty plan was important to me. Finally, I believed I would get my chance to find out if I had what it took to make my dream come true.

Secure in myself and where I was going, I worked hard and saved my money to get there. I felt good during this summer season of my life. In fact, life for me seemed to be just beginning. The years of waiting for love and career were not wasted, however.

Instantly my vacation travel adventures with girlfriends came to mind. Scenes, happy scenes, flashed in my mind of three particular trips. My travels to places I had only read about in books had been fun, but also there was no doubt that each adventure had significantly helped mature me and broaden my view of the world. *They were such fun!* I silently reminded myself, with a mischievous grin that spread across my face because my family still did not know of my experiences on those vacations.

With a long wistful sigh, I realized that until now I had forgotten those fun times. Laura and I normally talked about everything. But even when she and her girlfriend vacationed in Florida the spring of 1984, my own fun memories of being there had not surfaced to share with her. The year 1984 had been too dark and emotionally traumatic for me. No pleasurable thoughts of past fun, or for that matter, anticipated future fun, had crossed my mind. Now I wanted to remember.

The first of my travel adventures was in April 1955. My best girlfriend and I had saved our money and begged our parents to let us take our first vacation alone to Miami, Florida. We wanted to fly, but they would permit us to travel only by Greyhound. By the time we reached the first large city en route, we decided we were not going to make it to our destination fast enough, so we daringly took a taxi from the bus station to the airport and boarded a plane to Miami. It was the first time to fly for both of us, and it was very exciting. But when we phoned our parents upon arrival, they did not see it that way. They were more than a little shocked; they were angry. After being sufficiently chastised, we were cautioned to be careful of this and that—everything. But that had not dampened our spirits.

At once a smile animated my face as I recalled how we two girls from middle-class America had managed to find ourselves in the world-famous Fountain Blue Hotel, one of the ritziest playgrounds for the rich and famous in the 1950s. Obviously, we could not afford to stay there. Ours was a much smaller and cheaper hotel on the beach, within walking distance of the other. But once we spotted that fabulous hotel, we just had to explore!

After mornings on the beach, we would don our casual outfits and walk to the Fountain Blue. We meandered through the main lobby and gift shops, then out into the pool area, where we sat at a table sipping sodas and watching society's upper crust—the beautiful people, the international jet-setters—who were there legitimately.

We spent our evenings there too. We made sure we were immaculately groomed and perfumed, and dressed to the nines; then we took a taxi to the main entrance of that spectacular hotel, where the grand fountain stood in the center of the circular plaza. We strolled through the main lobby and into the lounge to listen to live music— and for more people-watching. After that we walked in and out of other public areas, even lingering in some for pleasant conversations with guests, just as though we belonged there.

We had not felt the least bit intimidated in those surroundings; rather, we felt unbelievably comfortable. However, we never forgot that we were only observers of how the "other half" lived. To our knowledge, no one suspected we were not guests. We never got into any trouble. It was a fun adventure, just an innocent deception, an exciting window on the world through which two rather sheltered, unworldly young women had peeked. At that time, in my wildest imagination, I would never have believed that one day my life experiences would take me on travels to beautiful cities of America and Europe, where I would be a legitimate guest in many equally grand hotels.

In 1956 five girlfriends and I flew to Fort Lauderdale, Florida, during spring break. Although we did meet guys and girls on the beach when we first arrived and our group ran around exploring the city together, spring break for us was innocent fun in comparison to the disclosed activities of more recent generations. The six of us crammed ourselves into a small efficiency apartment right on the beach during our ten-day stay; but we were in it only long enough to shower, snack, and sleep. Most of our days were spent on the beach. We spent most nights on the beach as well, where a group of us sat around a campfire, singing to the tunes one of the guys played on his guitar.

I took a weekend side trip on a Greyhound to a nearby city where I had been invited to visit my military guy's mother, who was living on a lake in a beautiful area of Florida. We exchanged his newsy letters and photos and became better acquainted. Also, we took the boat out and she taught me to water-ski. Our visit left me with a good feeling about his single mother, who had raised him, her only child, which could not have been easy for her. I boarded the bus to return to my shared beachside apartment. The rest of my days were spent lying under a burning hot sun, trying to get that deep Florida tan to show off when I arrived home, and daydreaming about my future.

The next memorable vacation was that long-awaited trip of a lifetime for me. It was in April 1957. My best girlfriend and I were twenty years old when we flew TWA to New York City. We were guests of my relatives. Also, I planned to visit certain art and design schools and to check out the Barbizon, a recommended Manhattan hotel-like residence for women only.

My elegant and cultured thirty-something cousin, the only single one of four beautiful girls in her family, took us all over Manhattan Island, starting that first day at the top of the Empire State Building, where we overlooked the glories of that great metropolis. She made a dream come true for me that evening when she took us to our first Broadway theater show to see the original cast perform the hot musical *South Pacific*. Another day she took us to see the famous, high-kicking Rockettes dancing at Radio City Music Hall. My cousin was a career girl in the fabric design industry, so we visited the garment center with its hustle and bustle of fashion activity, which was especially exciting to me. The day we toured Rockefeller Center, she treated us to lunch on the Plaza.

My girlfriend accompanied me on my visits to schools of interest to me in Manhattan. We rode the subway into the city and taxied to art and design colleges. For my focus of fashion design and marketing, some offered a bachelor's of business administration degree, and others offered an associate of arts degree. I remember that once I visited the Tobe-Coburn School of Art and Design, it was settled for me. I knew that was where I wanted to study. All these years later, I do not know if the school still exists.

And I remember that once my girlfriend and I visited the Barbizon, which was a boarding residence for women only and just three blocks from Fifth Avenue and Central Park, it was the place for me to live. Today the Barbizon is the Melrose Hotel.

Over the next two days we started our mornings exploring Manhattan, browsing bookstores, small boutiques, and Tiffany's, the jewelry store for which the Audrey Hepburn movie *Breakfast at Tiffany's* is named. Who can forget that famous break-of-dawn scene with elegantly dressed Audrey ending her night on the town by enjoying her breakfast, sipping her coffee from a paper cup and nibbling her pastry while doing some browsing of her own at Tiffany's display windows?

After filling our eyes with showcases of exquisite jewelry, we taxied to one of my favorite places, the Metropolitan Art Museum. There we filled our eyes with even more breathtaking artistry, the paintings and sculptures of great artists of the centuries. We spent the rest of the day seeing the places we had read about in *Vogue*. As we walked Fifth Avenue, Madison Avenue, and other streets, each one was buzzing with the energy of wall-to-wall New Yorkers. Naturally, people-watching was in order on our jaunts to Bloomingdale's, Saks Fifth Avenue, Bergdorf Goodman, Macy's, and Bonwit Teller. In each store, I made a beeline to the couture salons to check out the latest couturier design styles.

One of my aunts gave her son and his friend permission to take us out on the town a few evenings. They were older, in their mid-to-late-twenties, and lots of fun. They especially enjoyed showing off their city to girls who were, as they teased, from Cow Town U.S.A. The guys liked to dance, so they took us to classy places for dinner and dancing. The first evening they took us to the magnificent Waldorf Astoria Hotel, where we danced to the music of the Guy Lombardo orchestra—the same with whom my generation for many years celebrated New Year's Eve via television. Another evening they took us to the Rainbow Room supper club at the top of Rockefeller Center. Today's generation saw that famous night spot in a scene from the Barbra Streisand and Nick Nolte movie *The Prince of Tides*. Still another evening they took us to Birdland, a jazz club, where the music was fantastic and where, we were told, some of the great jazz musicians of all time had performed at one time or another.

It was all pretty heady stuff for twenty-year-olds in the mid-1950s. My relatives broadened and illuminated our world by exposing us to many new experiences that taught us more about life firsthand. But that trip held an even deeper meaning for me personally than it did for my girlfriend.

New York City was where I always knew my dream would begin. With my first taste of Broadway theater, I was even more convinced that I wanted to design for that entertainment medium. I fell passionately in love with live theater: its costumes, stage sets— the works! And I was even more excited now about the prospect of living in Manhattan, hopefully accepted at Tobe-Coburn and one day designing for theater and movies.

When it came to movies of the 1950s, it was an era of glamour and elegance. Unlike today, movies seldom contained violence or foul language, and they were never overly salacious or raw—at least the movies I saw were never like that. Moviemakers of the '50s took the moral high ground, delivering wholesome entertainment with high drama, fun musicals, and romantic comedies. I was dazzled by the costumes worn by stars such as Doris Day, Elizabeth Taylor, Audrey Hepburn, Jane Russell, Marilyn Monroe, and Lauren Bacall. They were made from the most exquisite, lush fabrics, decidedly feminine, and to coin a more recent phrase, *drop-dead gorgeous*. I dreamed of being like Edith Head, the renowned Oscar-winning costume designer for movies.

When I returned home, planning went into high gear to apply for design school, to work on my résumé to send to McCall Pattern Company located right in Manhattan with the hope of landing a part-time job, and to nail down my place to live. I knew my New York relatives would be there for me too. I was ready and eager to not only test the waters following my twenty-first birthday but to aggressively pursue my dream.

Chapter 3

Irresistible Force

M y excitement at the prospect of beginning my dream was hard to contain. Just prior to my scheduled departure for the Big Apple, my brother introduced me to his friend, Alexander Michael Lance. They had first met on the flight deck of their naval aircraft carrier during the Korean War. CJ had been a flight director with the navy, and Alex had been an aircraft in-flight electrician with the naval air force. Alex lived in a small town northeast of our home. When they each mustered out of the service, he looked up CJ after moving to our city to attend the Big Ten university.

Alex was only one of CJ's many friends who came to the house. It was no different now from the years during school when CJ's football buddies and classmates would stop by. All his guy-friends were three to four years older than I was, so I had never paid much attention to them nor them to me, except for always being respectful of me. To them I was just CJ's little sister. I never expected any of that to change because Alex now hung out at the house too. I certainly did not expect my life to change because of him!

As time went by, Alex was at our house fairly often, picking up CJ for evenings out with their buddies or for dates with girls, but we paid no special attention to each other. Alex was nowhere in my personal life. My total concentration was on my military guy, family, girlfriends, my job, and saving money for design college.

I was perfectly happy with my second love interest, my soldier. We wrote almost daily letters to each other. It was like sharing with a best friend. We could easily pen our thoughts and feelings and felt such a bond of friendship and deep caring that we were comfortable sharing everything about ourselves with each other. Because of that, as well as our shared religion, we imagined ourselves to be perfect for each other, although we still were not officially engaged. Knowing his plans for college and law school following military duty, I knew I could fulfill my own plans for a career.

Unlike with CJ's other friends, however, after a while, I sensed Alex had an interest in me; but of course, I had no interest in him and did not encourage his attentions. My full focus was on my dream, my future. Having selected the design school when I was on vacation, I had taken a leave of absence from my city school administration job in order to travel back to New York in early June to make arrangements to begin the fall quarter in September. I was anxiously awaiting that period to begin. Nothing could stop me now, certainly not Alex's special interest in me.

The day finally arrived. According to plan, I boarded the plane for New York City, with my large portfolio of design sketches tucked under my arm. One of my girlfriends accompanied me and would be staying with me in my hotel.

My friend, being a first-time visitor, was excited to be shopping and taking sightseeing tours around Manhattan on her own. Also, I took her to my favorite places. Everything had been going well. However, two days before she was scheduled to return home, she fell victim to one of the most shocking violations that can happen to a woman. She was fortunate to escape her attacker with her life.

It was hard for her to tell the details. I tried to comfort her, but the trauma was so severe that she was paralyzed with fear. We were both full of fear. She wanted to go to the airport immediately. But I just could not let her fly back home alone that night. She reluctantly agreed to wait for me, and we phoned the airlines to change our return tickets. I wrapped up my business the next day, and we took an evening flight. No matter how many times I told her there was no reason for her to be ashamed, nevertheless, shame gripped her and held her captive. She never spoke of her attack again, but it changed her.

Unexpectedly, my life also was altered by that sobering incident. I was traumatized. I felt as though I, also, had been attacked. Suddenly I did not want to leave the house; I did not want to return to work; I broke out with a terrible case of hives all over my body; and even worse, I entered a period of depression. I was so despondent that before thinking things through, I resigned my job. I did not know how I felt about anything or anyone—including my design career and my special soldier across the country.

Whenever I thought about that monstrous man and his horrendous act against my friend, I got sick to my stomach. Until that crime happened to her, the possibility of such a thing happening to me or any other woman had never entered my mind. Rape was inconceivable. In the 1950s, that kind of violence committed against women was unheard of in my city. At least I had not heard of it. Therefore, I had been fearless about walking the busy streets of midtown Manhattan.

Now I understood my father's initial concerns about my living there alone. In fact, I debated with myself about whether I should return. I decided to wait and see how my friend recovered. Besides, I realized I needed some time myself to recover from the shock of it all. I knew the fall quarter was no longer an option, but perhaps I could return to New York after the Christmas holidays.

In the meantime, Alex continued to hang out with CJ. Whenever he came to the house, I still paid no special attention to him. However, with each visit, including an occasional Sunday when CJ or my mom invited him to stay for dinner, he was becoming better acquainted with my parents and some relatives. During those times, Alex was also taking the opportunity to flirt with me. I must admit I was flattered by the obvious interest shown me by this nice-looking, mannerly, and likeable twenty-four-year-old, especially in light of the fact that I had not been able to see my guy for many months.

I told myself Alex was not irresistible, after all, so that was no excuse to allow myself to be charmed by him. But whenever he was around, I found myself enjoying his attentions like any other young girl would. I could not deny being enamored by Alex. However, at those times, I deliberately resisted his appeal and consciously refocused my concentration to my soldier; and finally, I began to think about my dream again.

Nonetheless, because of Alex's frequent visits with CJ, I felt uncomfortably stirred with some feeling I did not want to feel. With hindsight I know denial was my escape from facing the possibility of that feeling developing into a romantic relationship. I would permit myself only to consider Alex as CJ's friend and my "friend"— nothing more.

When Alex was not around, I could stuff that feeling for him— whatever it was—wherever people stuff those feelings they do not want to deal with or look at. But when he was at the house, that feeling demanded my attention.

Never forgetting my soldier, my deep feelings for him, my strong sense of loyalty to him, and my overactive conscience, I could not give myself permission to even begin to consider or examine what my feelings might be for Alex. I was not confused about how I felt for my guy, but I realized that I was confused by my mixed emotions about Alex. So I did the only thing I thought was right to do. I wrote to my guy telling him about my current confused state and my need to examine my mixed-up feelings. Also, having only alluded to meeting CJ's friend, I went on to ask if he would try to understand and give me time to sort it all out.

I recall that almost immediately after I mailed that letter, I had second thoughts, convinced that my depression following my friend's tragedy, coupled with my overly healthy conscience, had made me act too hastily; and I wrote to let him know. But it was too late. He did not respond.

Initially I believed that because we understood one another and shared our honest feelings on so many other levels, he would understand this too. Why in the world would I have expected him to understand this? Even I did not understand it yet! However, now I did understand his mother's words spoken to me before I left her Florida home, about the only flaw she knew in her son's nature. "Stubbornly," she had said, as though warning me, "he will give no second chances." She knew her son well. It was over. I was brokenhearted. At that point, I knew the same kind of pain I had inflicted upon him. I had received my just desserts!

Tears flowed like a waterfall for days, then on and off for weeks, before I could begin to let go. I tried to face my loss in a mature way, to face the reality I knew: that I had been foolish, that I had taken too much for granted, and that I had caused my own loss. Although painfully hard, finally I also faced the fact that my special guy did not want me in his life anymore.

I fought to change my focus. I began to think about my dream again. Knowing that I could still become a costume designer, even if I did not have him, helped me feel better about myself and helped me to move on. I concentrated on sketching designs to add to my portfolio, while thinking about returning to New York to start design school in January. But I knew even though I put all this passionate energy into making my dream come true, I would not forget him.

As the weeks went by, whenever I was sketching and thinking about design school, flashbacks came to mind and left me feeling anxious and fearful about returning to New York. Each time I deliberately put it out of my mind.

It was nearing August, and I knew I had to make a decision before Christmas. There was no doubt that I wanted to go to design school. However, some days I was excited about it, but other days I was not sure if I wanted to live alone in New York City after what had happened to my friend. Nonetheless, regardless of my confusion about New York, I knew I could not put off getting another job here, so I started looking.

I combed the classifieds and found an especially interesting job listing for an administrative position. However, besides the fact that it was in a totally unfamiliar field, I also knew I had neither a degree nor the qualifications and experience required. For that reason, I immediately dismissed it and went on reading other ads.

Nonetheless, the next morning the ad was unexpectedly in my mind again, and on a whim, I decided to go to that downtown association personnel office to try to land an interview. When I introduced myself and handed my résumé to the receptionist, she gave me an application to fill out. Knowing I was not qualified for the job made me feel I was being dishonest to apply, and I remember actually flushing with embarrassment.

To my surprise, the executive director walked into the area where I was sitting just as I completed the application. After being told why I was there, she looked me up and down, walked over to me, extended her hand, introduced herself, and told me to follow her. In her office, I sat quietly as she looked over my résumé and application. She had to know I was not qualified. While she was reading, my eyes examined her framed college degrees and commendation plaques hanging on the wall behind her. Her degree was in psychiatric mental health, and her honors were for many years of accomplishment in that same field; so I became a little anxious about this interview, feeling I—and my mental health—would be scrutinized like never before.

After she explained the position, I told her I was impressed with the association's work and was certain I could learn the job, that I was conscientious and would work hard. Her eyes gazed directly into mine as she listened intently to my every word—so intently, I felt she was seeing deep inside me. I had never experienced that before. When she responded, she actually said, "I know that. I see great potential in you."

I did not know what she was talking about. She had an office staff that was obviously qualified for this position and certainly experienced. Nevertheless, she decided to take a chance on me. She hired me on the spot. I would be assistant director and act in her absence. I was speechless! Like Mrs. Smith and Joann had seen when I was young, this woman saw something in me; and although I did not have a clue what it was, I was grateful to get the job.

I could not have had a better mentor for such a time in my life. She trained me herself. It was like taking a crash course, cramming for finals, and on-the-job training at the same time, all day and every day. I worked hard trying to live up to whatever "potential" it was she saw in me. I learned it all, and I learned it well.

It turned out, with my director's patient training and encouragement and my eagerness to learn and grow, I did rise to her expectations. She worked tirelessly, with me at her side, in the state legislature to lobby for educational needs, protective care, and service laws for the less fortunate among us, the mentally ill who could not speak for themselves.

With my position, I interfaced with the governor, mayor, state legislators, and other dignitaries in city and state governments. In addition, I worked closely with the association board of directors, which was made up of trustees who were some of the most prominent individuals in our state, such as our state senator, two state representatives, and others in the legal, judicial, educational, and medical fields.

My director was passionate about her work. I caught her vision and her passion. I knew I was working for an important cause. She trusted me to speak for her in her absence. Excellence was her standard, and excellence became the goal to which I also aspired.

My job included exciting perks and work-related social events where I met many other interesting, high-powered people. As a young lady from a middle-class family and a simple upbringing, I was clearly being given the opportunity to move in a whole different world that was stretching me mentally and emotionally and helping to mature me. My work was so exciting that although design school was always in the back of my mind, I was now even more uncertain about it. However grown-up I felt during those early months of my new job, I could not seem to make a clear, mature decision about returning to New York City.

During this time, I unexpectedly found myself glad to see Alex when he picked up CJ for their nights out. Nonetheless, I never let him, CJ, or anyone else know that. Then it happened. Soon after I got my new job, Alex asked me for a date. I accepted. *Why not?* I thought, especially since I had no one else in my life. In truth, I did not want any special guy in my life, but a casual date could not hurt anything.

I enjoyed being with Alex. He continued inviting me out, and I continued to accept. We were having a good time together, often double-dating with my brother and his girl. That was always fun, since CJ kept us laughing with his great sense of humor.

One night after Thanksgiving and nearing the holiday season, Alex and I had just arrived home from a date and were standing at the front door when I heard a car pull up and stop in front of my house. Although the night was pitch-black, with the light from the street lamp two doors away, I recognized the car. My heart leaped. *It's him!* I stared in disbelief.

My heart pounded as my eyes tried to penetrate deeper into the darkness to watch the moving figure of my ex getting out of his car and beginning his walk up the first set of steps from the street onto our property. *What is he doing here? He must be home on leave from the army. But why has he come? Maybe he wants to tell me off in person! Tell me how selfish I am, how disappointed he is in me. Oh dear God, I couldn't bear to hear that, even though I know I deserve it and he has every right to say it! I hate myself for what I did to him. Oh ... what am I going to do?* Suddenly I froze with fear.

The closer he walked toward the porch, the faster my heart pounded. Momentarily I actually forgot Alex was with me. Then I forgot my fear. Now I was silently crazed with excitement to see him. *I can't believe it! He came back! He came back! Oh ... what will he say to me? What will I say to him?*

The nearer he came, the faster my heart beat. Suddenly my mind went blank. Time stood still. My brain felt hazy, as though I were in a misty dream, everything moving in slow motion. He took the first of the second set of steps ascending the porch—and abruptly stopped. Immediately he spun around and walked back down the steps, shocking me from my paralyzed state. *He's leaving! What happened? Oh my gosh, it's Alex ... He's spotted Alex standing next to me. Did he say anything to me? Did I say anything to him? Did Alex say anything to him?*

Panicked, I opened my mouth to shout, *No! Wait! Please don't go! Let me explain!* but no words came out.

Instantly I was aware of Alex watching me. I flushed with embarrassment. Nevertheless, my mind raced: *Say something! Do something! Stop him before he gets to his car.* But again there were no words. Speechless and staring in unbelief, I watched him enter his car and drive off.

I stood there dumbfounded. It had happened so fast. The man I loved, the man I wanted to give my whole heart to, was here one minute and gone the next. I experienced the same emotional pain I had felt the first time our relationship ended. It was awful.

Sadly, I had too much pride to get in touch with him after that night to explain, to try to make things right. I had too much pride to tell him how foolish I knew I had been, how unkind I had been to him. I was too embarrassed about everything to tell him that I still loved only him.

I would never know if he had come back intending to break his own rule—to give our relationship a second chance—because I was too fearful of his rejection to ask. This time I knew our relationship was over for good. It was my private pain, pain I would feel for a long time. However, though I would not forget that night, I knew I must forget him, once and for all. I set my mind to never look back. I never saw or heard from him again.

Interestingly, Alex and I never spoke one word about that incident. The pain of my heartbreak lessened with each day, and once again I found myself enjoying Alex's company. Alex continued his pursuit of me with a whirlwind of dates—dinners, dancing, and other fun times—during the Christmas holidays. He even attended midnight Mass with my family and me on Christmas Eve.

On New Year's Eve while we were dancing, Alex declared his love for me and announced, with his boyish grin, "I'm gonna marry you!"

I was both shocked and flattered.

Kindly, but firmly, I let him know I did not want our relationship to go there. "Because," I emphatically stated, "I'm not ready to marry anyone! I'm going back to New York!"

Disregarding my resolve, Alex stepped up his determined pursuit. Without any suggestion or encouragement on my part, he also decided to convert to Catholicism and began instruction in the faith with our parish priest, Father Maloney. He was from Alex's hometown and could not have been happier to baptize his new convert. My parents were impressed. I was suspicious that this was part of Alex's whole design to win me over, his way of showing me he was serious about his marriage proposal. Nonetheless, he impressed me too.

Over time Alex fully charmed my parents, and, soon he completely charmed me in a way I would not have thought possible.

Before I knew it, I had been swept off my feet by this older, experienced, determined, and hard-to-resist young man, making me forget my passion for design and allowing me to move beyond my heartbreak. On the way to my dream, unexpectedly, I allowed myself to fall in love with Alex.

A year later on Christmas Eve 1958, we were engaged and planned to marry in the summer. I set my dream aside for the man I loved. My job was still bringing me a lot of satisfaction along with a good salary, but instead of saving my money for design college, now I was saving for marriage. I was no different from my sister and the other girls I knew in my generation who had set their career aspirations aside to marry.

There is something sad about past unfulfilled dreams. However, when my desire to become a costume designer first entered my mind and heart, and also when it was left behind for marriage, I had not figured God into the equation. But God does not forget. One day years later after committing my life to Christ, a remarkable, totally unexpected opportunity would open for me to experience an extraordinary piece of my dream.

The late days of the summer season of my life were filled with excitement for Mother and me as we shopped for French silk and lace from which I would sew the gown I had sketched, and together we planned every other needed detail for me as a bride and for the wedding ceremony.

During this preparation time, I also gave thought to my readiness to move into married life. I not only knew the kind of man I wanted for my life mate, but I had also learned a lot about myself. Before becoming a bride, I had been mostly outgoing, lighthearted, and spontaneous; and generally, I think I displayed my most favorable traits. I was, however, aware of a more private, serious, and guarded side of my personality. But for the most part, I believe I was resilient, optimistic, and positive in my perception of people, my life, and the world in general. Then again, in reality, those features of my personality had been tested only on a small scale as a young adult. Time and experience would be their proving ground.

I had been physically well before my marriage and emotionally stable—clearly grounded in my values, having adopted those my parents had lived before my siblings and me. I cared about people. They always had been important to me. I had enjoyed good relationships with my family and friends. Mine had been a transparent life.

Also before I married, I felt most fortunate that the summer season of my life had been packed full of interesting and varied experiences that had broadened my world and taught me about life. Even though I knew I still had a lot to learn, I felt I was ready for marriage. Both my spring and summer seasons had formed, not only my beliefs, my conduct, my ideas, and my attitudes about life, but also my concept and expectations for marriage, before I would begin to live them. I understood the true meaning of matrimonial union. I was in love. And I was excited about beginning my life with Alex.

In a strange way, recalling my life before becoming a bride and reminiscing earlier this morning about how life began for Alex and me are bittersweet memories. In an equally strange way, it was memorably beautiful to have been that much in love with a lifetime ahead of us; even though at the same time, those memories also serve to remind me that in reality, I only thought I knew Alex before we married.

Looking back on our courtship, although the characteristics I saw in Alex were exactly what I desired in a life mate, there was one area that had concerned me. Alex was reluctant to talk about his family. I was from a family whose open conversations had allowed Alex to know us well, but as we moved into a serious relationship, I became aware of my lack of knowledge about his family.

As time went by, when I questioned him he seemed uncomfortable, guarded, almost secretive, and disclosed very little. The two other young men with whom I had past relationships had lived in my area where their families were known and we had mutual friends. Because Alex was from another city, we knew nothing about his family and friends.

I rationalized that I should not press him for particulars, because the story behind those brief facts might be too painful for him to talk about. I was confident that one day when he was ready, Alex would freely add the details to the sketchy portrait of his family he had painted for me. A year had passed, but that still had not happened when Alex asked me to marry him. By that time, knowing him as well as I thought I did, his family background seemed less important to me.

Although I had believed everything I had been taught about God, now I know that I was still at a disadvantage spiritually. While my parents had been devout in their Catholic religion, with all due respect, they had never studied the Bible for themselves, nor had they introduced it to my siblings and me. Consequently, when making one of the most important decisions of my life, I did not know God's Holy Word as my source for wisdom and guidance. Instead, I relied solely upon the knowledge and guidance of my parish priest for my spiritual answers.

Years and experience also have taught me that although adult at age twenty-one, few of us really know ourselves, much less other people, beyond their obvious characteristics. Besides, we all put our best foot forward when dating and wanting to make a good impression. By the time I accepted Alex's proposal, I had the best impression of him. I ignored my previous concerns about his family background, rationalizing, as many brides do, *I'm not marrying his family, I'm marrying him!*

Today based upon my own experience and what I have learned from Scripture, that rationale seems borderline insanity to me. It is true enough in one respect; however, in another respect, Alex and I both carried into our marriage all the influences of each of our family backgrounds and lifestyles, both positive and negative, including any skeletons hiding in the closets. That is something for all prospective brides to consider.

This new vantage point serves to remind me of more reality. When we are young, we are certain of what we think we know about life. We are sure of our opinions and decisions. We are confident we can make our life just as we ideally imagine. But we cannot. Life has its own way of showing us, in one way or another, how much we have to learn. Life can wound us in our most vulnerable emotional places and bring us low with pain.

Slowly my thoughts drifted back to shocking awareness of the fierce wind and biting cold air almost stealing my breath. My daughter and I were walking fast against the wind, and I was conscious of a cadence in our steps as we walked the third and last block from the courthouse to the parking lot. Now I realized Laura and I had not exchanged another word for two blocks. I had been lost in my private thoughts. A deep melancholy sigh escaped me as I acknowledged the fact that so much pain might have been avoided if I had just gone back to design school in New York City as I had planned.

As Laura and I stepped up our pace, the heartbreak of shattered dreams was stinging my heart as brutally as the freezing wind was stinging my face. *Most people believe it takes both partners in marriage to cause divorce. But God knows, the children and I know—even Alex knows—that is not always true. Does the church forgive its own innocent victims of divorce?* I wondered, as Laura and I entered the Chrysler and she drove off the parking lot.

Stoically I mustered enough courage, real or false, to chide myself: *It's over, Alisha! Somehow, you will go on alone!* It was a frightening reality to ponder on our long drive home—a reality that quickly swallowed my courage.

As Laura exited the freeway and drove onto the country road that would take us home, I recognized another fear creeping back in: the opinions of others regarding my divorce. I knew it was sinful pride, for which I had asked God's forgiveness every time it had resurfaced throughout our court hearings.

I confess, Lord, I struggle even now about what Christians will think of me when they learn of our divorce today. They will all know soon enough from the public notice in the newspaper. I know it is a weakness of faith on my part to entertain such questions, but I can't help wondering what will happen to my public ministry to women. Will my life ever again herald to others the good news of Jesus Christ and His redemptive power?

Chapter 4

The American Dream Becomes a Nightmare

Laura pulled into the driveway next to the house, which was nestled in wind-tossed, overhanging trees. Sleeping ivy clung to the stone walls, and sculptured yews topped with crystallized snow lined the sidewalk leading to the front door, where we were met by Michael and Steven.

My sons' arms, linked with Laura's, circled me, feeling like the extended arms of God wrapping me in a warm blanket of His love and comfort. My three children needed my arms too, and the arms of one another. Alex's reward to all of us for our love and support had been grievous, a bitter pill to swallow. Not only had he broken all his promises to me and treated me treacherously, but also Michael, Laura and Steven had felt the sting of their father's broken promises and his final life choices that had changed their family life forever.

The ringing of the telephone broke our silent embrace, jolting me from my peaceful cocoon. I walked into the kitchen, hearing my children's voices floating out of the foyer and drifting up the stairs to their rooms. I reached for the receiver and put it to my ear.

"It's me."

That voice, though pleasant sounding, made a cold shiver go up my spine, because I knew it could turn harsh at any moment.

Suddenly I could feel my heartbeat increasing to a rapid, thumping rhythm.

"I just called to thank you," Alex began, in a soft, nonthreatening tone, "for not allowing your attorney to subpoena my customers. That would have ruined the business—and me."

I was sure he was right, especially since he had lived a public life that had been very different from his private one the last three years. Had Alex's customers been summoned to our court hearings, no doubt they would have learned something of his true lifestyle. I knew that could have jeopardized the good business reputation he had built and so carefully guarded for twenty-six years.

Silence hung between us.

How surreal this phone call feels. Our marriage ended only a couple of hours ago, and after everything he did to betray me and financially deceive me, he had the gall to phone to thank me for saving his business. His business!

We had both sacrificed everything so he could fulfill his long-time dream of owning his own business. I had agreed to mortgage everything we owned outright: our vehicles and, most scary of all, our nearly paid-for home. We even invested our only savings, our safety net should we need it, which actually had been earmarked as the college fund for our children.

Some wives might not have been willing to go along and take that financial risk for their husbands' dreams, when nearing midlife. That is such a precarious time for married couples. But at that time, I had believed in Alex's business expertise and experience, as well as believing in his relationship with God, whom Alex had taken as his partner. My faith also was in God to guide us with His wisdom in our new venture.

I had willingly joined Alex in giving up our financial security for his dream, and remarkably, with God's guidance and wisdom, the business was solvent within one year. Once again we owned all our assets. Alex and I together established his business to the financial success it is today.

All my sacrifice, my hard work and dedication to the business for which I received no salary, had in the end only ensured a future financial security for Alex—and his "other woman" to enjoy!

By now his kind, soft-spoken words, *Thank you ...,* were reverberating off the walls of my brain, sounding more like the embittered word *defraud,* polluting my mind and heart with resentment.

Suddenly thoughts of Alex's scheming made me shudder: *His deceptions got him what he wanted. Thanking me now feels altogether appropriate to him! Like pouring salt into my wounds!*

The truth made me feel painfully foolish. Regretfully, I had allowed myself to be cleverly manipulated by him who "loved" me. However, I confess I was the one who had not wanted to argue about money during the divorce process. This may seem cowardly or even crazy to some people. But in reality, I must admit that it would have been a different story if I had had dependent children to support. Then my claws might have come out, and I would have fought for money like a lioness protecting her cubs.

However, that was not the case. Each of our children was emancipated. Besides, Alex had written a letter to me before our court settlement, stating: "Whatever I have financially certainly was accomplished with your help, and you have always been a good and loving wife. I cannot fault you for this mess."

After that letter, when we talked about the settlement before our final court hearing, Alex had assured me he knew I deserved half of all our assets because we had earned them together; to which, of course, I agreed. He said he intended to tell his attorney he wanted to split everything right down the middle. Even though he had been deceptive with his adulterous affair and I did not trust him in most ways, because of his letter and his having had a relationship with Christ for twelve years, I dared to believe that perhaps his conscience had dictated that he be fair to me, at least financially.

Also, at this point in my Christian walk, I had learned through trial and error that choosing to do things God's way always worked out to be the best way for me. Therefore, it was my choice not to verbally scrap about money. I had also learned long before that God is faithful; He has His own way of righting the wrongs done to believers who place their trust in Him and obey His Word. Money issues were no different. In His faithfulness, God had led me to study certain Scripture I knew was His guidance for me.

The silence between us lengthened.

I do feel foolish about trusting Alex, but I cannot feel sorry for trying to go through this divorce without arguing about money.

The money deception had begun in Alex's heart months before, back in mid-1983, when I had given him that "one more chance" for which he had begged. I would have done anything to keep my family together—short of ever again being a victim of his abuse.

In the end, our final financial settlement was grossly unfair to me. But that was not the fault of my attorney. Again, I take responsibility for that. I listened to and trusted in Alex's words of promise.

The Bible proves true to me every time: "For the Lord sees not as a man sees; for man looks on the outward appearance, but the Lord looks on the heart" (1 Sam. 16:7b AMP). I *saw* and *heard* what I wanted to believe was honest and genuine in Alex. But only God had actually seen his heart. Nevertheless, what was done was done.

I broke the lull in our conversation and answered, "Alex, nothing in me would ever want to ruin the business or you."

My answer was defensive and cool. I wondered how he had known and lived with me so long but now found relief in the fact that I had not ruined him. He had to know I could not be vindictive or want to ruin him or anyone else.

After another uneasy lull in the conversation, Alex finally countered my coolness by saying in a soft, tender voice, "You know I really love you."

Silence again.

Unexpectedly, my emotions were aroused. His words were inappropriate at this point, purely gratuitous. Nonetheless, they were titillating, creating fragmented memories of the good years and the way we were together. I visualized him as he was when his eyes saw only me, pulled me in and embraced me, when his words *I love you* filled my heart with trust and made me feel safe. I could feel tears start to fill my throat. I was unraveling again; the image became blurred as tears pooled in my eyes.

How can this be happening to me? Was it the sound of his voice? The tenderness in the way he said, "I love you"? He's always known how to be charming when he wants to be. After all, he is the ultimate salesman!

I knew what I had to do. By a force of sheer will, I pushed my tears back somewhere deep inside and drove the sound of his voice and his words from my mind and my heart, letting go of the image. Part of me was sad to see the image go. But I knew it was the only way to stay clearly focused on the truth, no matter how painful.

Now that truth replayed loud and clear in my mind, aiding my surrender to reality, and I silently argued, *No, you can't love me! Love doesn't do what you have done to your wife, the mother of your children.*

As though reading my thoughts, Alex reaffirmed, "I'll never love anyone but you. I just can't live the Christian life," he confessed. "It's too hard. You're stronger than I am, Alisha," he softly defended, as if saddened by his own words.

Silence once again dominated us.

That's his excuse? He can't live the Christian life because it's too hard? As if that had been the real issue and not his own choices! If he couldn't live as a Christian, why couldn't he just live a good, decent life? Millions of non-Christian men do it every day! When did he lose his moral compass? Didn't he know God had watched him sneak back into his old life and watched him break his marriage vows before I knew it? Did he even have a clue that an insidious evil had invaded and poisoned his heart? Lord, I prayed so hard. Why didn't You rescue Alex before he wandered so far off Your path?

Then a Scripture passage softly moved across my mind: "Every person is tempted when he is drawn away, enticed *and* baited by his own evil desire (lust, passions)" (James 1:14 AMP).

I opened my mouth to scream at him, *Don't you dare say you love me or make excuses!* but no sound came out. It was not the first time I had choked on words that needed to be said.

Instead, I finally responded in a tone tinged with sorrow, but also reality: "That's sad to hear, Alex. But you're wrong about me. I'm not stronger than you. I couldn't make it through a day without Christ."

With that reminder, I thought about myself. I knew I was far from perfect, with my own weaknesses, inadequacies, and failings with which to deal. I wondered how I might have behaved toward him throughout the last three years and during this whole tragic divorce without the Lord being so indispensable to my daily living.

Clearly I could see it was only by God's grace and mercy, His influence in my life, that I did not retaliate in kind to Alex. That knowing alone now helped lessen my infuriation with him—and his words.

My voice took on a warmer tone, and I assured Alex, "God will be there for you too, if you ever decide you need Him again."

There was no response.

I wondered what he was thinking. I felt a shiver again, remembering I had never seen Alex happier than when he was living as a Christian. And I wished, again, there was a way I could edit my memories.

Now conscious of the silence that hung between us, I felt uncomfortable. It was an awkward moment. Two people who had spent twenty-six married years together now had nothing more to say to one another.

"Well, that's all I called for ... ah ... I just wanted to say thanks for saving the business ... Good-bye."

"Good-bye, Alex."

As I placed the receiver back on the phone, my heart grieved again for the death of my marriage and the breakup of my family, provoking the same sobering thought I had earlier in the morning and recorded in my journal: no matter how devout and true a Christian may try to be, life does not always turn out to be "happily ever after." My life with—and now without—Alex was shocking proof of that reality. It was a hard lesson to learn and one impossible to ignore.

I stood motionless, staring out the kitchen window, saddened by our conversation, saddened by the day and the last three years. It was an overwhelming feeling, quickened again by that single telephone call.

"I'm so tired," I whispered to myself as I leaned against the counter. Fixing my eyes on the coffeepot holding the cold remains of an early morning brewing, but no less appealing, I poured some into a mug and heated it in the microwave.

My life! I sighed. Taking my coffee from the microwave, I noticed it was in my favorite mug, given to me by my daughter. The inscription always made me smile: World's Greatest Mom.

Mug in hand, I moved to the glass sliding door to look out, staring but focusing on nothing.

Despite how it feels today, my life with Alex hasn't been all bad, I silently reasoned. *It just feels all bad today ... and I feel like such a weak Christian. I'm dealing with such an extreme mix of good and bad emotions.*

It was true. Conflicting emotions had been flooding my mind from early morning, exposing my weaknesses of self-pity, rejection, pride, fear, and shame. During the last three years, one or all of those crippling emotions had cropped up again and again, and each time I had asked forgiveness and released them to God. Therefore, they never plagued me for long periods, never took root, and never defeated my faith in God's protection.

For me His faithfulness had been tried and tested over many years. I knew He was in this fiery trial with me. But today it seemed to me that the finality of divorce had given those harassing sins of the flesh more punch, accentuating my weakness. I knew I had to keep on releasing them to God, if I were to be healed and whole again.

I took three deep breaths, slowly exhaling each one, trying to calm my roller-coaster emotions. It did not help.

Feeling out of control was not something I was used to for the last nineteen years. Before now, prayer had always turned my emotions right side up pretty quickly. I had been praying a lot, but now foreboding questions about my emotional instability pressed me hard into feelings of insecurity once again.

Oh dear Lord, my life has been turned inside out. How can I cope now when everything hurts so much? My feelings of sorrow for the past meshed with my fears for the future, growing so painful I could no longer express them, even to God.

"Oh God," I wailed, grabbing my churning stomach as the racking pain grabbed at my heart, my soul.

Deep sobs I had been unable to release gushed forth like torrential rains, and I groaned, "Help me, please … Oh God, take this pain away."

Then an inexplicable calmness came over me, and my sobs dissolved. I sensed a sweet peace enveloping me as a Scripture verse replaced all other thoughts: "I will turn their mourning into joy, and will comfort them, and make them rejoice from their sorrow" (Jer. 31:13 AMP).

"Thank You, my Jesus," I whispered.

I could feel myself drawing strength from that sweet reminder of God's words of promise, gently stirring my spirit, arousing silent praises. Courage was rising from within, renewing my confidence. It seemed that a load had been lifted from my shoulders. My chest had felt tight since early morning, but now the pressure had eased.

Calm now, I lifted my eyes to really look out through the glass door and saw that the wind was also calm. I focused my eyes and all my senses on winter's beauty. The trees were now standing straight and strong on a stretch of snow-covered lawn bordering the sixteen-acre lake framed by woods. I remembered how each season with its own special beauty had transported me into what I called my "great escape," when I needed one. Whatever the season, this particular view always lifted my spirit.

Gazing up at the sky, I could see it had also changed. Now it was brighter. Clouds were gracefully parting, clearing the way for spots of blue and, hopefully, a winter sun.

I needed this escape today. The anticipation of sun reminded me of spring, when all God's appointments of nature surrounding our home awakened to new life—when resident ducks floated gracefully on the lake or lounged on its shore, squirrels scampered over the lawn and joined chirping birds in the trees, and flowering dogwoods and perennials painted the landscape with glorious colors.

I remembered splendid summer days full of radiant blue skies glistening with blazing sunshine—happy days, when I stood in this very place, sat at the kitchen table, or sat on the back deck, sometimes with Alex, watching our children fishing from the boat, swimming, or rising swanlike up into the air from the diving board mounted on the dock or stretched out on beach towels, inviting hot sun rays to turn their beautiful bodies golden tan.

A broad smile spread across my face as images of my children when they were small appeared in my mind's eye and lingered. I could see them as they grew and developed into the persons they are today: Michael, firstborn, with his coal black hair and wise, hazel eyes; Laura, middle child, with that lovely combination of cornflower blue eyes and long, silky, chestnut hair; and Steven, the youngest, born a towhead, his hair turning color over the years from blonde to light brown to medium brown, with clear-as-glass blue eyes.

I feel a mother's pride when I think of my children. They're not perfect, but they have been good kids. Each one has a good heart, knows Christ as Savior, and has genuine respect for the Bible. They've been honor students throughout the years, each one graduating with honors from high school. That makes me proud too. Time passes so fast. They've become such interesting young adults. Now they're working equally hard to achieve in college, while holding down jobs. No easy task.

I loved mothering. Now I stopped to reflect on how the way I had been raised had influenced the way I had parented my own children. I realized that although I knew the satisfaction of having done my best during the spring season of my life, there had been a downside to living without parental praises. Sadly, I realized that back then I had not experienced a sense of genuine personal joy deep within for achievements or honors I received.

Nonetheless, despite my having lived without parental praise and demonstrative affection, gratefully, God had given me the capacity to be openly expressive with my love and praise for my husband, children, and others. It had given me pleasure when my husband had talked over the details of his days on the job and his achievements, or entrusted his disappointments and other heart concerns to me, for which I could encourage, praise, or console him.

Also, I had made sure to listen when my children had something on their minds, because I had missed that attention growing up. It had been important to me that none of my children feel alone, that they knew they were each a significant, valued individual in our family, that they heard my words of praise and emotionally felt my pride in them for their achievements, and that they each knew they were loved unconditionally.

I thought about the fact that while growing up, my children were exposed to more temptation in this current society with its modern morality than had my generation. I reminded myself that each of my children had come of age, and I knew I was no longer responsible for their decisions and life choices. All I could do now was love them, encourage them when they faced difficult circumstances, offer praise for their accomplishments, pray for them, and always be here for them. From now on, like their father and me, they would make their own choices—right or wrong, good or bad—for which they alone would be accountable.

Choices, I sighed. *Does Alex even think about how his choices have hurt his children?*

Now as I stood at the wall of glass, staring at the gorgeous view before me, I thought again about the wonderful times we had shared in this house, except during the last three years of Alex's raging anger. I had to admit that these past six months had been a pleasant reprieve from his threatening behavior.

After he left in July, it was finally peaceful and fun again, for the children and me. Summer Sundays were especially fun for us and for their friends who sometimes joined us. Michael would buy and cook his favorite surf and turf meal: crab legs and steaks on the grill. Steven, Laurie, and I would do our parts to bring the meal together, and we would all enjoy eating on the patio; then afterward the kids sometimes would swim or take the boat out.

Alex used to love watching the kids and their friends having fun in the water. Oh, why did he give up everything good in his life? When I think about the life choices he has made, I still cannot understand why he could not stay on track with Jesus when all the help of heaven was available to him. He said, "The Christian life is too hard to live." What was too hard about God having answered his prayers ... proven His faithfulness ... blessing him so greatly? What does one go back to that's better than knowing God's peace, having one's dreams come true, and living an abundant life?

Instantly I felt the tug of another melancholy memory, transporting me back to an autumn day when the trees were magnificent, full with brilliant fire colors. With perfect clarity, I can see Alex excitedly rushing us all to see the spectacular view from the back of this house high on a hill; his "dream home on the lake," he had called it. He was determined to buy it for his family, declaring, "I've worked hard for it," and promising, "We're going to be happier than ever in this house!"

Remembering that day and Alex's joyful declaration made today even sadder to me. My throat tightened as tears tried to push their way up again. Quickly I blinked them away and let go of the memory.

Again, it's strange how reflecting earlier this morning on the way we were when Alex and I began our life together, just as now recalling former happy times in this house, makes me feel more acutely alone.

Now I chided myself to remember reality again: *Things are not what I wish they were—they are what they are.*

As I recall, things were exactly as I wished them to be by the time I became a bride. Everything in my life seemed to be going well. My world still felt perfect when Alex and I entered his black Chevy on our wedding day to begin our life together. Having consciously dismissed all the negative from my mind, I began my marriage happily, with all the hopes and dreams of every bride.

Like other young married women, I expected the American dream of a happy home filled with love, and my expectations were realized throughout our honeymoon and the days that immediately followed. Little did I know that with my marriage, the day would come when I would make a desperate effort to hide my life from family and friends.

However confident about myself I had been before becoming a bride, however emotionally stable and physically healthy I had been before our wedding, however ideally perfect our marriage had begun, life with Alex would take shocking, unexpected turns, wounding me deeply. During the course of one evening, my American dream of a happy marriage and a home filled with love would become more like an American nightmare, and my life would drastically change.

Now a flashback came crashing to the forefront of my mind, reminding me again that I had no inkling of the heartache and pain that lay ahead for me when I married. Immediately that long-buried memory came into clear focus, automatically carrying me back.

I was a new bride. It was Friday, just two months into our marriage, when I rushed home after work anxious to try out the new entrée recipe I had found in a popular ladies' magazine. Having spent a lot of time cutting out recipes and reading my mom's cookbooks, I was hoping to learn some of her culinary skills, trying hard to become a good cook. Dinner was hot and on the table when I called Alex.

Waiting for him to take his place, I stood admiring our wedding gifts of white and aqua everyday china resting on white linen placemats trimmed with an aqua border, and matching napkins. After saying grace, silently we went about filling our plates. Handing Alex the last platter of the full-course meal, I awaited my new husband's delighted reaction.

I am not sure which I heard first, the shattering of the platter as Alex hurled it against the wall or his high-pitched screaming. His eyes were filled with hatred as he fired accusations at me. "Selfish!" "Disgusting!" "You stupid b— — — —!

I burst into tears. "What's wrong, Alex?" I cried. "Why are you doing this? Stop, please, stop!" "You made something with cheese sauce on it last week," he shouted. "Do you think just because you like cheese on everything, I do too? You selfish b— — — —, you only fix food you like! You don't care about what I like!"

"But Alex, I only thought ..."

"I don't care what you think. When I'm the one who works hard all day to put food on the table, I at least want something decent to eat." He continued to scream, describing my meal with obscenities and using the "f" word over and over, cursing such as I had never heard in my entire life.

I was sobbing. The more I tried to get a word in, the more filthy four-letter words Alex threw at me. The veins in his neck bulged, and his face was bright red.

"Get over there and clean up that mess!" he finally ordered. Cursing still, he got up, and I reared back, thinking he was going to hit me. Instead, he knocked his chair to the floor and stormed outside, slamming the door as he left.

I was stunned. *Alex seemed fine when he came to the table. He's never been a violent person. He's never used gutter language, and I know he'd never allow anyone else to use it in my presence! What's wrong with him? There has to be some explanation!*

Looking around the room at the debris, I saw broken china, and potatoes and cheese sauce dribbling down the wall and settling into yellow blobs on the tile. Cheese sauce was splattered on the dining room table and chair legs.

Robot-like, I tiptoed through the food, picking up the broken china. Tears blurred my vision. My hands started shaking. And then I remembered my dream of my faceless groom. In the dream I had not known the man I was marrying. Tonight I did not know the man to whom I was married.

I felt sick. I went to the bathroom, splashed cold water on my face, and looked up. There in the mirror was the image of a girl-woman, a new bride, stricken with fear of the violence she had just witnessed in her new husband.

After soaking a washcloth in cold water, I pressed it to my swollen eyes. Alex's words screamed relentlessly in my mind, bouncing around in my brain until my head began to throb. *None of the articles or books I read on marriage, none of Father Maloney's marriage counseling—nothing—could have prepared me for this!*

I looked in the mirror again. Everything was blurred, especially my American dream of a happy marriage to a wonderful man who would be my loving husband. In a split second, Alex had become someone else. *Was this what Jim had meant on my wedding day? Had he known this Alex? Had my brother CJ ever seen this side of Alex? No ... not a chance. I'm sure he didn't, or CJ would have told me ... He never would have continued a friendship with him, much less knowingly let his sister date and marry him! How did he hide this ugly temper from me and everyone else all this time? It seems impossible—but he did!*

I reached for a bottle of aspirin and fleetingly imagined consuming the whole thing, lying down in bed, and going to sleep forever. Instead, I swallowed two tablets and left the bathroom.

I considered calling someone for help. But who? I could not imagine telling my family or friends; how would they believe Alex could act like this when I could not believe it?

Almost mechanically I went back into the dining room to clean up the mess. In a flash, I felt a white-hot anger inside of me as I scrubbed the wall, table legs, and tile floor.

Who does he think he is, doing this to me, saying those ugly, foul words and calling me insulting names? I don't deserve to hear any of it—no one does! How could this possibly have happened?

Then my anger quickly gave way to unbearable despair. I was totally undone. I was in such shock that my mind, let alone my heart, could not even continue to try to process or make sense of all this. I went back to the bathroom and stepped into a very hot shower, hoping, I guess, to ease the tension in my muscles and the pain in my heart, probably much like a rape victim who tries to wash away the violation that has been forced upon her body.

I crawled into bed, trying to forget, trying to erase this insanity from my thoughts. But flashes of Alex's face, his cruel anger, his foul cursing and ugly name-calling brought fresh tears—and unanswerable questions—all over again.

It couldn't have been just the cheese sauce. That's ridiculous. This was no normal outburst; but then, what was it? Did I do something to make him that angry? Did I say something tonight, last night, this morning, last week, anytime? No decent husband would behave that way! So why did he? Should I leave right now and never come back? Divorce him and erase this chapter of my life as though it has never been? How could I? I've only been married for two months, and up until this day, I have been enormously happy. Oh God, I can't even think of it being over! Besides, I'm Catholic. I would be ostracized by the church ... my relatives and friends.

I felt betrayed, vulnerable. I was afraid for him to come home, but I was more afraid to leave. I was sure my parents would say, "Your place is with your husband." Even if they did agree with my leaving Alex, I realized at that moment I could not do it. I had loved him for a long time; this one event, as horrible as it was, surely should not erase that—and besides, I was not a quitter. The clincher was my own strong religious belief and commitment to my marriage vows.

I heard the car pull into the driveway and stop. My body tensed. The car door slammed, sounding louder than usual in the stillness of night. Listening to the back door open and close and to Alex's footsteps down the tiled hallway into the bathroom, I inched over as far as I could on my side of the bed, turning my back to Alex's side.

When he entered the room, I pretended to be asleep. He climbed into bed, and I could smell alcohol; and although he did smoke, tonight I noticed for the first time that rank smell of stale cigarette smoke on him. Obviously, he had been sitting in a bar for hours, something I would never have expected him to do, especially as a married man. But after his violent display, I realized there was a side of him I did not know at all. Because of that, I did not know what to expect next from him. To my relief, Alex stayed on his side of the bed.

The next morning I slipped out of bed gently, not wanting to "awaken the beast." The smell of coffee brewing brought him to the kitchen. I was nervous, not knowing what to say, and I kept my back to him.

He came up behind me, slipped his arms around my waist, and squeezed firmly. "What's for breakfast, honey?"

I was stunned at his casual tone. I kept my back to him, standing rigidly, as thoughts raced through my mind: *Is this the same man who yelled obscenities and ugly names, threw things and slammed doors twelve hours earlier? Is this the same man who screamed at his new bride before leaving the house for most of the night? I don't know that crazed man—but this man I know. This cheerful, affectionate man loves me, and God knows, every part of my being wants to deny what happened last night and go back to all that we had before that dinner.*

Turning me to face him, Alex folded his arms around me again, kissing me tenderly. "I love you, honey," he whispered.

Shrugging to break his hold, I began, "Alex, about last night ..."

He hung on tightly, repeating sweetly, "I love you, honey. I was just tired. The job has me upset. I didn't mean those things, whatever I said and did. I love you. You know that. I didn't mean to take it out on you. But please … no more cheese sauce, okay?" He ended his words with his irresistible, enticing boyish grin.

My pain, confusion, and anger were fading fast in eager, too eager, relief. I was faltering, caving in, a young bride who wanted desperately to understand her new husband and make her marriage a success. I knew that Alex loved me—really loved me—as I loved him. I needed to believe in this marriage and in Alex, and so I forgave him. Wanting to choose denial over reality, I reassured myself that the whole incident was behind us, and we would go on just as we were before it happened.

Nevertheless, questions stayed with me, haunting me. Alex's "dark side" had been so shocking to me because I had known him to be the same, even-tempered, nice guy day after day, month after month, for a year and a half. But now I wondered who that other frightening, abusive person was that my loving Prince Charming had turned into the night before? *How could he lose all control like that and scream at the top of his lungs at me, and use such vulgar language? How could he call me such filthy names? How could Alex speak to me or anyone else, for that matter, in that cruel tone of voice? How could he treat anyone that way? But especially me, the woman he claims to love?*

Looking back, I could see that when this dark side of Alex emerged over cheese sauce, my responses had been a series of emotions, actions, and reactions that exploded in me. They were unfamiliar, shocking emotions: everything from extreme terror, to extreme anger and confusion, to the most intense emotional pain I had ever experienced. Alex was like two people. His behavior was like that of Dr. Jekyll and Mr. Hyde.

That forced me to face agonizing observations, vexing questions, and poignant facts about Alex. An arduous mental exercise began, searching for a reason for my husband's violent behavior: *The nightmare of my faceless groom has come true. How did his dreadful dark side remain hidden from me all this time? What clues did I miss? Did my love for him blind me from seeing his anger before we married, an angry temperament that I might have excused?*

No! I had immediately known the answer to my latter question. It was definite. I was as certain then as I am now that had Alex displayed anything remotely close to that type of anger before marriage, I never would have married him—dream or no dream. The answers to my other questions, however, remained a mystery at that time.

As a young woman coming of age in the 1950s, I was typically naïve. Before Alex's abusive outburst, I had never seen that kind of violence or heard that filthy cursing coming from him or any other human being. However, considering that period in our nation's history, I now understand my naïveté. I had been brought up not only with a father who treated my mother with respect, but also in a more civil culture, part of the *Ozzie and Harriet* family television sitcom generation.

Nothing had changed by 1959 when we married. It was, culturally speaking, still a civil period in our nation. I saw no theater or television movies about family violence, or any that contained dialogue with the "f" word, or other cursing and filthy name-calling; neither had I learned from news media reports from television, radio, newspapers, or magazines about spousal abuse. If indeed the kind of abuse I had received from my new husband that evening was perpetrated upon other wives by their husbands, it must have been kept a deep, dark secret.

I remember the desperation, mental confusion, and conflict that horrible evening. Even back then, I did not believe that cheese sauce was the issue, although Alex had made it so as an excuse for his bad behavior. In fact, despite my lack of exposure to abusive behavior of any kind, I did not believe Alex's degree of anger toward me could be normal anger for anyone.

I recall part of my mental processing of the whole thing was recalling the year-and-a-half collection of good memories Alex and I had created during our courtship, engagement, and honeymoon. I remember convincing myself that all married couples need a period of adjustment. The combination of that rationale, society in the '50s and '60s, my fear of being ostracized by the Catholic Church, and the opinions of Catholic family and friends collectively formed my decision that divorce was not an option for me. I would try even harder to understand my new husband and to anticipate and meet his needs. Somehow I had to make this new marriage work.

Now a Scripture verse moved gently across my mind: "Do not boast of [yourself and] tomorrow, for you know not what a day may bring forth" (Prov. 27:1 AMP.)

I am reminded that as newlyweds, our marriage relationship should have been brimming with warm pleasures and happy discoveries about each other. Instead, for Alex and me, everything changed in an instant one night at the dinner table; and sadly, after that it turned cold, then oppressive. Without my realizing it, a stronghold of fear of Alex's Jekyll-and-Hyde personality took hold of me. Before I knew it, I was thrust into an even more painful, frightening new season of my life that I call my *autumn* years—and *winter* was just around the corner.

Chapter 5

Buried Memories Exhumed

The weight of reality of the judge's decree and an unknown future were hard to bear this morning, especially after Alex's phone call. My energy was sapped again, making me feel I was teetering on the edge of collapse. By now I felt drained of every ounce of strength I had marshaled to get through this morning's ordeal.

I refilled my coffee mug and walked from the kitchen to the sunken family room. Stepping down, I moved across the light cranberry colored carpet to the stone-walled fireplace where a fire Michael had laid was blazing up the chimney. A fire had always added to the already welcoming and comfortable atmosphere of this room. I settled into one of the two fireside wing chairs covered inside with a taupe, brown, and white print tapestry, the back and wings wrapped in coordinating brown velvet.

As I sipped the steaming coffee, my eyes perused the wood-paneled room that had an almost golden sheen wherever touched by light. Against one wall was the big brown velvet sofa with chairs pulled up around a French antique cocktail table for an inviting conversational grouping. Alex's comfy, beige recliner faced the wall of glass overlooking the back property and lake, a scene of which his eyes had never tired. Against the opposite wall stood the ceiling-high, three-piece traditional wall unit. Behind its top glass doors were shelved books, art pieces, and family mementoes, and the cabinet doors below hid games and movie videos.

I sat musing about former, happier times in this room where the whole family had gathered. Michael was the one who had usually laid the fires we enjoyed on winter evenings. The children had liked being with us in this room—just being a family—when their busy schedules had allowed them to be home watching sports on television or movie videos.

Suddenly I gave way to deep, agonizing groans. *Nothing will ever be the same again!*

Then reality washed over me. Being happily together in this room had ceased three years before when everything had gone sour. During that time, this had been their often drunken, verbally abusive father's spot when he was at home. It was the last place in the house the kids—or I—had wanted to be.

My eyes moved to the wall collage of brass-framed photos of family and friends above the sofa. I found myself gazing at the formal photograph of Alex and me on our wedding day, and my thoughts carried me back again to those early years, the autumn season of my life.

I remember Alex promised he would never again behave as he had that evening only two months into marriage when he first erupted in rage at the dinner table. He was sure of it. With that terrible scene behind us, my new husband could not have been sweeter to me. He kept his promise. Most of our days together were pleasant, leading up to our first Thanksgiving and Christmas as a married couple. However, during that happy season, only four months after his violent outburst, another well-hidden aspect of my new husband's personality was exposed to me.

We had decorated our first Christmas tree. Along with the excitement of decorating the house and shopping for gifts, something else even more exciting was happening. I had received an early, most precious gift when my obstetrician confirmed my hope: I was pregnant with our first child. I could hardly wait to tell my husband. It was his gift too. It would be a bright beginning to the New Year.

Alex was thrilled. We even planned our first party, when we would ring in the New Year 1960 by announcing the news to our friends. Twelve couples accepted our invitation, including Jim,

Alex's best man in our wedding, and his date, who drove down from Alex's hometown. That memory brought a gasp, as flashing scenes raced across my mind, triggering all-too-fresh emotions. Despite that and just as though I had no choice, I was back there again.

Congratulations, good music, and happy conversation flowed. The party was a success. I did not think anything could spoil my joy. Then …

I had just replenished a tray of hors d'oeuvres and was crossing the long hallway leading from the front of the house to the bedrooms, when I saw them. My heart sank to my toes. Alex and Cheryl, Jim's lovely blonde date for the evening, were embracing passionately at the end of the darkened hallway. Alex pulled away then leaned into Cheryl and kissed her again as she backed against the wall.

The conversation and music in the other room seemed to fade as I stood there frozen, watching—unnoticed—in disbelief. I started trembling and filling with anger. Wild thoughts raced through my mind: *Do I scream at them and expose Alex for the jerk he really is? Do I politely stride down to the end of the hall and softly ask them what they think they're doing? Should I ask the guests to leave, so I can throw Jim's date out and then kill Alex? Or should I just throw this tray of hors d'oeuves in both of their faces?*

The tray in my hands began to shake. I forced my feet to move toward the living room and approached Jim. Controlling my expression, I whispered for Jim to follow me. As we left the living room, hot tears slowly slid down my cheeks.

"What's wrong, Alisha?" Jim asked quietly, but with alarm.

"Look down the hall, Jim."

Jim looked then took my arm and quickly escorted me through the dining room into the kitchen. Through gritted teeth he looked at me and exclaimed, "Unbelievable!"

"Jim," I cried, "I'm pregnant! How could he do this?" I could see Jim was fuming inside despite his control. He hesitated for a moment before answering.

"Remember the question I asked you at the church the day you got married?" he softly asked. "Well, that's Alex!"

"Jim, for heaven's sake, we've been married only six months. We're still newlyweds! He already needs to make it with another woman? Neither one of them has had too much to drink, so that can't be their excuse!"

Jim looked at me with his own pained expression. "Try to get hold of yourself," he said quietly. "Don't worry about Cheryl. I'm not. She's just a date to me. Alex has known her for years. And believe me, she doesn't mean anything to him. Alex does love you; I know that too. Come on now," he gently urged. "Get hold of yourself, Alisha, for the sake of your baby."

We agreed to do or say nothing during the party. I put on my smile and rejoined our guests, disguising my hurt for the sake of our friends, my marriage, my unborn baby, and my own pride.

Alex and Cheryl rejoined the group, Alex resuming his role as charming host and happy expectant father without even a hint of guilt or unease. I was sure none of the guests even suspected. In fact, it was obvious that Alex and Cheryl believed that their disgusting secret exchange had not been discovered. It was all I could do to contain myself until the party ended.

As Jim and Cheryl were leaving, Jim kissed me on the cheek, gave me a long meaningful look, and squeezed my arm in a sympathetic gesture. Alex saw them to the door. Then together we said good-bye to our last guests.

I was so angry, I did not even so much as pick up a glass! Instead, I went directly to the bathroom to get ready for bed. Sounds of cleaning up could be heard coming from the kitchen as I switched off the light at the wall and climbed into bed.

When Alex finally came into the bedroom, he started undressing in the dark.

"Turn on the light," I calmly ordered. When he did, the light exposed it all—my pain and my hostility too. I glared at him.

"How could you do it?"

"How could I do what?" he asked innocently, keeping his back turned to me.

"You know exactly what you and Cheryl were doing in the hallway," I went on. "And, don't plead any excuse that you had too much to drink and didn't know what you were doing! I don't buy it! So why ... why did you do it? Don't you like being married to me? Am I ugly? Am I not passionate or affectionate enough for you, that you have to be kissing another woman? Or do you just need a little variety?" I finished sarcastically.

I started sobbing. "Kissing that woman ... and in our own home! How could you? Aren't you happy that you're going to be a father? What is it?"

"You're pregnant ... You're fat."

"Fat?" I screamed back at him. *He can't mean that*, I thought. *I'm 108 pounds! I don't even look pregnant yet!*

Crushed, nonetheless, I grabbed my pillow, screaming between sobs, "Oh, you'd like me to have your baby as long as I don't lose my figure? You say I'm fat, and you can't stand that?" I ran to the guest room and slammed the bedroom door so hard I half expected it to fall from its hinges.

I lay there in the dark, crying, feeling the sting of humiliation, hurt, and anger all at the same time. That scene of those passionate kisses kept replaying in my mind. *If the way I look in these early months of pregnancy has caused you to hold another woman in your arms right in your own home, what will you do when I'm near full-term and big as a barn? What will you do to me then, Alex?*

"Oh God, it hurts so much!" I cried. Even worse, though, was my husband's lack of remorse for what he had done and for the pain he had caused me. *Besides that, if he's capable of doing this terrible thing in our own home, what does he do when he's occasionally out late at night because of business meetings or entertaining customers?*

"Is he really with business associates or customers?" I moaned.

Then, remembering Jim's words, I sighed with exhaustion as I whispered them to myself: "Get hold of yourself, Alisha, for the sake of your baby."

Unbelievably, sleep finally came.

I awakened Sunday morning, wishing I could hide from the bright sun streaming through the windows—and wishing I could shrink from the reality of the night before. This time Alex's knife had slashed deeper than ever, wounding me in my woman's heart and wounding me in my woman's pride. *No wonder in my dream he had no face, only an empty black hole. That was because I really didn't know him. Did I marry a philanderer too?* With the pain of it still fresh, I wanted to erase Alex's presence from my life.

I remember skipping Sunday Mass to avoid seeing Alex, and, indeed, he left the house early in the morning and arrived home late that night after I was in bed in the guest room. By allowing him to leave the house before I got up for work, I avoided seeing him again until Monday evening when he returned from work. Throughout that time alone, I thought and thought about what I should do, how I should handle this devastating incident. I had to ensure that it would never happen again. Finally, I knew what I must say to Alex.

Dinner was ready. Even in my anger and humiliation, I believed fixing dinner was still my responsibility. But I did not have to be sweet about it.

"We can sit down and eat as soon as you change clothes, Alex," I said coldly.

"Smells good!" he said cheerfully. I could tell he was trying to erase the tension in the room.

We were silent through dinner. Now I was ready to talk. I had decided to tell him only one thing.

I looked him directly in the eye. "I have only one thing to say to you, Alex," I began, in a controlled and confident tone. "If it ever happens again, it's over between us."

Alex was obviously shaken by my confidence and control.

"It won't happen again. I swear it won't. I'm sorry," his voice quivered. "I must have had too many martinis. I don't know why I did it. Cheryl doesn't mean anything to me ..."

"Neither do I!" I interrupted.

"I didn't mean any of those things I said to you ... about being fat ... I'm glad you're pregnant," he said, smiling sweetly and leaning over to pat my stomach. "I love you, Alisha; you know I do."

Tenderness toward my husband tugged at my heart, but even so, I eyed him coolly. I heard his words, but still I did not feel very loved. Nor did I feel loving.

"I know you're sorry, Alex. Now let's forget about it. I can't talk about it anymore."

But I made it clear: "Don't ever let it happen again!" I knew I would continue to think about it, and I wondered if I would dare to trust him again and take the chance of having my heart broken once more.

Alex had appeared remorseful, and he had promised he would never behave that way again. He was sure of it. However, I was not so sure. I made very little effort to improve things between us. I was still cool, cautious.

Alex, on the other hand, tried to make up for his cheating actions by being especially attentive to me romantically and protective of me physically. I could not figure out how he could be so loving and kind to me one minute then say and do such cruel, terrible things to me the next. There was definitely a nasty Mr. Hyde living inside my loving Dr. Jekyll. I wondered if there was something in his family background that caused his changeable behavior.

Nonetheless, like any other newlywed, I could not have anticipated my husband's reckless incident of betrayal with Cheryl any more than I could have seen coming his first abusive outburst. I had forgiven Alex for his violent behavior and believed that with love and more understanding, I could help him overcome whatever it was that had caused it. However, I had to fight with my own conscience to forgive his behavior with Cheryl.

But then when I thought about my baby, it was inconceivable to me that it should be born without its father. So although it was hard, I did forgive Alex for the sake of our baby. Soon I found myself rationalizing once again. Since I was not a drinker and could not have understood the effects of too much alcohol, I considered that Alex may have been right. It could be true that he had had one too many vodka martinis at the party. *And after all,* I reminded myself, *it was just a kiss. It's not as though he slept with her.*

I believed I had to forget and go on, while at the same time I secretly planned to approach Alex, when the time was right, to suggest marriage counseling. But despite my resolve, as a result of my husband's illicit behavior with Cheryl, something began to happen to me. I decided I had to be a perfect wife; I had to look perfect, act perfect, keep a perfect house, and be a perfect cook. Perfect, perfect, perfect! I almost wore myself out every day trying to do it all, plus work a forty-hour week at my job. I had to be better than that "other woman," who might appeal to my husband in a future weak moment.

As the weeks went by, although I was still guarded, Alex continued to be sweet and attentive to me—like the man I had married. Although I could not deny there was a dark side to my new husband's personality, I made a concentrated effort to focus on the positive in order to rise above the difficult times, a common practice in my new marriage.

I filled myself with good thoughts about my baby and staying physically well, which helped to lessen my concerns about Alex's deceitful tryst with Cheryl. My worries faded with each passing day. I began to feel a little more secure with Alex. I finally let my guard down, and we began having fun together again.

Early in my pregnancy, I felt well; I had none of the morning sickness I had heard I should expect. I remember some nights Alex and I would lie in bed and he would place his hands on my belly, trying to feel that first movement. And I remember how much we had wanted this baby, and we loved talking about "him."

The first interruption to our neat little family plans was a three-day hospital stay for a threatened miscarriage because of breakthrough bleeding. I prayed hard for God to keep my pregnancy intact. The worry of losing our baby was short-lived, however, and the doctor assured us that everything would be fine. I returned to work.

A short time later, a second crisis came. I was hospitalized for five days, this time for toxemia. Again I prayed for God to save my baby. Again we were spared the heartbreak of a miscarriage, and I spent a few days at home before going back to work. Alex took good care of me in those days; he cooked our meals and even did our laundry! However, as the weeks went by, I began to worry about him again.

Alex did not erupt in anger, but his disposition became more erratic than ever. He appeared depressed. His mood changed unpredictably. He would be calm and easygoing one moment, then loud, nasty, and critical to me the next. For the most part, he would always apologize and cite some outside provocation: either the pressure of his job or he did not feel well. Then he would be especially loving and caring toward me once again. Although the words were unsolicited, he would often tell me, "You know I love you, honey. I've got the best wife in the whole world."

Suddenly flashing scenes of another long-buried memory came to mind, as though exhumed from the graveyard of bad memories in my subconscious.

I was back there again, plugging away at my regular routine while my belly was growing bigger and bigger. I usually spent my evenings and Saturdays sewing drapes for the nursery and painting secondhand furniture to complement the new crib my parents had bought for the baby. My last project for the nursery was to paint a wall mural of large scenes of Mother Goose rhymes to coordinate with the pattern in the drapery fabric. I looked forward to a free weekend when I could start sketching the nursery rhymes.

During my waiting period, we had bought a used car for me to drive, and it was Friday after work when I stopped at the grocery on the way home.

My car pulled into the driveway, and I maneuvered myself from under the steering wheel to exit the car and waddle to the trunk to retrieve the groceries. Both arms clutched two full bags, supported by my big belly, as I walked from the car to the house.

"Hi, honey," Alex greeted me at the back door with a smile. "How are ya?" He took the bags from me, peering into them as he carried them into the kitchen.

Suddenly he slammed both bags down on the floor. His back was turned to me, but I could see the back of his neck turn beet red. The bags ripped open, and tomatoes, lettuce, canned goods, and boxes slid and rolled across the kitchen floor and into the dining room.

Alex whirled around, his face now as red as the back of his neck. I was terrified and instinctively braced myself for yet another raging attack.

"Why," he cussed, "did you buy those things! You stupid idiot! They cost too much! Anyone knows you don't buy hothouse tomatoes this time of the year!" he screamed, following with a string of profanities. "You'd better clean that mess up!"

I did not say a word. I just stood there, locked in that same familiar fear, staring at him.

Alex yelled his order again as he bolted past me through the narrow doorway, knocking me hard against the door frame with his body, and slammed out the back door.

It had all happened so fast, I had not even set my purse down.

"Oh God ... not again ... not again ... We're going to have a baby ... I didn't think this would ever happen again," I cried. Grabbing my stomach, I wailed, "Not again ... I can't stand it! I can't take any more!"

Slumped against the wall, terrified, I burst into tears. My purse dropped from my hand, and I slowly slid to the floor and sobbed uncontrollably, surrounded by the mess that stretched across the tiled kitchen and dining room floors. Still crying, I started to slowly crawl on the floor, picking up scattered groceries—then I stopped.

"No! I won't pick up this mess ... He'll pick it up or it can stay here forever! There's no excuse this time ... I won't accept it!"

With that decision, I calmed down, got myself off the floor, went into the bathroom, and stepped into the shower. I did not care where Alex went tonight, what he did, or if he even came home—ever. *This is Alex's problem! I refuse to allow his problem to further spoil my life!* Divorce was on my mind. But then I reasoned with myself and muttered, "This baby growing inside of me needs two parents. I have to make this marriage work!"

This determination helped ease my nerves. I did not know how I was going to manage anything from now on, but at this point I decided to let go of my anger and settled in the guest room with a novel. I was still awake when I heard Alex come in the back door. It was eleven thirty. Soon I heard rustling in the kitchen, cupboard doors and the refrigerator quietly opening and closing, and realized he was cleaning up the mess. Quickly I turned out the light, tugged my propped pillow down, and went to sleep.

The next morning I was up early, determined for my unborn baby's sake not to be affected by Alex's cruel behavior the night before. This Saturday I was going to sketch the Mother Goose scenes on the nursery wall, and I intended to enjoy myself.

I could hear Alex moving around in the kitchen, and soon I smelled coffee and bacon. I thought he was making his own breakfast, too embarrassed to face me or ask me to make it for him.

"Honey," Dr. Jekyll beckoned sweetly, standing at the nursery room door, "I've made breakfast. Will you come to the table?"

"No, Alex," I answered flatly.

"I cleaned up that mess ...," he coaxed, as if that would fix the problem.

"Yes, I saw you did. It was your mess!"

"Honey, I don't know what got into me. Come on and eat, and we'll talk about it," he insisted.

"No. No more excuses, Alex. I don't want to hear them. There's no excuse for that kind of behavior." I abruptly turned back to my sketching.

"Honey, please, just come in and sit down and eat with me," he pleaded.

I knew I would have to confront him sometime and thought it might as well be now. "Okay ... okay," I relented. "I'll be there in a minute," I said, concentrating on the sketch of the "Old Woman Who Lived in a Shoe".

When I sat down at the table, he immediately began talking about something else, carefully avoiding the subject completely.

"What about last night, Alex?" I interrupted.

"What about it? I just got mad ... Just don't buy hothouse tomatoes anymore," he stated with a grin. I did not respond, but I was fuming inside at his ambiguity, his guiltless shift of blame to me for his violent behavior.

"I'm sick of your refusal to take responsibility for your bad behavior," I finally declared in a raised tone. "If you can't control your temper, if you have to rage and curse, you better get some professional help, because I don't want to see those actions or listen to that vulgar language. It's unacceptable behavior in human society! And I certainly will not expose our baby to it!"

Alex seemed stunned. Finally he spoke.

"You're right, honey. I won't do that again ... I won't. You'll see."

After breakfast he was so loving and especially attentive toward me, profusely complimenting me on the nursery scenes. "I'm the luckiest man in the world to have you. The baby's lucky too!"

His sweet talk did not turn me. I had heard it all before. I was cool toward him and initiated no conversation between us the rest of the weekend. In the weeks that followed, although Alex was occasionally moody and critical once again, paradoxically, he was also the caring, charming, and lovable man I had fallen in love with.

I was back in the present again.

Unnerved by that last memory and still staring at our wedding photo, I told myself that once in a lifetime would be too much to experience that kind of violence in marriage. The reality for me was that I had lived through all those abusive incidents within our first year!

Although my husband's verbal abuse and betrayal during that period was indefensible, I recall telling myself: *I can't throw in the towel this early in our marriage. Who divorces her husband after only two months ... six months ... one year? Besides,* I rationalized, *the fear of becoming a father might be causing some of Alex's stress. There must be natural anxieties about this new role and the responsibilities that come with it—for every man.*

Alex was under some pressure with his job, and with my having almost lost the baby twice, I further rationalized that maybe his behavior was not so unusual after all. It was such a confusing time for me. All I knew for sure was that I wanted my baby to have its father.

I know it seems lame now, but it made perfect sense at the time.

Again I had made a choice. I would continue to try hard to keep the peace, to be the perfect wife, and to find a way to fix our marriage. But still I was waiting to find just the right time to speak with Alex about the two of us getting professional help. My baby just had to be born into a peaceful union, a peaceful family, a peaceful home.

Perhaps new-millennium women would not agree with my choice. In today's culture, I can understand why women might be wondering why I did not go ahead and divorce Alex.

Looking back, 1959–60 was a time in our society when things were also different when it came to divorce. It was a time when divorce rarely happened. Divorce was the big taboo. As far as I knew, divorce happened in Hollywood, but not in the general population, and definitely not in my little corner of the world.

It was a time when divorce was not socially accepted in most circles. If there was a divorce, it must have been only whispered about behind closed doors. I believed, for instance, that a divorcée became a marked woman. Her character and reputation were held in question, and she endured shame.

However, spiritually speaking, it was also a time before we found out that divorce was *not* the unpardonable sin, and remarriage was *not* an automatic one-way ticket to hell, contrary to the belief of some religious people back then and perhaps now.

It was a time when couples did not have the same choices for legal grounds to obtain a divorce as they do today. No-fault divorce, dissolution, incompatibility, and irreconcilable differences were unheard of as legal grounds. Legal grounds for divorce, such as adultery, for example, were stringent and had to be proven.

It was also a time when, by and large, people stayed in their marriages no matter what and for various reasons:

- Women stayed no matter how oppressed they were by abusive, alcoholic, or philandering husbands.
- Men stayed no matter how miserable they were.
- Some women stayed for economic reasons. They simply could not support themselves and their children, nor were there day-care facilities for children available to single mothers as there are today.
- Men stayed for their own economic reasons.
- Many couples stayed for the sake of their children.

Others stayed for religious reasons: one who was divorced risked being ostracized by his or her church clergy and congregation.

- Roman Catholics risked being ban from receiving the church sacrament of Holy Communion if they remarried; the same ruling applies today.

Each of these reasons became scenarios looming vividly in my mind after that "hothouse tomato" incident, just as they had after Alex's first violent outburst and his betrayal. However, I also could not let go of my own ideals about what marriage and family should be, what it could be—what I knew it must be for my baby.

Now, my eyes still fixed on our wedding photograph, I was conscious of an invisible line that had been drawn today, separating my past from my future. I had been a wife for most of my life. Now I was in my middle years—not old, but not young anymore—and alone.

Alex may have had the right to choose his future, I silently groaned, *but who gave him permission to order mine?*

Never in my wildest imagination would I have believed my future would be lived as a divorced Christian woman. For me the word *divorcée* felt like a descriptive tag with worldly connotations that did not fit comfortably. Nevertheless, I would have to wear it like a garment.

Alex's departure from me and the children and from the scriptural principles he had espoused for twelve years in order to embrace his old lifestyle and new life choices had been painful to watch—but tormenting to live through. There was no limit to his life choices; they were not restricted to shattering my dreams. They reached further than that, shattering my life, my children's lives, our family.

This day of the divorce climaxed that terrible three-year period in our marriage. Alex's assaults upon me were over. But I knew the assault upon my mind, my heart, and my soul would last far longer.

I refocused my eyes on our wedding photo, remembering all too well how the handsome, innocent-looking face of my groom with his boyish grin could change in a split second to a cruel-looking face with a sadistic, even menacing, smile.

My emotions of anger and bitterness were aroused again, not only from my memories of the old Jekyll-and-Hyde days, but also because within the last three years, Mr. Hyde had reared his ugly head again and taken my loving Dr. Jekyll to a new level of cruel deception and sinister antics. My reality this morning reminded me that I will never again live with that dark, deceptive, abusive personality, Mr. Hyde. That truth overcame my negative emotions and filled me with a sense of relief. Nevertheless, automatically I walked to the sofa, yanked our wedding photo off the wall, walked into the laundry room, and threw it hard into the trash!

"Help me, Lord!" I whispered, as I walked back into the kitchen to heat another cup of coffee.

Chapter 6

Clouded Joys

Gripping my hot mug, I climbed the stairs to my bedroom. The children were still in their own bedrooms. *Probably studying, or perhaps they, too, are remembering the good and bad times, feeling their own kind of pain—or anger,* I silently considered.

How terrible for innocent children of parents like us whose life choices or divorce are forced upon them! They can do nothing about their family breakup. Although Michael, Laura, and Steven understand it all, I know it has to be hard for them.

I could hear faint sounds of music coming from their stereos as I passed their closed doors. The volume on each was unusually low. *No doubt they sense I need to have quiet time alone.*

I closed my bedroom door and walked to the night table next to my bed, on which sat my clock radio. It was already tuned to the local FM Christian station I had listened to the night before. During the last six months alone, I had had the freedom to listen from bed each night. First, I was encouraged by the program *In Touch with Charles Stanley* and his vital spiritual lessons for daily living, followed by the soothing music and comforting words of Bill Pearce on *Night Sounds*, after which I usually drifted into a peaceful sleep. If I could not sleep, I would set my sleep timer and go on listening to *Grace to You* with John MacArthur and the next program, the Word of God ministering truth and comfort to my heart, assuaging my feelings of loneliness or other emotions until, finally, sleep captured me.

I moved the tuner dial to the classical music station to which I occasionally listened while cleaning the house and set the volume low. I pressed the "on" button, and my favorite music filled the room: Rachmaninoff's Symphony no. 2 in E Minor.

Moving to the window-wall, I drew the white, sheer glass liners fully open to expose the afternoon view. It was a fairyland with ice crystals, still clinging to the trees, that sparkled like diamonds in the bright light.

It's turned out to be a nice day after all, I sighed.

After retrieving my journal, I cozied into the chair in front of the windows—my special corner—ready to unwind from my emotionally draining morning. Placing my coffee mug in the coaster on the table beside me, I stretched my legs and propped my feet on the ottoman. I was ready to release my heart feelings to God and to my journal.

I thought about the volumes of boxed journals stored in the back of my closet. Most were personal, but some, which I had labeled "Spiritual Lessons for Daily Living," were filled with significant Bible teaching notes taken from Christian books, radio, television, or tapes, as far back as 1966 and up to the present. Over the years, I have regularly watched on television or listened on radio to an array of church ministers and evangelists who adhere to the Bible. I have always received "fresh bread" and the "meat of the Word" from these preachers whose teachings nourish me spiritually. I can never thank God enough for these men and women He has called and anointed to edify the body of Christ. I would never want to be without these continually inspiring sources of wisdom and knowledge to help me grow in the Word.

It had always been my intention to catalog my "Spiritual Lessons for Daily Living" journals for easy reference, since they had over the years served me with helps when facing a problem or studying Scripture for spiritual growth. I did not know, however, why I wanted to catalog my personal journals that recorded my thoughts, feelings, prayers, and observations of incidents and events as they happened in my life, my marriage, and family.

Perhaps for posterity, I smiled.

I never got around to that task.

Maybe I'll tackle that one day soon, since all I have is time now, I thought, with a hint of sadness and a touch of resentment.

Opening my journal, I was tempted to read my thoughts during more recent traumatic incidents leading up to this morning but resisted. With that I turned to the page titled "January 15, 1985, D-Day!" and flipped the pages to where I had left off this morning. Staring at my words *"More later ... if I survive this morning!"* brought a smile to my face.

"Yes! I did survive this morning! Thank You, Lord!" Somehow that reminder made me feel somewhat strong. I picked up my pen and began with those same words:

Yes. I did survive this morning. But all these memories of our early marriage before Christ rescued us reminds me that the last three years have felt just like the "American nightmare" revisited! I have that same deep ache in my woman's heart as I did back then.

Flashbacks interrupted my writing, immediately taking me back to the autumn season of my life.

After the hothouse tomato incident, I made the decision that divorce was out of the question for me because of the baby I was carrying; paradoxically, I recall feeling I wanted to run from this new husband whose personality showed a side I had never known before saying *I do.* Nonetheless, I did not run; and life went on for us, with my Dr. Jekyll trying in his usual loving ways to make up for everything Mr. Hyde had done.

Although still cautious and cool following Alex's last abusive incident, I began feeling a little more secure with him after a while. I let my guard down, and we were enjoying one another again and making lots of plans for our baby. One of primary importance to me, with Alex in agreement, was to resign my job when the baby arrived to be a stay-at-home mom. We knew without my income we would not be able to buy extra things. But we also knew we could live without the extras. We believed it was the right decision for us.

I am sensitive to the fact that unlike my generation, many of today's mothers do not have that option to be a stay-at-home wife and mother because it takes two incomes just to meet family and household expenses. My heart goes out to those mothers, many of whom I meet in my ministry.

I recall that back then my close girlfriends questioned how I could give up my career position. Although I was unaware at that time, now I believe that job was part of God's plan for me, one of His divine intentions for my life, based upon what He promises in the Bible: "For I know the thoughts *and* plans that I have for you, says the Lord, thoughts *and* plans for welfare *and* peace and not for evil, to give you hope in your final outcome" (Jer. 29:11 AMP).

Looking back, my on-the-job memories are reminiscent of how everything about that particular position was significant to my own personal growth as well as my spiritual journey. I worked for a cause bigger than myself. I liked that. My distinguished director was tops in her field. During her tenure, she was officially recognized by American presidents and state governors, by proclamation of the state legislature several times, and requested by the President of the United States to serve on his national mental health task force; and I witnessed her induction into the prestigious state Hall of Fame. I understood why not only her work but also her entire life was successful. Her intelligence, abilities, and hard work took her to the pinnacle in her field, but it was her good character that kept her there.

After meeting Alex, she asked specifics about him. Of course, I enthusiastically told her all his good qualities and how happy he made me. She and her husband threw a fabulous engagement party at their home for us. They and several association board members attended our wedding. Later she and her husband, as well as those board members, embraced our children and shared in some of our special family gatherings. We remained close friends.

After I resigned, over the next few years when needed, I worked with her on association special events. When she was ready to retire, the association board members requested that I plan her black-tie dinner/dance retirement party, which notables in our state and around the nation attended.

I have learned that even before we have a personal relationship with the living God, His divine intentions for our lives can be taking place while we are yet unaware. We never know the people and experiences God is permitting in our lives for our mutual blessings as well as His eternal purposes.

After I committed my life to Jesus Christ, my special director-friend knew me well and did not doubt one detail of my extraordinary experience. Having received my story with joy and awe for God, subsequently she made her own commitment to Jesus Christ. In turn, through sharing her story with others of her board members, they, too, were introduced to our living Lord.

Because of her testimony, several of those particular luminaries accepted her invitation to attend a Christian dinner meeting in a local hotel at which I had been invited to share my story.

From the time she became totally converted to Christ until her passing into heaven, where one day we will be joyfully reunited, we had precious discussions about the Lord and Scripture.

Yes, perhaps it would have been difficult for some women to give up such a job back then or one like it today, working daily with important public figures in the city, state, and the nation; but for me, it was an easy choice. To my mind, being a stay-at-home mom molding little lives was a much more important job for me. I felt those child-rearing years would be a season of my life that would pass all too soon. I did not want to miss anything! When that season was over, there would be time enough to pursue the same or another career, if I so desired. Right now I wanted to concentrate on my baby, my firstborn, who would soon arrive and I would have no problem resigning my job.

The remainder of my pregnancy was filled with all the normal expectations. The nursery was finally ready, crib sheets on and booties waiting for whenever "baby" decided it was time.

The baby decided to arrive on a hot August day in 1960. Despite the possibility of a breech birth, everything went smoothly.

"It's a boy, Alisha!" Dr. Donaldson called out.

"A boy ... how wonderful," I sighed.

Alex came into my room smiling, after visiting his son in the nursery. Unlike today, during the '60s fathers and other family members were not allowed to be with the mother in the delivery room.

"Isn't he beautiful, honey?" I said excitedly.

"Yes, he's great!"

Finally a nurse brought baby Michael in and laid him in my arms.

"You're so precious, my little son … We love you," I said aloud, looking up and smiling at Alex. I lifted Michael to my breast for the first time, watching him nurse. It was the happiest moment of my life.

The day Alex brought baby Michael and me home, he said, "I missed you so much, honey. I'm going to make up for everything I've ever done to make you unhappy. I love you, and I'm going to take good care of you and our son." There was no doubt in my mind at this point that Alex had resolved to be a good husband and father.

Instantly a flashback came, then another. I gasped. Now with that remembrance, I felt a quiver and stiffened in my chair. My eyes looked over to my dresser where Michael's photograph was displayed among others of the family. The joy of his birth had appeared to be a new start for our marriage.

Baby Michael and I had been home from the hospital only three days when I began feeling sick, and hot inside. After taking my temperature, I was not surprised to discover it was 102 degrees. By midday I ached all over, and I noticed an odor emitting from my body. After two days of illness, my mother took off work to stay with me and help take care of the baby. When she arrived, she realized how sick I was and also noticed the now strong odor. She immediately called my obstetrician, Dr. Donaldson, who thankfully (back then) made house calls.

"What's the problem, Alisha?" Dr. Donaldson asked upon arrival, concerned.

"Doctor," I hesitated, embarrassed, "I not only feel terrible, I smell terrible too! Alex couldn't even sleep with me last night!"

He shoved a thermometer into my mouth and then began to examine my heart and lungs, saying, "The odor is just your imagination, Alisha. You don't smell bad."

Irritated by his condescending reaction, I pulled out the thermometer and emphatically explained that the strong odor *was not* my imagination. I had bathed, and my mother had changed the bed sheets and scrubbed the tile floor with Lysol just before he arrived. He would not hear me. Instead, he gave me an all-knowing smile and shoved the thermometer back into my mouth.

After taking my vitals, he diagnosed a mild infection that he said was common to new mothers. He told me to stop breast-feeding to protect Michael from possible illness. I understood the logic, but I would miss the oneness I shared with my son during breast-feeding.

The doctor handed Mother a prescription for an antibiotic. "That will clear up the infection. You'll be feeling better soon, Alisha," he said cheerfully as he left.

But instead of feeling better, I became worse. By now I also had constant severe pain in my lower back, and the odor was still obvious.

Finally, at my delayed first postnatal examination in the doctor's office, he found the problem.

"A ... a ... sponge!" he declared.

"A what?" I asked, shocked. "You found a sponge inside of me? What do you mean? What kind of sponge are we talking about, Doctor?"

Instead of answering my question, he explained, "Now that we've removed the source of the odor, we've solved that problem. Now bear in mind," he continued, "you do have a slight infection; but as I told you before, it's one that's common to all new mothers. We'll get that cleared up too. And as far as your lower back pain is concerned, that, too, is common to all new mothers. After all, you're not used to carrying a baby around all day. Don't worry about it. It will pass," he concluded.

"What kind of a sponge was left in me, Doctor?" I pressed.

"Oh, it's about the size of a fifty-cent piece," he answered evasively, and then muttered, "a surgical sponge."

"You mean that sponge has been in me all this time? Is that what caused the infection?"

He dismissed me right then, with my question unanswered. His condescending attitude offended me.

Alex was infuriated about the sponge, and afterward he was sympathetic about my illness—and patient. For example, when he returned home from work each day and occasionally found a chore undone, I would explain, "Alex, I felt so bad today, I just couldn't get to it," promising, "I'll do it another day this week." Usually he would just patiently go ahead and do it for me.

It was Dr. Donaldson's suggestion to see me once a month. But three months passed, and despite my taking a different antibiotic, the infection had not cleared up; my body aches and fatigue became overwhelming some days. At those times, I found myself barely able to care for the baby, much less accomplish my household chores. Baby Michael came first.

Each day I mustered all the strength I could to keep up with the house and laundry, but still I could not manage everything as I had before. Despite my efforts, there were always more things left undone. That was not good enough—neither for Alex, nor for me— not with the burden of perfectionism I had placed upon myself and to which Alex had grown accustomed.

In the following weeks, I was still complaining about the same symptoms, and the doctor's examination still resulted in his same diagnosis. Again he prescribed another kind of medication, but it did not alleviate my symptoms.

As my health continued to deteriorate, Alex became less patient with me. And I became more vulnerable to his sarcasm and criticism. Some evenings he would walk in from work and seem calm and congenial until he observed some chore he thought I should have accomplished in the house that day but had not; then he would instantly blow up and become abusive, for instance, over something as insignificant as the time I left the newspaper from the day before by his chair.

"All you do is sit on your a—— all day!" he raged at me, following with vile name-calling and cursing. "You don't care about the house or me or how hard I'm working!" he further accused.

Alex demeaned me with ugly descriptions of my body; then with vulgar, disgusting words, he charged that I was faking my illness and screamed, "You loaf around; that's why things don't get done in the house! You're a lazy, worthless good-for-nothing!"

His vulgar language, sharp criticisms, and cruel tone of voice made me shudder and landed powerful blows to my personal dignity, my self-esteem, and my confidence. And to make matters even worse, Alex would often berate me with the doctor's diagnosis. "The symptoms you're complaining about are common to all new mothers," he would say with a contemptuous tone and menacing smile. Then he would add, in his most convicting tone, "Can't you take it?"

After each of those or similar terrible attacks played out, my sweet Dr. Jekyll would be sympathetic and loving once again. His personality changed from Jekyll to Hyde day to day, and his reactions to me and my illness changed accordingly. I prayed and tried to think positive, to overcome his ugly slurs—and my own guilt—but after several months of Alex's verbal battering and my physical illness, I was just as emotionally weak as I was physically weak and fell into depression.

I decided that maybe Alex was right. Maybe my condition was all in my head. And so, I pushed myself harder and harder, trying to ignore my sore body and fatigue until I became so exhausted that my body felt near collapse at the end of each day.

I had been sick for almost a year, still experiencing lower back pain, abdominal pain, and overwhelming fatigue. After monthly examinations and the different medications tried, which had not alleviated my symptoms, my doctor continued to stand by his original diagnosis of a common, mild infection. Then ...

One hot day in early July, Michael was napping and I was standing at the ironing board finishing the last of Alex's white shirts when I suddenly felt a gush of blood. I was hemorrhaging. Instinctively I ran to the bathroom, stepped into the bathtub, and stood there, watching in horror as the blood gushed and ran down my legs. I grabbed the towel from the bar over the tub and clutched it to my body to catch the bleeding. I was alone, and Alex was not due home for hours.

"Oh God, what do I do now?"

Just then from the open window above the tub, I heard a car pull into the driveway. *Alex! He's home! I can't believe it!*

Alex never came home for lunch, but sure enough, there he was! As he opened the car door, I yelled to him from the window, "Alex, come quick! Oh thank God you're here! Hurry!"

Alex dashed down the hall to the bathroom door, saw me and then the blood, and cried out, "Oh my God!"

He bolted from the bathroom to the kitchen and started dialing the telephone. I realized he was speaking to someone in the office of a doctor whose name I did not recognize. When he returned, he said, "Come on; I'm taking you to the same doctor who did Joe's wife's surgery." He called our neighbor, who came to sit with the baby, and we took off.

I discovered that Alex had been carrying this new doctor's phone number in his wallet for a long time, despite his belief in my obstetrician's continued insistence that my symptoms were not uncommon for a new mother. At some point, obviously, doubts had entered his mind, and he had already been considering the need for a second opinion.

By the time we reached Dr. Jamison's office, the bleeding had stopped. In the examination room, I nervously explained to him that I had not had a menstrual period since Michael's birth. I also told him all about the surgical sponge and that I was worried about my lingering illness.

"Don't you worry now," he said kindly. "We'll find out what the problem is," he smiled. His words brought a hope of being well again, a settling to my inner anxieties and frustrations.

After examining me, he questioned me at length about my symptoms then asked me to dress, and he quickly left the room. I could hear him talking to Alex in the adjacent office.

"Who was the SOB (only he used the exact words) who did this to her?" Dr. Jamison asked in an elevated, angry tone, no doubt speaking of the sponge that had been left in me. "She's so full of infection, I don't know how she got out of bed every morning!"

Though I was not glad to hear I was that sick, it was good to know, finally, that it had not been all in my head. The pain and fatigue were still there, but at least I could let go of the guilt I felt for my inability to keep up with the house, and I hoped Alex's nagging criticisms would stop.

After I joined them, Dr. Jamison explained what it would take to get me well again. "You're one sick girl, and we're going to start treating this condition immediately!" he said as he wrote out four prescriptions. "We've got to get rid of that infection before we can do anything else," he said, answering my silent question about taking so many medications but raising another.

"What else is wrong with me?"

He explained that he had discovered a cyst the size of a lemon on my left ovary.

"We want to clear up that infection and dissolve the cyst, and then we'll see how you're doing."

I was shocked—I had had no idea. But I was grateful to be under skilled care and ready to get on with the treatment.

But after a couple of weeks, I was not improving. The medications were obviously not working. Dr. Jamison prescribed other antibiotics, but again, no response. Within that month, the cyst grew considerably larger, and I was feeling excruciating pain. The doctor took a biopsy and prescribed another type medication.

A few days later, the pain abruptly ceased. I happily called the doctor with what I thought was good news.

"I was afraid of that," he said. "Get into my office as soon as you can."

That afternoon Alex drove me to the doctor's office, where Dr. Jamison and both of his OB-GYN practice partners, one of whom was a surgeon, Dr. Bailey, examined me.

"Based on our examinations," Dr. Jamison began, "and the result of the biopsy taken of the cyst, we concur that a complete hysterectomy must be performed without delay."

A hysterectomy? Oh God, no! I silently moaned.

"No, Doctor! I just turned twenty-five; I want to have more babies. Try something else— another kind of antibiotic! Please, not a hysterectomy!"

Alex said nothing while the doctor explained that the different antibiotics should have cleared up everything by now.

"The medication is just not working, and your immune system is not cooperating at this point. We have no other choice. It all has to be removed, Alisha," he insisted.

Alex and I had looked forward to having more children. I wanted an even four. I was brokenhearted to think that there would be no more little ones.

That Thursday night, I lay in bed full of fear. The pamphlets I had read on cancer and its warning signs made me think that I might be a good candidate for it. The next morning, I anxiously made an appointment for that afternoon for further consultation with Dr. Bailey, the surgeon. I had questions for which I needed answers before my scheduled surgery.

"Doctor, I want you to know that I prefer to know what I'm dealing with; then I can handle it better." I took a deep breath and asked, "Doctor, is ... do you think I might be a ... a good candidate for ... ah ... cancer?"

Dr. Bailey stared long at me before answering. "Alisha, I can't say that you do [have cancer], but I can't say that you don't; we won't know until we go in."

My prayer life up to this point had consisted of bedtime and morning prayers memorized from my first Holy Communion and Confirmation sacraments. That night I found myself praying to God, not with someone else's words of prayer, but with my own words—just talking to Him as I always had about the abusive relationship in my marriage—but now also praying more specifically about my illness.

Please, God, no matter what the surgeon finds—even if it is a life-threatening condition—please permit me to live long enough to enjoy Michael and even see him grow into manhood. If that's not Your will, then please, God, help me to accept whatever Your will is. I'm so terrified.

Instantly I felt something strange, like a faint electrical current moving through my body. It lasted only seconds, and then I felt complete peace. Without fear I entered the hospital Monday morning for next-day surgery.

On Tuesday, though groggy, I was conscious of lying on a hospital cart being wheeled from the recovery room to my semiprivate room.

"It's over," I moaned. *It's something that just had to be. No more babies ... but thank You, God, that I have my son.* I drifted off again.

"Alisha." My eyes opened to see my surgeon at my bedside. "Has anyone told you the good news yet?"

Still groggy, I answered, "I don't know anything. What do you mean?"

"Alisha, when we opened you up, we couldn't believe how clean you were inside. We only had to remove the cyst that had already consumed the left ovary and do a little repair work. We didn't have to take everything as we had thought we would. You can still have children with one ovary. Although it might be more difficult for you to conceive again, you will. You can have more children!" he said, his lips curling into a broad smile.

"I don't understand, Dr. Bailey. I thought you had to take everything, that ... "

Instantly I remembered my prayer and the faint electrical sensation that had passed through my body. *Did God answer my prayer? Did God make the difference? Alex! Where is he? I have to tell Alex!*

"I'm so happy, Doctor! Have you told Alex yet?"

"No. I looked for him after surgery but didn't see him around anywhere. We even paged him, but he didn't respond. You'll have to be the one to tell him the good news," he said with a smile as he left the room.

My disappointment in Alex overwhelmed the happiness and gratitude I felt. My parents, who had waited throughout the surgery, came in to see me. They had not seen or spoken to Alex either. All day into evening, I kept waiting for him to walk into the room any minute.

"Visiting hours are now over," the faceless announcer's voice came through the intercom. It was eight o'clock. My parents kissed me good-bye. *Where is my husband?* Tears welled in my eyes. Despite my happiness about the doctor's extraordinary news, I felt painfully alone, abandoned by Alex and embarrassed. *Why didn't he stay to learn the outcome of the surgery?* A sense of rejection filled me. I gave myself up to the sedative the nurse brought me, numbing my emotions and my expectations.

The next afternoon, Alex walked into my room with a big smile on his face. He did not explain his absence the day of my surgery, and I did not question him. I wanted to. I wanted to tell him how selfish and insensitive he had been again. I wanted to tell him that I could not depend on him. But when I shared the good news with him and saw the obvious wave of relief that came over his face, I rationalized that we had both been under a lot of strain and that it would be best just to forget about it. Alex was with me every night after work for the rest of my hospital stay.

I arrived home just a few days before our son's first birthday. As I held my sweet baby boy in my arms, everything felt right. Michael was happy. I was happy. The prospect of being able to have more children made my recovery seem easy, notwithstanding my surgeon's caution that it might be difficult for me to conceive.

In spite of everything, I felt like I had a great deal for which to be grateful. I remembered after my doctor's good news being left with serene thoughts about how my baby boy, Michael, had survived two possible miscarriages and was born healthy; and I remembered how my surgery had turned out extraordinarily better than my surgeon or Dr. Jamison or even I had anticipated.

Back then I neither knew Jesus Christ personally as I do today, nor did I know the Bible. Nevertheless, God knew me. Now I am certain that God did indeed intervene to change the outcome of my medical problem. I believe I experienced a miracle in my body after my prayer, when I felt that sensation of a faint electrical current go through me.

Some Christians who espouse divine healing might not consider the positive outcome of my surgery a miracle because medical physicians were involved. And, of course, that is their prerogative. I would never be offended by another's opposite opinion on this. However, I do believe God will intervene by working through those in the medical profession. In my case, my surgeon could have stuck to his plan, but instead he displayed wisdom in recognizing the unexpected, sudden inexplicable improvement in my condition and stopped short of performing a complete hysterectomy.

Now back in the present, with the last sip of my lukewarm coffee, another memory surrounding the birth of our second child, our daughter, Laurie, came softly stealing into my mind, along with a sigh of thanksgiving. It was pretty remarkable that she had been conceived at all. Nevertheless, seven months after surgery, I did become pregnant, contrary to my surgeon's prognosis that conceiving again might be difficult. We were thrilled. Alex and I both thought a baby girl would be perfect!

I started redecorating our guest, or third, bedroom into "early toddler" for Michael: lots of reds and blues, wooden soldiers and drums, fun fabric patterns for the bedspread and drapes, which I thoroughly enjoyed sewing. My creative projects had always been therapeutic for me, relieving my mind and emotions, if only temporarily, of the extreme stress I had lived in for over two years.

We had a peaceful, nearly normal home life for a time. Then unexpectedly Alex's mood swings and erratic behavior returned. I decided I could wait no longer. It was time to act on my secret plan. We needed professional help before our second baby arrived.

One night I cautiously approached Alex with the idea. He flatly refused. He treated discussions about his extreme personality changes with the same firm rejection.

Another night I warily tried a fresh approach. "Alex, if you won't see a marriage counselor with me, would you consider talking with Father Maloney? He'll listen to whatever is bothering you—whether it's your work or problems with me or, perhaps, a problem that could even stem from your past."

He did not respond. He just glared at me.

"Alex, honey, something has to be affecting you," I said softly. "At times you're just not yourself. Please, just think about talking to Father Maloney."

Then his reaction to that statement came as swiftly and violently as a tornado.

He hurled a filthy four-letter word at me and screamed, "There's nothing wrong with me! You're the one who needs help! All this stuff about something being wrong with me! You're paranoid! That's what you are. You'd better see a psychiatrist. You're the one who's crazy."

I gripped the side of the sofa. Again, his quick switch from Jekyll to Hyde caught me off guard. But over the last two years, I had discovered some techniques for defusing his temper. I tried one.

"Crazy?" I answered with seeming surprise. "Is that why you think I'm asking you to talk to Father Maloney? Because you think that I think you're crazy? No, that's not it," I softly said. "I just thought that with the relationship you and Father Maloney developed during your Catholic instruction, you would feel more comfortable telling him things that are stressful to you. Things you don't feel comfortable talking to me about that might be causing you to have such a short fuse sometimes. That's all."

His face began to relax. More confident then, I continued reasoning: "I just mean, Father Maloney likes you; he's someone you could talk to. I want to understand, Alex. I love you."

His face softened, and he responded, "I love you too. I'll try to do better, but we don't need any help." I dropped the subject.

At that time, I still knew very little about Alex's past. When it came to his background, I further realized for the first time how strange it was that the common family-related remarks usually interjected in normal conversations between married couples was always absent from ours.

I recall that in the weeks that followed, it appeared that Alex definitely tried to keep his promise to do better. However, I was certain my kind Dr. Jekyll could not sustain self-control for long. When Mr. Hyde resurfaced with the same malevolent and sadistic verbal attacks leveled against me without provocation, I was convinced beyond question that my husband was not a man with an uncontrollable temper, as bad as that would be; but rather, I believed his behavior was mentally and emotionally abnormal.

When his dark side was raging with criticisms about something I did or said, and I tried to defend or explain myself, sometimes he would scream at me, "You should be committed! You're nuts!" along with other cruel accusations. Nonetheless, although I knew it was his problem, his powerful words planted a seed of self-doubt within me, and his words kept washing over me: *"You're crazy; you'd better see a psychiatrist."*

At first I ignored his words, and then I argued with them; but they continued repeating over and over in my mind until I was emotionally tired of battling his accusations. *Maybe I should see a psychiatrist,* I thought.

The doctor who had done my surgery recommended a Dr. Sterling, and I immediately made an appointment for the following week. I wanted to make sure I followed through, if only to relieve the self-doubts that had taken root in my psyche and were growing rapidly.

The day finally came. As I settled into my chair opposite the psychiatrist, I wondered how to begin.

"I've been married almost three years, Dr. Sterling. I ... I ..."

"Yes, Mrs. Lance, go on," he urged.

"I love my husband, Doctor. But he's ... he's so different from the man I thought ... "

Tears welled in my eyes. I was used to protecting Alex. By covering up his actions and making excuses for him, I could protect myself too. I would be embarrassed if my family and friends knew Alex verbally and psychologically abused me.

Suddenly I had an urge to just run out of the office—to push all of these marital skeletons back into the closet. It was safer to hide them and deal with my private terrors alone. My personal life was now an ugly world, and I was ashamed to let anyone in to see it.

"I guess I'm nervous, Doctor, because I'm feeling disloyal to my husband. It's difficult for me to tell you the terrible things he does. What I mean is," I said quickly, "he's different at times. Someone I didn't know before we married." Why could I not just say *abusive?*

When I finished telling the doctor the whole ugly story, I waited for his response—his answers. But instead of answers for me, he had questions about our relationship when Alex was not in one of his violent rages.

"When Alex is himself, he is respectful of me in every way. He never insults or criticizes me. We discuss everything openly—his work, our decisions regarding finances, and little Michael. We've always shared the same basic moral principles, the same sense of responsibility and respect for home and family—at least I thought we did. That's the reason, Doctor, that I feel Alex has a ... problem. He's like Dr. Jekyll and Mr. Hyde.

"But he won't hear of seeing a marriage counselor, psychiatrist, or psychologist. He won't even talk with our parish priest. How can I help him? Or how can I help myself? Is it me? Maybe the times I've been sick ... Maybe I expect too much from him ... Am I the problem? Am I crazy, as he always tells me I am, whenever he's in one of his moods, especially when I try to have a discussion with him to find out what the problem might be? If I'm the one who needs help," I went on, "then please, Doctor, help me! I want to save my marriage. I want a normal, solid family for my son and the child we are expecting soon."

The tears I had been fighting now came rolling down my cheeks. There was so much pain. I had been pushing the pain, disappointments, the unhappiness in my life down deep inside, trying to be strong, trying to keep control. There seemed no more room inside of me for pain—I was full.

The doctor straightened in his chair and clasped his hands together. The room suddenly seemed very quiet.

"Mrs. Lance, I don't believe you are the problem in your marriage. I think you are mentally and emotionally sound; and don't worry: your reactions to your husband are normal."

With that I sighed with relief.

"You cannot help the fact of your illnesses," he continued. "It's unfortunate that you've been sick. However, neither are you the cause of your husband's changeable personality. You are perfectly normal to feel as you do about his abusive behavior being a severe problem. But I cannot help him unless he is willing to come in and talk to me. If you think he will, then we'll get to the bottom of this.

"In the meantime, don't be so hard on yourself, Mrs. Lance. Just remember, you are not the cause of your husband's bad behavior, and you cannot change him. Neither you nor your son is deserving of that kind of treatment."

His words of reassurance of my own sanity instantly overcame Alex's nagging accusations. The long-repressed, painful facts of our relationship had finally been told, and the relief of it all made my chest feel light, as though a crushing weight had suddenly been lifted.

Looking back, I remember how my mind raced to sort out everything as I drove home: our relationship and how it had reached this desperate state. Also, I was lamenting all my rationalizations for Alex's behavior. But I did glimpse some reality:

- My first rationalization had been made when we were moving into a more serious relationship and I had questioned Alex about his family background, still a mystery, which he had avoided sharing. Lacking this knowledge robbed me of important information that was significant for me to know and consider before choosing a life mate.
- My rationalizations about Alex's first violent outburst and his first infidelity had enabled his subsequent abusive behavior over the hothouse tomatoes and continuing abuse toward me—all of which had brought me nothing but grief.
- My rationalizations had changed me into someone else: someone I no longer knew, someone I no longer liked. I had become angry, bitter, resentful, and defensive; and even if I did not express those emotions all the time, they seethed inside me.

That day I only knew I was no longer happy, optimistic, or trusting as I had been as a new bride. I had failed at marriage. But vital truth had come out of my session with Dr. Sterling: he had helped me realize that I could neither fix our marriage nor could I fix Alex.

Now I realized for the first time that all my early rationalizations for Alex's behavior had laid the foundation upon which many more unhealthy rationalizations would build, facilitating and giving impetus to my husband's abuse toward me. Between Alex's violent outbursts, his behavior seemed normal.

The cliché "When he is good he is very, very good, but when he is bad he is horrid" perfectly described Alex. He always confused me with his ambiguous words and actions. His pattern was always the same. When he was good, he was kind, thoughtful, and loving. When he was bad, he was verbally and psychologically abusive.

Afterward he seemed sorry for what he had said or done, and I would think he really was going to try to overcome his terrible anger. But in the end, he did not accept responsibility; in fact, he would turn the tables on me and in effect insinuate that his violent outburst had been my fault. No matter how much positive effort I had invested up to now trying to improve my marriage, nothing had worked. I did not know of one more thing I could do. I felt my last-ditch effort, my last hope, was in Dr. Sterling.

I remember as I drove into our driveway, my last thought was more of a prayer: *Oh God, I just hope Alex will let Dr. Sterling help us.*

That evening I was relieved that Alex was in a good mood when he walked through the door. Without dark Mr. Hyde to deal with, I hoped it would be a good time for us to discuss my visit with Dr. Sterling. After dinner I bathed Michael, distracted by the anticipation of my talk with Alex. Michael and I went through our usual tucking-in ritual. Michael squirmed and squealed as I tried to put his pajamas on him, and my anxiousness dissolved in the joy of playing and laughing with him. I held him in my arms and read him a story until he fell asleep.

Gently I laid him down, pulled his blankets up around his peaceful face, and left the room. As I carefully closed his door behind me, under my breath I moaned, "Something has to change, or I have to get us away from here." *But where would we go? I can't go back to live with Mom and Dad and put an extra burden on them, but something ...*

Walking into the kitchen, I turned on a low fire under the Pyrex coffeepot to heat the remains from dinner.

This is it! I silently declared, as I brought two cups of coffee into the living room, placing Alex's on the table next to his chair. Sitting quietly on the sofa, I tried to regain the courage to bring up the possibility of marriage counseling again. I began cautiously.

"Alex?" I softly called, to make sure I had his attention before going on.

He looked up.

"I asked Dr. Bailey if he would give me the name of a psychologist or psychiatrist for marriage counseling … "

"I'm not going to any psychiatrist with you or anyone else!" he interrupted. "There's nothing wrong with me. You think you've got a problem—then you go!"

"I did go, Alex. I went to see Dr. Sterling this afternoon."

"Well, good, so you went. What did he tell you?" He quickly changed the question before I could answer. "Or, what did you tell him about me? Did you tell him how hard you have it?" he asked sarcastically. I said nothing.

"Yeah, you have it so hard," he went on. "You live in a nice home, have someone to pay all the bills, and someone to take care of you when you're sick!" His face reddened. Hatred hung on every word. "Did you tell him that? Yeah," he cursed and went on, "you've got it so bad, don't you?" His voice was getting louder and louder, as a few more four-letter curse words and disgusting names came at me.

"Alex," I said calmly while my stomach began to quiver, "Dr. Sterling said he would like to see us together. He said he would be glad to help us in any way he can."

Alex glared at me, boring into me with his cold eyes.

"We have to get help, Alex!" I said desperately, with the nervousness in my voice resonating in my ears as he continued his icy stare. I broke down and began to cry. "We need to understand what's happening to us. Don't you realize how cruel you are at times? And what about the baby we're going to have? Don't you want to get some help before a second child comes?"

The obvious pain on my face, the desperation in my voice, did not faze him. He was indifferent to my pain, unmoved by my tears.

He started cursing and screamed, "No!" rushing across the room for his coat. He left the house, slamming the door behind him. I listened to the car back out of the driveway, and then to the dominating silence that settled in the room. The calm after the storm of my husband's wrath always left me to fight the backlash of his cruel words, alone to face the problems in our marriage.

I was frustrated and angry. *Nothing works! Nothing! No matter what I do… no matter what I say… no matter how nicely … or gently*

I say it! He won't hear that we need help! He doesn't think there is anything wrong with him! It's me! I'm always "making an issue out of nothing" whenever I mention our marriage is in trouble.

"But, it's not my problem! Dr. Sterling said it's not my problem!" I yelled out, pacing the room.

A few moments later, the door opened, startling me. Alex walked swiftly into the living room, grabbed my hand, and sat me down beside him on the sofa.

"Honey, I'm sorry I yelled. I'm sorry for the way I acted," he said sheepishly. "But there's nothing wrong with us. Look, I love you," he pleaded. "We love each other. We've got almost two beautiful kids," he grinned, "and a nice house. We don't have any problems that we can't solve on our own. We don't need a psychiatrist or a marriage counselor. I'll do better. I'll try not to fly off the handle from now on."

I stared at him, unconvinced.

"I love you, honey," he coaxed, "I'll do better. You'll see. I just get uptight, but I don't mean anything by it. Give me a chance to prove that I can do better, okay?" he pleaded, taking me into his arms and holding me tightly. "It will be okay ... trust me ... you'll see!"

Ironically, Alex's disposition was pleasant after that evening. He was usually in a happy, playful mood. He even played with Michael. I still could not figure out at that time how Alex could so quickly change from the loving, sweet guy I married to the cruel, violent husband who seemed to be randomly controlled by some invisible, evil force.

I knew Alex was self-deceived. He had tried so many times but could not keep his promise to control his temper, and the cycle of abuse would start all over again. Gratefully, his abuse was never directed at Michael, but I knew Michael had to be affected by his father's loud and cruel tone of voice when attacking me.

My 1961 journal reminds me that I thought at the time that perhaps knowing I had actually talked to a psychiatrist about our problems not only surprised Alex but showed him that I was at the end of my rope, not willing to put up with any more of his excuses for his bad behavior. It appeared that he knew he better shape up because I intended to do "something." I am sure he did not know what I might do next. In fact, I was not sure what I would do next. But I hoped Dr. Sterling held my answer at my next scheduled session.

The following Wednesday, I related to Dr. Sterling my unsuccessful attempt to get Alex in to see him.

"Mrs. Lance," Dr. Sterling responded, "I don't see any reason for you to continue seeing me unless your husband is willing to come with you. It isn't that I mind your coming if you think there is anything else you need to talk about." He paused. "But your problems stem from your husband's behavior, and I don't see that I can do anything about that unless he is willing to accept my help." He rose from his chair, walked me to the door, and said, "Now if you ever need to talk to me again, don't hesitate to make an appointment."

My heart sank. This time I left his office feeling an overwhelming hopelessness. I had so wanted—so hoped—that things would be better before the child inside me entered our world.

Driving home, I suddenly felt panicked, like I was trapped in a room without a door. The psychiatrist had been my last hope.

What is there left to do that I haven't already tried to do? Do I want to keep trying? Do I want to continue my marriage? I just don't know. But Michael and my baby ... I have to keep trying for them. But is that the right thing to do? Maybe it's better to leave with them after the baby's born.

My religious convictions about divorce had not changed, but the alternative of staying in my marriage seemed impossible.

"Please help us, Lord," I whispered. I wanted our children to have their whole family—a normal family.

Looking back, I was blinded to exactly what was happening to me, to my personality. I was unaware that focusing only on Alex's needs and neglecting my own, striving for perfection and taking on the self-imposed burden of full responsibility for keeping our marriage from failing, had taken root and promoted other self-deceiving, unhealthy patterns. They were the prelude to an even greater self-deception during those early years: believing that my love and commitment to my husband were strong enough to keep his dark side from emerging and to make our marriage relationship harmonious. Without my recognizing it, my self-confidence, my spunkiness, my sense of humor, my individuality—my very identity—were being whittled away little by little.

But then I did recognize that I had made one of the best decisions of my life when I met with the psychiatrist, Dr. Sterling, who made clear to me that my husband's abusive behavior was a serious mental and emotional problem, but definitely not my fault. Although all my efforts had been futile to get Alex to agree to marriage counseling before our second baby was born, at least I was emotionally empowered by Dr. Sterling's medical diagnosis of me, assuring me that I was mentally sound, which gave me strength to keep my family together because I believed my children needed two parents.

In the weeks following my last session with Dr, Sterling, surprisingly, Alex was still in control, keeping his promise to do better. One beautiful sunny April morning, I heard a car door slam, then Alex entering the back door.

"Honey, where are you?" he called to me excitedly.

"Hi! What are you doing home from work this time of the morning?" I asked with surprise.

"How soon can you be packed for Florida?" he said, grinning.

"Are you serious?"

"Sure, I'm serious."

The next morning, we were on our way—Alex, Michael, and I, with "baby" tucked under my heart.

The sunshine, warm temperatures, the beach, and the lazy days of R & R were a welcome relief. Some days we took excursions to surrounding popular tourist sights. Other days, while Alex fished in the morning, Michael and I walked the beach and picked up shells; then Alex joined us for swimming and picnic lunches on the shore. Afterward Michael napped under the shade of the beach umbrella, while we sunbathed next to him.

I felt perfectly well those ten days. Alex appeared relaxed and rested. And Michael was happy. It was a good vacation, without incident—a needed vacation.

Alex's temper was still under control. His more normal disposition made my pregnancy easier. As the birth date neared, I began preparing Michael for my hospital stay and for his new baby sister or brother, whom I would be bringing home with me. He was excited. Alex and I were very excited too.

During Michael's naptimes, I enjoyed sewing new baby clothes and even a pink, yellow, and blue crib quilt and pillow, both of which were trimmed with ruffles in the hope that we would be blessed with a baby girl. With added touches of pink to the already blue and yellow color scheme, the nursery was finally ready to greet "her." The remainder of my pregnancy was pleasantly filled with all the normal expectations of motherhood. And in a corner of our bedroom sat my already packed suitcase.

Back in the present again, I recall that after Alex's last terrible outburst, I made the choice to continue honoring my marriage vows *for better or for worse,* since our second child was on the way. But I had no idea then, how bad *for worse* would become. At that time, I also had no clue of the pain, anxiety, shame, self-neglect, and loss of self-esteem that would take hold of my life. Nonetheless, although I had been unaware, God was watching over me and my children, and yes, He was working behind the scenes.

Taking my journal in hand, I penned my last thoughts of the afternoon:

It occurs to me now that remembering the past and all of what God has brought me through, while also facing this present hard reality of divorce and recording my thoughts, has been emotionally therapeutic and spiritually encouraging. With grateful hindsight, I can know God has always been with me, intervening to protect me and my children. Recalling parts of my early married life before Christ, and having lived through the last three equally painful years, I realize how fortunate, how blessed I am to have come through it all with my faith still intact. I know the Holy Spirit has been my "keeping power." Now, Lord, I pray that You will please keep on helping me to recover from the death of my marriage, so that one day I can begin again and live out my purpose—my destiny ...

Gently I placed my pen on the open journal and looked out the window again. I noticed the winter sky was losing its afternoon light, fading fast. It was dinnertime.

I quickly picked up my pen again and signed off, ***More later ...*** This time I placed my journal on the table beside me.

Standing to my feet and stretching to loosen my tight muscles, I closed the sheer glass liners and the drapery, and I walked downstairs to the kitchen.

Chapter 7

Terror!

Mentally I dismissed the course of my day, but an obscure heaviness lingered. Nonetheless, I managed to cook dinner and even slice a "hothouse tomato" for our salad. When the kids came to the table, we sat eating and chatting about everything accept the sadness we each felt today—the day that had changed our lives forever. At the same time, after having lived through a grueling year of court hearings with their own traumatic incidents, I think we all felt a sense of relief that it was finally over. After dinner Laura insisted that I should rest and she would clean up the kitchen. I was grateful. Although I knew she needed to study, I also knew I felt utterly wrung out from the day.

I lay on one of the sofas in the living room, listening to the conversations of my children as the boys cleared the table and Laura loaded the dishwasher. My eyes roamed from the foyer, across the living room, and into the dining room—all of which flow into one another with an overall color palette of ivory walls, carpet, and window drapery, with furnishings covered in burgundy, soft coral, and pale aqua fabrics. The large foyer has a flagstone floor on which a long Georgian chest stands against the wall, which is covered with a Waverly floral within wide stripes; and above the chest hangs a gold-framed Queen Ann mirror. A crystal chandelier hangs from the ceiling, with its shimmering prisms reflecting in the mirror.

One step down from the foyer is this large sunken living room. It is traditional in style, but eclectic, like the other rooms. It has a cathedral ceiling with natural wood beams. Opposite the entrance to the room is a stone wood-burning fireplace that rises fourteen feet to the ceiling, with a raised hearth upon which is a long, pale coral velvet pillow for extra seating. A tall cherry wood secretary stands on one side of the fireplace, and on the other side stands a tall walnut étagère with glass shelves holding the stereo and a collection of Chinese urns and plates.

Flanking out from the fireplace are the two large burgundy velvet sofas. Between them is a large square brass cocktail table with a glass top upon which sits a silk floral centerpiece. Beneath the table is a large oriental carpet in a design of muted shades of coral, aqua, and burgundy.

There are two wing chairs pulled up and angled to the sofas, each covered inside with an ivory wool tapestry in a crewel-embroidered floral with multicolored wool yarn, with the outside wrapped in burgundy velvet. There is a baby grand piano against one wall. On the opposite wall is a wood and brass writing desk with a glass top, and pulled up to it is a high-back cane chair with an upholstered pale aqua velvet seat.

Rather than feeling overly formal, the room is homey and inviting, with its overall quiet color scheme and sink-in, comfortable furniture.

The dining room is one step up from the living room, with wraparound windows that bring the outside in, offering our dinner guests spectacular views. It is furnished with a secondhand traditional eighteenth-century Georgian dining suite that Alex and I bought in 1967. It came out of a very grand home in our city's most elite residential area, as did our solid cherry wood bedroom suite. Both were fifty years old then, but only the dining room pieces were in need of refinishing. Back then we had the eleven pieces professionally refinished for an unbelievable cost of nine hundred dollars.

Many school nights, Michael, Laura, and Steven sat at that dining table doing homework, but its top is no worse for wear. Although old and secondhand, it served our family well for "lo, these many" years and holds little evidence of that continual use. In fact, it still looks new. A Williamsburg brass chandelier hangs over the table.

When the kids were small, I told them our home belonged to our whole family, and each of us had to help take care of it and keep it nice, stressing that even though some of our furniture was old and secondhand, it was new to us. Somehow that stuck. They were always respectful of our home and furnishings, and they took good care of their own toys and other personal belongings.

When it came to decorating our home, instead of overly formal (or whatever was the newest trend in furnishings), Alex and I both liked timeless, classic pieces, whether old and secondhand or new, which made for an easy, quiet interior. Being a stay-at-home wife, mother, and homemaker for twenty-six years, I felt it was important that our interiors be decorated as nicely as possible, but equally important for them to be comfortable so our family could really live in our rooms. I wanted my husband and children to walk into our home at the end of a day to find refuge and rest from the hectic outside world of work, school, and now college.

Alex and the boys always preferred the family room, where they could stretch out, put their feet up, and lounge. The boys rarely sit in the living room unless we have guests gathered here. But Laura and I enjoy its comfortable, serene ambience; oftentimes we spend evening hours in here—Laura on one sofa, I on the other, having long mother-daughter chats or reading while listening to classical, jazz, or Christian music. These times are some of my most pleasurable and memorable in Alex's dream home on the lake.

Now Laura, having finished in the kitchen, came into the room and turned on the stereo before stretching out on the other sofa to read. Easy listening music filled the room. She looked up at one point, and her eyes met mine. Her smile warmed me. Without a word, her eyes returned to her book.

Watching my daughter now made my heart swell with pride for the person she has become. *She's such a special young woman, smart, responsible, hardworking, and gifted. Her heart is special too. I don't know if Laurie really knows how special she is. Her brothers think there's no girl quite like their sister. They are proud of the fact that while she is pretty and as "girly girl" as can be, she also*

135

has enough tomboy in her to enjoy playing, watching, and talking sports with them. They are quite a threesome. How wonderful that God gave them to me!

Now I remembered like it was yesterday that my pregnancy with Laura, as well as her birth, had been so easy—easy, like her personality. Those glorious days of October 1962 had felt like Indian summer, making my last month of carrying her even more pleasant. Finally that day came when our precious Laura Nichole blessed our world with her presence.

"This is our china doll," said the nurse as she walked into my room and laid baby Laura into my arms to nurse for the first time.

"The staff named her that because we all agreed that she looks like a china doll, with her creamy white porcelain-like complexion and slanted-looking blue eyes. Look how her thick black hair grew in a natural pixie style around her face," she smiled. "In fact, the photographer took her picture to be featured in our hospital newsletter."

"How nice. Yes, it's true," I said proudly, "she does look like a beautiful china doll." I smiled back at the nurse, holding Laura to my breast. We wanted this baby girl—planned for her.

"Thank You, God," I whispered. My husband and I had been twice blessed with two beautiful, healthy children.

Alex even sent me a dozen red long-stem roses for Laura's birth! In the hospital, he told me he was determined to be the husband and father that the children and I needed and deserved. At that time, I thought this precious new addition to our family offered Alex a fresh start, incentives to control his temper and do things right as he had promised. I remember things did go along smoothly and happily for Alex and me at the time of Laura's birth—until terror struck from another direction.

I was not feeling well on Thursday morning after Alex brought the baby and me home. Déjà vu.

I had picked up what I thought was a simple cold in the hospital. Alex volunteered to stay home the rest of the day with the baby and Michael so I could go to bed. Later I began running a fever. *Oh no! This feels too familiar. Does something always have to spoil my joy?*

Over-the-counter medication did not help. So far, the baby was still well; but because I was breast-feeding, I was concerned about passing the "bug" on to her, so I stopped. The next morning, our family physician, Dr. Schwartz, diagnosed a staph infection that I had obviously contracted in the hospital and gave me a shot of penicillin.

In the middle of the night, the excruciating head pain started. The pain persisted, and my condition worsened throughout the night. Alex said he would call the doctor in the morning.

Before noon the next day, Saturday, we made another trip to the doctor. He said I was having an "internal reaction" to the penicillin and gave me a shot to counteract it, along with a prescription for an oral medication.

Immediately, I sensed an "external reaction" from Alex. He seemed to be exasperated with me for being sick again. When I needed his emotional support, he reacted with indifference and hostility. It was almost a punishing attitude. But why?

Later that same day, after taking the oral medication, I became sick to my stomach and vomited. Alex called the doctor to explain my condition. He ordered that I stop the medication and meet him in his office Monday morning at eight o'clock.

Throughout the night, the pain in my head continued. By mid-afternoon on Sunday, it was getting hard to breathe; a suffocating feeling overwhelmed me. I was terrified that each forced breath would be my last.

I told myself I was being ridiculous, that the doctor would have admitted me to the hospital if there had been any real danger. By late afternoon, my fear grew as my condition worsened.

"Alex, help me!" I gasped, grabbing at his arm, "I ... feel ... like ... I'm drowning! I've got to get to the hospital!"

But Alex was not convinced and tried to calm my hysteria. "You're going to be all right. The doctor will give you something in the morning." I was still frightened. Helpless to do anything for myself, I tried to calm my fears by watching the clock on the dresser, believing that if I could just hang on fifteen more hours, I would be in the doctor's office at eight o'clock in the morning.

It was only a few minutes later, around five o'clock that afternoon, when I heard my father's voice. Alex was explaining to him about my condition as they walked the hallway to our bedroom.

My father took one quick look at me and shouted, "Alex, we have to get her to the hospital! She can't breathe!"

At the emergency room, the doctors and nurses were swarming around me, but I was oblivious to who was doing what to me. I felt cold. *Is this what death feels like? Am I dying?*

I heard someone shout, "It's not working!"

"Call in Dr. Anthony!" another directed.

Lying on the cart in that cold ER, I felt relieved that I had hung on. By now I was only catching words here and there.

"It's working!" a voice shouted, the words startling me.

Dr. Anthony, a highly respected internist, had found the right combination of antitoxin, and I could sense the relief in the emergency room.

I was not sure how much time had elapsed when Dr. Anthony came into my private room to see me and speak with Alex and Dad. I listened as he told them my reaction had caused all my vital organs to swell, including my throat!

No wonder I felt like I was drowning!

Alex explained that I had been scheduled to see our family doctor at eight o'clock tomorrow morning to receive another shot of antitoxin.

"Mr. Lance, your wife would not have been alive at eight o'clock tomorrow morning!"

Alex's face turned ashen with shock. Dad's expression was one of total relief, and I lay there grateful. *If it had been up to Alex ... Oh thank God, Dad came to the house, or I would be dead!*

Looking back, I have no doubt that just as the outcome of my earlier surgery had been remarkably changed, God intervened and changed the outcome of this near fatal crisis by giving my father the desire to come to check on me just in the nick of time. Sometimes we forget that God uses people and leads them by His Spirit in extraordinary and mysterious ways to intervene in the circumstances of His children in order to help them. He uses people to share His heart of caring and compassion; His mind to share His knowledge, wisdom, and revelation; His feet to take Him to meet us at our place of need; and His hands to do what is needed in service.

I am thankful God used my dad, the ER staff, and a physician to save my life—or I would not have been alive to encounter the living God, Jesus Christ, a few years later when I would receive eternal life. God knew me when as yet I did not know Him. The Lord tells us in the Bible that He knew us from the womb: "My substance was not hid from thee, when I was made in secret" (Ps.139:15).

After I survived that crisis, Alex confessed to me his fear of having almost lost me. I wondered how my husband could profess his deep love for me and his fear of my dying when at times he had shown such unloving reactions to my unpredictable illnesses and had emotionally—and physically—withdrawn from me when I had most needed his love and support. However, Alex did visit with me in the hospital each evening after work while I was recovering.

Ten days later, I was released to go home and soon was as good as new. For the first time since Laurie was born, I finally felt well enough to enjoy our sweet baby girl and my sweet, patient son. Both she and Michael brought me great happiness.

But sadly, Alex did not appear to enjoy his children the same way I did. Just as with his baby son, he paid little attention to his new baby daughter. Unlike most proud fathers, Alex showed little enthusiasm toward her "firsts" and usually dismissed my excited conversations about them, just as he had with Michael's firsts.

Recalling Michael's sweet nature, I remembered it had been hard for anyone to resist him; but except for brief interludes, Alex had managed to do so. He was either too tired after work to play with him, too preoccupied, or complained of not feeling well. When Michael was a baby, I was concerned that he did not spend enough time with his father to bond. There were times when I asked Alex to please give Michael attention. I remember his answer and how it grieved me: "I don't know what to do with a baby. You're with him all day; he gets enough attention."

It was true. I treasured every moment with Michael. No matter how sick I had been all those months after he was born, I delighted in taking care of him. My only joy was caring for him, playing with him, and watching his development. But it had been sad for me, knowing that most of the time Alex could not find that same kind of joy in holding him, or romping and playing with him.

Alex had seemed to lack normal parenting skills that come naturally to most fathers. That was troubling, and yet I continued to patiently encourage him to spend one-on-one time with Michael. When I sensed Alex was in a good mood, sometimes I pretended to be too busy to give baby Michael his water or juice, so Alex would have to hold him in his arms. Now I was doing the same thing with baby Laura.

I believed that as a toddler, Michael needed to spend time with his daddy, so I would find some reason why Alex must take him to the store or wherever he was going. When Alex agreed, it was almost always with irritation, but afterward I could tell he had really enjoyed those times.

Despite my concerns, however, I knew Alex loved his son. I also knew he loved his baby daughter. He seemed to have controlled his temper and bridled his tongue since Laurie was born, so during this time our relationship improved. However, my secret plan was still with me. I would choose just the right time to speak with Alex again about marriage counseling. If he agreed, I hoped he would not only receive help for his unpredictable disposition and Mr. Hyde tendencies but also gain insight into his attitudes toward parenting.

After my near fatal medical problem, everything seemed to settle down again, and I was thoroughly enjoying baby Laurie and Michael. I thought the hard times were behind us and my life would finally be free of crises and the overwhelming stress that had become my almost daily companion. But I could not have predicted the incident that would happen next and how it would bring my greatest fear as a mother.

Our "big boy" Michael was having a bout with tonsillitis again. Despite my efforts to get his temperature down, it continued to rise late one evening. Fearing he would have a convulsion, as he had the last time he had run a fever, I called Dr. Bunter, our pediatrician.

The doctor calmed my fears and said, "Give him two baby aspirin and rub his body down in an alcohol and tepid water bath until his temperature drops." In spite of our efforts, his temperature remained high. Four hours later, Alex went to the kitchen to open a new bottle of baby aspirin and give him two more tablets. About two o'clock in the morning, Michael's fever broke and Alex put him in our bed where he could keep an eye on him, while I slept in Michael's room so I could get up for the baby's four o'clock feeding.

"Mommy."

"Mommy." I slowly awakened to Michael's faint call and opened my eyes in time to see him vomit a little bit of pink liquid. Instantly I remembered the new bottle of pink baby aspirin that Alex had opened the night before and screamed, "Alex!"

I heard him jump out of bed.

The moment he saw Michael standing beside the pink liquid on the floor, he cried, "Oh my God ... no!" and ran into the kitchen, calling back to me, "He ate 'em all ... He's taken the whole bottle!"

Instead of placing the container back into the cupboard on the top shelf as he normally would have done, in the urgency of the moment, Alex had retrieved the aspirin and left the open bottle on the counter. Michael had slipped out of bed very early and eaten ninety-eight aspirin tablets!

Immediately Alex drove Michael to the emergency room. It was around six o'clock. I stayed with the baby and nervously paced, waiting for them to return.

"Finally! Thank God!" I said. Peering intently out the window, I could see Michael sitting in the front seat. Anxiously I opened the back door.

"He vomited a little again in the car on the way home," Alex said wearily as they got out of the car.

"Michael, Mommy was so worried," I cried, taking him from his father's arms, hugging and kissing him.

"The hospital's not that far away; what took you so long?" I asked.

"They made us wait a long time before they pumped Michael's stomach and took a test for the toxin level in his blood."

"Why?" I asked, angry that the hospital would have made such a sick child wait.

"There's only a skeleton crew on duty on Sunday mornings."

"This is too serious. Why would they wait so long?" I asked angrily. "Oh well," I caught myself, "he's home now, and he's going to be all right—that's all that matters!"

"The nurse said they will call us if his test results show that a dangerous amount of toxin entered his bloodstream," Alex said.

"What?" I spun around. "Why on earth would they send him home—especially before they had the test results—if there's a chance he could have a dangerous level of toxin in him?" I asked, incredulous.

Alex shrugged.

Knowing how impatient Alex could become, I wondered if his impatience had gotten the better of him and he had decided to leave the hospital before the test results were known. I hoped not.

Michael was weak. I carried him into the living room and laid him on the sofa where I could watch him while I prepared breakfast. I did not believe completely that he was out of danger. My body felt tense, anticipating the phone call from the hospital, dreading what I hoped would not happen. I kept up a constant line of chatter with Michael.

"Michael, Mommy's making you pancakes, your favorite. Won't they taste good?" I called to him.

I continued questioning him, and he answered each one. Suddenly I realized Michael had not answered my last question. I peered around the corner to see if he was still on the sofa. Michael lay motionless. *Oh God!* The sick feeling in the pit of my stomach turned to chaotic fear—and then to terror—as I ran to the sofa. His face was ashen. A lump formed in my throat as I leaned close to him. He was barely breathing.

"Michael!" I shook him. "Michael! Oh God ... Michael!" I screamed, shaking him again to make sure he was conscious. His eyelids fluttered slightly. I shook him again. He appeared only semi-conscious. I screamed, "Oh no, God ... no!"

Alex heard me and rushed into the living room. At that same moment, the phone rang. I knew it was the hospital.

"Okay, I'll take him right over to Children's Hospital. Yes, I'll take him right in!" I heard Alex answer.

"Grab a blanket," he yelled grabbing his and Michael's coats. "The test registered a high level of toxin! Let's go!" he ordered.

"I can't; the baby is still sleeping. I'll call Will and Susan!" I yelled back, grabbing a blanket off the bed to wrap Michael in.

Will, our neighbor, instantly raced across the street to the passenger side of Alex's car, and Alex placed Michael into his arms. I watched the car speeding down the street and wondered if I would see my little boy sitting in the front seat when the car pulled into our driveway again.

I paced and prayed, prayed and paced. *Oh Lord, I want to be with Michael. I want to be at the hospital.*

Five minutes later, Susan, Will's wife, came to the door. She offered to sit with the baby, and she also offered her car so I could drive to the hospital. *What would we do without good neighbors?* I thought, backing out of the driveway. I broke the speed limit all the way to the hospital. "God, please don't let him die," I pleaded over and over again. *Why didn't Alex just stay at the hospital until he knew the test results? We've lost so much time.*

By the time I arrived, I felt numb. I walked toward Alex and Will, seated in the waiting room, feeling as though I were in a dream watching everything happen in slow motion.

"Where's Michael?" I asked.

"Alisha, if it hadn't been for that policeman, I know Michael wouldn't have been alive when we got here," Will said.

"What do you mean?" I asked, my fear rising.

"We were driving over the speed limit, and a cruiser stopped us. Alex was so nervous trying to explain … but the officer took one look at Michael and said, 'Come with me!' I jumped into the cruiser with Michael, and the officer motioned for Alex to follow us. He turned on the siren, and we zipped through traffic. I kept looking down at the little guy's face. I think he might have stopped breathing a couple of times on the way … God, I've never prayed so hard in my life!" he said, with tears in his eyes. "But he's gonna be all right, Alisha; the doctors have been working on him."

Mechanically, I sat myself down next to Alex. As usual, he shut me out. He did not even look at me; he just stared at the floor, saying over and over again, "Please God, don't let him die!"

My voice trembling, I asked, "What have the doctors said?"

"Nothing!" he snapped, jumping to his feet. "I haven't even seen them to ask a question." He began pacing back and forth. I watched him angrily for a few moments. *Why didn't he press someone for answers? Why didn't he insist on immediate attention for his son earlier this morning? He makes me so mad. If he'd just stayed at the hospital the first time, Michael might not be critical. Why can't I count on him to take charge in a crisis?* As frazzled as I was, I knew that underlying all these emotions was the fact that Alex was unable to meet even my most basic expectations for his natural support as a husband and father.

After what seemed like hours, Alex and I were summoned to where Michael lay on a hospital cart. The medical staff was in and out, working with him.

"Why is he still so gray-looking?" I asked. Michael looked so small and limp lying there.

"They were barely able to get a blood pressure reading on him when he was brought in," said a familiar voice. "He'll be all right now." I turned, grateful and relieved to see Michael's pediatrician, Dr. Bunter.

"You'll be able to take him home in an hour or so. He's out of danger, but we just want to watch him for now."

I did not want to leave my son's side, but Dr. Bunter politely urged me to do so. As I was walking to the waiting room filled with worried parents like us, the image of Michael's gray, limp body lying on the hospital cart would not leave my mind. I was relieved, however, that the danger seemed to be over.

Releasing my initial reactions of fear and anger, I sat down close to Alex. I reached for his hand, and he took mine and held it tightly. We did not speak for a few minutes. We only gazed into each others eyes from time to time, squeezing our clasped hands simultaneously as we read one another's thoughts. This trauma was somehow momentarily washing away our relationship struggles. There was no distance between us at this moment, only a love for our son and our shared relief.

We rode home in silence, emotionally exhausted. Will followed us in the car I had driven to the hospital. We thanked Will and Susan for their help and they left, expressing their happiness that Michael was safe.

I held Michael as close to me as possible. We cuddled without speaking. He held on to me tightly; I knew he was glad to be in his mommy's arms. My thoughts drifted to the police officer who had rushed Michael to the hospital. *If not for him, Michael would have died.* And I thought at the time that God in His mercy might have intervened again in this near fatal tragedy.

Looking back, I remember how terrified I was of losing my son, but how grateful I was to the police officer, our neighbors, and the pediatrician and medical team at Children's Hospital. Although I was grateful, believing that God had changed the outcome, silently I was groaning about all we had gone through during our first three years of marriage. I could not help but question God: *Why? Why have all these terrible things happened in the first place...to me... and now my child?*

I remember how I attempted to settle back into my Sunday routine after the near death of my little boy, but the possibility of tragedy crept into my mind. Its reality shadowed even the happiest occasions of my life. I had passed through a dark, dark tunnel—a mother's worst nightmare—and had emerged into the light. But from that time, I no longer took for granted that there would be no more dark tunnels in my life or that I would pass into the light the next time. I had seen the flip side of the American dream: the "American nightmare." Now, at twenty-six, I felt wiser to the world. I knew that no matter how smooth the ride seemed on my life's road, tragedy could rear its ugly head in an instant.

The dual responsibilities that I had taken on—fending off Alex's verbal attacks and trying to keep the peace to prevent his violent outbursts, while fearing another tragedy—changed the way I traveled through life. I was now a defensive driver, alert for the next tragedy that might strike at any moment. Alex's Jekyll-and-Hyde personality notwithstanding, I rationalized that some of his on-again, off-again behavior might be caused by the stress of waiting for the next crisis to happen. I could understand that. I was under the same strain.

In the weeks following Michael's crisis, a real weariness settled upon me, coupled with resentful thoughts: *Why should I be the only one in this marriage who always has to do the right thing? Forgive. Forget. Try harder to better our relationship; meet all my husband's needs… be a good wife, a good housekeeper… keep the peace at any cost. Alex doesn't do his part. It's not fair!*

Some days I wanted to stubbornly refuse to do the things for Alex that I knew were my duties, because I did not think he appreciated a good wife. There were times when I was more resentful and rebellious than others. Then I wanted to say, *Cook your own meals … do your own laundry … iron your own white shirts!*

At those times, my father's words to me as a teenager would steal across my mind, and the memory of them would loom vivid again. "Don't ever compromise your own high standards to fit in with someone whose standards are below yours. Don't let them bring you down to their level," he'd say. After hearing my dad's words replay in my head at those rebellious times, I would determine all over again not to fail in what I believed were my responsibilities as a stay-at-home wife. I would choose to do the right thing.

Regardless of everything Alex had done, I still bent over backward to be loving to my husband, showing him personal attention, always expressing interest in his job, praising his efforts, and encouraging him, always sensitive to his male ego. Surely my nurturing would keep his dark side, Mr. Hyde, tamed. But I still resented feeling I was alone when it came to caring for our children.

Despite my efforts and being pleasant to Alex, instead of becoming more sensitive to the emotional and physical strain I had been under, whenever he was in one of his moods, he blamed everything on me. The physical crises I had endured and put behind me were now used as Alex's weapons against me. It was "my fault" our marriage had gone sour, because I was always "sick." He alone had suffered because of me. My illnesses were now the reason we were financially strapped, causing him to be "under pressure all the time," as he often accused—even though 80 percent of our medical expense was paid by insurance.

Alex was becoming more successful in the company and still working hard at his position. He was out even more nights of the week, entertaining customers or meeting with business associates. Now he was coming home later and later—and tipsy. *Why does he have to go out so often, and why does he have to drink so much?* Before we married, to my knowledge Alex had drunk only socially, and very little. Now I was worried that he was becoming an alcoholic.

When he was out on business, I always waited up for him. One night when he arrived home unusually late, I was ready to question him. Carefully using a nonthreatening tone, I cautiously asked why he had to stay out so late for business and why he was often smashed when he got home. He answered with a sneer that it was none of my business how many nights he went out, where he went, what he did, how late he came home, or how much he had to drink. Then I got mad.

"Doesn't seem like business to me!" I sarcastically retorted, glaring at him.

The pattern was always the same. I could not get through to him. My pleadings to limit his nights out and not to drink so much always ended the same. I would always break into tears, just out of frustration, telling him that the kids needed him to spend more time home with them. He ignored me. Alex was never moved by my reasoning, my tears, or my complaints. He just got angrier. There was no reasoning with this man.

The tension between us became unbearable. Our children were all we had in common now. However, Alex was seldom in the mood to talk or play with them. Mostly, it appeared he did not want to be bothered with them. When he was at home, there were times when he could not tolerate even their normal laughter, their frisky sounds, their playing with each other. Although he was never abusive to them, at those times he would curtly order me to silence them. More times than once, I responded with something to the effect, "Lighten up, Daddy! They're just having fun. You need to be more sensitive to the children, Alex."

How strange. Isn't there such a thing as paternal instinct too?

By now Alex stayed home on a weeknight only to mow the lawn or take care of other home maintenance needs. Although he was usually home all day on Saturday and Sunday, I was noticing that he was restless and agitated much of the time. I did not know why. If we did not have a family or business function to attend on Saturday, Alex was now going out to play poker with his friends. I had no objection to Alex's going out occasionally with the guys, but many of those Saturday nights he was coming home inebriated. Even so, we never missed going to Mass on Sundays, and sometimes we visited my parents. Fortunately, Alex was always the good Dr. Jekyll in front of my parents and relatives.

Soon he was coming home from playing poker, full-blown drunk. Then he started bringing beer by the case into the house, to which I strongly objected. But he did not pay any attention to me. Those nights when he did stay home, after the kids were in bed, he began drinking. He drank one beer after another. The more he drank, the more he talked about regrets in his life. Then he would drink a little more and start slamming me. I was a "good-for-nothing wife" and one of his biggest regrets. I would have to retreat to the bedroom to get away from him and his vulgar slurs. I knew it was the alcohol then. He would drink until he fell asleep or passed out, whichever came first. Nonetheless, curiously, he was up early the next morning and off to work. He never missed a day of work.

When he crossed into addiction, Alex started drinking his beer as soon as he got home from work—and I took immediate action. Usually I took the children for a drive to the store, or in warm weather, to the park to swing; other times I took them to visit my parents. If none of that was feasible, I gathered them together in one of their bedrooms to play games or read stories before bathing them and tucking them in for the night.

I was angry about Alex's drinking. I was also angry about his footloose and fancy-free attitude of going and doing whatever he pleased, which the children and I had to live with, like it or not.

Fortunately, I did have the companionship of women friends who had children too. We would visit each other's homes some days, or we would go shopping together. But I always felt sad when

I listened to them talk about their husbands' obvious interest in them and their children. I saw the joys of family life and marriage fulfilled in my friends' lives, but unfulfilled in my own. It was a heartbreaking comparison. I saw our family life as severely abnormal.

Alex resented the time I spent with my friends. He felt I should never be gone from the house. He often ridiculed my friends and family. If they dropped in unexpectedly, he made them feel unwelcome. I tried to counteract his indifference by being even more hospitable, while inside I choked on my embarrassment and hoped he would not expose his dark side. We almost always argued after every social evening. He found fault with my family and friends, totally misjudging them, and I found myself defending them and trying to reason with him to change his negative opinions of them.

However, he was different toward his friends and business associates or customers—always hospitable, the perfect host. My wonderful Dr. Jekyll ensured his good image and business reputation when we entertained his boss and his wife or when we attended a company party. At those times, Alex donned the smoothest of social graces and treated me like a queen, enjoying the admiration his business contacts showed me. Secretly, I was always uncomfortable at those times, feeling I was being paraded like a trophy wife. Obviously, he thought he was boosting his public image.

Even our children seemed to be paraded as his trophies at times when kids were included. He always portrayed himself as the perfect husband and father with the perfect family, although we were far from perfect and hardly even a real family at all since I was the only one in the marriage who was "married." Nevertheless, it was all about appearances, all about doing what was necessary to build on his good image and his business reputation, and to maintain it.

Of course, his public image was a far cry from his private one. However, he was charming in those business social gatherings, and I admired him then; his finesse, his good manners, and his ability to make articulate conversation were what I had found attractive when we had met. But now I saw his deception too, and there were times I detested him for giving his best to his company associates and customers and his worst to his family.

No matter how disappointed I had been about the autumn season of my life back then, I still tried hard to keep my home calm and peaceful. Nonetheless, even when things were going smoothly, Alex often started an argument just so he could justify leaving the house. It was emotionally and physically draining for me to always be on alert, trying to anticipate his moods, trying to get the children and me out of his "cruel zone," to stay out of his line of verbal fire. I had to keep one step ahead of Mr. Hyde to hopefully keep my little ones from the effects of his personality. But I became weary of combating it all. It was hard, and I felt I had no more emotional strength.

The truth was that by now Alex and I only existed under the same roof but had no real relationship. We both felt trapped. I approached him again about marriage counseling. His answer was still, "No!" followed by the same old accusations that all the problems in our marriage were my fault. When I tried to reason with him, an argument ensued. Alex could out-talk me and out-yell me, and only after he had stomped out the door, leaving me in a heap of frustration, anger, and tears, could I think of hateful comebacks.

When his drinking at home escalated, Alex's verbal and psychological abuse toward me felt even more threatening as I recognized that Mr. Hyde was becoming more dominant than ever. I feared another violent outburst.

One evening I gave Alex an ultimatum: he must agree to professional help, marriage counseling, or he would have to leave the house and we would have no choice but to legally separate. He again refused the professional help. He also refused to leave the house, telling me that if anyone left, it would be me and the kids.

Eventually Alex would understand his complex and changeable personality—and so would I—when Mr. Hyde was fully exposed. But not before my life was threatened.

Suddenly the memory was vivid in my mind.

The children and I were asleep when Alex came home very late. He turned on the overhead light, waking me. My eyes opened to see him standing at the foot of the bed. I squinted and blinked before clearly refocusing on him again. Fear grabbed me. He was holding a double-barreled shotgun pointed directly at me.

"I'm gonna kill you tonight," Alex calmly declared.

"Alex," I tried to softly plead, "don't be silly. Put that away, honey. Come to bed." I half smiled, trying to hide the terror gripping me. But I was trembling so hard that I was sure Alex could see the bedcovers shaking. My thoughts raced: *Oh God, help me. Keep my babies from waking up. What's wrong with him? He doesn't seem drunk.*

As fearlessly as possible, I spoke again. "Come on, Alex," I said sweetly, "please turn the light out and come to bed."

He smiled back. "No. I'm gonna kill you. I am."

"Please, honey, you don't mean that," I tenderly answered.

Coldly, calmly, with a menacing grin, he said, "Yes I do. I'm gonna kill you, if you try to leave me."

I did not answer. I was terrified. Now his face was hard; his look, fierce.

My eyes locked with his in a piercing stare, trying to act as though I were not afraid. I did not move a muscle.

"Get out of that bed!" he ordered.

"Alex … please … please Alex, don't wake up the kids. Please put that away," I begged, watching his face. His eyes did not even twitch. My nerves were so raw, I burst into tears, so worried about my little ones.

"I told you to get out of that bed!" he demanded.

Cautiously, as though moving in slow motion, I slithered like a snake out of bed onto my knees. He came around to the side of the bed and stood over me. I was trying to suppress my sobs and praying silently: *God, please don't let Michael wake up and come in. Please don't let my babies wake up. Please don't let him hurt my babies!"*

I lifted my head slightly to turn and look at Alex. He lowered the gun about a foot from my head. I believed I was going to die, because I could feel the gun moving closer to the back of my head.

"Please, Alex, don't shoot!" I begged in a whisper. "Oh God, no! Alex! No!" I cried, hunching down and curling into a fetal position as if to hide from him. I choked on the scream rising in my throat. But no sound came out. I could not scream. I could not speak again.

Alex stood over me as I lay on the floor in complete submission—waiting, waiting, waiting for him to pull the trigger. He made no sounds but kept the gun pointed at my head. I resigned myself to the fact that these were the last moments of my life. I actually saw my life pass by me in one wave of hopelessness. I was terrified that he would pull the trigger any moment and then kill the children.

"Oh God, protect my babies," I sobbed.

After several moments, Alex started laughing. It was a frightening, sinister laugh. Startled, I looked up at him, only to stare into the gun barrel, and quickly looked down again, locked in fear. He stood over me, laughing as I cowered even lower, shaking.

"I was just kidding," he said. "What are you so scared about? I wouldn't kill you; you know that," he said, still laughing as he took the gun away and walked out of the room.

I remained crouched on the floor, paralyzed by fear. Then I began to shake violently. I clenched my teeth trying to stop their clicking. *I know for sure now—he's sick! Oh God, he's so sick! A normal person couldn't do such a thing, even as a joke. I have never felt so glad to be alive. I've got to get the kids out of here. I've got to get them as far away from him as I can ... but where can I take them this time of night? Oh God, help me!*

I had to get to my kids. I tried to stand, but my body would not obey my will. Like an animal, I crawled on hands and knees to the door and reached for the doorknob to pull myself up. My legs were like rubber. I made a second effort, and finally on the third, I was able to stand. I made my way into the hall.

Reaching the baby's room first, I sighed with relief as I heard her breathing softly in a peaceful sleep. I lifted her, grabbed a couple of diapers and her blanket, and moved quickly into Michael's room. *He's fast asleep; oh, thank God!* I quietly shut and locked the door. I wrapped the blanket around Laura and tiptoed to the chair and slid back into it. The kids had slept through the entire ordeal, and we were behind a locked door; but my insides were in knots.

Gradually I let my shoulders relax, and my arms loosened their grip on the baby. I took a deep breath and tried to go back over what had just happened. Unexpectedly, my mind was amazingly clear.

Unbelievable! He has some sadistic need to control me, to rule me. I realized that all his verbal attacks of the past—everything— was done from his throne of control! *That's enough! Enough!* I was beyond trying to figure Alex out. It did not matter anymore what the reason was for his behavior; this insanity had to end. *I have to get out of here before he tries this scare tactic again—or worse, before he does kill all of us!*

I sat all night with baby Laura in my arms, thinking and plan- ning. *I'll call a lawyer in the morning. Threatening me with a gun is the last straw! I won't live with this madman another day!* Now I did not care about my marriage vows, the Catholic Church, what my parents would think, or anything else. I thought only of my children, myself, and our safety. I dozed off and on throughout the night.

Sounds of Alex showering for work aroused me, and I checked my watch. It was six o'clock in the morning. I sat very still, not wanting to waken the children, at least not within the next hour before Alex would leave the house. My arms felt paralyzed from holding Laura all night. I stayed in Michael's room until I heard Alex's car pull out of the driveway.

After feeding and dressing the children, my intention was to call an attorney, but I did not know one; and at that moment, I was too nervous to make inquiries. For some reason, Father Maloney came to mind, so instead, I dialed his number, wondering how much I should tell him. He and Alex had become friends before our marriage. He thought Alex was a great guy, as did almost everyone else.

"Hello," he said as he came on the line.

"Father Maloney, this is Alisha Lance."

"Alisha, how are you? And how is Alex? What can I do for you?"

"Well ... I ... I don't think you can ..." My voice cracked. There was a huge sob sitting on my chest.

"It's okay. Take your time. Just tell me what I can do for you. Is it one of the children?"

"No, Father, they're fine ... It's Alex." He waited silently while I forced myself to regain my composure. I took a deep breath and began again.

"Father ... It's really bad!" I started tearing. "Alex has done some terrible things since our marriage, but last night was the worst. He held a gun on me and threatened to kill me!"

Now the words were coming quickly as I poured out the ugly details about his abusive behavior. "I can't stand any more! I'm terrified of his violent temper, but also, he's ... well, he's ... sadistic!" I blurted out. "Really, Father, he is that way to me—in our home!"

Waiting for his response, I wondered if he was remembering the recurring dream of my faceless groom and my fears about marrying Alex, shared with him before our wedding.

"I think you should see Dr. Herald," Father Maloney said. "He's a psychologist, a Catholic, and works with married couples. I think you and Alex should see him soon."

"Oh no," I quickly replied, "Alex won't see him. He won't even talk to you. He wouldn't want you or anyone else to know the things he's done."

"Well, if Alex wants to talk to me ... if he changes his mind ... I'd be glad to schedule some time even this evening for the two of you." He made no comment about the horror of Alex's threat to kill me.

I can't believe it. No reaction at all ... as though Alex's abuse wasn't even shocking to him. This is my priest! He's known me since birth. Doesn't he care about what Alex did to me?

I was frustrated. I wanted him—someone—to realize the seriousness of all this and help me!

Why doesn't he even offer some spiritual counseling for me? Tell me what to do ... Tell me to get out ... Point me in a new direction! Give me hope that my children and I can start a safe life without Alex. Did Father really hear what I said?

I was full of resentment that Father Maloney seemed apathetic about it all. Then like a flash, I had the thought: *Perhaps he was trained to not show emotion in such extreme cases. Maybe he is in shock. Maybe he is finding it hard to believe that Alex is capable of such an act.*

After all, he did not know I had been emotionally and psychologically tortured by Alex for over three years. Neither he nor anyone else, for that matter, knew how hard I had been trying to avoid splitting up my family.

I had pent up my feelings and pain; and I had hidden Alex's abuse from him, my family, and friends—from everyone except Dr. Sterling. *But no more! This is it for me! I'm through! I have no choice but to get as far away from him as possible!*

"No, Father. Alex definitely won't see you," I reiterated. "But I need to talk to Dr. Herald."

Father Maloney gave me the phone number, and I made an appointment for that very afternoon. I packed diapers and nursing bottles and some clothes for us in a suitcase and drove to my parents' home to stay. Mom was at work, but Dad agreed to babysit while I went to talk to Dr. Herald. I had to talk to someone who could help me shake the effects of Alex's cruel, violent dark side and this last nightmare I had just lived through.

I was back in the present again. As I lay there on the sofa, my eyes wandered over to the baby grand and fleetingly moved across the grouping of family photographs displayed there, resting on one taken during those terrible autumn years. The memory of when that photo was taken brought a frown. *Ah, yes ... Alex and me and the kids. We're all smiles. The kids' smiles were genuine, but Alex's smile was covering his dark deception; and mine ... mine was hiding relentless emotional pain.*

Part 2
The Healing Begins

Chapter 8

Evil Unmasked

Now I felt myself gasp. I looked up. Laura was still sitting across from me. My memories had been hard-hitting tonight, all day, for that matter. For someone who had spent a lot of mental, emotional, and spiritual energy during the past year shaking off memories, today I was doing nothing but remembering. In fact, the good and bad memories seemed to be fighting for control of my soul. Then I wondered if God Himself had exhumed them one by one from my subconscious where they had been buried so many years ago, buried in the cemetery for bad memories.

Maybe the cemetery was necessary during those early years: for self-preservation and as the only way I could survive until that time when I would meet Jesus and begin to deliberately trust Him with all the hard issues in my life.

But what value is it to dwell on the past today? For what purpose? How will memories, especially bad memories, help me? Is it a psychological trap to keep me from moving on, concentrating on my future?

Somehow I feel I can never escape all these bad memories of my life with Alex. But they are my life, like it or not. I own it! The apostle Paul remembered his past from which God had rescued him. That was his testimony. That is the testimony of Christians down through the centuries. How can I separate myself from my memories, shake off twenty-six years of my life? Yes, it is my past. But it's also my testimony of what God has brought me through by His amazing grace. It's my story.

Then it occurred to me that perhaps remembering even the bad times from this new vantage point could be a catharsis. Maybe this was needed to bring closure to my life with Alex: "face my demons"—like the favorite secular cliché for facing problems—that sort of thing. Perhaps this was actually a necessary step to healing, deliverance, and complete recovery in order to put my memories of the past behind me once and for all, before God could lead me to take my next step into whatever He had for me. *Time will tell whether I am right or wrong. But for now, I need to remember.*

Staring at Laurie, I remembered how hard I had tried to convince Alex that we needed marriage counseling before she was born. As a young married woman who knew nothing about spousal abuse and domestic violence during the 1950s and '60s, without knowledge of agencies, printed information, or shelters for abused women and children (which is readily available to women today), I was ill equipped to deal with the unexpected cards of life I had been dealt.

I tried everything I knew, but I could not keep Alex's inner rage from attacking me without provocation and without warning. Alex had not physically touched me, but he had stabbed me deeply with every abusive, vile profanity imaginable, with revolting, ugly names, and with mean criticisms, wounding my heart.

But the gun incident, Alex's threat to kill me if I left him, was the end—Mr. Hyde's last blatant, sadistic threat against me. I would take no more chances! To protect my children and myself, I made a dramatic decision to turn from the fear of living with Alex's dark side to that of which I had been equally fearful: divorce.

But first I would meet with Dr. Herald, the Catholic psychologist. Because of my decision, Alex's life would take a dramatic turn, and mine would as well.

I remember my session with Dr. Herald like it was yesterday. My emotions had always been suppressed around my children and others; but now I had no more strength to restrain myself, and I poured out my pain and fears to the psychologist. He asked if I would submit to a psychological test, which I did. It was the ink-blot test. Dr. Herald left the room with my answers and returned a little while later to announce, "Mrs. Lance, the results of the testing prove you to be mentally sound in every way." I was neither surprised nor relieved. Dr. Sterling had already assured me of that.

The doctor asked more questions about our relationship, and I gave long, painful answers. I began with the first incident of violence over cheese sauce on potatoes, continuing up to the gun incident. He listened without interruption and without any expression of emotion. After I finished, Dr. Herald told me to take a few moments to relax.

We sat in silence until Dr. Herald finally responded: "Mrs. Lance, I believe that while Alex's threat to kill you is a definite sign that he does have a serious problem, I also believe he had no intention of killing you. He was only trying to control you."

I strongly objected, "Yes, I understand the control thing, but that validates only part of my own concept." I concluded with an emotionally charged defense: "Doctor, you don't know Alex. You have not experienced his unprovoked violence! It was more than a scare tactic or domination ploy for control! All the things Alex has done to me have been vicious cruelty, pure sadism!"

The doctor reiterated his words, but they were no consolation for me, since he had not yet examined Alex to know exactly what was wrong with him. However, he did tell me that it was a good idea for me to separate from Alex for a while and quickly added, "You're a Catholic. Don't be hasty to initiate divorce until we can convince your husband to see me."

"Doctor, Alex will never agree to see you!" I said firmly.

"Do you love your husband?" the doctor asked. "Now, think about this question before you answer."

His question threw me. I sat there silently sifting through the horrible things I had told this psychologist, just as I had told the psychiatrist before him. I could hardly believe my young married life had gone this way, that all these terrible things had happened in only our first three years. My life had turned out so differently from what I had expected. My hopes and dreams had all gone unrealized, except for my children, who met all my greatest expectations and brought my only joy. I knew I was a good mother. But beyond that confidence, I had no clue to who I was anymore. *Oh God, what happened to the "me" I used to know, before Alex?*

"Does your husband have any redeeming value in your mind?" the doctor prompted, startling me. "Is there enough love for him left that would cause you to want to see him helped and therefore save your marriage and prevent the breakup of your family?" he coaxed.

"No! I don't trust Alex. I'm terrified of him. No, Dr. Herald, you're asking too much of me. I came here for you to help me shake the effects of Alex's abuse and get on with my life and … make a safe home for my babies and me! Alex doesn't want any help. God knows I've tried," I ended sarcastically.

"Mrs. Lance, I believe you will be safe. Your husband doesn't understand his own behavior. He probably doesn't understand why you want to leave him. By his threat, he hopes to keep you from leaving.

"I don't expect you to do anything you don't feel comfortable doing. I asked you that question because if you do still love your husband, I believe I can help him if he would permit me to," he said confidently.

"You don't understand, Doctor; he refuses. He insists that I am the one with the problem. I know he'll never see you!"

"How about asking him to come see me about you? If he thought I wanted to talk to him about your problem, do you think he would come in?" he asked. "Do you care enough to use this strategy to help him? Do you still want to keep your family together?" he repeated firmly.

Yes! No! I felt like I was in a catch-22. *Why is he pressuring me to do this? Here it goes again … Forget about how Alisha feels … How can we help poor Alex?*

Suddenly, I felt so quiet inside that I was not sure if my heart was still beating. It was a strange sensation. *He seems so sure he can help Alex. He's Catholic too, so I'm sure he doesn't advocate divorce. Maybe that's good. But can he really help an abuser and an alcoholic change?*

To my surprise, I found myself saying, "Okay, Doctor, I'll try, but only for Alex's sake. He does need help. But I can't live with him any longer, and I can't have my babies around him. I am planning to divorce him."

"Well, then, you will ask your husband to make an appointment to see me, using that special strategy. Go ahead with your plans to separate, if you feel you must. Don't worry; you and your children will get along all right. These things are never easy, but you said you have parents who will help you. Actually, this is a positive decision to consider before doing anything drastic. It could ultimately save your marriage, if that's what you want. You're doing everything you can do. The rest is up to your husband," he said, ushering me to the door.

I left the doctor's office, wondering how everything had gotten turned around. I wrestled with my emotions as I drove to my parents' home. Dr. Herald had completely changed my objective to receive help for myself. *Here I go again. How much more can I take?*

When I arrived at my parents' home, I knew I had to suppress my frustration and conceal my pain for the sake of my children. I prepared dinner and played with them before tucking them in for the night. The shopping center was open until nine o'clock, so it was after eight when Dad drove to the department store to pick up Mom from work.

When they came home, the three of us discussed my marriage problems for the first time, as well as my session with Dr. Herald and his special strategy to get Alex in to see him. They were shocked to learn of what I had been living through but had covered up all these years. Finally, I told them of my plan to separate, assuring them that the *Catholic* psychologist was in agreement. And, I tried to prepare them for the possibility of divorce.

Now it was time to leave. I had to approach Alex while I had my nerve. Driving home that evening, I thought about my parents. Because they were strict Catholics, I knew it would be a real shame for them to endure a divorce in the family. It was hard to hear their opinions and feel their disapproval of what I might do. I still feared divorce myself, for all the same reasons.

No one wanted my marriage saved more than I, but only if our family could be normal; that is, healthy and safe. I wanted my children to live in a stable atmosphere. At this point, it was not Alex, but my children, who were my only concern. They were my only focus. I was glad they were with my parents, since I anticipated a scene when I approached Alex tonight about seeing Dr. Herald.

I pulled into the driveway. The house was dark. *Alex is out again tonight? Obviously, he's not the slightest bit worried about where the children and I are! Maybe he doesn't even remember what he did last night.*

"I'm tired, drained. Oh God, I'm so tired," I moaned as I walked into Michael's bedroom and threw myself across his twin bed. *Oh God, I need someone to hold me and tell me everything's going to be all right, and let me drift off to sleep—maybe forever.*

How good just the thought of that felt. *Am I actually thinking about suicide? No … I could never do that! But to go to sleep and escape all the pain, the worry, and the responsibility for my babies, just until I knew I could wake up and be strong enough to cope. I'm so tired … tired of fighting Alex's abuse … tired of trying to hold up under it all, for the kids … tired of being tired.* I drifted off to sleep.

I awakened to the faint sound of the television. *Alex is home.* I turned on the light and squinted at my watch to check the time. *Almost midnight. That's unusual. Normally he comes straight to bed when he comes home this late—and more often than not, he's drunk.*

I remembered those times and how I hated the smell of his body and his breath when he had been drinking in the bars. His hair would stink of stale cigarette smoke, and the sour smell of beer would permeate the whole room. Sometimes the smell was so nauseating that I had to move to the living room and sleep on the sofa.

I pulled myself up from the bed and walked into the living room. Alex was lying on the sofa. *I might not see him tomorrow. I have to talk to him now … get it over with before I lose my nerve.*

"The children are at Mom and Dad's," I said, to get his attention. He did not even acknowledge that I was in the room.

"I've seen a Catholic psychologist," I said, testing Alex's reaction. He did not respond. I cautiously continued.

"The doctor gave me some psychological tests. He feels he should talk to you about me. He wants you to call to make an appointment as soon as you have time. It must be serious!"

The lie terrified me. *What if he can tell I'm lying?*

Alex sat up, looked at me in his superior, arrogant manner, and sarcastically asked, "What's wrong? Did he find out you're nuts? I could have told him that." He grinned smugly. "Yeah, I'll see him. I want to hear this for myself. You make the appointment and I'll go."

"You're sure? You'll really go?"

"Yeah," he said with a smirk, "the sooner, the better. I want to hear what a psychiatrist has to say about you!"

Alex was scheduled to go to Dr. Herald's office on Friday after work. I spent the day with the children at my parents' home and then came home early in the evening—and worried. I was not used to lying. My conscience bothered me. The doctor's plan had been rather deceptive. *But it worked! The doctor was right. Oh, but what will happen if Alex finds out the truth? Have I opened Pandora's box?*

The fear was real. I was scared.

I went along with Dr. Herald's deception for Alex's sake ... to help him. Never mind that. If he feels he's been tricked by us, I'm the one who will pay for it!

When Alex arrived home, he seemed to be in a good mood. I breathed a sigh of relief. But I was curious to know for sure if he had kept the appointment. If so, he did not talk about it, and I asked no questions. Then he surprised me by casually mentioning he was going back to see Dr. Herald in the morning. *On a Saturday? That surprises me.*

I was back and forth between my parents' house and my own all weekend. The times I saw Alex, he was amazingly calm. He still did not talk about his sessions. Although we had no conversation at all, I saw no hostility, no anger in him. What was going on?

Barely able to curb my curiosity, early Monday morning I telephoned Dr. Herald, hoping he would shed some light on his time with Alex.

"I tested your husband, Mrs. Lance. He does have a serious problem. I explained that to Alex. I told him he can be helped, that actually he's not bad enough to be hospitalized but that he needs ongoing therapy. I suggested that if he doesn't deal with this now, it will only get worse as he grows older. He's scheduled to come in again tomorrow, Tuesday, at four o'clock. I'd like you to come with him."

"No, Doctor, I can't. I mean, I really shouldn't, because I'm planning to see an attorney this week."

"Mrs. Lance, I believe I can help Alex, and I think you want that, don't you?"

"Yes, for his sake. I do want Alex to be helped, but … ," my voice faded to a whisper, "I'm not sure if …"

"It's up to you, Mrs. Lance. It's your decision. I won't insist. Just think about it. And incidentally, I agree with a separation period for the two of you, and I'll try to convince Alex that it would be good for him, temporarily, until he gets better. But please don't file for divorce yet. I believe Alex will get well and your marriage and family can be saved."

I mentioned Alex's unusual calmness during the weekend and the fact that he had not talked to me about their two meetings.

"Let's hope he is considering what I've told him and that he'll follow through. Alex has accepted the fact that he has a mental illness, and …"

"Oh?" I interrupted. "He didn't tell me that. What exactly is wrong with him?"

"He's manic-depressive."

Oh no! I remembered hearing the name of that mental disease within my former work environment, but I did not remember in-depth knowledge about the disorder.

"Tell me more about that problem, Doctor."

"We'll talk about that later. But Alex is treatable … and he's facing the truth. He wants to get well. I think I can help him. You said you do want to see that happen, Mrs. Lance."

"Can I be certain his condition is treatable? I believe he's addicted to alcohol too. Can he get better … stop drinking? Are you sure?"

"Yes. Can I count on you to come in tomorrow?"

"I'm not sure. I'll think about what you've said, Doctor. I must admit, while I want to believe you can help my husband change, to be honest, Doctor, I'm afraid to hope for that. But yes, we will definitely separate. I don't think I should disrupt the children's lives by moving them. Alex will need to move. Will you suggest that to him?"

The doctor agreed. I hung up the phone, knowing I had a big decision to make. After a lot of thought, I called Dr. Herald back.

"I'm sorry, Doctor, but I've decided not to join Alex tomorrow. He will have to do this on his own—without me. Anyhow," I stressed, "he should do it for himself."

On Tuesday Dr. Herald obviously managed to convince Alex that we should separate, because that weekend he moved into his bachelor friend's apartment.

Alex's therapy was expensive and not covered by insurance. Now he was paying shared rent and utilities with his friend and also giving me money to pay our mortgage, car payments, and all the same monthly bills. Although Alex had become more successful in his job and his salary had increased accordingly, we still had little savings to fall back on. I hated the thought of leaving my children during the day to go to work, but with two places for Alex to pay for now, I felt I had to help carry the load.

A battle began vis-à-vis my mind and emotions, because I did not want to be apart from my little ones for eight hours a day. I was about to do the very thing I had always sworn I would never do. I remembered what I had missed as a child because my mother decided to take a job. I had always told myself nothing I could buy with money from a job that took me away from my kids would be worth it to me.

However, my circumstances were very different from my mother's when she chose to work. My children were still babies. Nevertheless, I argued with myself that there was no denying it: getting a job now was absolutely necessary if I was eventually going to be on my own and making a living for us. I had no other choice. But I hated leaving my babies in someone else's care.

Get a grip, Alisha! I chided myself. *That's how it is for many other mothers who have no choice but to trust their kids to another's care every day while they work in order to keep a roof over their little ones' heads and food in their little tummies.* Still, the thought of leaving *my* kids was heart-wrenching for me.

Before searching the classifieds, I telephoned my former employer and friend. She could give me part-time work, but she was disappointed that she had no full-time position open for me in the association administration office. However, I passed the state civil service test, and almost immediately I interviewed for a job as executive assistant to the director of the student union on the campus of the Big Ten state university and was hired.

Fortunately, Susan and Will, our neighbors across the street, loved our kids and actually offered and were delighted to take care of baby Laurie; and I learned about a Catholic day-care facility for Michael that had just opened. It was perfect timing. It was in a church school located up north near the university, so I could easily drop him off and pick him up as I drove to and from work.

After only a couple of days, Michael was already looking forward to going to "school" to be with his new friends. It was a good arrangement for the kids; although as most single mothers can relate, it was sometimes tough for me to juggle everything. Mostly, I was sad to be missing this important time with my baby girl, watching her develop and accomplish her firsts.

Nevertheless, I made the best of it and tried to be as cheerful as possible about it, especially with the kids.

Alex's weekend visits with the children began and were going well. After several weeks, I had to believe he was responding positively to his treatment. I could see he related with the children better. He was more patient and even appeared to be having fun with them. Baby Laura seemed contented when he held her, and Michael never wanted him to leave. After he did, Michael would often ask me the same question: "Why doesn't Daddy stay home with us?"

His questions tore at my heart. I always told him Daddy had to travel to other cities throughout the week to do his job, which was partially true, but that he would always come home on weekends to be with us. Alex did travel for his job, and it was the most simplistic answer I could give to Michael, a toddler who must have felt his little world was out of sync. When he had other questions, I tried to come up with answers to assuage any worries he might have.

Also, on Alex's weekend visits, he was sharing a little about his sessions with the good doctor. It appeared to me that Dr. Herald had been able to help Alex, just as he had promised.

After Alex had completed several months of treatment, I received another phone call from the doctor, again requesting me to join Alex at his regular biweekly evening therapy sessions. He would make time to see each of us separately, then together. I told him I would think about it.

We ended our conversation, and I called my dad. Because he was retired, I could call him anytime during the day if I needed him. I could always count on Dad to listen, to be as objective as a father could be, and to offer sound advice. As a rule, even if it was something I did not want to hear, I always considered it, because I knew my father had my best interest at heart.

"Hi, Dad," I said when he picked up the phone. "I just talked to Dr. Herald ... and he suggests that I go with Alex to his next session."

"Does he say Alex has improved?"

I explained as much as I knew. When I finished, he was silent for a few moments then said, "I think you should go, Alisha. How do you feel about it?"

"I guess I should, Dad, but I'm scared."

"Sure, you're scared, and you don't know if Alex will continue to let the doctor help him. I understand. But if he does, that could make all the difference in your future, for you and the kids. I know you don't want to get a divorce. That would be so hard on the kids. Your mother and I hate to see you do that too. Divorce would be a bad thing for everybody."

In the words my dad did not say, I picked up on his fears, and, no doubt, my mother's fears, about my getting divorced. Even though they knew I was living in unbearable circumstances with Alex's abuse and did not want me to suffer that kind of heartache and pain, or for their grandchildren to be exposed to it, they still were concerned about what other people would say. It was obvious they would feel shamed by my divorce.

"You're right, Dad. But I have to be honest. You should know I'm still going to get a divorce if this treatment doesn't work for

Alex. I can't live that way anymore … I can't have my kids in that kind of environment."

"Do what you think is best. But you asked my opinion, and I think you should give this a chance," Dad concluded.

Now all things considered, I believed our children needed to interact for many years to come with a mentally healthy father, whether he ever came home to live with us. With that thought, I mustered the courage to do the right thing, for the right reason— again!

Before I joined Dr. Herald to begin couple counseling, I determined to learn everything I could about Alex's disorder—exactly what we were fighting. I remembered before Laura was born, Dr. Sterling had told me I could not fix my marriage nor could I fix Alex. However, he had not advised me how to handle Alex and his insane, out-of-control behavior, nor did I know how to stop myself from trying to fix everything.

Now that a professional had diagnosed Alex and his problem actually had a name, I decided to go to the library that evening to research mental health books to understand more about my husband's disorder. Finally, I got it. Now I knew beyond a shadow of doubt, this was something I could not fix. However, I gleaned from my reading that I needed appropriate coping skills with which to arm myself, skills to use for my children's protection as well as my own during this "iffy" period. I listed them on a piece of paper so I would not forget them. In fact, I wanted to read them to the doctor.

The next morning I phoned the doctor to make an appointment to discuss all this with him before agreeing to the joint counseling.

The following Saturday, Dr. Herald was ready to listen, and I began.

"I have thought this through and decided to join Alex for counseling. I'm scared to do this, Doctor. I admit it."

I paused because I was nervous and my voice was quivering. When I gained my composure, I began again.

"Since I have decided to give this a try, I will make every effort to stand with Alex as he continues to "tough out" his therapy—but it will not be at the expense of me or my children," I said emphatically.

"I am determined to fight by Alex's side until his battle is won. However, you should know, Doctor," I boldly declared, "only if it can be *on my terms.*"

Without waiting for the doctor's response, I went on to explain I had learned some coping skills in order to deal with Alex's abusive behavior, should I see it again during this joint counseling period.

"Dr. Herald, I'm reasonable. I don't expect all this to go perfectly … this joint counseling. I don't expect Alex to be perfect. I'm far from perfect. No doubt we'll both say stupid things at times. That's understandable. Alex is definitely trying to get well, but I don't know how to deal with him on a personal level right now, other than by using these rules for myself.

"However, I must tell you this: If I have to use these rules for coping even once to combat one of Alex's violent outbursts like those in the past, it will be once too often. You have to understand that I can *never*—I will *never ever*—put up with that abusive behavior again … even though he's still in treatment and isn't well yet. No more! If that happens one more time, it will be over for me. No more counseling. No more chance for reconciliation. I will immediately initiate divorce. I think you should tell Alex this."

I took a deep breath, wondering if I could maintain the kind of boldness and determination I was feeling at this moment.

"Doctor, do you want to hear my new rules for coping, discovered from researching Alex's disorder and how to live with one who is manic-depressive?"

"Yes, I do, Mrs. Lance."

I looked down at my list and began reading.

"First of all, I will mentally and emotionally erect my boundary, an invisible line that will separate me from Alex's violent outburst, should he ever have one again. I will not cross that line. I will cope, but I will not stay.

"I am determined to never again get caught up in Alex's frenzied behavior by trying to reason with him, distract him, or stop him. I will cope, but I will not stay.

"I will neither take into myself his insults, his obscene name-calling, or criticisms, nor will I defend myself against them or any of his false accusations. I will cope, but I will not stay.

"Should any of this behavior occur while in counseling or during Alex's weekend visits with the children, my plan is to leave: to get myself and our kids away from him and then call the police. In the past, I would simply leave his presence, take the children from the house to keep them out of earshot when he was being loud and belligerent or to keep them from seeing him drinking one beer after another. If I could not leave the house, I would immediately remove the children and myself and go to one of their bedrooms and redirect their attention by some means to deflect their father's behavior. As I said, that was in the past. Now, should Alex begin that insane behavior with me—anytime or anywhere—I will leave and then call 911. This is the way I will cope, but I will not stay.

"That's it!" I said, looking up again.

Before the doctor could respond, I went on to tell him: "This is a last-ditch effort on my part. For me it is risky. I am taking a big chance and putting a lot on the line, investing all of myself and a whole lot of time to see my husband well. And I know if things do not go as planned, if everything backfires and Alex walks away from his treatment, I will be the one who will get the fallout of Mr. Hyde's behavior. Anything could happen. However," I reiterated, "with my new mind-set, my boundaries firmly drawn, I believe I will at least be armed mentally and emotionally to cope in a healthy way throughout Alex's continued treatment and our joint counseling."

Dr. Herald agreed. In fact, he said, "You've found good coping skills. Let's hope you don't have to use them. You're going to be fine. I think we'll have success. I'll see you on Tuesday evening."

Our biweekly, two-hour sessions began with Dr. Herald talking with Alex and me about our marriage, first separately, then together. Alex was very cooperative. When I expressed my feelings, he did not get hostile and interrupt. He listened without agitation. He did not deny anything I told the doctor about his behavior, his violent outbursts, his lack of parenting—everything negative he had said and done to me over the years. He just sat there calmly, admitting each wrong and agreeing with whatever the doctor suggested.

During the next several weeks of counseling as a couple, we learned a great deal about ourselves, each other, and our relationship. Finally, in one of my private sessions, Dr. Herald revealed to me that Alex had confronted his horrifying family background, and he was dealing with not only that but also with his alcohol addiction and his abuse of me.

Then he went on to tell me that Alex had lacked the kind of basic security I had taken for granted while growing up. I asked him to please put the pieces of this puzzle about his family together for me because I had to understand what I was dealing with or I could not go on with this counseling. He agreed. It was hard for me to hear the details about my husband's traumatic childhood. It had been filled with fear and abandonment.

When Alex was young, his father had left the family alone on their rented farm for several weeks in the dead of winter. One Sunday when his aunt and uncle visited, his uncle warned them that their only cow seemed to be sick and should not be milked. That warning had come too late. They had all been drinking the milk, but his mother was the only one who became ill with undulant fever.

Soon afterward the family ran out of food. They had no telephone to call for help and no transportation. Being so far out in the country, there was no way his mother could get into town to receive medical help. So Alex, the eldest of the four children, but only twelve years old, became nurse to his mother, and parent and provider to his brother and two sisters. Alex trapped rabbits, skinned them, and cooked them for the family's meals—he was responsible for their very survival.

When he realized his mother was getting worse, he ran through the snow a long distance to the nearest farm to get help. It was owned by a wealthy couple from whom Alex's parents rented their home. They took his mother to the hospital.

Alex told me privately that he remembered sitting on the back porch of his maternal grandparents' home, praying that God would not let his mother die. Despite his prayers, his grandfather came out and said, "Alexander, Mother's gone."

I wondered what must have happened inside him emotionally at that moment. I could not imagine what that must have felt like. If I had been the one, so very young, would I have ever again trusted my prayers to a God who had not answered my most earnest one?

When Dr. Herald mentioned that after Alex's mother died, his father gave his youngest daughter to his cousin and her husband to adopt as their own, I instantly had a flashback of the shocking way I had first learned about her and the adoption. It was three days before our wedding when I received a letter from a girl who claimed to be Alex's baby sister. It was stunning news. Alex had never told me about a baby sister. That evening when I confronted him, he apologized and explained that she had been two years old when his mother died and his father arranged for relatives to legally adopt her.

I was astonished for two reasons: one, that Alex had not told me long before that he had another sister; and two, that regardless of whatever Alex's dad's reason might have been, I could not imagine that any father could give away his child. I remember Alex and I immediately responded to her letter by phoning to invite her to the wedding. She was thrilled.

At our wedding rehearsal, she was reintroduced to her father and brothers, seeing them for the first time since she was a toddler. She was a beautiful young girl, who, I learned, had just a month before graduated from high school, where she had been homecoming queen. Finding out about her so late in the game had been a daunting situation that turned delightful for the three of us. We enjoyed our time together.

This session with Dr. Herald stirred another memory about yet another Lance family mystery. Before our wedding, I recalled being curious about the only sister Alex had told me about (who turned out to be the eldest of two sisters), whom I still had not met by the time we were writing our invitations. Alex had not invited her to the wedding, nor had he offered an explanation for excluding her.

I also learned during this session that after his mother's death, Alex's father took his younger son and elder daughter to live with him in another city. The wealthy farmer and his wife wanted to adopt Alex, but he chose to live with his maternal grandparents. What must it have been like to lose his mother and then be separated from his father and his siblings? The desperation to hang on to some stability must have been extreme. A short time after his mother's death, Alex's grandfather died at a young age. In fact, Alex had been with his grandfather when he suffered a massive heart attack.

From that time on, his grandmother took on the sole responsibility for raising him. It was difficult for the two of them. Her home was located in the poorer neighborhood of the small town. The house had no indoor plumbing or conventional heating system. There was a wood-burning stove and a free-standing bathtub in the basement. Even so, Alex had fond memories of that time with his grandmother. However, only a few years later, his grandmother became ill with cancer and died. It was another heartbreaking loss. Then Alex went to live with his mother's sister. She also died of cancer.

Amazingly, Alex remained an "A" student throughout the entire trauma. When he graduated from high school, he entered the naval air force. Four years later, he came to my city to enroll in the university. It was then Alex was reunited with his father, who was living here in town with his second wife and her children.

The reunion was not an easy one. His father told Alex he could stay with them while he was going to college and then put him on the back porch where he slept on a cot. The porch was unheated and very cold in the winter months. This was where he was living when we met. A short time after we married, Alex's father died suddenly. Alex did not say much about it, but I remember thinking, this was another painful loss for him because the father that never was, was still his father!

Dr. Herald was right. Compared to Alex's childhood, mine had been trouble-free and simple. Finally I understood why Alex had been reluctant to talk about his family during our courtship. Back then I had loved him too much to demand answers.

During a following private session with Dr. Herald, I wanted to talk more about Alex's family history. I did not doubt that he had endured and overcome in many ways; but I believed that somehow those traumatic events had twisted themselves into something ugly and evil inside him, rearing up and striking out at me without provocation. I alone seemed to be his target.

That was the result of deep psychological distress Alex had suffered as a child with the deaths and separation from those he loved. I now understood that without professional help Alex had been left with emotional scars and unresolved anger with which he had never dealt. Therefore, he had carried them into adulthood and into our marriage relationship. They negatively affected his ability to love and care for me and his children in an emotionally healthy way.

Obviously, his unresolved rage and his disorder undermined his ability to deal with any stressful situations that arose in different areas of his life. He was rendered incapable of settling minor as well as major differences in our relationship or dealing with the medical crises in our family.

Learning these well-hidden details of Alex's childhood helped to make some of my husband's behavior patterns clearer to me. Alex had known so much illness and death in his early years. I realized, therefore, that when he had encountered the same in our marriage, he might have experienced that same fear of loss all over again.

My past resentment and bitterness toward Alex was now replaced by compassion. Our joint therapy sessions were going better than I had expected: no abusive behavior, no violent outbursts from Alex, no superior attitude, no more disrespectful words thrown at me, no more Mr. Hyde. My husband was definitely getting well.

Because of that, my fear of Alex was gone. With my mental and emotional boundaries firm in me, over time my confidence in his steady, consistent, normal behavior increased until I finally could let my guard down. That was a big relief from the stress of having it up, moment to moment, for almost four hard years by now.

Alex continued responding positively to his private therapy as well as to our joint counseling. Nonetheless, I knew we still had a long way to go before we could consider our relationship healthy and functioning successfully. And, a great deal depended upon Alex. My husband knew he had betrayed my love for him when we were newlyweds; now he had to prove to me that it was not too late for us. He was being smart, cautious, taking it slow. And it was working.

Alex offered to start picking me up for our joint evening sessions. After several more weeks, one night on the way home, I actually felt a new kind of affection for Alex when he kissed me good night. He wanted to stay, but I did not have that much confidence in my feelings.

A few more weeks passed, and then Alex asked if he could move back home; but I told him I was not ready. I did realize, because of the good doctor, that Alex and I had made a lot of progress. We were finally on the same page. For once Alex and I were both happy at the same time and happy for the same reasons: happy with each other, happy and grateful to have our two healthy children, and happy to be "one" for the first time in our marriage. It felt good. It felt right.

I decided to phone Dr. Herald to ask how he felt about Alex's coming home. He believed Alex had done so well over the last year that he was indeed ready to move back home. He added that it would be good for the children.

After much thought and prayer, I asked Alex to come home. It seemed God had answered my prayers.

With a deep sigh, I was back in the present again. Now I stepped across to the other sofa where Laura was still reading and said, "Good night, sweetheart. Thank you for everything this morning. I'm sorry we haven't talked all day. I just haven't felt like it ... you know?"

"I understand, Mom," she smiled.

"Love you, Laurie," I said, leaning down to kiss her on the cheek. She reached up, hugging my neck. "I love you too, Mom."

I walked to the foyer entrance to the family room and called to Michael and Steven, "Good night, boys."

"Are you okay, Mom?" Michael asked with a serious, concerned tone in his voice.

"Yes, honey, I'm fine, thanks. Sorry we haven't talked more today, but we'll catch up."

"Boys, I love you both."

"Love you too, Mom," Michael called back.

"Good night, Mother. I love you too," Steven answered in his usual cheerful tone.

Chapter 9

Second-Chance Marriage

After changing into my robe, I settled in my special corner of the bedroom to read. Instead of opening my novel, however, I opened my journal. I simply was not finished writing my thoughts about today's infamous event that I felt had marked me and changed my life forever.

Tonight my mind was rather chaotic, with a mix of emotions. I knew God was with me, but in a human sense, I felt lost out here in the world by myself. Who would I be now after twenty-six years, if not a wife? Someone else would, no doubt, soon be Mrs. Alexander Lance. That reality made me feel like my identity had been ripped from me again, stolen right out from under me.

I looked at my journal and thought my writings tonight might end up reading like the ramblings of an unbalanced woman, a hodge-podge of unintelligible words coming out of my dazed and confused brain: negative and positive, sublime and ridiculous, reality and imaginings.

"But that's okay," I muttered. "God knows my heart ... and He knows my flesh."

Flipping the pages to the last entry, I began there in the middle of the page. With a snicker, I began my journaling by writing the date and an appropriate title:

January 15, 1985—D-Day PM!
Ramblings of a Brokenhearted Wife—the Divorcée

God has been with me today. On and off, I have felt the intimacy of His presence. At times my spirit has been lifted by His peace and Scripture. Thank You, my Jesus. In reality I know my identity is in You, Lord, not in my husband. Forgive me. Knowing You, Lord, are with me is priceless; I'm grateful. But no matter how sound I feel spiritually, my heart is aching. I didn't want things to turn out like this. I have long believed that the family based on the sanctity of marriage is God's original design and the only one that works like a well-oiled machine, needing only a minimal amount of continual repairs. I wanted my marriage to be a rock-solid, happy, faithful, God-fearing, and vow-honoring "until death do us part" union.

I fought hard for Alex and to keep my family together. I gave it all I had. The truth is, I'm a casualty of that battle. I know I'm whining, complaining, and, yes, full of self-pity right now, but I can't help it. This divorce is a bitter pill to swallow. I'm humiliated before my family and friends. I feel like a blight on the church. I'm especially afraid of what my community of believers will think of me. I'm embarrassed and ashamed of my new marital status, "divorced," that I will have to circle or check from here on out on all government, medical, employment, or even travel forms. I'm being cynical, I know, but there is reality to accept. I have joined the ranks of those who make up the statistics of a fallen society. I am "the divorced," part of the evidence, along with, of course, the increase of other statistics like crimes of murder, rape, robbery, adultery, drugs, and perversions that prove the traditional American family is going to hell in a hand basket.....

My words gave me pause.

Immediately I asked forgiveness for my sins, my vain imaginings, and my ramblings and released them to God. Cynicism and sarcasm were not normally part of my thought-processing or expression, at least for the greater part of the last nineteen years since Jesus and His Word became my life. Tonight those negatives had crept back into my psyche. I definitely had been pessimistic about my new status, and I had let my imagination show me the stigma, the *scorn* I would bear as a Christian divorcée, just as though I had not been given God's promises. *Why am I doing this—vacillating? I know better. Why have I allowed my negative emotions to control me like that? How can I feel strong and full of faith one minute and so weak the next? My Jesus, please help me. No matter how strong I feel at other times, this heartache is too hard to bear. Will I ever be strong again?*

Then I remembered the Scripture, Hebrews 13:5b: "I will never leave you." I took a deep breath and calmed myself. I could feel a quiet assurance again that I *would* get through this. With that, I took hold of my pen to continue writing, but this time, with a clearer head:

Thankfully, it feels the Lord has stopped me from going off into the deep end and drowning in my negativity and pain. My thinking is turned right side up again. Now I recognize I allowed my emotional pain to make me forget the promises and power of Scripture God gave me. I realize now I am in a different kind of battle with my flesh than before, but it is the same enemy. I am grateful to be rescued from my negative attitude and words. Words are powerful. I have learned my words can change my whole perspective, change my mind-set, and change the atmosphere around me; they can change my direction and put me on a different path. I know I can bless or curse my life with my own words.

Yes, I am thankful for this reality check. With what just happened, it feels like God is keeping an invisible rope, a lifeline, tied around me. When I get too far out there—like tonight, wallowing in negative emotions—He lets the Holy Spirit bring to my remembrance Scripture, and that pulls me back into my safe zone in Him. This is a lesson for me now. I have to watch myself, to guard my heart and psyche to keep from getting negative again, taking me out there too far. Like the Bible says, "Be sober and vigilant, cautious at all times; for the enemy roams around like a roaring lion, seeking to seize and devour whomever he can."

Also I am reminded that the past can be a wise teacher. I have learned lessons from the past—past brokenness and past healings. One must be so sure that healing is part of God's gospel of love for His children. I must be sure—sure of God's covenant with me and His plan for me now—so that all the reasonings in my own mind and all the reasonings of the best men and women cannot shake me! I believe I will be healed again! I believe I will survive again! No! I believe I will thrive again!

I closed my journal. My mind was quiet. I rested my head back on the chair and closed my eyes. But before I knew it, my mind was in motion again, this time transporting me back to that turning point in Alex's life that gave him mental and emotional stability, back to that turning point in our relationship, back to our second-chance marriage. Through that emotional time in my life, I learned from Dr. Herald how to *survive*, until the day came when I learned from God how to *thrive*.

Dr. Herald had made a promise that he could help Alex get well, thereby saving our marriage and keeping my family together, and he had delivered. Because of Dr. Herald, Alex had made wonderful progress. There was no doubt in my mind that my husband was well. Laura, just a baby, and Michael, a toddler, were also a big reason I went along with Dr. Herald's medical determination that Alex was well enough to move back into our home. I so desired, prayed for my children to have a real family with both parents.

I remembered the day Alex moved back home.

It was nearing the Christmas holiday season. Laura had turned one in October, and she was too small to know what had been going on, but Michael was so happy. As Alex and I stood in the living room, with Michael's arms wrapped around his daddy's legs, Alex smiled and pulled me to his chest.

I was stiff. As though realizing I was still cautious, he repeated that same statement he had already made several times since our joint counseling began: "Honey, you have to forgive me for all those things I did to you." I did not respond.

What's wrong with me?

My thoughts raced: *I think I've forgiven him. Oh God, I'm still afraid of this. I thought I was ready for him to come home, but I guess I'm not. I'm afraid to let go ... let myself love him as a wife again. I'm so confused. He's really happy to be back with me and the kids. I don't want to spoil this.*

With that last thought, I finally responded by putting my arms around his neck, and we kissed.

That evening the anticipation of bedtime was difficult for me. I found myself sorting through my personal feelings for Alex again. I had gone over them in my mind a hundred times before tonight. I remembered his weekend visits during his months of therapy. Every affectionate gesture he had made toward me made me quiver and at the same time repulsed me, and I rejected him. Even so, my every rejection of his loving advances left me hungry for his arms the next day. My changeable feelings confused me then. Now I was confused again.

I hope Dr. Herald is right. I hope he's well enough to be home. Oh God, please take my memory of that night away—permanently. I know that man who threatened to kill me is not the man he is now. I can't think about that anymore. He's here now. I agreed to start over, to give him and our marriage a second chance. Please let it last this time. God, help me trust him again ... to love him again—really, deeply love him. Help Alex stay well, and help us be a real family.

Tears welled in my eyes. I reminded myself that since our biweekly sessions with Dr. Herald, we had been sharing a warmth and tenderness that had been lost to us since our honeymoon. *I need to keep remembering we have something better now, something to build our love on. Concentrate on the positive, Alisha. At last we're on solid ground.*

Now we were in bed together. It was good to be lying in my husband's arms again, talking about our relationship, our kids, and our future plans. It was good to be really communicating. Alex's body moved closer to mine. *He smells so good. No alcohol on his breath since he hasn't been out at bars.*

Alex cautiously put his hand on my shoulder, pulling me closer to him, and softly kissed me. Alex whispered, "I love you ... I love you … I love you." I felt my tight muscles begin to relax. Now those old warm feelings flowed through me. I was his again.

When Alex fell asleep, I carefully inched myself out of his arms, looked over at his peaceful sleeping face, and whispered in a barely audible voice, "I'm sorry you had such a painful childhood." *It doesn't change the pain you've caused me, but at least your past behavior makes sense to me now.* I closed my eyes and drifted off to sleep.

The next morning I awoke to the smell of coffee brewing. Only the sheer white window liners were closed, so since I had forgotten to also close the drapery last night, bright sunshine now flooded the room. *What a beautiful morning!*

"Hi, honey. You ready for a cup of coffee?" Alex asked, peeking around the bedroom door.

"Yes, I'd love it!"

He came in and sat beside me on the bed. "I'm so happy to be home. Last night was wonderful, honey," he said softly, looking down at me with his boyish grin. "That was love last night. You love me, Alisha. You still love me; I know you do."

"Yes, Alex, I do still love you … but it will take more than one wonderful night to make our marriage work. Dr. Herald says you have to stick with your therapy. Are you willing to stay with it—go the distance—no matter how long it takes?"

"Yes, honey, I only know that I want you and the kids more than anything in the world, and I'll do anything to keep you."

Together Alex and I decided we could get along financially now without my salary. Before Christmas my boss, the director, and my fellow employees threw a big going-away party for me in the student union, attended by a lot of friends (personnel and students) I had made at the university, as well as by Alex and the kids.

I was so glad to be home with the children again. I hated the fact that during the time I had worked, I missed hearing Laura's first word and seeing her take her first step. We all wanted to make up for lost time with her. Christmas was especially happy for us because we were celebrating our new life together—our second-chance marriage.

The New Year 1964 started off perfectly too. Our days were indeed very happy days as a family. However, unbeknown to us, our joy would soon be marred with another physical crisis—mine *again.*

The second week of January, I became ill. When my fever persisted and my joints began to ache, Alex took me to our family doctor and he ran tests. During my follow-up visit, Dr. Anderson told us I had contracted an acute case of rheumatic fever.

Soon after the onset of this new illness, I discovered I was pregnant. Although I was happy about my pregnancy, I soon learned that both my obstetrician and my family doctor were more than a little concerned. During my next scheduled appointment with Dr. Anderson, he told me that I could recover from the rheumatic fever with medication and bed rest, but the pregnancy complicated things. "There are some dangers involved for your baby, Mrs. Lance. We'll have to keep a close watch on the two of you," he smiled. "You're a pretty sick woman."

Oh God, no! Not my baby! Haven't I had enough? Haven't we all had enough?

When Alex came home, he was silent as I told him everything the doctor had said. *Will he withdraw from me when I need him most, like he used to? Oh God, I couldn't bear that! And I couldn't stand to see his old look of disgust because we're facing another problem caused by my getting sick again.*

He finally spoke. "Don't worry, honey, you're gonna be fine. The baby will do fine too." I sighed with relief. I noticed, however, Alex quickly dismissed further conversation about possible danger to our baby. That bothered me.

Maybe he's acting nonchalant about it so I won't be more alarmed, or maybe he's trying to apply what he has learned in therapy about dealing with unexpected, stressful, and potentially threatening problems. I need his arms wrapped around me now, assuring me that he'll help me get through the months ahead.

The next moment Alex had his arms around me, assuring, "Everything will be okay, honey. We'll get through this together."

A long sigh escaped me.

Though there was excitement and cheerful conversations about our coming third child, it was a physically tough time for me. However, Alex was sensitive to my condition. Although difficult, I managed caring for my little ones throughout the day, with Alex taking over after work. He was enjoying his children. Everything was going quite smoothly. I was still a long way from being well when Alex threw me a curve.

"Alisha, I don't think I need to continue seeing Dr. Herald. We're doing fine, and therapy is costing too much money. I'm not going back." Disappointment stabbed me, but I was too sick to argue his decision. I did not even question him. I did not fall apart. By this time, I was well acquainted with disappointment. *Go ahead, quit, Alex. It's only our lives you're quitting!*

Alex was sure he would continue to be well. At this point, I had to trust in the insight Alex had gained in treatment. Still, I braced myself for the old days of worrying about his mood when he walked in the door from work, never knowing if he was going to attack me or love me. However, all my worry was in vain. To my delight, he maintained his stable disposition.

As the weeks passed, I grew more positive, grateful for each day of peace when we were together. Alex was very good to us. Everything was still going more smoothly than I had dared to believe.

Warm spring days were finally here and begged us out of doors. I was not well yet, but I was happy to be outside soaking up the sun every chance I got. Weekends were pleasant. Alex liked to fish, and he often fished on Saturday mornings with his boss or other friends. He would leave before dawn and was back home by midmorning.

In the afternoon, he worked in the yard, and with my limited energy, I delighted in planting a few annuals in pots and in beds around the house while Michael and Laura played in the sunshine on the patio. We went to Mass on Sundays and sometimes visited my parents, who were very happy about our successful lives and their coming grandchild. Other times we went for a drive in the country, always keeping an eye out for a home with acreage, since we had a desire to live outside the city. Often we stopped for ice cream on the way home. They were carefree days that held real happiness for us. One day Alex came home from work and told me he had learned about a new home for sale. "It's up north, honey. It's larger and has a basement. Let's take a look at it, okay?"

"I don't know, Alex. I don't know if I can make a move now."

However, after quickly going over the idea in my mind, I decided perhaps this was a good time to make a change—a new home to welcome our new baby.

"Let's take a look at it," I enthusiastically agreed.

In many ways, I welcomed a move from this neighborhood where I was no longer comfortable around my neighbors. I felt humiliation knowing they must have overheard Alex's rantings and some of our quarrels those early years. Although they had not heard anything in the last year, I still liked the idea of moving to another area.

Before I knew it, our house was sold to friends of ours, and Alex and I were packing to move. I was still weak but managed to work a couple of hours each day before I became fatigued and had to rest for a while. Then while Laura napped, Michael and I would lie down to read a book; he would soon fall asleep, and I would get some good rest before starting in again. Alex was a great help to me, packing each evening after he arrived home from work and then unpacking in our new home.

We had a lot of rain before we moved in, and on our final courtesy walk-through before the purchase closing, Alex discovered one of the basement walls was cracked and bowed. The owner promised to get the builder back to fix it. We agreed to rent until the wall was repaired; then we would schedule another closing.

Finally I recovered from all symptoms of my illness, and day by day I was regaining my strength. As the weeks went by, I attempted a new craft. I reupholstered one of two small occasional chairs we bought secondhand. I hoped to finish the other one before the baby was born.

On a hot day late in July, I was pounding in the tacks on the last section of the chair when I felt a sharp pain. It was too early, so I thought my pain was false labor. Then another pain came ... then another. I had been wrong; I was definitely in labor. Several hours later, I gave birth to our second son, a beautiful blonde, blue-eyed baby whom we named Steven. He was born perfect, with all his fingers and toes, and Alex and I gave a sigh of relief. All was perfect in my world too, as my arms held our precious baby Steven and I put him to my breast to nurse for the first time.

The day we brought Steven home from the hospital, Michael, Laura, Grandma, and Grandpa were there to greet us. The kids thought their new baby brother was quite special. They peered into the bassinet, watching Steven closely, their eyes filled with wonder. We all delighted in playing with Steven. Michael loved to entertain him, and little Laura, hardly more than a baby herself, was already mothering her little brother.

Stevie was an exceptionally contented baby. And he loved our smiles. His eyes would brighten in response, and he would get so excited that his little arms and legs would move every which way as though he were dancing in his bassinet. Oh, how he enjoyed our smiles! The pediatrician finally put to rest my silent fears carried over the months, when at Steven's first regular checkup after birth, he told me Steven was a healthy baby boy in every way. Alex and I were greatly relieved by that medical confirmation and relaxed into our normal family life.

It was a wonderful, emotionally freeing time for me. And although Alex had stopped going to his counseling sessions, he was still happy and stable, which made everything brighter. He was at home most nights and only occasionally stayed out of town overnight for his job. In fact, he told me he often skipped lunch to cover his sales territory for the day so he would not have to be out overnight.

We were warmly embraced by our neighbors. Our children played together, and we parents enjoyed dinners at one another's homes and group family outings.

One day I noticed two chairs and an ottoman piled at the curb in front of our elderly next-door neighbor's house, obviously there for refuse pickup. When I asked, my neighbor was glad for me to rescue and restore them, since she expected delivery of two new chairs that very day. When I dragged them home, I discovered they were Chippendales of high quality with well-constructed frames; only the fabrics were worn. As busy as I was, I made time to shop for fabrics and found beautiful, high-grade tapestries, which had been greatly reduced in price because they were ends of rolls and on clearance. For our bedroom, I upholstered one chair in pale gold brocade. For the family room, the other lounge chair with its matching ottoman was covered in a heavy wool weave of deep gold and copper threads, which I finished just in time for Christmas. The chair with ottoman was my gift to Alex, and he loved it.

*   *   *

New Year 1965 began with more broken promises from the builder of this new ranch house. The cracked and bowed basement wall was still not repaired. By then two scheduled closings had already been cancelled. A February closing was set up. When that closing had to be cancelled for the same reason, Alex called the owner to withdraw from our contract. Naturally, he was angry and gave us a three-day eviction notice. It was early March, and the city was still deep in snow. We would be lucky to find a vacant apartment or house to rent in three days, much less a home to buy.

After two unsuccessful, exhausting days, we got worried. That night an idea came to us. We would start out the next morning and go to residential areas we liked and then drive up and down streets, keeping an eye out for rental or For Sale signs. Fortunately, around four o'clock in the afternoon we spotted a sign, For Sale by Owner, in my favorite residential area of the city.

We really liked the house outside. Alex rang the doorbell. The owners, an older couple, came to the door. We learned the house was empty, but they *just happened* to be there because the carpet was being cleaned. We were invited to view the inside.

It was a lovely, spotless, older, well-built two-story. We liked it better than the brand-new ranch we were leaving, and it was larger. The owners were sympathetic to our predicament. They accepted our purchase offer and down payment, and they agreed to rent the house to us until the closing in thirty days. They gave us immediate possession. We wrote up the purchase price and terms on a contract form which they had there at the house, and we all were perfectly comfortable about the whole thing. Alex immediately phoned an area moving company, which agreed to move us early the next morning.

Back then we had not figured God into the equation. But driving home, Alex and I went over the amazing details of how everything remarkably came together when we were down to the wire—the eleventh hour—evicted, with only three days to find a place offering immediate possession, and having to hunt for it during the coldest, snowiest days of the year. Nevertheless, everything had gone unbelievably smooth that last day. From the time we made the decision to drive up and down certain area streets, it was as though we had been led to that house by an unseen guide. Then the whole purchase transaction seemed to go through like it had eyes.

By six o'clock that day, we were home for dinner with my parents and the kids. After the little ones were tucked in, Mom and Dad helped us pack until quite late; then they retired. Alex and I packed all night long. Amazingly, we were ready for the movers when they arrived at eight o'clock the next morning.

We were so pleased with our new place; it exceeded all our expectations and was more than we had thought we could afford. Michael made friends quickly, and we met the parents of his playmates and other neighbors and enjoyed all of them. The year was a happy one for us.

Christmas came and went. We rang in the New Year 1966 with relatives, neighbors, and friends gathered at our home for a fun evening, and the following winter months were happy times for our family. Then spring brought forth its glorious colors in different perennials dotting the flower beds around our yard, a gift left for us by the former owners. The flowers were a magnificent sight I enjoyed every day, especially the rose garden.

However, also with spring came changes in Alex. They were only subtle at first. Then I noticed mood swings. He was never nasty, but sometimes he seemed to be indifferent toward me and the kids; then, paradoxically, at other times he showed interest and was just as sweet as could be to all of us.

When I began to feel him slowly withdrawing emotionally from us, I got worried. At those times, he seemed to be preoccupied and restless, ignoring us. Other times, he seemed to be fine. This all-too-familiar behavior pattern was beginning to scare me, and I prayed—a lot. Now he often came home late from work. I learned he was spending those afternoons at the spring thoroughbred horse races, then stopping afterward at a bar for a drink with his buddies.

As spring passed into summer, gradual negative changes in Alex became more obvious. Sometimes he appeared irritated whenever I suggested he do something with the children. They needed him to hold them, talk and play with them, like he had done before. It was not long before I knew that Michael and Laura were feeling confused. There was no doubt they were picking up on their father's changeable reactions to them. I knew their little world was definitely out of sync when Michael asked, "Mommy, what's wrong with Daddy? Doesn't he like us anymore?" Oh, how that hurt!

By now, though Alex was coming home from work at the usual time, after dinner he left the house to make the night harness horse races and then the bar scene for the rest of the evening. He reeked of alcohol when he returned and fell into bed, hours after I had been in bed worrying. I imagined women involved in his late-night escapades.

As the last days of summer passed, Alex seemed to have no conscience about rejecting his children. They longed for his arms, but as their father, he felt no obligation to hold them. I was overly stressed by my worries for my husband. My emotions were up and down like a yo-yo. Alex ignored my pleadings for him to resume his therapy with Dr. Herald.

It was hard carrying the burden of concerns for the children alone. And it was hard living with Alex. He was getting worse. Immediately I applied the coping skills I had learned, and though they helped me, they could not stop Alex's downward spiral. Then it happened—Mr. Hyde suddenly reappeared.

Now besides Alex's razor-sharp criticisms, I was hearing something new: "You and those kids of yours are a millstone around my neck!" Alex had fully resumed his old lifestyle. To my chagrin, bottles of beer now took up most of the top shelf of our refrigerator. I was infuriated every time I had to reach around them to get the milk. Even worse, on the nights when he did come straight home from work and stayed home, he drank one beer after the other. I was heartsick. *How could he have let this happen again? And why? What went wrong?* I entered a dark valley of despair.

It was September 1966, seven years into our marriage—seven hard years, save three. With Mr. Hyde back on the scene, I absolutely could no longer count on self-absorbed Alex to recognize my needs or the children's needs. My pain and frustration were overwhelming.

During this time, no matter how difficult daily living became again, my children kept me functioning. My only conscious, healthy rationale at this time was that I had to stay emotionally strong for them. I guarded their little psyches from their father's behavior like a mother lioness fiercely protecting her cubs. I was a good mother. But I felt I had failed miserably at marriage—at living.

As the days of September passed, I was becoming more and more depressed. Although I had been applying the coping skills I had learned, they were no longer helping me. I felt powerless to change anything about my life. In fact, by now I believed God had turned a deaf ear to my prayers, to my cries of anguish. I felt isolated, trapped in my frustrations with my husband—his dark side, Mr. Hyde. I had taken another chance with Alex and thought I would never see Mr. Hyde again; but despite all we had learned in therapy, our relationship was back to square one. Nothing had permanently changed after all.

I was still holding up for the sake of my children, but only barely. I tried to give them plenty of attention because I knew they needed all the love and emotional security I could give them. But despite my outward functioning, inwardly I was again hopelessly ensnared in fear, anxiety, self-pity, anger, depression, and deep pain. So deep was my pain, there were times when I wanted out of my life—one way or another. And so deep was my hopelessness that I believed I was forgotten even by God.

A wistful sigh left me as I remembered where I was at that point in my life. However, the extraordinary events that began unfolding are indelibly etched on my heart and my spirit. At that dark, hopeless, desperate time, I could not have known that God was never more near.

It was a beautiful, early October morning, my favorite time of the year. Standing in the kitchen by the back door of our home, I held the screen door open wide, watching Laura, our almost four-year-old, step carefully and deliberately down each of the porch steps, proudly jumping the last step down to the sidewalk. The sun pierced through the branches of the majestic oak in our neighbor's back yard. Brilliant orange and red leaves cascaded from the old oak's branches, gracing our lawn with patches of vibrant color. For the moment, the quiet peace of my favorite season replaced the anxiety that hovered over my long days and sleepless nights.

Squealing and dancing about the yard, Laura made sure she had my attention then reached down and scooped up as large a pile of leaves as her little arms could hold.

"Look at me, Mommy!" Gleefully she threw the leaves high into the air, giggling as they filtered down over her head.

"Have fun, baby!" I yelled, laughing and clapping my hands together as though applauding a grand stage performance.

Six-year-old Michael was playing outside too, with his little buddies. Two-year-old Steven, always near me, was amusing himself with his Slinky on the kitchen floor.

The early morning chaos of fixing breakfast for five and getting Alex off to work was behind me. Lingering at the screen door, I watched Laura playing in the leaves.

This day feels so good. It started out so right—like a day of hope—unlike the past few days when everything has felt hopeless. I closed my eyes and inhaled the warm Indian summer air, savoring its wonderful freshness, relishing the quiet peace that for the moment replaced my anxiety.

I returned to the kitchen sink to finish the morning dishes, and my thoughts wandered. *Why haven't the answers come? I've prayed every day and every night, and I've lit candles at Mass for the special needs of my family ... and oh God, we have so many. Why hasn't anything changed?*

"I'm tired ... so tired of it all," I whispered.

Lurking like a dark cloud over and around me was a creeping, suffocating fear that I could no longer cope. I felt totally inadequate. Under that strong exterior that others saw was a frail spirit. No one, especially not Alex, realized my frustrations—frustrations compounded by his harsh criticisms, his total indifference to me one

193

minute and then his exuberant expressions of love for me the next, his indifference to our children.

I could feel the panic and agony rising within me again, and my thoughts were mixed with prayer as I stared out the window. *I feel lost. I have no more hope. I feel like You've forgotten me, God. Why? I've tried to do what's right. Why haven't You answered my prayers?*

I turned and smiled at Steven. He glanced at me out of the corner of his eye, keeping his attention on the Slinky now flip-flopping slowly across the linoleum floor. Then he crawled across the floor, following his Slinky until it lost its momentum and stopped beside the kitchen table.

As I returned to drying the dishes, memories—painful memories—rushed into my mind, ugly, horrible scenes from the past seven years: *the platter with potatoes and cheese sauce smashing against the wall ... Alex's cruel tone of voice, his profanity screaming in my head ... filthy, four-letter words and names ..."B————! Stupid b————!" ... grocery bags crashing to the kitchen floor, splitting open as they hit; boxes, cans, hothouse tomatoes rolling and sliding across the tile ... cowering on the floor, curled into a fetal position in paralyzing fear as Alex held the shotgun pointed at my head ... waiting ... waiting for him to pull the trigger ... his sinister laugh.*

Now I leaned against the sink, grabbing my head. *What's wrong with me?* Again more memories were assaulting my mind. I could see them. I could hear them screaming in my brain: *"You're worthless! Worthless! You and these brats of yours ... You're all a millstone around my neck!"... Alex storming out the front door and slamming it behind him ... the echo of the slamming door ... waking in an empty, lonely bed in the middle of the night, wondering where he is—if he's with another woman.*

I thought I had put all the ugly memories behind me. They had been buried deep in my subconscious, seven years of painful memories buried in the graveyard of my life's junk. I had to bury them. I could not have survived day to day, otherwise.

Stop, Alisha, stop! Get hold of yourself! With the last of my emotional strength, I forced the memories back into my subconscious and walked over to the kitchen door to check on Laura.

Staring at my little girl sitting on her swing made me remember her and Michael at Steven's age, the cute things they both had done and said. I took in a deep breath of fresh morning air and exhaled. *My kids ... I have so much to be thankful for, to live for.*

Stevie got my attention with his whining for something, pulling me back to the present. I turned.

"What do you want, honey?"

I went through the process-of-elimination game, trying to figure out what he might want. I had done this a hundred times before, but today my nerves were raw and it was all I could do to keep from falling apart right there. It was not about Steven; it was about me. I wanted to scream. I wanted out of my situation, out of the pain. I wanted out of my life!

Rationale immediately kicked in again and dispelled the crazed thoughts in my mind. *What am I saying? My children need me. I can't let myself think such awful things! I can't fall apart!*

In my own preoccupation, I did not realize Steven was still trying to make me understand and give him what he wanted. With that realization, somehow I managed to gain some control. I took a deep breath and exhaled slowly, and then in a deliberate manner, I asked, "What ... do ... you ... want, Steven?"

He could not express what he wanted, but his little face was getting red and he seemed as frustrated as I was.

My heart splintered with pain as I saw his anxious attempt to tell me what he wanted. I knew he was also reacting to the anxious feelings that he was instinctively sensing in me, and that only made me feel worse. I turned abruptly and cried aloud, "Oh God, why? How can I care for my children if I can't take care of myself and I can't even figure out what my Stevie wants right now? God, oh God, why? Why did You give these precious children to someone like me?"

Steven's voice grew louder.

I turned to look at my little boy again. His mounting frustration was more than I could bear. I could not stop what was happening to him—or to me. Now I was emotionally teetering on the fine edge of control.

Steven looked at me. Suddenly, in his own frustration, with all his tiny strength, he pushed the kitchen chair to the floor, sat down, and began to sob. My heart broke.

I burst into tears and ran to him, dropped to my knees and gathered him into my arms, rocking him back and forth.

"Steven ... oh Steven ... I'm sorry, baby," I whispered. "Mommy doesn't know what you want." His face was buried in my chest as he sobbed so hard I was afraid he would lose his breath.

"Oh, why is everything so hard?" I muttered, my lips resting on his forehead. "My sweet baby, I'm sorry ... so sorry Mommy is such a mess."

I held my son tightly, rocking, rocking, rocking. Tears were running down my cheeks, unchecked. His sobs were muffled as he nestled into my chest. *It's all so hard ... seven hard years ... one thing after another.* I was hurting more than I had ever remembered hurting before—hurting and hopeless!

Then, from somewhere deep inside me, there came a heart-wrenching plea: "God, *if* You're *really* here now ... please help me!"

Time stopped. A kind of calm settled over us, and my tears stopped. Then Steven's sobs broke into soft whimpering. The sweet smell of baby shampoo and talcum powder lingered from his bath the night before, but only a trace now, mixed with the hot sweat of our bodies and tears. He was limp in my arms. An inexplicable stillness was all around us, a sweet peace.

I continued holding him. I felt limp too, drained of all frustration, drained of all emotion. I was spellbound by the extraordinary calm, unable to move, without desire to move. Steven, lying silently in my arms, seemed content now. I relaxed my grip on him. Looking into the face of my usually happy and bright little one, I thought, *He has been such a joy.* "Thank you, God," I softly whispered, as I smoothed Steven's damp hair and kissed his head gently.

He was asleep now. *He looks like a little cherub.*

Slowly I managed to lift myself off the floor, careful not to jolt the sleeping cherub in my arms. Cautiously I moved toward the living room sofa and gently laid him down.

I was beginning to feel better. But also I was feeling something else, something I had not felt much of in the last seven years. I felt very calm, peaceful inside. I dared to believe that in some strange way, I had been redeemed from the dark hopelessness I had felt locked into just a half hour before.

Back in the present now, I sat there in my chair motionless, sensing the presence of the Holy Spirit. I felt as though I had just relived that early October morning in 1966. I had not forgotten the smallest details of that extraordinary incident. The details were just as fresh now as all those years before when they had captured me. It was easy recall. I knew it would always be fresh because it was alive in my heart. It would stay there forever. Gratitude and silent praises filled my spirit.

Now I glanced at my watch. It was eleven o'clock and time for *In Touch with Charles Stanley.* With my journal and pen in hand, I walked over to the bedside table and turned on my clock radio. Pushing the FM button, I heard the program intro music. Quickly turning down the comforter on my bed, I propped the pillows against the headboard and slid in, ready to listen.

The words of Dr. Stanley always ministered to my spirit, and they were also a good application for everyday living. And tonight was no exception. After the program ended, I jotted down notes and quotes to be remembered in my journal of "Spiritual Lessons for Daily Living." Then I opened my personal journal to record my last thoughts for the night, which were more of a prayer:

I feel peaceful. It's been a long day of dealing, with good and bad memories and mixed emotions. Oh God, how sad! I never would have believed that this would be the last day of my married life. The morning began with dread and trepidation, but because of Your unfailing love, it is now ending with hope for Your redeeming intervention.

Chapter 10

Renewal

The next morning I awakened before dawn. Lying there in the dark, I wondered what my day would bring. It would be different from all other days. Today would be the first full day of my life as a "single again" woman.

But there was no rejoicing in me because I was free. I could not rejoice over the tragedy of our divorce and the breakup of my family. Yes, God had encouraged and comforted me all along, but even so, I still knew there was a sadness about it for me and my children.

I intended to keep a semblance of family for us. But I was alone. I know the middle years cannot be easy for any woman—wrinkles, tummy bulge, menopause—whether married, divorced, or single. At that age, we are not old, but we are not young anymore.

I even felt I was fortunate to have landed a good-paying job at my age. Nonetheless, I was alone at this most precarious time in my life: alone to make important decisions, maybe life-altering decisions; alone with no companion by my side; alone perhaps for the rest of my life. *Alone* is the reality that had made my mornings hard to face during the last six months. Besides, I still choked on the word *divorcée*.

Maybe it would help if I knew and could talk to a woman who is a divorced Christian leader … who could encourage me, affirm that I can live out my future as a Christian divorcée and still fulfill God's purpose for my life.

I don't know why, but I can't shake the feeling that when the church learns of my divorce, I will be a "marked woman," who might as well have a scarlet letter "D" hanging around my neck. But why not my husband?

That question carried me to a place of righteous indignation for the injustice I saw to Christian wives, which I believed was a blind spot in church vision. When it came to the marriage relationship, it was clear to me that there was an imbalance in teaching. From some church pulpits and some radio ministries, I heard preaching that a wife must be "submissive to her own husband." I believed that to be true and had obeyed that Scripture. Submission for wives was the one and only teaching on the marriage relationship I had heard over and over throughout the mid-1960s, '70s, and early '80s. But I knew that was only half the story.

When are some preachers going to bring balance to teaching on the marriage relationship, giving equal time to God's truths in the Bible commanded for husbands? How about, "Husbands love your wives and be not bitter against them"? Then there's, "Husbands love your wives as your own body," and "Husbands love your wives as Christ loves the church." If these Scriptures for husbands were preached at the same time as submission for wives to their husbands, I can't help but believe that balanced teaching would bring justice for Christian wives and truth for couples, which could be a deterrent to divorce. I don't think Alex ever heard those Scriptures for him as a husband preached from the pulpits of churches we attended—at least not when we attended together. But I sure heard exhortation for wives about submission!

I know that regardless of how the church or other Christians might judge me for being divorced, no one but God can truly know, 100 percent, the circumstances of my marriage ... what I've lived with ... Only God can judge why I'm divorced.

At that point, my thoughts moved into prayer: *Lord, I surrender to You ... again ... the mess I am. I surrender all my anxieties about facing my new life as a divorcée ... the opinion of the church and the opinions of other Christians ... and my fear of being alone in my middle years. I surrender my singleness, my future, and everything else to Your care, Jesus.*

Sadly, I was aware, and confess now, that my whining and complaining had gotten the best of me again that morning before I finally prayed. Sometimes it takes me awhile before I realize nothing is going to help me until I pray. Then ...

- When I admit to God that I am not strong as I think I should be,
- When I am completely honest about all my weaknesses,
- When I am utterly without confidence in myself to rise above my problems, conflicting emotions, or vain imaginings,
- When I yield, or surrender, to God and ask for His help,
- When I become totally dependent upon Him and His Word,
- Then God will reveal His guidance and wisdom and more of His promises to me.

With that reminder, I decided to read Scripture. I knew it still had to be dark outside, too early to get up. I turned on the bedside lamp, propped my pillows behind my back, and reached for my Bible. Instantly Isaiah 43 came to mind, and I turned to the chapter and began reading at the first verse: "But now thus saith the Lord that created thee ... and He that formed thee ... fear not: for I have redeemed thee, I have called thee by thy name; thou art mine ... when thou passeth through the waters, I will be with thee; and through the rivers, they shall not overflow thee: when thou walkest through the fire, thou shalt not be burned; neither shall the flame kindle upon thee."

I paused, sighing with gratitude for those promises. I had no doubt God was speaking to me through His Word once again. I leaned my head back, pondering God's faithfulness to His Word in the past and His encouragement to me with these verses now.

Thank You, my Jesus.

My eyes returned to the Scripture, continuing to read on to verse 18: "Remember ye not the former things, neither consider the things of old. Behold, I will do a new thing; now it shall spring forth; shall ye not know it? I will even make a way in the wilderness, and rivers in the desert."

My spirit quickened, and my heart felt like it leaped. Simultaneously, I felt God's presence, His peace—peace I can only describe as feeling like waves of warm oil moving through my body as though being perfectly navigated to touch every part of me. With His Word and His peace, I knew God the Holy Spirit was comforting me again, encouraging me to trust Him for everything in my single life.

"God, Your Word is so good to me," I whispered as I closed my King James Bible. Now for some reason, I focused my eyes on the cover, feeling the faux leather now tattered on the edges and holding gold-edged pages—dog-eared and marked with highlighter and colored pencil underlining and margin notes—some pages with torn corners repaired with scotch tape, some pages loose, some no longer attached to the spine, from years of use. But worn or not, it was still precious to me, and it was in a black leather carrying case to keep it all together.

"Thank You, Lord, for Nora ... not only sharing her testimony with me, but also for this ... my first Bible."

Every time I thought about Nora, which was quite often over the years, especially every time I shared my own personal testimony, I asked God to give her a special blessing that day. Today was no exception, and I silently prayed, *Give Nora a big one today, Lord!*

Feeling comforted by Isaiah 43 and God's peace, I left my bed and walked to the window-wall. Drawing back the drapery, I pulled the liner curtain back just enough to peek out. Dawn was breaking. The grounds and lake, still illuminated by the moon, looked like a winter wonderland.

I walked downstairs to the kitchen to make a pot of coffee. Waiting for it to brew, I thought about Nora again. *If not for her, where would I be today? Oh Lord, I hate to think of that!*

Returning to my special corner, I turned on the light, set my steaming mug on the coaster, always in the same spot on the table, and slid back into the old comfy pale gold Chippendale. After only sipping my coffee, I knew it had to cool a few minutes before I could really drink it.

I leaned back and rested my head for a moment. Immediately Nora was in my mind again—one flashback, then another. They were taking me back to my memories of fall 1966. For me those were the worst of days and the best of days.

The stress of my life hit me hard that early October morning. By then I had come to the end of my own strength—to the end of myself. No books, no counseling, and no coping skills had permanently changed me, changed my life, or changed my painful circumstances. I had tried it all.

But when I cried out that morning in desperation and pleaded, "God, *if* You're *really* here now, please help me!" something began to change for me. I felt more relaxed. I found it easier to care for my children, even alone. I began coping better with everything. And I dared to believe that God had, indeed, *really* heard my prayer. However, that morning I had no way of knowing the unbelievable and creative lengths to which God would go to fully answer my plea.

It was a rainy Tuesday afternoon, only a few days following the incident in the kitchen. It was time to pick up Michael from kindergarten. I was standing on the front porch trying to balance an open umbrella while holding Steven in one arm and pulling Laura close to me with the other, hoping to keep them dry on the way to the car.

Just as I was starting down the porch steps, my neighbor, Nora, came running across the street and up onto the porch. I had last seen her when we first moved into our home months earlier.

"Alisha, I see you taking the children to the car every afternoon. I know you're going to the kindergarten to pick up Michael, but you must be waking the kids from their afternoon naps, aren't you?"

"Yes," I answered quizzically.

"Why don't I just come over each school day at this time and sit with the children so you won't have to disturb their sleep?"

I hardly knew what to say! "Thank you, Nora," I finally responded, "but I can't allow you to obligate yourself to my schedule every day."

"I have nothing to do at this time of the day," she gently insisted. "I would like to do it. In fact, you go on now, and I'll sit with the children today. I insist!" She smiled warmly.

Driving to the kindergarten, I went over the scene in my mind. I hardly knew Nora. Why would she want to do this for me?

Waiting in the car for Michael, I found myself returning to Nora's words, pondering and analyzing each one. *Why would anyone want to obligate themselves to another person at a specific time every day?*

I decided Nora was indeed an unusual person. I remembered meeting her the day we moved into our home. She seemed different from most people: very nice—and warm—but different. I had wondered back then what the difference was, but I could not put my finger on it. I had even mentioned it to Alex, although I could not explain why she left me with that impression. *What is it? She seems so sincere, but why does she want to do this?*

When Michael and I arrived home, Nora and the kids met us at the door.

"Hi!" I said, looking down at the little ones. "Were you good for Nora?" I asked, especially wondering how she had managed with little Stevie. Nora smiled at both of them and said, "Yes, indeed! They were very good! We got along just fine, didn't we, kids? And I'll be back tomorrow!"

What do I say? She wants to do this. She really wants to. And she's so nice. How can I say no?

"Please allow me to do this for you, Alisha," she said, as though she had read my thoughts. "It will give me something to do while I'm waiting for Melody to arrive home. She rides the shuttle bus to and from kindergarten because I don't drive."

"Oh! Well, then, she can ride to and from the school with Michael."

"Thanks, but she enjoys riding the bus. She has made some special friends and looks forward to being with them every day."

"I understand," I said. "All right, Nora. If you insist," I smiled. "I am very grateful. You're right about the kids being wakened from their nap time. Thank you. But if there's ever a day you can't come, or if it becomes difficult for you to continue, I'll understand. And if I can do anything for you, please don't hesitate to ask me. Okay?"

Nora lingered there at the front door for a moment and looked directly into my eyes. "Alisha," she said softly, "Jesus loves you. He sees your burden, and He will help you with it."

Without waiting for my response, she stepped through the open door and down the porch steps. I stood there flabbergasted, dumbfounded, speechless, while still holding the door open, watching her cross the street. *What on earth? Why did she say that? What's happening to me? I want to cry.* When Nora reached her front door, she turned and waved.

Why had I been so deeply moved by her words? No one I knew had ever mentioned the name *Jesus* to me in conversation. That was a name spoken only in church by the priest or spoken to me by my catechism teacher when I was young. Nora's words went over and over in my mind the rest of the day: *"Alisha, Jesus loves you. He sees your burden, and He will help you with it."*

The next day, Nora arrived promptly and convinced me again that it was convenient for her to stay with the children. I had to admit, it was a lot less trouble for me, and I was grateful.

I was even more impressed with Nora that day after Michael and I got home. The children wakened and came downstairs carrying their shoes. I watched Nora help Steven with his shoes and praise Laura for knowing how to tie hers. *She seems to have such a loving way with the kids.* The children had responded to her warmth and affection immediately the day before, and today they seemed glad to see her.

On the third day, Nora shared an experience that both she and her husband had one night in a little church they had been invited to attend by friends who had become Christians. This experience, she said, changed their lives.

"After preaching the gospel message, the minister gave an altar call," she said. "Ray and I went forward, knelt at the altar, and gave our lives to Jesus Christ, and we were born again. We're not the same people we were before that church service, Alisha. Ray used to be an alcoholic, but that all changed too," she said, and went on to share the rest of her story. Then she declared with joy, "Oh, it's been wonderful these last few years!"

My heart was pounding; my thoughts were racing: *I've never heard anything like this in my life! I don't understand the meaning of "altar call" and "born again," but I believe her completely.* It was her genuineness and sincerity that caused me to believe every word. Had it been someone else—maybe someone not so kind, not so real—I might have hoped the phone would ring or the children would interrupt.

"How wonderful, Nora! God has really been good to you and Ray."

"Yes," she smiled, "and I praise Jesus every day for the new life I have—Ray too. I love Jesus with all my heart, Alisha. I just never would have believed we would be in a church that night. Neither of us was ever a churchgoer. But I'm sure glad we accepted that invitation. Jesus not only changed us completely, but He's changed our future."

Oh God, this is real. I'm certain of it. All my life, I've wanted to believe this is the kind of thing You do for people.

"Nora, I believe you!" I said with enthusiasm and quickly added, "I've always believed in Jesus ... and God, and I've gone to church all my life."

A long silence filled the room. Nora gazed directly into my eyes—just as she had that first day. She firmly but lovingly asked, "Yes, honey, I know you believe, but have you been born again?"

I was taken aback, really puzzled! *What is she talking about? What does she mean by "born again"?* Nora was still smiling. Being Catholic, I had absolutely no idea what Protestants believed or how they expressed their beliefs.

This was no time for pride, so I asked the question: "What do you mean by born again? I've never heard that phrase used to describe a Christian."

"Alisha, that's what it means to be a Christian."

I wanted to know more. "I still don't understand, Nora. Is that what your Protestant church calls being a Christian?"

She smiled and said, "No, honey, that's what the Bible calls it. That's what Jesus said in John 3:1, 2, and 3: "You must be born again ... ." After quoting the verses entirely, she explained, "It's not Protestant or Catholic, Alisha—it's Bible! It's a command from

Jesus to everyone; *whosoever* will come to Him, believing in Him with all their heart, can be *born again.*

"Think of it like this, Alisha. In the natural, we're conceived in our mother's womb, and nine months later we are born; we're alive, and we have physical life—we're born of the flesh. When we're born again, we come alive spiritually—inside—our spirit is alive and we're born of the Spirit."

That made some sense to me, but I still did not understand *how* one became born again.

"I'm very happy for the experience you and your husband have had, Nora, and I'm glad you told me about it. But I must admit that it provokes a lot of questions for me."

"It's all in your Bible, Alisha," she declared cheerfully and quoted another Scripture verse, which amazed me. Clearly Nora was not trying to impress me with her ability to memorize Scripture. On the contrary, she was so humble when she spoke those verses that I was deeply moved. *I need to buy a Bible. Nora assumes that I have one. I can't tell her I don't own a Bible. What would she think of me? I call myself a Christian but don't even own a Bible?*

When Nora left, I pondered her story and the Bible verses she had quoted. Despite her explanations, I still was not clear about her question, *I know you believe, but have you been born again?*

Have I? I'm thirty years old and have never heard this.

I wondered how I could have lived all these years, attended Mass every Sunday, and yet could not recall having ever been taught or encouraged to become born again. *Why not? Especially, if those words were so important that Jesus Himself spoke them—and they're in the Bible.* I concluded that if I did not spiritually understand what that phrase, *born again,* meant, then I almost certainly had not been born again as had Nora.

Although I still had lots of questions, there was a kind of peace inside me, meshed with a nervous excitement, as Nora's story played over and over in my mind.

Could God change me as He did Nora? Could He change Alex? Could he take Alex's alcohol addiction away? Maybe the gambling, too. Mostly, oh God, mostly, I wish You could free Alex once and for all from his illness, that other ugly, dark side of his personality.

Nora is so happy, God. I love what You did for her and her husband and family.

Thinking about Nora's story made me more conscious of God in a real way, more conscious of the reality of His actual interest and involvement in the everyday lives of people. I could tell how close Nora was to Him. When she shared her story, she radiated such happiness. Her relationship with God seemed direct, as though she did not have to be in church to feel close to Him. She talked about Jesus as though He was her dearest friend. I envied her in a good way, and my wish was more of a prayer: *I wish I knew God and the Bible like Nora does. If I did, maybe God could change our lives too. Oh God, I wish You would.*

Michael left the house to play with his friends, and I decided to take Laura and Steven out in the backyard and watch them play. The sun was still bright and felt warm as I sat on the porch steps. Watching the children made me happy — and grateful.

It's too bad Alex rarely takes the time to watch them at play — to really see them as the precious gifts they are. He could experience such joy being with them, and they need his attention too. The truth is, he's not interested in them or me. We all come somewhere behind his job, the racetrack, and the bars. What does that make us? Fourth ... or maybe fifth? Is he really with his buddies or customers every night as he claims? Could there be another woman too? I don't give him a reason to seek out another woman. Oh God, I try not to think about that, but why is he gone from the house night after night? I've tried to make Alex happy. You know that, Lord. But why do I even try anymore? Nothing works!

I looked around the yard, then up at the sky. *What a beautiful October we're having this year.* I took in a deep breath and sighed. *I love the smells of fall.* "Everything God made is beautiful," I muttered, crossing the yard to the beds of brilliant impatiens. I bent over and gently brushed away a new blanket of leaves, unleashing colors of red, pink, and coral. I wanted to enjoy them as long as possible.

Returning to the porch, I sat on the top step. My eyes scanned the trees left and right in the neighbors' yards; some trees were still holding their brightly colored leaves. Laura's squeal got my attention, and I watched her motion to Steven to follow her up the ladder and down the slide. And I remembered Laura playing in the leaves just a few days before. *That day was the same kind of day as today. Strange that I was feeling so hopeless that day … but today I feel hope once again. Everything is so pretty, Lord. Thank you for the trees and the flowers. I don't think I've ever thought about or thanked You for everything You've created.*

I lay in bed that night, my mind absorbed with the details of Nora's story and our conversation about Jesus and the Bible. My thoughts shifted to my own relationship with God. It had been humbling to admit just how ignorant I was of God's Holy Scriptures, especially since I had attended Mass almost every Sunday of my life. *Yes, I've heard portions of the Old and New Testaments read at every Mass, the Epistles, and the Gospels; but there must be a whole lot in between I've missed.*

I was further humbled by the obvious contrast between Nora and me; that is, our spiritual understanding about knowing Jesus, and I had questions in my mind—lots of questions: *I feel like there is a big gap between Nora's knowledge of Jesus and my own. I know I have been just as attentive in Mass as members of my family or any other Catholic; and I always believed what I was taught about God and Jesus in catechism classes. Have I taken my Christianity for granted because I go to Mass each Sunday? As a baby, I was baptized a Christian. But that Scripture Nora quoted about Jesus saying you must be born again and the way she refers to Jesus as her "personal" Savior disturbs me. Is it possible that without knowing that Scripture verse, I have only been believing intellectually?*

Nora had not been a churchgoer throughout her early years and the years of her marriage; but she had an experience one night that changed her life and caused her to know Jesus, her "living Savior," as she called Him, and to know the Scriptures. And she spoke of Jesus not as an historical figure, but as a personal *friend*. I had never heard another Christian—Catholic or Protestant—speak of Jesus Christ as Nora did. Despite my years of church, admittedly, I did not know Christ or His Bible as she did.

Also, Nora knew I was Catholic, but she never indicated that she was interested in discussing the differences in church doctrines. I was impressed with that. She had not even mentioned the name of her church. She only told me about Jesus, the Christ. None of her words contradicted what I already believed, but rather, her words amplified the foundation of what I already believed about God.

The next day Nora and I talked again. She had brought her Bible with her. It looked worn from use.

"Nora," I started slowly, "I want to tell you about something that happened to me in my kitchen just a few days ago. Tell me if you think God really answered my prayer or ... "

"Or not?" Nora finished my sentence. She paused a moment and then continued. "Alisha, I believe already that He hears your prayers."

"Do you, Nora? I mean ... even if I haven't been born again, like you? God has heard my prayers all these years?"

"Yes, of course, Alisha. God hears every prayer."

When I finished sharing the details of what had happened that memorable morning, I said, "Nora, I remember I felt very peaceful afterward. I've had a similar experience of feeling an unusual calm, a peace, in the past, despite the extreme circumstances I was facing. It was right before a major surgery. When praying about my condition, I felt what I can only describe as a gentle electric current go through me. I know that sounds bizarre, but after that I felt peaceful and I slept wonderfully; and everything about the surgery went better than expected. I wondered then if it was because of God—because He had heard my prayers. Nora ... do you think it was?"

"Yes I do," she boldly declared.

How can she be so certain?

Then suddenly I had the answer to my earlier question. It came like a flash into my mind. I realized that I had always believed in God and understood, intellectually, everything I had been taught about Him. I believed that God was everywhere. But that morning in the kitchen, deep inside my inner person, I was more aware than ever of that inexplicable void I had felt most of my life, which I had never been able to identify. Despite my believing and my prayers all those years, still I always felt *there was something missing.* That morning in the kitchen, I think I realized for the first time that I was not sure I really knew God after all.

All my life I had never questioned anything I had learned about God. I was now full of questions for Nora. Listening to her answer each one with Scripture was amazing, but humbling too. Each day that week, Nora left me wanting to hear more about the Bible. I longed to know Jesus Christ in the personal, intimate way she knew Him.

Nora gently introduced me to more and more of the Holy Scriptures, and I would spend the rest of the afternoon and evening reflecting on them. I had my Sunday Catholic missal, but I still did not have the nerve to tell her that I did not own a Bible. However, I intended to buy one soon.

The following Monday morning, Nora invited me to her home for coffee. There she showed me a Bible her church had awarded her for perfect adult Sunday school attendance.

"I have been praying that God would show me who I should give it to," she said, "and you are the one!"

"Oh, how nice … thank you so much, Nora." *She doesn't know I don't own a Bible*. But then I realized that God knew. Nora had prayed about it, and I was sure, even though I had known her only a short time, that God answered her prayers.

After I got home, I held my gift tenderly, inspecting it carefully. Rubbing my hands over the white faux leather cover with embossed metallic gold letters, I read, *Holy Bible*. I whispered, "Thank you, God." Turning it on its side, I read, "Red Letter Edition, King James Version." Opening the cover to the first page, titled in Old English lettering, I read, "Presented to," with my name, followed by Nora's name and the date. I reached for my pen and proudly wrote under Nora's name: "My Christian friend and neighbor."

I thought about Nora: her generosity, her thoughtfulness, her genuine concern—her love for Christ and her love for me. Instantly I realized that was what I had felt when I met Nora for the first time. *It's love. That's why I felt she was different! She's not only a Christian, but she radiates God's love! It's genuine love. I can never thank You enough, God, for sending Nora into my life.*

My daily routine changed after she gave me that Bible. Before, I did get up early, long before my family, to have my time alone. It was my time for pleasure reading of novels and magazines, to study articles on parenting, or to do my sewing—whatever required uninterrupted time. Now I began using that time for reading my new Bible.

Usually I tried to read a chapter or two, only to find myself absorbed and reading on and on, looking into the reference verses, until I had studied several chapters before the family awakened and prompted my morning routine. I had an insatiable hunger for truth about God, truth about myself, truth about everything. I simply could not get enough of the Scripture. Often questions would come to mind during the day as I moved through my household chores. I would stop what I was doing and search for a verse that offered an answer.

I recognized how vast is the knowledge of God and the knowledge about God, and how little I had known about Him. Also, this Bible was revealing to me how much more God expected of me, if I was to be a true Christian. Discovering these new insights, these truths, was exciting to me. They were like newly found treasure—as exciting as I can imagine the discovery of a mother lode is to one who mines for gold.

Early in the morning on October 29, 1966, something not just unusual, but startling and utterly phenomenal, happened to me during my Bible study time. First, a peculiar feeling came over me. The only way I can describe it will seem overly dramatic. Nevertheless, the truth is that I felt suddenly suspended in time, as though everything in the universe had stopped. Instantly a thought came that I should turn to the book of Matthew. When I found it, I felt compelled to turn to chapter 22. I did, then began reading from verse 1 with full concentration. When I came to the red-lettered words of Jesus in verse 37, I was stunned by what I saw.

My eyes are playing tricks on me! What's happening to me?

What was happening was indeed unimaginable, incredible. I understand if others find it hard to believe. I found it hard to believe myself.

My eyes locked onto what appeared to be highlighted words, almost like neon lights, and I read each one: "Thou shalt love the Lord your God with all your heart, and with all your soul, and with all your mind, this is the first and greatest commandment."

I winced, refocused my eyes, and re-read each word slowly.

Instantly the knowing came to me that although I had believed in God my whole life, I had not kept that commandment. He had not really been first in my heart or in my mind. *I have not truly loved You, God. I've put myself, my husband, my children, and others I love before You, Lord. I've even put my Catholic Church before You.*

Truth was rising within me, and I welcomed its conviction, unearthing confessions about myself that had been hidden from me before now.

As I looked down at the page to read on, it happened again. The next words popped out at me like before: "And the second [commandment] is like unto it, thou shalt love your neighbor as yourself."

These two commandments grabbed at my heart and dug deep into my soul. Strangely, I did not feel condemned by them; but however familiar they had been to me all those years, I felt as though I had been blind to their deepest meaning. I continued reading the words of Jesus: "On these two commandments hang all the law and the prophets."

My mind was racing: *Wow! If these two commandments are the most important and the ones all Bible truth hangs on ... and I haven't observed them ... I've been way off base for thirty years! How could I have believed my entire life that I obey the Ten Commandments, when before now I not only didn't know what Jesus said about them, but I also didn't realize I haven't even kept the two most important commandments? Have I been asleep spiritually? God, I need help!*

Those thoughts stayed with me. I had kept all my Catholic traditions, read my prayer book, said the rosary, and observed all the religious rituals. In fact, when I was a teenager, I faithfully attended Monday evening church novenas to the Blessed Mother. I was trying to draw close to God. Often, following the novena, the priest would ask me if I wanted to go into the convent after I graduated from high school. I think that was because I was the only teenager there on Monday nights. At one point, I thought I should consider it and even made an appointment to speak with a priest about becoming a nun. Simply, I was trying to *really know God and how to please Him.* Somewhere along the way of my growing up, that notion of considering the convent left me. Even so, that longing to know God never left me.

It amazed me that I could have lived my whole life without really knowing the deep spiritual significance of these two commandments that Jesus said are the most important of the ten. In that moment, I realized if all of God's people sincerely kept those two commandments, there would be no prejudice, no racism, no anti-Semitism, no need for civil rights laws or a mandate to enforce those laws.

For the rest of the day, I reflected on those powerful, red words of Jesus in Matthew. Metaphorically speaking, they seemed to have fastened to my brain, bringing more confession: *How much time have I given to You, God? Sunday Mass ... observing church rites ... praying ... Yes, but I've never read the Bible before now. I've never shared my love for You with others, as Nora does. It would never have occurred to me to do that. She has unselfishly given her time and her help to me. She told me about You. That's what Your Bible tells Christians to do, although it would never have occurred to me to do that, either!*

In the secret places of my mind and heart, I had always had a longing to know God, and that day I knew I wanted Him to be first in my life, more than anything. But I did not know how in the world to put Him there. I only knew I wanted to obey those commandments. As I pondered them, a litany of prayerful, soul-searching thoughts disclosed more truth about me: *I thought I loved people, looked for the best in them. But I guess I've never loved with Your kind of love, God. I try to love Alex. But now I have to admit that I'm not sure if I really, down deep in my heart, love Alex anymore. He's so difficult to love. You say that I should love others as I love myself. God, how do I love myself?*

I concluded that I really did not know how to love at all, because I knew I did not love myself. "Me? Whoever I am ... what's there to love?" I moaned.

That night as I lay in bed, suddenly I awakened from a sound sleep. It was still dark outside, but I was alert and felt completely rested. Almost immediately I began thinking about God—nothing specific, not even the Scriptures I had pondered throughout the day. God was just at the forefront of my mind. Curiously, I felt that same sensation come over me again, like I was suspended in time. I knew I had not imagined all I had experienced earlier in the day, because with those Scriptures in Matthew, new truth about God and myself had been revealed to me. But I could never have conceived in my wildest imagination what was about to take place.

I now know what happened to me next was rich with the convicting power of the Holy Spirit and the amazing grace of Jesus Christ. If I had not personally experienced this, I would find it hard to imagine it to be true—but it is absolutely true.

My eyes were idly fixed on the wall in front of me, opposite the foot of the bed, when suddenly, something—something I can only describe as a scene on a home movie screen—appeared on the wall, shocking me. I quickly turned my eyes away.

Then I looked again, squinted, blinked my eyes, and refocused them. The picture on the "movie screen" was still there. *Oh, come on, Alisha; it's a blank wall—you know that!*

Then suddenly another scene appeared on the screen, followed by another, and another. I was frightened. *Oh God, take it away. What's happening to me? Am I losing my mind? Is this a dream?*

"But it can't be a dream," I softly muttered, blinking my eyes and refocusing them again. "I'm awake!"

But if it isn't a dream, what is it?

I stared, intently now, at the images on the screen before me—and recognized them. *It's me!* It was a scene from my past. Then another scene flashed and another. Now they were moving one by one across the screen in staccato rhythm, like photo slides.

"I'm sorry, God," I whispered. "I'm so sorry."

As soon as I spoke those words, somehow I understood that God was revealing my sins. Not only my sins of the past, but also various painful experiences flashed before me, particular incidents of Alex's abuse I had suffered and two other people who had deeply hurt me years before. And, to my amazement, there was the scene of the last time I saw my ex–love, my soldier, when without a word he suddenly turned and walked off the porch of my home. Now I saw his face and what I had not seen in his face that night. I saw the depth of pain I had caused him all those years ago. "I'm so, so sorry," I whispered.

No one ... not a living soul knows these things. Only God could know. Oh God ... oh God ... I'm so sorry ... so sorry.... . Please forgive me, Lord.

The movie screen was gone!

Deep sobs collected in my throat as I recalled every scene, every detail. I quietly got out of bed, grabbed a box of tissues, and went downstairs to the living room.

I dropped to my knees in front of the chair and let go of the sobs as I again begged God to forgive my sins.

The painful scenes of Alex's violent, abusive rages replayed in my mind, the despicable things he had said and done to me over the years. I tried to force them back into my subconscious, but God seemed determined to exhume them again, one by one.

My tears stopped. I could feel bitterness, resentment, and hatred for my husband rise up from within me. *I hate him for what he's done to me.* The ugly scenes remained until something began happening inside me.

"Hate!" I said aloud. "What a terrible thing! I didn't think I could hate anyone," I groaned.

I broke into deep, agonizing sobs again, as conviction forced out of me heartfelt repentance: "Oh, dear God, please, please forgive me for this terrible bitterness, resentment, and hatred I feel for Alex." I had had no idea that I actually harbored those sins in my heart for my husband. "And I forgive Alex for everything he has ever done to me," I quickly whispered.

Something lifted. I felt light-headed and put my head down on the seat of the chair. Then more scenes replayed in my mind: those of two people who had hurt me deeply over the years. At that moment also, I was forced to face the resentment I felt toward them.

"God, please forgive me," I cried in a muffled tone. "And I forgive them too."

Instantly I felt quieted within, and peace settled around me. The tension was gone. I sat back on the floor, thinking about what had happened to me, and to my amazement, I clearly understood everything.

I had thought I was a good person all these years. But I was not. I had committed sins, and I had held sins against Alex and others. They were sins that I had never thought of as sin: negative thoughts and unkind words spoken about those who had offended me. They were all sins. I had given myself the right to resent those two people who had wronged me. I had pushed those painful incidents to the back of my mind and had not remembered them — until tonight. Although my sins had not been obvious to those persons against whom they had been harbored, and others could not see them, nevertheless, I now realized they had been grievous sins to God. He had seen them all. And instinctively I knew that soon I would have to humble myself to ask their forgiveness.

Buzz-z-z-z-z. I was startled by the sound of the alarm clock in our bedroom. I heard Alex walk into the bathroom. I remained downstairs because I did not want him to see that I had been crying, and I did not want to field his questions. How could I explain this? Gratefully, the alarm had not wakened the kids.

I hurried into the kitchen to splash my face with cold water and dab my swollen eyes with ice. I felt light as I prepared breakfast. Seeing the truth of my sins and repenting for them had been freeing, but for some strange reason, I did not feel this encounter with God was over.

I was tempted to tell Alex some of what had happened to me when he came to the table, but I reminded myself again that I could not explain such a bizarre experience. There was only one person I felt I could tell. I just wanted Alex to leave for work so I could telephone Nora.

"Nora ..." I said. Strangely, I could not go on with what I intended to say. My voice began trembling. I began to cry again.

"What's wrong, Alisha?"

"I don't know what's wrong with me, Nora. I guess I need help." I could not speak anymore. All I could do was cry.

"Would you like to come to my house?" she asked gently. "Please!"

When the children and I arrived, two of Nora's friends from her church were there. Nora introduced us, and then she took Laura and Steven to the playroom and I joined the other ladies. When Nora returned, without questioning me about why I was crying earlier, she quietly asked if I would like them to pray with me.

I answered, "Yes, please," as Nora took my hand, gently leading me into her family room. The four of us knelt, and they began to pray. I listened at first. *I don't know how to pray like they do.*

Then I found myself caught up with my own thoughts. The Scriptures I had meditated on the previous day and all that had happened during the early hours of the morning came back to my mind. I knelt there silently in my own deep reflection. Then I just started talking to God in my mind: *God, I want to really love You... love You with my whole heart. And I want to love others too. I want to know You ... really know You like Nora does. I want to be born again like her ... and like Nora, I promise I will do what she does ... I will tell people about You.*

I was oblivious to everything except my desire for God.

Unexpectedly I heard myself quietly plead aloud, "Please, dear Jesus ... forgive me for all my sins ... and please forgive me for living my whole life without putting You first ... for not loving You with my whole heart, my whole soul, and my whole mind ... I do love You now, Lord Jesus ... I love You with all my heart!"

After a moment, I felt as though I had been lifted up with the Lord, as though I were totally alone with Him. I believed if I died that moment, I would be with Jesus.

Suddenly I was aware that the women, still kneeling, had stopped praying and were silent. I recognized the peace that had settled over us. It was like the sense of calm, perfect tranquility that I had felt around Steven and me in the kitchen a few days before, again yesterday, and in the wee hours of this morning. I knew for certain now that it was God's presence, His peace.

This was remarkable! I no longer felt that deep, inner void I had felt all my life. Instead, I felt fully saturated with love. I felt loved with a kind of love I had never known before or imagined I could ever feel. I felt complete and pure love for the first time in my life. It was the sense of being utterly, absolutely, unconditionally loved.

I opened my eyes and saw three sweet, smiling faces gazing back at me. We all stood up, and one by one Nora and her friends hugged me. I found myself saying to each of them, "I love you ... and I love Jesus so much!"

They laughed and said they loved me too. I felt so much love inside that I wanted to run outside and shout *I love you* to the whole world! The ladies just kept smiling at me and at one another.

"Oh Nora, I feel wonderful! I feel like an enormous weight has been lifted from me! I feel like I've just had a shower inside and I'm squeaky clean!" I laughed. "I feel so much joy ... I feel brand-new!"

"You are," Nora said with a smile. "You are brand-new — you've been born again!"

"I have? Yes ... yes, I know I have, Nora! I really know I'm born again!"

Only minutes before, the words of Jesus in the Gospel of John, *You must be born again,* were still a mystery to me; but now, like Nora, I knew that I knew that I knew, experientially, the reality of those words. And I knew my spirit had come alive within me.

Now I was back in the present with my heart full of praises for my Jesus. I will never forget, not for a moment, all that God rescued me from that day, October 30, 1966. And I never want to stop remembering. It had been my divine appointment.

After being born again, I knew beyond a shadow of doubt that God had led us to that house. When we had only three days to find a place to live and had already spent two unsuccessful days searching, I believe God gave us the idea to drive up and down streets in areas we liked. He led us to my favorite neighborhood in the city, to that particular street, and to that particular house — directly across from the home of His faithful one, Nora. This, too, was awesome to remember again. It brought to mind a Scripture verse in the Old Testament: "For I know the thoughts *and* plans that I have for you, says the Lord, thoughts *and* plans for welfare *and* peace and not for evil, to give you hope in your final outcome. Then you will call upon

Me, inquire for, and require Me as a vital necessity and find Me when you search for Me with all your heart" (Jer. 29:1–12 AMP).

I believe these verses were promises from God that have proven true in my life. I know they also are true for everyone who will embrace the same promises with faith, believing.

Having been comforted earlier this morning by the presence of God the Holy Spirit and with His new promises in Isaiah 43—and remembering the remarkable circumstances the Holy Spirit used to draw me to Jesus—once again, my faith was stirred and increased by His amazing grace. With all the encouragement I had received, the joy of the Lord was with me. By now I was feeling strong and more than confident. I felt empowered to meet the day. I was ready to shower, dress, and go to work. I was ready to step out with expectation into the "new thing" God had promised.

Chapter 11

Recovery

The house was dark and empty when I arrived home from my first day back to work. There were only a couple of fellow employees who knew I was getting divorced, and they asked concerned questions, but nothing too personal—nothing I could not answer with only a few words. The kids had returned to college and were working their evening retail jobs until ten o'clock, so I would not see them until eleven. I did not mind eating alone tonight. For now I did not feel like seeing or even talking with my family or friends. After dinner I skimmed through back issues of the newspaper I had saved for a couple of days, and I read today's paper.

I carried my coffee mug to my special corner and set it down on the coaster, turned on the light, and closed the drapery against the long night ahead. Inching back into the chair, I lifted my novel from underneath my journal on the table, ready to unwind from the day by finishing the last two chapters. After a couple of pages, I realized I could not concentrate because my mind kept wandering from the lives of the story's characters back to my own. I closed the book, leaned my head back, and shut my eyes. I found myself reminiscing again about that most important turning point in my life, that day when I *began again* because of God's unfailing love.

When Nora came to sit with the children that afternoon, I was still excited. I was anxious to tell her of the unusual experiences I had had the day before while reading Matthew 22 and seeing the "movie screen." I also wanted to tell her about my hopes for Alex.

"I know Jesus can free Alex as He did Ray, Nora. I just know it!"

"Ray and I have been praying for him," she said.

"Oh?" I responded, surprised. I quickly asked, "Why have you been praying?"

"We hear him screaming at you sometimes ... you know, obscenities when he's angry," she said, lowering her eyes with embarrassment.

All the way across the street? Momentarily I felt that same old humiliation I had felt when I knew our neighbors had overheard Alex in the first neighborhood we lived in. I wondered what all she and Ray had heard, but I did not pursue it further, and she said nothing more about Alex. I was so full of love for Jesus that the feeling of humiliation left me instantly.

After I shared my experiences, I quickly added, "Do you believe me, Nora? Have things like this ever happened to you?"

"Yes, God leads me ... but no, not exactly like that. But I think it's wonderful, Alisha. Yes, of course, I believe you. Why wouldn't I? That's what brought you to salvation!" She went on to tell me she was "blessed" to know how the Holy Spirit had been preparing me for this morning's event, and concluded, "Praise the Lord, Alisha. God can do anything!" I had never heard anyone exclaim *praise the Lord*, but I liked it.

Alex arrived home earlier than expected from work. I was upstairs wiping the tear stains from my face. To my relief, Dr. Jekyll was standing at the bottom of the stairs looking up at me as I ran down to meet him.

"Gee, you look pretty, honey."

"Really?" I asked, unbelieving. *What? Crying all day and he thinks I look pretty?*

"Yes, really!" he said, smiling as he put his arms around me, giving me a big bear hug.

"Thank you, Alex. I'd like to talk to you when you finish changing clothes." I was so anxious to tell him what had happened to me, especially knowing he was in a good mood. My heart pounded with excitement as I waited for him. He found me in the kitchen.

"I have something to tell you, honey."

Alex might have realized something had been happening to me during the past three weeks, but maybe not. His pattern of indifference to my interests during the last few months was a fact I could not ignore. Usually Alex seemed to only half listen to what I had to say.

But today he listened intently as I shared every detail of my experience—including the flashes of my sins across a "movie screen."

"Can you believe that, Alex? It was like our own home movie screen ... honest! There can be no other way to describe it."

"After everything that's happened to you? Sure, I believe you. Of course, I believe you!"

"Well, it was so remarkable, so bizarre, I wondered if you, or anyone, would believe me."

"What do you care if people don't believe you? You and God know what happened to bring you this kind of happiness. I think it's great, honey!" I was so pleased that he was genuinely interested and happy for me.

"I kind of understand what happened to you," he said. "When I was young and living with my grandmother, she used to take me to her Baptist church. I was twelve or thirteen when I went to the altar ... and I was immersed in water baptism too."

"Really?" I said, surprised to learn this about my husband after all these years. "Why haven't you told me about this before?"

"Well, to tell you the truth, I forgot about it until now."

That answer took me aback. It made no sense to me. *I can't imagine anyone having that spiritual experience and not remembering it. Especially if his "going to the altar" meant the same thing to him as it had meant to Nora and Ray.*

"Alex, why do you suppose you forgot about such a meaningful decision in your life?"

"I guess ... well, I think I went to the altar and got baptized more because the preacher and my grandmother told me I should... that was all. I just did what I thought I was supposed to do. What's happened to you is different. I never ... well ... felt about God the way you do now."

"Alex, I must ask ... will you forgive me for everything of the past? Everything I have ever said or done to hurt you or make you unhappy? And I forgive you too," I quickly added.

"Sure, I forgive you," he enthusiastically answered.

I was disappointed that he did not ask my forgiveness for his wrongs against me. Nonetheless, I appreciated that he had been open with me and quickly asked, "Honey, would you like to commit your life to Christ?"

"Well ... no. I didn't say that."

When I attempted to say more, I could tell he did not want to talk about his commitment. Wisely I dropped the subject.

As I lay in bed that night, I was still too excited to sleep. I was feeling the afterglow of my personal experience. My mind was full of the details. Before today my prayer life had always been private, silent, certainly never praying above a whisper. I marveled that I had actually prayed aloud in front of Nora's friends, who were strangers to me, and my display of emotion and free-spirited gestures also had been a bit out of character for me.

My phenomenal experiences throughout the past month went over in my mind again. Each of these happenings would have been unimaginable to me before I experienced them. Having been supernaturally led to read Matthew 22 and all that followed with the movie screen had to have been the work of the "Holy Spirit," as Nora said. There was no doubt God had revealed His truth and my sins to me, and this had removed blinders from my eyes. I understood that what I had experienced had bypassed my mind and had taken place in my heart and spirit.

To me it was all fantastic! ... Still, it might seem bizarre to some people. I could never deny it though ... not one extraordinary, merciful detail. But what if my family doesn't believe me?

Suddenly I felt a tinge of fear about telling them. My thoughts raced. They became somewhat of a prayer, a conversation with myself and with God at the same time: *That might happen. Oh Lord, they might find it all hard to believe, especially Scripture appearing highlighted on the page and my sins flashing on a movie screen! It might sound off the wall, weird to my parents, Mary, and CJ. I don't know, though; there's a lot of unexplained mystical things in the Catholic Church, so maybe my experiences won't seem too strange to them. But still, what if they don't believe me?*

I paused to think about that. "No! Lord Jesus, I can't let that get to me," I muttered.

Like Alex said, "What do you care if people don't believe you? You and God know what happened." He's right. Either way, their opinion will not ... cannot ... does not change one iota of anything I've experienced. For me, Lord, my personal spiritual experiences are not debatable!

Pondering those things, I knew that before I told anyone what Nora called "my testimony," I had to give serious thought to how I would handle it, should they reject the whole thing.

It's realistic to consider there probably will be some people I know, who, if I tell them, will no doubt be nice and polite enough to listen, but they might privately pooh-pooh the whole thing. Or some might even flat out reject it to my face. But that will be okay. After all, everyone has the right to disagree.

I was feeling less fearful now.

For me ... I know I could never deny what only the love of Jesus Christ and only the power of the Holy Spirit could have done for me ... did do for me.

With that solid assurance, I closed my eyes and fell into a restful sleep.

I felt vibrantly alive after that day. There was no longer the feeling that something was missing in my life. Now I knew it was God who had filled that void in me. There was no more questioning. My search was over. I had a matchless peace in my heart. Calm assurance replaced worry.

Also, my overwhelming fear of Alex's bad temper, his verbal abuse, was gone. I was no longer afraid of his dark side, Mr. Hyde. The suppressed hatred, resentment, and anger I had felt toward him also were gone. I felt only forgiveness and love for my husband now.

It was wonderful being free from severe stress and tension, to be genuinely happy in my daily life that first week. Caring for my children was still a constant joy. And I would soon find out how others would respond to my testimony.

The following Sunday I decided to go to my parents' home alone, wishing to not have distractions from the children while sharing my experience with them and my siblings. I had prayed and prayed the night before and that morning at Mass that God would give me wisdom, especially when I spoke about being born again. That was a phrase I knew might sound as strange to them as it had to me when I first heard it from Nora. But I was prepared to answer their questions with the same Scriptures Nora had used to answer mine.

I waited for an appropriate time after dinner, telling them I was excited to share with them about the most wonderful thing that had ever happened to me. I had their attention. While joyfully sharing with Mom and Dad, and Mary, CJ, and their spouses, I became aware that their listening seemed to fall somewhere between mild interest and complete disinterest, with the exception of my father, who was listening intently to my every word. When I finished speaking, however, there was no response, not even from Dad. There was only uncomfortable silence.

In their silence, I felt time stood still for me. *Was it the words "born again?" Perhaps they had not sounded "Catholic" to them, so that made everything else I said questionable.*

Rather than that uncomfortable silence, I would have preferred them to challenge me with questions, as I had Nora. But they did not.

Finally, my mother made the only comment: "I don't know what you mean about all this, Alisha. You've always been a Christian. You're not a sinner; you're a good girl." I was eager to give more details, but there was clear indication that she did not wish for me to explain further. I felt Mother and the rest of them feared I had joined the camp of the Protestants. But I had not joined another church. I was not part of some fringe group of fanatical religious people. It was not about religion; I had simply entered into a personal relationship with the living God, Jesus Christ.

No doubt, Mom was concerned about my reading the King James Bible, which she associated with Protestantism, because she immediately gave me the family Catholic Bible, but without explanation and without a word of criticism. At that time, she did not realize that all the truth of my having been born again was, in fact, validated on the pages of the Catholic version as well as the King James. Nothing more was said.

Driving home, I thought again about that uncomfortable silence. My family had no idea how their lack of response had affected me. However, I knew that even if they disapproved, they were all too nice to say anything unkind to me, face-to-face.

When I arrived home, I guess I looked a little down, because Alex asked me how it went. My emotions got the better of me, and I poured out my disappointment about the family's silence and how I felt it was their unspoken disapproval and that I might even be an embarrassment to them. Immediately Alex put his arms around me and said, "That's okay, honey. Don't worry. Give it time to soak in. They'll come around."

That night I lay in bed thinking about how different my family's response to my testimony had been from my husband's response. When I began praying about all this, I had a knowing within, that my family simply had not understood my testimony. I remembered the remark Nora had made to me, which in effect was the same thing I felt impressed of now: that if God the Holy Spirit had not drawn me and prepared the way for me, I would not have understood Nora's testimony. Then again I had a profound knowing that I should not initiate further conversations with my parents and siblings about Jesus or the spiritual things I was learning. But rather, I should only love them and be "the message of Jesus." That was deeply puzzling.

However, the next morning, providentially, I found verses in the Bible that seemed to address that concept: "Ye are our epistle... known and read of all men.... Forasmuch as ye are manifestly declared to be the epistle of Christ ... written not with ink, but with the Spirit of the living God; not in tables of stone, but in fleshy tables of the heart" (2 Cor. 3:2–3).

I began to pray that God would teach me how to become the message of Jesus, His epistle. I had a lot to learn. I was not only eager but also determined to learn it well. Naïvely, I had no clue then how hard it would be. But for now, my emotions about all this had been turned right side up again. I felt impressed to believe that one day all my family members would understand my testimony and we would talk often with one another about our Jesus. I was learning to have faith, to take God at His Word.

After that Sunday, my family and I never discussed my spiritual experience; but interestingly enough, my father began consistently asking me to pray before meals when the family and guests were gathered around my parents' table. I was rather timid the first time, but after that God gave me the grace to say a prayer, not by rote, as usual, but to pray whatever was in my heart. Never, however, did my praying invoke a comment from the hearers. God was teaching me not only to have faith but also to trust Him more.

I had a burning desire to share the love of Christ with others as Nora had with me. However, I had no idea how soon an opportunity would come to do so.

We still had not spent our tax return money for the last eight months. Four hundred dollars had been sitting in our savings account to use for an emergency, a family vacation, or a need of some kind. One day soon after I had shared with my family, out of the blue Alex said, "Honey, why don't you use the income tax money in savings to buy that piano you've always wanted?"

He knew that had been a long-time desire of mine, but I never felt we could afford a piano. Nevertheless, Alex insisted; and delighted, I immediately combed the classifieds of that day's newspaper. There was one used piano advertised, but it was a baby grand. The price was not listed, but I knew we could never afford it. I was looking for an old upright or spinet.

The next day, I kept feeling I should call the phone number and make an appointment to see that baby grand. But why? It made no practical sense to me to waste my time and the seller's time. Finally, on a whim, the next morning I picked up the phone and called. I found the address of the piano seller was located in the most affluent residential area in our city.

That afternoon I found the seller friendly and warm as she showed me her baby grand, but I sensed her smile and cheerfulness were masking a heavy heart. I did not know why I felt that. When she told me the price, I could only compliment the beauty of her piano then quickly add, "I'm sorry I took up your time. As much as I love it ... it's way out of our price range."

One thing led to another, and she began telling me why the piano must be sold after being in her family since she was a little girl. Her husband's company was transferring them to New York City, and the new apartment was not large enough. I felt she was distressed about selling her piano and disappointed it could not remain in her family.

Before I knew it, she was offering me a cup of tea. Sitting at her kitchen table chatting, I do not know how or why, but I ended up sharing a small portion of my testimony with her. She reacted to hearing it, in effect, the same way I had reacted to Nora's words. When I was ready to leave, she thanked me for sharing my story and told me my coming had meant a lot to her. I gave her my phone number and asked her to feel free to call in case she felt like talking further about her move.

Driving home, I no longer cared about that baby grand; but I rejoiced because I had met the seller and had actually stepped out in faith to share my beliefs with her, and she had positively responded. Everything had been spontaneous. I prayed that God would bless her and her husband, that she would grow to better accept giving up her piano, and that they would be happy in their new location.

The next afternoon, she called me to say she had told her husband about me and that he agreed with her that she should sell me the piano.

I was shocked.

"Thank you, that's so nice; but again, we can't afford to buy it ... nothing even close ... We have only four hundred dollars in savings to spend for a piano. But thanks anyway."

"That's fine, then. You may buy it."

I was dumbfounded.

"If you don't mind, my husband and I both play, so we would like to tape record some of our music before we part with it."

"Really? You want to sell your cherished piano to me for only four hundred dollars?"

"Yes, really!" she laughed. "It's yours."

"But I won't actually be paying for your piano ... you know that. This can only be called a gift."

She laughed again. "I know it will have a good home with you."

"Oh, I don't know what to say. My husband will be in shock too. I don't know what to say except thank you ... thank you so much."

I could not believe it! What is more, she not only sold me that valuable, magnificent piano, hand-built in New York City in 1912 and in perfect condition, for four hundred dollars, but she also paid to have it delivered to our home and set up in our living room by professional piano movers. I had no doubt that the desire of my heart for a piano was known to God and He had granted me my desire with that particular piano as my gift because of Jesus in my life. That baby grand was over and above any piano I could have imagined or dreamed possible to own. It would always be a reminder to me of God's grace. My new life was becoming quite an adventure, and I could not wait to see what would happen next.

A short time later, I shared my born-again experience with Sister Miriam, a Catholic nun with an order in our city. After she heard all the details, she rejoiced with me, saying, "My dear Alisha, we are kindred spirits in Christ, and I understand completely." It was a blessed meeting of two women who personally knew and loved Jesus.

Next I shared my testimony with one of my oldest and dearest friends, my childhood mentor, Joann. She, too, received with joy my born-again experience. I had the privilege of praying with her, and she became born-again and totally committed to Jesus Christ. It was a glorious experience for me to witness God's blessing of her life. Like me, her search was over.

Soon after, something else totally unexpected—in fact, something astonishing—happened to me. It unfolded one day when Joann phoned to tell me about an upcoming charitable event for which her sister-in-law was chairperson. It was a luncheon and fashion show to be held in the most prestigious country club in town at that time. The show would feature wedding gowns of the last one hundred years, and they needed a local dress designer who could create the "wedding gown of the future."

Her sister-in-law remembered reading the newspaper article and seeing my photo from years earlier about my having designed and made my own wedding gown. Knowing Joann and I were friends, she asked Joann to see if I would be interested in designing the needed gown for the show. I accepted the offer with excitement and immediately began my sketching and my plan for appropriate fabrics. I started with the futuristic premise in mind and came up with the idea of using a paper fabric, which I knew looked and felt like cloth.

When I had my sketch, I made an appointment with the manager of the fabric department in a major downtown department store. He was impressed with my sketch and my idea to make it completely from paper fabric and synthetic materials. Right then and there, he phoned a New York fabric manufacturer and related the whole plan, and requested samples of its paper fabrics. That person asked the manager to send him a copy of the design sketch.

The samples of paper fabric arrived at the store, and I selected one, asking the manager to place the order. It was then he related something surprising. The New York contact had phoned him after receiving a copy of my design sketch and said he was so intrigued he would donate the many yards of fabric needed on one condition: that following the event, I would send his company the finished dress to use for display in its showroom. I promptly agreed.

Then, again to my amazement, the manager offered to donate everything else I needed to make the dress if he could display it as well, to which I also readily agreed. To my absolute shock, in addition he told me he would arrange for one of the professional models who worked the store's fashion shows to model my gown at the event. I was astounded. This ordinarily very expensive project would not cost me or the organization one dime.

From the time I received the fabric and was given carte blanche to select the other items of my choice, I gathered all my materials and began creating the gown I had sketched. A pattern was made to the size of the beautiful, raven-haired model, the white paper fabric was cut, and I started sewing. My mother helped me hand sew thousands of seed pearls and iridescent beads on the bodice and beaded appliqués that adorned the front and back of the full, flowing long gown with a graceful three-yard-long train. A wide band of delicate white synthetic flowers sprayed with white pearlized paint amazingly became an elegant headpiece with an attached full-length veil of white nylon tulle.

The well-publicized luncheon and show drew not only a large audience of the most affluent women in town but also the media. The century-old gowns that were modeled still were beautiful, and the fabric had been well preserved. To my surprise, mine was the featured gown of the show. I gasped when I saw the lovely brunette model, the only professional one in the show, standing at the top of that ornate bridal staircase, wearing my creation, illuminated by the light of the hanging crystal chandelier.

The musicians began playing again, and I stared in awe as the model in my design gracefully descended the stairs and walked the runway, with cameras flashing, as the commentator at the podium described every detail of the "wedding gown of the future" and the materials of which it was made. There was a buzz throughout the room, then a burst of applause. The commentator introduced me as a "local dress designer" and asked me to stand. I gasped again. I was not a "local dress designer." I was just a woman who was experiencing the thrill of a young girl's dream, now come true.

My gown closed the show. Immediately there were photographers flashing pictures of my model and me, and a microphone was in my face. That evening the event was a segment on the six o'clock news of a local television network. Alex, the kids, and I watched intently. There was my design. The kids cheered and applauded Mommy.

As a result of the event and the television exposure, the telephone started ringing off the hook with requests from women to make their daughters' wedding gowns, special-occasion gowns for themselves, and, actually, all kinds of clothing.

According to my agreement, the wedding gown was put on display at the downtown store, with a plaque that read "Wedding Gown of the Future, Designed by Alisha Lance." To see my creation on a mannequin and to read that plaque was both elating and humbling at the same time. Then the manager shipped the gown to the New York fabric manufacturer for its period of display.

With the media bringing attention to my talent, and the local requests to design, I realized that this was my dream come true. I was more than grateful. But I knew then that though I had long forgotten my dream of becoming a costume designer (which I had set aside years before to marry Alex), God had not forgotten. I had no doubt that He had given me an extraordinary opportunity to live out a small piece of my dream.

I chose, however, to decline all requests to design, because that career held no interest for me now. God had realigned my priorities, so there was no difficulty in making that choice. I was content with my life, and it was full. Besides, I was sure now that God had His own particular design and purpose for my life, that there was something more He had for me to do even though I could not see then that it would ever go beyond my priority of being a wife and mother and simply caring for my family.

This delightful incident, like the other extraordinary happenings, was more than I had ever imagined could take place in my life. It was exciting. These experiences obviously were by-products of my total commitment to Christ and His very real love for me.

I had a yearning to really know the ways of my God. I recognized that not only had my spirit come alive to know Jesus, but also the Bible had come alive to me. Now God was not only revealing more about Himself and His ways to me through the Bible, but He was also revealing to me *who I was!* The Bible became a mirror to me. I could clearly see my reflection, and I wanted to change in every area. I welcomed the Bible's corrections and discipline. I desperately wanted to become the woman God created me to be. And so, day by day as I learned more truth about the triune God as well as myself, "precept upon precept," just as the Bible declares, changes came.

With the guidance of God and His Word, I soon found my emotional wounds being healed; the psychological effects of seven years of abuse, as well as codependency, were no longer active in my psyche; and eventually I completely recovered.

Looking back, my problems did not go away like something magical. My healing, deliverance, and recovery came through a daily process of allowing the truth of the Bible to renew my mind and reach deep into my inward parts—into my heart and soul.

Searching for Scriptures in my new King James Bible to help me change, to teach me how to live my married life God's way, and to believe for Alex's conversion proved to be the best way for me to begin "walking my talk." I learned the order of God's priorities for my life: Christ and His Word first; next, my husband and my children; and then, others. I determined to keep my priorities, to honor them, believing if I did so, God in turn would honor my prayers.

I discovered verses that were giving me continued hope for Alex's salvation: "For the unbelieving husband is sanctified by the wife" (1 Cor. 7:14). That Scripture assured me that because I was now a committed believer, my husband was separated and set apart by God and given the opportunity to choose Him, to become His.

I chose to believe God for my Dr. Jekyll, because I learned that a believing wife who will live her quiet Christian faith before her husband, who is always watching her life, can win him to Christ, even if he is not reading the Bible. This was exciting news! I vowed to obey those Scriptures.

However, a couple of verses in that chapter tugged at my heart: "For what knowest thou, O wife, whether thou shalt save thy husband? or how knowest thou, O man, whether thou shalt save thy wife? But as God hath distributed to every man, as the Lord has called every one, so let him walk. And so ordain I in all churches" (1 Cor. 7:16–17).

I knew that meant I must serve Christ according to His Word, whether or not my husband, children, or other loved ones chose to commit their lives to Him. I distinctly recall that a provoking thought stirred my emotions at the time: *I guess there is no guarantee.*

But those verses did not dampen my faith for Alex's conversion. After all, with all God had done for me, I knew He could do the same for Alex if he would allow Him. Like Nora had said, "God can do anything!"

I found a strong Scripture verse God charges husbands to obey: "Likewise, ye husbands dwell with them [wives] according to knowledge, giving honor to the wife, as unto the weaker vessel, and as being heirs together of the grace of life; that your prayers be not hindered" (1 Pet. 3:7).

In my daily study, I wanted to find Scriptures that spoke to Alex's problems. But, no, God had something else in mind. Instead, each time I opened my Bible, I felt impressed to read verses that were clearly suited to my own need for change—designed for nothing short of my own total makeover. Deep within I felt impressed that if I would yield to the Word's transforming power, that same power would be there for me to overcome every battle waged against me. I understood this was not mere human mental or physical power to overcome, but the power of the Holy Spirit of God.

The Bible taught me something else that was very important: even though God desired my obedience and thereby would favor me accordingly, He left me my free will. Interestingly enough, I sensed that while these scriptural exercises were to conform me into the woman God created me to be, I had a *choice* whether I would obey what His Word was telling me. For example, I could choose whether to love Alex when he was downright unlovable, just as I had chosen to forgive him. I knew that Alex, too, had to choose to allow God to change him.

God's condition of leaving the choice to the believer made sense to me. My Lord was a fair and just God. I recognized that He does not want mindless, robot-like followers. Rather, He wants His people to choose Jesus Christ—to love Him enough to trust Him, to obey His Word, and to believe His promises are true.

I also found that desiring to obey God's Word and His will is a far cry from actually, consistently doing it. One of the hardest things for me to learn was how to separate Dr. Jekyll from Mr. Hyde: the

Alex who sometimes behaved like the loving and kind man I married from the Alex who exhibited that horrible dark side. But that became easier once I grasped the concept Jesus taught: hate the sin, but love the (sinner) person.

Finally, through an exercise of trial and error, I learned to be only a "spectator" when Alex was nasty. On those occasions, I turned inward to my consciousness of God, and I found Alex's false accusations, unfounded criticisms, and sometimes degrading declarations did not penetrate me mentally, emotionally, or spiritually. I sought God to teach me how to control my tongue, since the Word says, in essence, that it is our worst enemy. In the concordance of my Bible, I found many Scriptures about the tongue and studied each one. That study is rich with the convicting power of truth—and self-discovery—if one dares to go there.

Although it was difficult to control my tongue, when I failed, I prayed and prayed, determined that the next time I *would* obey. I wanted to master my tongue, and God helped me exercise that control. I saw for myself that when I was able to make the choice to bridle my tongue and to forgive my husband in spite of his behavior, that right choice changed the atmosphere in my home. I was learning a practical principle: my *right choices* could make all my tomorrows better, despite Alex's problems.

However, every day brought a new lesson. By now I was leaning more on the Lord and less on myself to make right choices and to exercise obedience in order for Scripture to help me cope with my everyday circumstances. Now I was able to love my husband when he was unlovable.

As the months went on, I learned more nuggets of Bible truth to help me live my new life. I was pleased when I discovered a store in my area that sold all kinds of Bibles and Bible study books. When I saw *Strong's Concordance* and the *Amplified Bible,* which I knew Billy Graham touted, I had to have them. These, I thought, along with my other versions, would surely help me to "rightly divide the Word of God," which was a Scripture verse I had discovered that exhorted believers to do just that.

I further searched the Scriptures that pertained to marriage, and specifically to wives, using my concordance and reading my different Bible versions. They virtually all said the same thing. In addition to my private study, I was regularly listening to Christian radio preachers and teachers. I was receiving good teaching from them most of the time. I knew that, because I always checked to see if what was being said lined up with what the Bible taught.

When it came to a wife's being in submission to her own husband, that was easy for me to understand and accept. It made perfect sense to me that the husband should be the head of the family. When there is a stalemate in a marriage or family decision, someone has to break that deadlock by making the decision. Besides, I wanted to obey God's Word.

However, when I heard some radio ministers preach on the subject of wives and elaborate on their duty and conduct in general and submission in particular, it seemed to me that their teachings were biased, especially when it came to ministering for God. To my understanding, their words implied that God did not call women to preach or minister for Him.

Their interpretation of Scripture on wives did not seem right to me, especially when it came to ministry for God, since I had already read in the New Testament that Mary Magdalene and the women were the first to see Jesus after He had risen; and He told her to "go and tell." And in the Old Testament, I had already read about Deborah, who was a patriotic military advisor and a judge. Did she have a husband? I do not know, but she certainly had an impressive ministry to the people on behalf of God (Judg. 4:4–10). Then there was Esther, used mightily by God, who became Queen Esther and risked sacrificing her life for her people (Est. 4:16). Needless to say, after knowing about these women of God, I could not accept teachings on wives that limited them.

Although those particular radio ministers preached other Bible truths that lined up with Scripture and with which I wholeheartedly agreed, I believed that when it came to the subject of wives, there was a blind spot in their spiritual vision. Their teachings left me with the perception that a Christian wife should be this quiet, docile, rather subservient woman whose primary spiritual duty was to be submissive to her husband and remain in her place—behind him and his authority, with his leadership exclusively. Never mind the intellect, capabilities, or giftings God had given her that could benefit her husband and children. I was by no means rebellious, but this was another reminder to me that I was still living in a man's world.

On my own, I was still searching out Scriptures on the subject, and there was more of God's truth yet to be revealed to me. When I studied Proverbs 31 in my Amplified Bible, it changed my perception completely. I was thrilled when I read in that particular Bible version, which *amplified* the meaning of certain words, thus giving a better understanding of a wife, that she was an altogether different kind of woman of God from what I felt was being portrayed by some Bible teachers. I knew I had found more truth to treasure.

In capsule form, the king's mother advises him in the first nine verses about how a young man should live and the kind of woman he should seek for his wife, and the king in turn passes on this advice in verses 10–31. Learning from God Himself, who had inspired those Scriptures, I knew they would further help me learn to be the woman and wife I should be. I knew I had a long way to go to be like that Proverbs 31 wife, described throughout the chapter to be the kind of woman a man would be fortunate to find for his wife. But I saw this woman as an excellent example for me and other Christian and Jewish women; in fact, for all women. In my opinion, she was a woman with whom twenty-first-century married, divorced, and single women could identify on one or more levels. My identification with her was based on the fact that she, too, was a wife, mother, and homemaker—and totally committed to her God.

I gleaned from my study, which was purely subjective interpretation, what kind of woman she was and what kind of woman she was not. Immediately I recognized she was neither a Pollyanna nor a prima donna; she was not docile, wishy-washy, and definitely not a doormat; and she was not an emotionally needy wife who was dependent on her husband to make every decision for her, the family, and their home. On the contrary, I recognized the following:

- She was her own person. Her identity was in God.
- She was a woman of God first—before being a wife, mother, homemaker, daughter, sister, friend, or neighbor.

- Although she was submissive to her own husband, her submission was to God first.
- She was strong in her faith and strong in character, and she was a capable, virtuous woman in whom I saw great dignity.
- She was a good wife, who comforted and encouraged her husband, who was "well-known in the gates." In turn, her husband trusted her to hold the family and home together while he was with those in authority: the elders, the nobles, and the judges. In modern society, he might be a rabbi, minister, carpenter, politician, judge, lawyer, physician, teacher, engineer, entrepreneur, corporate CEO, or any other white-collar or equally important blue-collar gentleman — definitely one of the good guys, away from the house and working to make a living.
- She was a good mother, parenting her children with love, teaching and disciplining them according to God's principles, or laws.
- Whenever she counseled and instructed (ministered), she did so with skillful and godly wisdom and kindness.
- She was not a gossiper or a busybody. She minded her own business.
- She was kind and benevolent, extending a helping hand to her friends, neighbors, and others in need.
- She ran her household with ease. She rose early and directed her household help; she was a prudent shopper and always prepared for the changing seasons by buying fine fabrics from which to sew proper clothing for herself and her family; and she also made coverlets, cushions, and rugs of tapestry for her home. In modern society, she might not sew, but she, too, is a prudent shopper and will make sure she and her family are properly clothed for all seasons and her home is comfortable, attractive, clean, and safe.
- She was industrious and creative and made fine linen garments and other items to sell for extra money, and she was a knowledgeable merchant as she sold her homemade pieces in the marketplace.

- She was smart, keen-minded, and a decision-maker. She not only had the intelligence to survey, evaluate, and consider a field to buy it, but also she had the wisdom and discernment to judge its worth and negotiate the price; then she had the confidence to purchase it. Moreover, that Scripture verse indicates that she bought that piece of real estate on her own, without her husband's input.
- To top it off, she was strong in body as she planted her own vineyard in that very field she procured.

Imagine! I realized this woman was amazing! Perfection!

This chapter told me the Proverbs 31 woman was appreciated by God and her husband, not only for her spiritual virtues, but also for her intelligence, abilities, and competence to carry out practical, everyday duties and to make important decisions that benefited her husband and children. Obviously, she was not intimidated by her husband. And, obviously, her husband was not threatened by her intelligence and capabilities.

But why would he be? This woman had no ulterior motives in being accomplished and doing what she was capable of doing to be a good helpmate to her husband. She was not the kind who had to prove she was smarter than or as smart as her husband. She did not do all she did to "one up" him. She blessed her husband and children by being a woman who was caring and whose works and decisions were all influenced by her intimate relationship with her God.

No wonder one verse told me, that *the heart of her husband trusts in her confidently and relies on and believes in her securely.* Another verse told me, that *her children rise up and call her blessed; and her husband boasts of and praises her.*

One of the closing verses showed me the secret to this woman's success. It was a reminder to the man who was looking for a wife, exhorting him to understand that *charm is deceptive and beauty is vain and does not last* [even for Miss Universe], *but* [the secret is] *a woman who reverently fears the Lord will be praised.* The chapter ended, telling me this woman's rewards for living her life under the influence of God: "Give her the fruit of her hands and let her own works praise her."

Knowing this woman in Proverbs 31, why would anyone sell Christian wives, or women in general, short? How could they interpret Scriptures about wives in regards to submission to indicate a wife is limited in any way from accomplishing anything her God-given intelligence, abilities, and decision-making skills can perform to benefit her husband and children, or to preach the Word, if she is so called by God?

Yes, Scripture revealed to me that husbands are the spiritual covering for their wives, a protection for her designed by God. But Proverbs 31 made clear to me that her covering was never meant to smother her or to limit her from being led by her God in performing her duties as wife or her ministry for Him to others. In fact, in this God-inspired word, this woman is described as being "more precious than jewels; her value is far above rubies or pearls" to the man who is lucky enough to make her his wife.

I wanted that kind of affirmation from my husband. And so I aspired to become that kind of wife and mother. I knew I might never meet the perfection of that woman—most of us will not—but I could try to develop and attain to her qualities. That was a big challenge for me and a tall order for God. But I was determined to try.

With my added new insight into what God created a woman and a wife to be—and the high value He places on her—I now studied submission again, but this time using the whole of Scripture. I learned God's kind of submission to my husband. The Holy Spirit helped me to rightly divide the Word on this subject, to gain a healthy balance. It was even more freeing when I learned what God expects of a husband, and that He also clearly teaches husbands and wives should be subject (or submissive) one to another (Eph. 5:21–25 AMP).

Then it all came together for me when I found Romans 8:29. That verse told me God wanted to conform me to His image. I likened that to all He had been trying to teach me. I could see the correlation: that God's molding and conforming was what I needed to become the woman God created me to be, and at the same time, to become a clear message of Jesus, an "epistle" known and read by others. I knew this was all about learning to live and love God's way, which goes against human nature. But that was my goal. I had no inkling then of how hard it would be or how much it would cost me in the long run to love God's way.

As I applied the Word, choosing God's way despite my circumstances, I could feel myself becoming uncompromisingly strong in my faith and more consistent in my daily living. I found my obedience was not only affecting change in me and improving my relationship with my husband but also positively influencing my ability to cope with every other area of my life. Gratefully, I was seeing less and less of Mr. Hyde. I believed Michael, Laura, and Steven, as well as Alex, were feeling the effects of my new life. I was no longer a "victim." I was free.

In short, with the Holy Spirit's guidance and the truth of the Word, I learned what God says about me, and my sense of self-worth was restored:

- The Bible taught me a healthy love for myself and others.
- My personal dignity was restored, as well as confidence to be my own person, as I learned that I am of great value to God.
- I learned my identity is not in my husband, and he is not responsible for my happiness; but rather, my identity is in God, who is my first source of true happiness.
- The power of God's truth in the Bible delivered me from all symptoms of codependency, which had enabled and given impetus to my husband's verbal and psychological abuse.
- The Bible opened to me a whole new way of living my life God's way, regardless of my circumstances.

During the months following my born-again experience, I recognized God was definitely softening Alex. But, of course, Mr. Hyde was always lurking, hiding under the surface. Nonetheless, I knew Alex had been taking notice of the changes in me since October, and I could tell he liked it.

Although Alex was happy with my total commitment to Jesus, he still did not show a desire to have his own personal relationship with Christ. Nevertheless, he appeared to admire my faith. He saw that when problems came up in our family or household, I would pray for or about them. He was seeing good results. Oftentimes Alex would ask me to pray about situations relating to his job. But nothing would test my faith and prayers like what happened next.

Summer had arrived, and warm days were beckoning the children to play outside. One early afternoon, Laura and Steven wanted to ride their tricycles on the public sidewalk. I put a meatloaf in the oven and planned to sit outside on the steps to watch the kids while it was baking.

Laura and Steven hopped on their tricycles and immediately started pedaling down the sidewalk. I called out: "Wait a minute, kids. Laura, just ride to the corner; then turn around and ride back. Watch your little brother. Make sure he turns around with you. Mommy will sit right here on the steps and watch you."

"Okay, Mommy," she said as she threw her arm up in the air to signal Steven to follow her.

Back and forth, back and forth, Laura rode her big tricycle with Steven following along on his little one. The sidewalk was lined with mature maples, with their branches extended over it like huge umbrellas. I could hear the older neighbor boys playing a little farther down the street, near the corner. They were laughing and jumping around on the bank in front of the home.

As Laura and Steven started from our house to once again ride to the corner, I ran in to check the meatloaf. I was in there only moments when I heard screaming.

I dashed out of the house and down the steps. Laura reached me first. She was terrified and crying so hard she could hardly speak but managed to get out the words, "Bees, Mommy. Bees!"

But Laura looked fine, just scared. I was confused for a moment. Then I looked up and saw Steven.

He was running toward me, and I gasped. His whole face, neck, and all bare parts of his body were black—covered with hornets. Not a feature on his face was visible.

"Oh, dear God, no! Help me! Can someone help me?" I screamed, running to Steven. I began scraping the hornets off his face first, with my bare hands. It was already swollen beyond recognition. "Oh God! No!"

Jane, my next-door neighbor, came running across the yards, shouting, "Oh my goodness, what can I do?"

"Jane, call the doctor ... Dr. Bunter ... He's on Kingston Boulevard ... Ask him what I should do. I'm going to put Steven in the tub with baking soda ... Oh God! ... Jane, I don't know what else to do!"

I carried Steven into the house and upstairs to the bathtub, stripped off his clothing, and scraped the remaining hornets off the rest of his body. Hornets were flying out of his clothing and buzzing all around us. I sponged him off with the cool baking soda water. *His little face ... it's grotesque ... The pain has to be excruciating ... Oh, this is terrible! ... Please, Jesus, please help my Stevie.*

Jane came in and yelled from the bottom of the steps to tell me the doctor said Steven needed emergency treatment. "He'll be right over ... He said five minutes," she assured.

"Thank God!" I called back to her.

Thank God he's so close. Stay calm, Alisha ... stay calm ... don't panic ... don't upset Steven. Jesus, please heal my boy ... please ... please.

"Poor thing ... poor, poor little guy," I muttered to myself.

I lifted my swollen son out of the tub, wrapped him in a big towel, then grabbed a sheet from the linen closet and wrapped it around the towel. I picked him up and carried him downstairs and laid him on the sofa in the living room.

"Can I help with anything else, Alisha?" Jane asked.

"Thanks. Could you take care of the one sting on Laura's ankle? Oh, and turn off the oven; then call Michael home from the Bennings ... Just keep an eye on them, Jane."

The doctor arrived only moments later. He took one look at Steven and immediately opened his medical bag, took out a syringe, and gave him a shot. Steven lay there whimpering.

"His condition is severe," he began. "Stings cover 75 percent of his body. I gave him an antitoxin, and I will wait here and watch him in case other measures are needed." I did not know what he meant and did not ask; I was praying and believing God would heal Steven and thanking God that Dr. Bunter had rushed over more quickly than I could have gotten Steven to a hospital. "We will watch the boy until I know he is out of danger. He must be watched constantly during the next six hours."

I placed my hand on Steven's head. His hair was still damp from the reckless sponging with the baking-soda water. *Thank God for Dr. Bunter. Lord, please let the antitoxin work.*

The memory of the incident replayed in my mind, and I recalled it for the doctor.

"Stevie had on little boxer shorts, a short-sleeved T-shirt, long socks, and cowboy boots. The hornets actually swarmed inside his clothing, even inside his underwear, socks, and boots, Doctor. Can you believe that?" I sighed.

The doctor only nodded, not taking his eyes off Steven's little swollen, limp body. We were watching and waiting for the first sign that the swelling was receding.

I wonder what town Alex is working in today. He says he doesn't preregister at a hotel when he is only staying overnight ... Wherever he stops for the day, that's where he looks for a hotel ... so I can't even phone him. What if Steven doesn't pass the six-hour wait? Oh God, I can't think about that! He will! I know he will! He has to!

Surprisingly, after only an hour or so, Dr. Bunter said, "The antitoxin looks like it's taking effect already, Mrs. Lance. The swelling is going down. This is wonderful. He has responded remarkably fast. I think it's safe for me to leave now. He's out of immediate danger. I'll be at my office, only five minutes away, if you need me before six o'clock; after that I'll be home. I've written my home number on this," he said, handing me a sheet from his prescription pad. "You call me anytime and let me know how he is. But I think he'll be fine now."

When the sixth hour was over, I could see the swelling was completely gone. Steven looked like my little boy again. *Thank You, Lord ... Thank You, thank You, thank You!*

I called Dr. Bunter to tell him the good news and let him know how grateful I was for his immediate emergency attention. I could hear the sigh of relief in his words: "Good. He'll be fine now."

Jane told me the incident had caused a lot of commotion in the neighborhood and that several neighbors had called to see how the children were.

The mother of one of the boys whose yard they had been playing in called again later and cleared up the mystery of what had happened. She told me she had not been aware of what the boys were doing until afterward. Now she explained what had taken place.

Standing on the six-foot bank in front of her home, her son and the other boys had been throwing rocks at a hornet's nest hanging on a large maple branch extended over the public sidewalk where Laura and Steven had been riding their tricycles.

"Seeing that the stones had loosened the nest and it was ready to fall, the boys yelled, 'Run!' They all scattered away from it … and so did your daughter, but," her voiced cracked, "I understand your little boy must not have heard them and didn't respond quickly enough. He was sitting on his bike right under it." She paused as though tears were collecting in her throat. "The hornets swarmed him. The boys said your little ones arrived at that very spot exactly as the nest began to fall. I'm so sorry."

My heart ached at the memory of Steven's blackened, hornet-covered face, and the picture of his swollen, grotesque-looking features. I prayed he would not remember it.

When Alex came home the next evening and listened to the story, he felt bad that Steven had to suffer such pain. I did not understand why the hornets had been allowed to attack my son, but there was no doubt in my mind that God had saved his life through Dr. Bunter's quick response and treatment.

Over the years, Alex's ambition and hard work to succeed in his career had not only paid off monetarily, but he had also been recognized as Salesman of the Year at an all-industry conference. But after eight years with the company, Alex was notified that he was being transferred out of state. He wanted to stay in town, but he was told the company needed him to expand another sales territory—and the relocation was non-negotiable. This move would be harder than the others made in town, because I would be leaving Nora as well as being far away from family and other friends.

Nonetheless, immediately upon notice, we put our house on the market. Alex and I spent two unsuccessful weekend trips to the new area to house hunt. We found ourselves down to the wire again the next weekend.

House-hunting all day Saturday had been futile. It was now Sunday, the last day we had to find another house before having to vacate our home. By three o'clock in the afternoon, we were discouraged and felt we had no choice but to shift our focus to finding a house or an apartment to rent.

We went back to our hotel room to concentrate on the newspaper rental ads. Alex and I were ready to check out of our hotel and run down the selected rentals when suddenly I felt impressed to say, "Alex, before giving up on a house to buy, let's pray about this. God knows exactly where our new home is."

"Yes. Okay, honey, let's pray."

We got down on our knees together, held hands, and Alex asked me to pray. I began speaking aloud, telling the Lord what He already knew: that we had exhausted our efforts, but that I believed He knew exactly the home that would meet our family's needs and our price range. I ended by praying simply, "Lord, please lead and guide us now."

Only moments after prayer, an idea came to Alex to call one of the builders in the city, who might have a new spec home or know of a vacant house for sale or rent. The idea seemed rather farfetched. But Alex thought it might be our answer, and I encouraged him to go ahead. Under my breath I said, "Thank You, my Jesus; I know You will lead us."

Alex literally flipped through the telephone directory yellow pages of building contractors, randomly selected a builder, and dialed the number listed. The builder himself picked up the line. Lo and behold, that builder was planning to sell his own personal home but had not yet listed it with a realtor! Within the hour, we viewed it. Not only was it perfect for us, but also it was within our price range. Our purchase offer was accepted, and we signed the contract.

The builder was flabbergasted by the way it had all happened. Alex and I were amazed and grateful. In fact, Alex could hardly contain himself on the long drive home. He felt good because he had acted on that idea and believed, as did I, that it had been given to him by God.

The new home was located in the country, ten miles outside the city. The kids loved it. There was no racetrack nearby, so Alex was always home evenings. Now he spent his free time working around the house and yard. Over the months, he worked hard and sales increased dramatically. I found that my country isolation offered precious time alone with God to continue studying His Word.

Soon my fourth pregnancy was confirmed. I was thrilled, because I had always wanted four children. But the sad interruption to our new joy came only too soon. I carried my baby only five months when the contractions started. While lying in my hospital bed, I laid my hands on my tummy and dedicated my unborn child to God. A short time later, I asked God to fill my emptiness.

I was hardly recovered from the loss of our baby when, after only eight months, Alex's company ordered another non-negotiable transfer. This time we would have to move from the Midwest to the East Coast. Alex and I discussed the pros and cons of relocating again. I was pleased when he asked me to pray with him about the situation. After joint prayer, Alex made the decision to resign his job and return to our hometown.

Part 3
Grace upon Grace

Chapter 12

A New Dimension

Alex and I were learning that God is interested in our everyday practical needs and will lead and guide us regarding important decisions to be made if we pray and ask Him to do so. I was especially pleased when my husband requested that I join him in prayer for this last big job decision. It offered me more than a glimmer of hope for his conversion to Christ. He was not only showing respect for me and my faith, but he was also placing confidence in the God to whom I prayed.

We were all happy with Alex's decision, knowing we were going home. The following Sunday, our country home was listed "For Sale by Owner" in the newspaper. It was March, and the area had a big snowfall on Saturday; it was still snowing on Sunday when we left for church. Since we did not think prospective buyers would be driving to the country looking for a house on such a day, we decided to stop in town for breakfast.

When we returned, the phone was ringing as we walked into the house. Unbelievably, a couple wanted to view our home. Forty-five minutes later, two couples got out of a late-model car. The men instantly walked to the back to see the garage, and the ladies came in the front door to view the house. We all met in the breezeway between the two; one gentleman asked his wife if she liked the house, and she said she did. He told her he liked the garage area and said, "We'll buy it!"

Alex and I were once again dumbfounded. It was then we learned Alex's heading on the ad, "Four-Car Garage," is what had attracted an Indy 500 champion race-car driver. He and his wife did not question our asking price, and there was no negotiation for terms and possession. Everything was agreed upon. His wife did talk him into at least looking at the inside of the house. After they did so, we signed the purchase contract.

Alex took off work the next day to drive home to interview with another company and to look for a house to rent until we could later check out the real estate market.

In a nutshell, we sold our home, found one to rent, packed, moved, and Alex began his new job, all within a month, and did not even skip a paycheck. I knew God had answered our prayers. Alex knew it too.

Once we moved into our rented home, we intended to take a breather from the whirlwind of the last eight months.

The Bible continued to be my "mirror," and at the same time, it checked me when my actions and reactions did not line up with what my daily study was telling me. Little by little, day by day, as I made right choices to react to difficult situations God's way instead of my own, I gained more self-control, especially with Alex.

One Saturday afternoon soon after we were settled into our rented home, my friend Joann telephoned to tell me about a small group of Christians from all different denominations who regularly met on Sunday afternoons very near our home.

"What kind of service is it?" I asked, curious.

"I only know that they pray and study the Bible together. And I know they believe God still heals people today."

"Do they believe as we do, Joann? I mean ... in Jesus Christ? I hope they're not one of those fanatical religions!"

"I know a Catholic couple who attend. If it were some far-out group, I don't think they'd be part of it. I understand the people are wonderful, Alisha. Do you think you'd want to go tomorrow?"

"It sounds interesting. Thank you, Joann. I'll call you in the morning and let you know."

Immediately I told Alex about the group and said, "I'd like to go. I'd like you to go too. What do you think?"

He had a suspicious look on his face.

"You don't know anything about those people. You do whatever you want. But I'm not going."

I took little Steven with me and met Joann at the meeting, and the three of us were warmly greeted at the door by a man who introduced himself as Judge Stahl and shook our hands. He had a hearty laugh and a kind of contagious joy, I thought, as I watched him greeting others he obviously knew with a big hug and "praise the Lord!" I found out later that he was a practicing judge in the city. We found seats, and the people sitting nearest us introduced themselves.

After prayer and group singing, we listened to a tape recording. A Catholic priest was talking about the miraculous physical healings as well as spiritual healings taking place in the lives of clergy and Catholic laypersons and, specifically, professors and students on the Notre Dame University campus.

I am not overly suspicious, but, on the other hand, I am not gullible either. So after becoming born again, it became my habit to prove by the Bible everything spiritual or religious that I was hearing on Christian radio programs, to make sure it lined up with what God says. What I was hearing on the tape recordings would be no exception.

To my delight, immediately following the taped testimonies, the man who was leading the group did that for me as he invited us to open our Bibles to Scriptures regarding miraculous physical healings in the four Gospels. We read them, and he expounded on each one. I had previously read all these particular Scriptures at one time or another, but reading them now brought new understanding.

Little by little, the leader's words seem to fade from my hearing and consciousness as my heart and spirit absorbed all the Scriptures, especially the words of Jesus Himself, about healing. I found myself feeling as though I were locked in with God alone, reasoning all this out with Him. I considered that Jesus claimed the healings and other mighty works He did were all done only according to His Father's will. So then it made perfect sense to me that divine healing definitely must be the will of God for His people today as well.

Now once again my mind was conscious that I was not alone. My eyes perused the room then settled again on the leader standing at the podium, and I listened. He pointed out that we Christians today are as important to Jesus Christ as those He healed during His ministry on the earth, that miraculous healing according to the Father's will is what Jesus preached as "the full gospel" and what Jesus commissioned His followers to preach to the ends of the earth.

Then the leader directed us to turn to another Scripture from the Old Testament, Isaiah 53, stating that Jesus Christ had fulfilled this verse on the cross; and my heart leaped within me as he read aloud: "He *was* wounded for our transgressions, He *was* bruised for our iniquities: the chastisement of our peace *was* upon Him; and with His stripes we are healed" (v. 5).

I read and re-read that verse. It stood to reason that God had even tried to tell us through the inspired writings of the Old Testament that we could expect, in His time, that Christ would pay the price for our complete salvation, including our healing.

Slowly my eyes and ears drifted from the speaker's words again, and I reasoned with God to better understand. I felt as though my mind were being cleared of cobwebs. And I recognized something significant about healings in the Gospels; that is, in several cases Jesus commented on the healing recipients' own faith: that *their faith* had healed them, that their healing had been done unto them according to *their faith,* and, in fact, that Jesus had *marveled* at the *faith* of some. With others it appeared their healings were done simply because of His compassion and mercy. So it seemed reasonable to assume that receiving their miracle healing was dependent on their faith working with the faith of Jesus.

However, there was also one qualifying factor that could not be ignored. Jesus had already taught that He did nothing in His ministry except what the Father told Him. Spiritually, I understood that while active faith was important for one praying for healing, receiving healing was primarily based upon what our all-knowing God's will was for an individual's life. It made perfect sense to me.

More understanding came, based not only upon the Scriptures about divine healing, but also based upon other scriptural truths I recalled that were simple, plain, and easily understood; truths such as, "God is no respecter of persons" and "Jesus, the same yesterday, today, and forever." For me, recollection of those facts brought everything into perspective and made the case for divine healing today virtually a no-brainer. God is God, and He does not change.

Metaphorically speaking, it seemed as though the scales had fallen from my eyes or blinders had been removed. The Spirit of truth was stirring within me and now my thoughts were racing: *I remember the times before I was born again when I believed God had intervened more than once and changed the negative outcome of a physical crisis to a positive one. I've always been grateful, but now I know for sure that it was not because I had great faith; rather it was God's compassion and mercy for me that moved divine healing into action! Through this small group of people whom I don't even know, I'm fully persuaded by the Holy Spirit and God's Word that divine healing is for people today as part of the full gospel of our salvation. No believer should remain blind to this truth. Clearly I can see from Scripture that divine healing is the demonstrated compassion of Jesus for His people everywhere—and in my opinion, His full gospel of salvation should be preached from every pulpit. After all, the Bible's words are not written on a page simply to teach us church history, to learn about what our God "used to do" for His believers. He is a just God, who will do the same for all of us, if it is our all-knowing Father's will and plan for us. As believers, we should expect healing in our lives.*

The reality of all those verses in the Gospels, along with the one from Isaiah 53, "with His stripes we *are* healed," brought the promise of healing to the present for me. That day divine healing became a viable promise for me. Spiritually, that truth was solidified in my mind, written on my heart, and implanted deep in my spirit. For me, it was common sense to believe that Jesus had never stopped healing according to the Father's will down through the ages —even today.

My private thoughts settled. In the end, I could understand that I, too, could receive divine healing in the name of Jesus if I truly believed and if it was the Father's will, based upon what He already knew His purpose and plan was for me. That was comforting to know, and it took the struggle out of my hands.

Suddenly I was again conscious of the group of people I was sitting among. I thought about the fact that this was a different religious gathering from any I had known. The people's faces glowed with obvious happiness in knowing the Lord. There was much joy as some shared personal testimonies, and we heard responding words of "praise the Lord" coming from not only the judge but also intermittently from people behind and all around us. I had not heard that expression since the day I was born again, when Nora had spoken it. The praise and worship and singing seemed free and joyous. I liked it.

Before the close of the meeting, the gentleman leading the group asked if anyone was in need of prayer. Several requested prayer for the salvation of their loved ones and for physical healing for either themselves or others. I watched and listened and prayed right along with the group.

When the meeting ended, several people introduced themselves and invited us to join them again. Each one appeared to be very much like my friend Nora, possessing that same quiet, pleasant demeanor. Among them was the Catholic couple Joann knew, and we also met several other Catholics and Protestants from mainline denominations, who briefly shared their personal testimonies of having the experience of being born again. Until then Joann and Sister Miriam had been the only Catholics I knew personally who had experienced what I had.

I was still curious about these people and had the opportunity to ask one of the women how their group had started. She explained that it was a gathering of people who had been acquainted with the leader from attending the Full Gospel Businessmen's Fellowship dinner meetings. "He is an officer of the local chapter and a wonderful Christian," she said. "The judge is too.

"This isn't a church per se," she went on. "We are all from different Catholic parishes and Protestant denominations. We attend our own churches on Sunday mornings and gather here for Bible study, prayer, and fellowship. We're just people who love the Lord Jesus, and we're very pleased to have you with us this afternoon, Mrs. Lance," she concluded with a warm smile.

Eventually I would come to understand that God the Holy Spirit had been going before me, making a way for me to be in the right place at the right time to meet the right believers to help me take the next step in my spiritual growth. I was learning that the full gospel of Jesus Christ encompasses all I need as a believer: He is ever the same — His dependable character and His unchanged ministry. I did not know how or where I would be led next, but I believed God was taking me on a spiritual journey toward His purpose for my life — my destiny.

Later that evening after I tucked the children in for the night, I shared with Alex my experience at the meeting and my newfound faith in the Bible verses for miracle healing. I told him about the judge and some of the lovely Christians I had talked with. He listened but made no comment.

* * *

It was June 1968. The family had had a restful three months, but now it was time to begin house hunting again. Alex and I began searching the real estate ads to purchase a home before school started, but to be honest, I dreaded another move.

We followed up on a newspaper listing, and our family made a trip across town to view the house on the outside before making an appointment to see the inside. We liked the area, but having quickly rejected that house, I continued driving slowly while we scrutinized the rest of the houses on that block, until reaching the corner stop sign. Looking to the left, I spotted a For Sale sign in front of a house on the adjoining street. I drove to it and stopped. All of us really liked the outside.

It was a large, stately, two-story white colonial with green shutters. It had a big front porch with white pillars. A mature oak stood at the top of the steeply banked front yard. I could already imagine electric Christmas candles in each of its long-paned windows and a lighted Christmas tree in the large front window.

As the family stood on the sidewalk viewing the exterior, I had an eerie feeling, a kind of knowing inside that this was our home. I figured it must be my imagination, since I had no idea what the interior was like, or, for that matter, did not even know if we could afford such a house. I said nothing to Alex. However, I could not shake the feeling. We made an appointment to view the inside that very afternoon.

We gasped as we stood in the large foyer. The ceilings were ten feet high. The house had natural woodwork and hardwood floors. Double French doors framed the foyer, opening on the right to the living room and on the left into the dining room; and another door led into a very outdated kitchen. After we viewed the rest of the house, the real estate agent told us it was a one-owner home and showed us an old, yellowed newspaper clipping with a photograph and description of the fifty-year-old house featured as the 1918 Decorator Show House in our city. It had been well cared for, but it was in the original state as when built.

Alex led me to a corner and whispered, "Let's buy it! We'll remodel the kitchen and bathrooms, and you'll do wonders with your decorating. Let's make an offer now! Remembering the feeling I had about the house initially, I had no problem agreeing.

Driving home, I smiled as I remembered the thought that came the instant we stood in front of the house. *So then, it wasn't my imagination after all! Thank You, my Jesus.*

On July 1, 1968, we moved into the house. While I was unpacking, my left eye began bothering me. It felt as though there were something in it all the time. My mother urged me to see an eye doctor. But I figured it would eventually go away.

Gradually the vision in my left eye became blurred. I tried over-the-counter eye medications and waited a couple of weeks, hoping it would clear up. But the medications did not help. The blurring continued, and then my eye became sore.

My next-door neighbor, an ophthalmologist's wife, visited me several times a week, and one day I told her about my problem. She encouraged me to talk with her husband. He referred me to a Dr. James Long, an eye-disease specialist.

Dr. Long thoroughly examined my eyes and made a diagnosis of uveitis. Only my left eye had been affected, but unfortunately, I had waited too long; the bacteria in my left eye had built up considerably, and Dr. Long said that it could spread to my right eye. I was shocked that he wrote a prescription for thirteen cortisone tablets to be taken each day, along with eyedrops to be administered four times a day.

"It's at a chronic stage. We need to get that infection arrested," the doctor said. "I need to see you twice a week. We'll see how it responds to the medication."

He explained that the medication would arrest the disease, but that I would need to be on a maintenance dosage of cortisone for the rest of my life.

"The rest of my life?"

"Yes. We can control the disease with medication, but there is no cure for uveitis," Dr. Long said, "We're working on it."

He further explained that this disease carried the risk of blindness.

"But, Dr. Long, how did I get this disease? I haven't had a recent virus or anything."

"I can't tell you what caused this, Mrs. Lance. It is unfortunate, but hopefully we can get it arrested for now and then keep it that way."

After sharing Dr. Long's diagnosis with my physician neighbor, he told me that Dr. Long headed a team of researchers at the state university hospital, seeking out a cure for uveitis. I felt assured that I was in good hands.

I settled into a mind-set of doing whatever I had to do to save my vision. And I prayed. I did not allow my eye disease to slow me down. My days were filled from sunrise to sundown. Michael and Laura had a lot of playmates in this new neighborhood, and Steven met a friend his age. They were having the time of their lives! My schedule was hectic with the remodeling my father began, with all my household chores, and with the children's needs. I managed to fit in my decorating projects, because I enjoyed them so much and regarded them as therapeutic for my daily stress.

In September Michael started second grade, and Laura entered kindergarten, attending the morning session. Our kids loved walking to and from school with their neighborhood playmates and the new friends they had made in their classes.

One beautiful fall afternoon, I was cleaning in the sunroom when I heard Michael calling at the door. Opening it, I said, "Hi, honey. How was school today?"

"Okay," he said in little more than a whisper.

"Michael, do you feel okay?"

"Yeah," he said.

"Honey, after you change your clothes and do your chores, will you take Stevie outside in the yard with you for a little while?"

"Okay!" he answered, bounding up the steps.

When he came downstairs, he walked into the sunroom and sat down.

"Honey, is there anything wrong?" I worriedly asked.

"No-o-o-o-o." He clearly had something on his mind.

"Is there anything you want to tell Mother?"

He got up and walked close to me, and I reached out and pulled him into my arms, thinking maybe he just needed a hug. He hung on to me and leaned his head into my chest. *He's so sweet ... such a good kid. I wonder what he's thinking. He's always seemed so much older and wiser than his years. Just bless him today, Lord.*

I broke from our hug and looked down at my black-haired, handsome little guy who had just turned eight. Ruffling his hair a little, I smiled at him. Michael looked up at me and smiled.

"Mommy, I want Jesus to come into my heart ... like He came into your heart."

I gasped in surprise. *When did he decide this?*

Michael was smart, thoughtful. I knew if he had made that decision, he had given it a lot of thought before telling me. Then I quickly answered, "Michael, honey, Jesus wants that too. Would you like to ask Him right now?"

"Yes ... " his voice trailed to a whisper.

"Sweetheart, we can kneel down right here in front of the sofa and talk to Jesus."

"I don't know what to pray," he said.

"Well, would you like Mother to pray and you can say the words after me?"

"Okay."

We knelt down on the floor, and I watched Michael bow his head with such sweet reverence. I began to pray, with Michael repeating my words. My heart was so touched hearing my little boy humbly asking Jesus to forgive him of all his sins, and as he went on repeating my words: "... and please come into my heart, Jesus ... and live in my heart forever." We knelt in silence for a few minutes, my arm still around his shoulder.

"Michael," I softly said, and he lifted his head to look into my face, "you have a Savior and a friend, honey, and He'll always be with you to help you."

"Yeah," he whispered.

"You know when Jesus came into my heart, and you know He's always with me. And now, He's always with you too—forever!"

Michael responded with a big smile and his face bright and shining, and then cheerfully said, "Thanks, Mom!" and instantly was up off his knees and out of the room.

I remained on my knees, amazed at what had just transpired. *Thank You, Jesus. You said in the Bible, "Whosoever will humble himself as this little child ..."*

Alex had been taking notice of what was happening with answered prayer up to now, and he was obviously touched when I told him about Michael: that he was one happy little fellow after his prayer and said, "Thanks, Mom!" before he scampered off. Alex laughed and said, "Well, good; that's great!"

Although Alex's mood swings were present some days, his disposition was pleasant a good deal of the time. He was still drinking, and he had bought two thoroughbred race horses, so he spent a lot of time at the racetrack with his horses and trainer. I earnestly prayed that just as with Nora's husband, Ray, the time would come when Alex would no longer need to drink or gamble.

We continued going to church every Sunday as a family, just as we had for the last nine years, but Alex still showed no interest in committing his life to Christ. I did not speak with him about it either—I just prayed. We were not without problems, but I was no longer emotionally poised for the next tragedy to occur. Since 1966 I had been perfectly well until the uveitis, and my husband and I were getting along. Alex was still enjoying his new job. He established an outstanding sales record by the end of the year and was determined next year would be even better.

As the year came to a close, family life was good, and my hope was solid in Christ for my husband's conversion. Dwelling on the positive distracted my concerns about my eye disease. Besides, from the Bible I had become fully persuaded that my Lord Jesus could heal me as well as having saved me; I believed that nothing was impossible for God.

By Christmas Day, our big fifty-year-old colonial had been completely transformed. Alex, with young Michael's help, had painted the outside while I stripped wallpaper and painted the entire inside. My father's efforts were major, as he not only helped me wallpaper certain rooms, but he also worked tirelessly every day, with Alex's help only on weekends, to completely gut and remodel the kitchen and bathrooms.

Alex and I enjoyed updating the house together. Our Christmas tree stood in the sunroom in front of the large front window, and an electric candle lighted each window in the house, just as I had imagined the first day I saw it. Alex watched and listened with an admiring smile as the kids and I sang happy birthday to Jesus and blew out the candle I had placed on top of His cake to remind my children *who* we were celebrating on Christmas Day.

* * *

I felt expectant as New Year 1969 began. I was full of hope. It was obvious to me that God had been with me and my family in a special way over the past two-plus years. There had been extraordinary answers to prayer that had changed our circumstances—and changed them fast! Since I had become born again and committed to Christ and His Word, our marriage and family life had been far from perfect, but it had been much better. It appeared that Alex's dark side, Mr. Hyde, had been miraculously stayed as though by an unseen hand. And I lived with hope that Alex would soon make his own commitment to Christ, and when he did, I believed I would never see Mr. Hyde again. Then not only Alex's life would be normal, but also our marriage and family life would be normal too.

However, all too soon my hope for Alex began fading. Although gratefully Mr. Hyde was not showing himself, after the time understandably needed to succeed at his new job, Alex made his two thoroughbreds his second priority, and all his free time was given to their needed care and attention. It seemed to me the horses were taking over his life. It was obvious that he was gambling on the races too and losing money, which made him angry with himself. Naturally his anger spilled over onto us, exhibited in various ways.

Slowly I slipped into a bout of self-pity and resentment, with nothing but negative thoughts about Alex bombarding my mind again: *He is more self-absorbed than before—just as unpredictable as he used to be—and gambling on the horses even more. If I want to buy a pet for the kids, pay for dance lessons for Laura or piano or swimming lessons for the kids, his decision is always, "No! We can't afford it." Oh really? But we can afford your horses?"*

I was so frustrated with Alex over all of this, I could not stand it! It was bad enough putting up with his difficult personality, but for my children to be shortchanged because of his horses was something else. I told myself and God, *I can't do this anymore!*

My anxiety was mounting daily. It was the last Sunday in January when my frustration, anxiety, and resentment got the better of me and I became angry. I was angry with Alex and angry with myself. By now my thinking was definitely out of whack, and I was back to square one, believing—and fearing—that Alex would never change. I was anxious and weary of waiting. I believed I could not go on in this marriage.

After Sunday dinner, I felt my anxiety building to the point where I wanted to cry and scream at the same time. It was about six o'clock in the evening when I slipped out of the room where the family was watching television and went upstairs to our bedroom.

Dropping to my knees at the foot of the bed, I poured my heart out to God in prayer: *Oh Jesus, what can I do about my life? I feel so alone in this marriage. Alex makes everything so hard. When are things going to change with him? Please, Lord, You are the only one I can turn to. If You want me to go on in this marriage, I need more of Your strength. I feel like such a weak Christian. I feel defeated again. I need more faith. I need more of Jesus.*

Instantly a beautiful peace came, and I felt silenced within. By now I knew this kind of peace was the very presence of God, and I was struck with a sense of awe—a deep reverence that humbled me, bringing me to repentance. *Forgive me, Jesus, for being so angry with Alex. It feels like I am the only "married" one in this marriage. It hurts so much, Lord, but forgive me for being so weak and giving in to my anger.*

I began to quietly sob, and it seemed all my emotional pain and anger was being flushed away with my tears. My nagging doubts and anxiety seemed to drain completely and were replaced by God's sweet peace within. I knew Jesus had once again forgiven me. He had cleansed me on the inside. But I felt something more than that. I felt love for my Lord fill me up until I felt wholly saturated inside with love for Him.

"I love you, Jesus," I whispered earnestly, repeating the words over and over. Then something extraordinary happened that with my logical mind, I found difficult to believe. For the first time in my life, the word *hallelujah* came from my lips as an involuntary utterance, and I began repeating it, feeling a higher level of praise for Jesus than I had known before.

All of a sudden, syllables began quietly rolling off my tongue and flowed. They sounded like a foreign language, beautifully melodic and smooth. But I had never spoken any other language besides English. I had studied Spanish in high school, but I knew this was not Spanish. *What is this, Lord? What's happening to me?* I was praising God in my mind and in my heart, and simultaneously questioning Him, while this strange language softly rolled off my tongue.

My knees seemed glued to the floor. I was fully submissive to God—to His presence—unable to move and seemingly unable to stop speaking, bewildered by this language but not wanting it to stop. Unbelievably my spirit felt as though it had been lifted up and was soaring beyond the confines of my room. I do not know how long I continued praising Jesus in my mind and heart, still conscious of the strange syllables tumbling from my lips.

Abruptly they stopped. I felt silenced within again as peace seemed to gather itself around me like a warm robe. Then …

"If you will obey My voice and keep My commandments, I will give you the desires of your heart."

The words startled me. They sounded like Scripture. They had shot through my mind, and although they were not audible, they were authoritative, as though someone standing right next to me had given me a non-negotiable directive.

What's happening to me, Lord?

Immediately I realized I had heard God's voice, and the peace I felt within gave me assurance that it was truly God who had spoken to me. The stillness in the room—the peace—felt so heavy and thick, as though I could gather it into my arms.

Just then Alex's heavy footsteps jarred my consciousness, and I realized that he was walking up the stairs. Still kneeling at the foot of our bed, I looked back over my shoulder and through the open door, just as he reached my line of vision. I felt self-conscious, wondering if he had overheard me.

He paused for a moment and turned to see me looking at him. We gazed silently at each other through the spindles of wood on the hall banister. Then, without a word, Alex turned and walked back down the stairs, as though he instinctively knew he should not intrude. He said nothing and asked me no questions that evening.

The next morning, Alex still said nothing and still had no questions about the incident the night before. I was grateful for that, because I could not have explained to him or anyone else what had happened. However, there was a quiet excitement within me. As my thoughts dwelled on my experience, for some strange reason, the story in the Bible about Cornelius, the Gentile Roman centurion, came to my mind. I did not know why, but I made a mental note to read it again sometime that day.

I found my mind reliving every detail of last night. I realized I had once again experienced something deeply spiritual and totally unexpected. I had no foreknowledge of such an experience, and I had never heard anyone I knew tell of anything like it—not my parish priest, not a minister on Christian radio, not even my former neighbor Nora, who shared her testimony with me. Nonetheless, I rejoiced in my mind, heart, and spirit because deep within I felt I had been given what I had prayed for: more faith to go on. And I felt certain that the presence of God the night before had caused something extraordinary to happen to me.

It had been wonderful but puzzling, especially that altogether phenomenal, utterly incomprehensible, fluent language that felt as though it had come from deep within me. There was no question. I was speaking a definite language, albeit, totally foreign to me. It had been mysteriously spiritual, although a bit scary, and too amazing and blessed to ignore. Like all that I had spiritually experienced that led me to be born again, this, too, had been so profound within me, I knew I could never deny it, even if my life depended upon it.

Also, because I knew this experience was from God, I knew I would find it in the Word. It was imperative that I find out from Scripture as quickly as possible just exactly what spiritual significance this experience held for my Christian life. I would not tell a single person about it until I had my answers.

I could hardly wait to get through my morning routine of preparing breakfast for five, getting Alex off to work, seeing the children off to school, and completing my necessary housework so I could start my Bible search.

When I began, I felt impressed to use my concordance to read Scriptures listed under "Spirit," looking into all the reference verses. Obviously the Lord knew I had a lot more to learn about the Holy Spirit. My only knowledge of the Spirit had come to me, as though automatic, at my salvation.

For example, even as a new believer, I knew the Holy Spirit was within me. I knew from the Bible that it was the Spirit of God Who had wooed me, or had drawn me, to Jesus Christ in the first place. And I knew that when I was born again, my spirit had come alive to know Jesus Christ as Savior.

I had already learned that the only way I or any believer could know that Jesus is the Christ was by divine revelation. This truth already had been made clear to me when Scripture told me how it had been revealed to Peter. When Jesus asked His disciples, "Who do you say [yourselves] that I am?" Simon Peter replied, "You are the Christ, the Son of the living God." Then Jesus answered him, "Flesh and blood [men] have not revealed this to you, but My Father Who is in heaven" (Matt. 16:15–17 AMP).

Admittedly, my understanding of the Holy Spirit was limited to His being the third person of the Holy Trinity and equal with the Father and Son. I simply did not understand God the Holy Spirit's extensive function in the world and in the church today, nor did I understand the extent of His function in each believer's life—even in my own life. I was soon to discover that the Holy Spirit's ministry was much more than my limited knowledge had grasped.

In the process of my search, just as the Lord had prompted earlier, I went on to read the Scripture about the Italian Gentile, Cornelius, in chapter 10 of the book of Acts. I recognized that God obviously had been watching Cornelius's life, because the Bible declares that Cornelius was "a devout man, and one that feared God with all his house, which gave much alms to the people, and prayed to God always" (Acts 10:2).

At once Scripture came to me as a reminder that *man looks on the outward appearance, but God looks on the heart.* I thought about the fact that our heavenly Father recognized Cornelius was a God-fearing man, and his prayers and his alms had been going up before the Lord. With that I reasoned that God must have looked upon Cornelius's sincere heart and liked what He saw. Obviously, having seen his heart, God orchestrated the miraculous circumstances by which Peter was sent to preach salvation through Jesus Christ to Cornelius.

Then I discovered something as Peter preached Jesus to Cornelius and those with him: "The Holy Spirit fell on all who were listening to the message. And the believers ... [the Jews] who came with Peter were surprised and amazed, because the free gift of the Holy Spirit had been bestowed and poured out largely even on the Gentiles. For they heard them talking in [unknown] tongues (languages) and extolling *and* magnifying God" (Acts 10:44–46 AMP).

I understood Peter and the Jewish believers recognized the evidence of the outpouring of the Holy Spirit upon Cornelius and his household as being the same they had received on the Day of Pentecost, because Cornelius and the others were also praising and worshipping God in unknown languages. Instantly I knew beyond a shadow of doubt that God also wanted me to recognize that while that prayer language was rolling off my own tongue Sunday night in my bedroom, I had been praising Jesus, *extolling and magnifying God*, like Cornelius and his household. My heart had felt saturated with thanksgiving, praise, and love for Jesus, just as their hearts must have felt.

I was awestruck by the story of Cornelius. Instantly a thought came that this detailed account should encourage non-Christians to believe that Jesus knows them, just as He had known Cornelius. His story proves the incredible and very great lengths God will go to in order to create His divine appointment with an individual whose heart sincerely cries out to know Him. Our living Lord does not miss a thing! Nothing is hidden from God!

Then I was struck with another thought about the Scripture describing the Day of Pentecost: *All we believers in Christ are no different in God's eyes from the 120 believers who were gathered in the Upper Room to tarry for the promise of the Father, just as Jesus had directed. Included in the 120 were Mary, the mother of Jesus, and the other women, when the Holy Spirit came upon them; and exactly as Jesus foretold, they were all empowered with the gift of the Holy Spirit and were extolling and magnifying God in unknown tongues. That and the other Scriptures about this are clear. I believe that same promised experience is for all believers! This is wonderful!*

At the end of the day, it was inspiring for me to realize that God the Holy Spirit had actually led me to re-read about God's visitation with Cornelius, as well as having opened to me so many other Scriptures about the Spirit. Now I understood that the Holy Spirit is not only the third person of the Trinity and equal with the Father and the Son, but He is also the power of the Godhead. His power notwithstanding, God the Holy Spirit never speaks about Himself; He always speaks about and glorifies Jesus.

My own experience was wonderful, and the substance of this Bible study proved to me its validity, purpose, and benefit to my Christian life and service to God; but more importantly, it reemphasized to me that God's Word stands as absolute truth—eternally. As a willing student, I had learned more about the Holy Spirit's functions in the world, in the church, and in a believer's life, assuring me that the love and promises Jesus gave believers who walked with

Him on Earth and throughout the New Testament, He still gives to believers today. He never changes.

That Sunday evening in my bedroom, I had not known enough to ask for His promise of this free gift of the Holy Spirit and my treasured prayer language, but I conclude that God, seeing my heart and knowing my need, shed His grace on me. In His love, He graciously answered my ongoing prayer to know God and His ways, and He heard my pleading that I needed more of Jesus. I knew that I knew that I had entered *a new dimension.*

* * *

It was bitter cold on the following Wednesday, but by afternoon the sun was shining brightly as I drove to Joann's house to drop off the children—Laura, who had already attended her half-day kindergarten class, and little Steven—while I kept my regular two o'clock eye appointment.

As I drove, I thought about what an exciting adventure my life had become since Jesus had come into my heart. Even though there were still some rough times, it was exciting for me to see how God gently guided me through to the other side of each one. Remarkable! Jesus always rescued me when I needed Him most. I remembered Nora's words, spoken two and a half years earlier: "Jesus loves you, Alisha. He sees your burden, and He will help you with it!"

This time it was my ever-worsening eye problem. Biweekly the doctor kept a close watch on my right eye, hoping to prevent it from becoming infected. After my last exam, the doctor had been discouraged. The bacteria was at its highest level, and he was talking about possibly injecting cortisone directly into my left eye, a drastic measure, I thought.

I realized that my examination was taking longer than usual. Dr. Long repeatedly shifted the special equipment with its light back and forth from my left to my right eye, and I started to get nervous. When he began concentrating on my right eye as much as my left, I feared that the bacteria had spread.

My fear got the better of me, and when I questioned him, he hushed me and said he would discuss his findings after he completed the examination. His evasiveness fueled my anxiety. I knew the disease could spread to the right eye and that blindness could occur if the bacteria did not respond to the cortisone, the only medication known to arrest the bacteria. Finally Dr. Long motioned for me to take the chair next to his desk.

From the beginning, I perceived him to be a no-nonsense physician. He was direct. I liked that. Never during the past seven months had he engaged me in small talk. I was pleased that each of his examinations had been so thorough, but I feared hearing the results of today's exam.

The doctor sat silently for a few moments with his eyes fixed on me. Then he smiled and made a comment that seemed completely out of character for him. He said, "Mrs. Lance, do you know another word for *hallelujah?*

I was startled. He had no way of knowing that precious word had been rolling off my own lips for the first time last Sunday night.

"What do you mean, Doctor?"

"Mrs. Lance," he said, still smiling, "there's not one trace of bacteria in your eyes!"

I was stunned.

"What's happened to it?" I asked. "Just last week you said the bacteria was at its highest level. How could the bacteria have disappeared so quickly?"

"I simply don't know what's happened," he answered, bewildered. "I've never seen anything like this happen with a uveitis patient, but you definitely have absolutely no bacteria in either eye."

"Dr. Long, you said this disease is incurable, that it could be arrested with treatment, but that I'd have to remain on a maintenance dosage of cortisone for the rest of my life."

"That's what I said, Mrs. Lance. And all I can say now is that you are a very fortunate young woman."

"Do you want to see me again … I mean, should I keep my Friday appointment?"

"Only if you have another problem with your eyes. As far as the uveitis, the bacteria is gone. There's nothing to treat medically."

I left the doctor's office in a daze.

Driving to Joann's home to pick up the kids, I began thanking Jesus. There in my car, I felt the same peace settle over me that I had felt in my bedroom only three nights before. Those strange syllables began rolling off my tongue, just as they had that night. Then I realized I had paid no attention to my eye problem since that Sunday night. Instantly I believed that Jesus had healed me of the eye disease that same night without my even realizing it.

I had not asked Him to heal me or baptize me with the Holy Spirit that night; I only pleaded for more faith—more of Jesus. But I had believed the Scripture that says God often does give us more than we know we need or can expect: "Now unto Him that is able to do exceedingly abundantly above all that we ask or think, according to the power that worketh in us" (Eph. 3:20).

When I arrived at Joann's, she met me at the door with a big smile. Bursting with joy, she flung the storm door open, put her arms around me, hugged and kissed me. With tears of joy in her eyes, she said, "Alisha, your eyes are healed! I know it! While I was praying for you this morning, I felt ... I knew you would find out today that you're healed!"

I was flabbergasted!

"Yes, Joann! Yes, the eye disease is totally gone!"

Joann had a guest that day. She introduced me to this lovely Christian woman whose name was Nora, ironically the same first name as the lady who had shared Jesus with me. This Nora was my senior, and to my delight, I learned she taught a Bible class at the Christian radio station in my area. She was exceptionally pretty, and seemed to radiate the joy of the Lord. I perceived her to be a real, genuine, intelligent, balanced Christian; and to my mind, she was a beautiful representative of Christ.

For some unknown reason, immediately I felt our meeting was another divine appointment for me and my lifelong friend and mentor, Joann. God knew exactly the right person with whom I could relate the details of my recent experience of receiving the Holy Spirit.

When I shared with her and Joann, Nora told us she, too, had been baptized in the Holy Spirit. After we went over all the Scriptures about receiving the Holy Spirit, Joann expressed desire for this promised gift of the Father also. We prayed for her, and she, too, received the Holy Spirit, with the evidence of speaking in tongues. It was an extraordinary experience for me to witness. I knew God had sovereignly intervened in my life again and led me to be in the right place at the right time to meet the right person—but also to bless my caring and loving Joann.

Nora told us that beginning in the mid-1960s, there had been a continuous worldwide outpouring of the Spirit upon millions of clergy and believers in all the mainline Protestant denominations as well as upon Catholic clergy and laymen. The reality that this same phenomenal experience given to New Testament believers was also given to Nora, Joann and me, and other Catholics and Protestants throughout America and the world was utterly astounding news.

That evening Alex listened to every detail about Dr. Long's examination and his medical determination that the uveitis was completely gone. He was genuinely happy with the news, saying, "That's great, honey. This is wonderful for you. It's a miracle!"

Then I filled him in on the fact that my miracle must have happened on Sunday night, without my having realized it, while I was praying in my bedroom, because something else extraordinary and also totally unexpected was happening to me as well. Puzzled, he asked what had happened.

When I shared the details with him about my having received the gift of the Holy Spirit, he did not pooh-pooh the whole thing as I considered he might. I briefly shared the Scriptures the Lord had led me to read that validated my experience.

Even though up to now, Alex had not indicated that he wanted to commit his own life to Christ, he never doubted my born-again experience was genuine; and he respected my commitment to Christ and my prayers. So now, he was again sincerely happy for me; and although he did not understand my experience completely, he believed every detail about it as well as the Scriptures I shared.

It was then he confessed that on Sunday evening when he had left the family room and passed through the foyer on the way to the kitchen, he heard what sounded like someone speaking in a foreign language coming from upstairs. He knew I was the only one up there. He was curious. That was when he walked up the stairs to check things out.

"I didn't understand what was going on," he said, "but when I saw you on your knees, I stopped... and as we stared at each other, somehow I knew God was involved in whatever was going on and ... well, I just sensed I should leave you alone."

* * *

There was an undeniable change in my spiritual walk in the following days. I was aware that supernatural things were happening to and for me. It was as though God had baptized me with a deeper level of love and compassion for others as well as a desire to serve Him. I found a Scripture that explained what I was feeling: "Such hope never disappoints *or* deludes *or* shames us, for God's love has been poured out in our hearts through the Holy Spirit Who has been given to us" (Rom. 5:5 AMP).

Also, I recognized that my prayer life was changing. Not only was I growing in my knowledge of the Lord and the Bible and becoming a stronger Christian, but also as I prayed in my new private prayer language for my own needs and interceded for the needs of others, my prayers were getting remarkable answers. Although before that memorable last Sunday in January, I had known I was totally committed to Christ and His Word, now with all the new truths I had learned, I was aware that I was becoming even more deeply devoted to the Holy Scriptures and beginning to witness more to others about the love of Jesus. It was obvious to me that this was the work and the power of the Holy Spirit within me.

I got excited when I read this passage of Scripture: "But as it is written, Eye hath not seen nor ear heard, neither have entered into the heart of man, the things which God hath prepared for them that love Him. But God hath revealed *them* unto us by His Spirit: for the Spirit searcheth all things yea the deep things of God" (1 Cor. 2:9–10).

As I learned to yield daily to the Lord, I was strengthened in my "inner man." However, by virtue of the simple fact that I live in a fallen world, there were always problems to face and difficult circumstances.

On and off, I was definitely facing the hard issues of life with Alex, but amazingly, even while they were happening to me, the effect of them seemed outside the perimeter of my inner man and did not touch the peace of Jesus I felt within. Although that made everything easier, it did not mean my flesh did not feel the stress, pressures, and pain of my circumstances. So surrendering myself wholly to Jesus and the guidance of the Holy Spirit each day now became instinctive for me.

Although just weeks before, my husband had been so happy about my experience of receiving the baptism in the Holy Spirit and my having received my miraculous healing from uveitis, he was again making things hard for me in various ways. I watched as he gave into his dark side in subtle ways, and I feared seeing Mr. Hyde again. If so, I wondered what I was going to do. I knew I could not live with Alex's abuse ever again. I knew God did not want me to live in an abusive marriage relationship.

By now I was on guard every day, hiding in my faith, hiding in every Bible truth I had learned, hiding in Jesus. Although it was still not easy for my flesh, I no longer tried to escape my difficult circumstances, because in them I knew I was learning my most valuable spiritual growth lessons, one of which would be my lesson in patience.

At this point, I recognized some of the characteristics of Mr. Hyde showing up as he tried to force his way back to dominate my husband. I prayed and prayed for Jesus to rescue Alex. However, I was experiencing an especially rough time, and my flesh was weakening again. My prayers became coupled with complaining about Alex: *He's wonderful for a while, Lord, and then in a flash, he's playing to his dark side again. He's been so much better for quite a while, as though he's trying hard to keep himself in check. And I know I've been better at obeying the Scriptures. But I'm so tired, Lord, and I have run out of patience. When is he going to change?*

I knew my spirit was strong, but my flesh was very weak. I went on to earnestly beg God to help me gain more patience or I did not think I could go on in this marriage. Suddenly words passed through my mind: *My daughter, you ask Me for patience. How can you learn patience unless you remain in a place where you can do nothing but be patient?*

Once again, those words were not audible, but they were powerful within me and left me feeling peaceful and encouraged because I knew God was seeing it all. He knew what I was going through, and He was with me.

Now my hope was energized by more faith for the healing of my marriage. I believed the Spirit of truth would show me exactly how to walk it out with patience and that He would be with me every step of the way. Emotionally I had been fortified by the Holy Spirit's words of knowledge for me about patience, and they would help me to keep on keeping on, leaning hard on the Lord. From that time on, God's words, as though branded on my heart, readily came to mind whenever I needed to be conscious of having patience with Alex, my children, or in any other situation.

Chapter 13

A Completed Family

Good was definitely working behind the scenes in our family. My husband's personality was a dichotomy; in the days following my plea to God for patience to go on, yet again, Alex became a "mellow fellow." He appeared more like my lovable Dr. Jekyll. He was more attentive to the children and me. Alex, the quintessential successful businessman, although self-absorbed, often absent, and living his own life, was obviously amazed by not only the emotional and spiritual restoration in my life but also the miraculous physical healing he could not ignore. Even though he did not fully understand what had happened to me that Sunday night when I received the gift of the Holy Spirit and he heard me speaking in another language, he still appeared impressed by it. He even seemed to enjoy taking part in conversations about God with Christian friends who visited our home.

In the process of searching the Bible to learn more about my recent experience, I studied 1 Corinthians again. There Paul teaches in chapters 12 through 14 about the nine gifts of the Holy Spirit: what they are; why they are to be greatly valued by believers, personally, in ministry to others and in the church; how they benefit the believer as well as the church; how they should operate in and through believers; and the proper practice of ministering these gifts in the church.

Paul's last words in chapter 12 exhort believers to earnestly covet the gifts, and then he adds something interesting: "Yet show I unto you a *more excellent way.*" Right in the middle of his teaching on the gifts of the Holy Spirit is chapter 13, in which Paul goes on to explain what he means by the "more excellent way." I gleaned from that chapter that the gifts are to be desired but should be ministered *from a heart of love* to others, since Paul makes it clear that love is the greatest expression of God. Immediately I thought that the nine fruits of the Spirit, which are the characteristics and behavior of Christ that Paul teaches about in the book of Galatians, chapter five, coupled with the nine gifts of the Spirit, which I thought of as being the power tools of the Holy Spirit, would be the perfect combination to minister the more excellent way in love.

Now I was in pursuit of learning more about practicing the more excellent way by love. Also I was pursuing truth about something else to which I had been previously ignorant: that is, hearing the voice of God. I knew I had heard God's voice that Sunday night in my bedroom. After that I recall wondering if it were possible for me to actually *expect* to hear God's voice as needed whenever I prayed for direction. My search of the Scriptures gave me my answer.

I dared to believe, with my simple faith, the many Scriptures that run throughout the Bible about hearing God's voice: *Listen for* the voice of God, and *listen to* the voice of God; *hear* the voice of God; *hearken to* the voice of God; and *obey* the voice of God. It only made sense to me that if the Bible commanded God's people to *listen, hear, hearken,* and *obey* His voice, then if I believe the Bible, I should expect to hear God's voice for my specific guidance when I pray. After all, I reasoned, why would I want to believe in a God who does not hear my prayers, speak His direction, and guide my way? I believe in the *living* God, not a *dead* one! Then, my answer had come experientially when I prayed for patience, when I was ready to give up again on my marriage. Those words from the still small voice of God had taught me a valuable spiritual growth lesson I knew I would never forget. They would benefit me forever.

I also was learning in that study more about the importance of being in God's will, that it was my only "safe harbor." Although I prayed that Alex and I could live harmoniously, I had no clue about

278

what would happen from one day to the next with my husband's changeable personality. So I also prayed constantly to be in God's will. I agree with a statement my adult daughter made years later about facing the unknown, when we do not know what tomorrow will bring. Laura said, "The only time the unknown feels safe is when we are in the will of God."

Sometimes it was a fierce struggle for me to remain in God's will, because it was always easier to react to Alex my own way instead of biting my tongue and choosing to react God's way. But the Holy Spirit helped me to yield time after time. I vividly recall when I came to the conclusion that God's way was not only the best way for me, but also the only way that would keep me in His will. Another valuable spiritual growth lesson finally was learned: obedience to the will of God brings not only His presence, but also His protection.

With February came snow and lots of it! The children and their neighborhood playmates built a big snowman in our front yard. They laughed and played in the snow after school. One day I watched with delight from the window — all of them lying on their backs, making snow angels by moving their arms in arcs. They popped up giggling at one another's angels. The entire yard had a pattern of angels over it, and the steep hill in front of our house made for a good slide. The kids were happy, I was happy, and Alex was happy — on and off again.

Early in the month at a Christian Literature Crusade luncheon meeting, surprisingly, I met Judge Stahl again. I had first met him in that small fellowship Joann and I had attended in April, the year before. We were seated at the same table. Curious, I asked the judge about himself and when he became such a bold witness for Christ.

He explained he had been a practicing attorney before becoming a judge. At the age of twenty-five, he held the office of assistant attorney general for our state. He also had been a United States senator for two terms. He told me he had served in World War II as a major in the Air Corps Paratroop Command. He laughed and added, "Oh-h-h-h ... but that was back in my evil days!" He told me his lifestyle had changed drastically since he became a Christian.

He was so open and enthusiastic as he said, "I've got a fire burning inside me to serve Jesus Christ ever since I received the baptism of the Holy Spirit."

"Me, too, Judge!" I said. "I just recently had that experience. It's wonderful! That's my desire too. But I don't know how to serve God exactly. I'm open to whatever way He chooses to use me that will bring honor to Him."

In conversation I learned he knew my former employer, and he knew her husband, who worked in government, as well; the judge had a lot of respect for the programs and services for the mentally ill written into state law because of her efforts. It was nice to share that little connection with Judge Stahl. Although I was at the luncheon only to do my friend Joann the favor of taking her place, by now I believed meeting the judge again was another divine appointment for me. But more than that, I felt God had a reason that was bigger than just the two of us meeting.

That evening I told Alex about seeing the judge again and what I had learned about him. I liked the judge. He was a happy Christian and an interesting man.

To our surprise, Judge Stahl phoned a few days later to invite Alex and me to attend the local Full Gospel Businessmen's Fellowship International monthly dinner meeting the upcoming Friday. As an officer of the chapter, the judge told us the guest speaker was a Roman Catholic and a professor at a Catholic university. Alex agreed to go.

When we arrived in the banquet hall of this upscale hotel, people were moving about the room greeting and hugging one another before dinner, and Judge Stahl used that time to walk Alex and me around to the speaker's table to introduce us to the other chapter officers and their wives.

Kevin Ranaghan, the speaker, shared his personal testimony of being born again in Christ, including his experience of being baptized in the Holy Spirit with the evidence of speaking in an unknown language. Alex was hearing from another person about these same extraordinary experiences his wife had had. The speaker told about the transformation for good in his personal life and about his intense desire to serve God and others since receiving the Holy Spirit. He also spoke of a Lutheran minister who had been a great inspiration to him.

"His name is Harald Bredesen," he said. "Pick up the book *They Speak with Other Tongues,* and you'll read about him there. I highly recommend it to those of you interested in this spiritual experience." I intended to buy that book for Alex.

That gathering made a profound impression on Alex and me. Most people lingered afterward, and Judge Stahl introduced us to several of them. Their kindness touched us.

Driving home, Alex commented that he had never seen so many happy people gathered in one place. He enjoyed talking to other businessmen who were Christians. Alex was taking a genuine new interest in spiritual things now. We looked forward to future monthly meetings.

Judge Stahl invited Alex to attend the Full Gospel Businessmen's prayer breakfast the third Saturday in March. Alex was impressed again. At that time, he had learned that the FGBFI chapter in his hometown would hold its prayer breakfast the next Saturday. To my surprise, he planned to attend. That Saturday morning he was up at five o'clock, left the house at six, and drove fifty miles to make it to the seven o'clock meeting. I was optimistic.

Furthermore, I had been studying the more excellent way of God and trying to put it into practice with Alex and others, as well as getting to know from the Bible that many times God is practical in His dealings with people. I could understand why God would lead Alex to meet other businessmen with whom he could identify and have rapport—and perhaps develop friendships that could ultimately lead to His conversion to Christ.

Although he did not share his thoughts with me, there was no doubt in my mind that Alex wanted to commit his life to Christ. I hoped it would be today. I prayed for him throughout the morning and into the afternoon.

"Alisha!" Alex finally called, opening the back door. "Where are you, honey?"

"Right here," I said, entering the foyer where Alex was hanging up his coat. "How was the meeting?"

"Good," he said, closing the closet door.

"Do you have anything to tell me about?"

"Yeah ... plenty. Honey, I went forward today for prayer ..."

"Oh, how wonderful, Alex!" I interrupted excitedly.

"Let me finish," he scolded softly. "Something unusual happened to me."

"What do you mean ... unusual?"

"Well ... at the meeting some men laid their hands on my shoulders when they prayed for me. I didn't feel anything especially spiritual happening to me then. But after the meeting, a fellow named Bill Scofield invited me to his home, along with Bob Landon and another guy," he said, pausing.

I was so grateful to hear that because I had previously met Bob and Bill at the Christian radio station where they served on the board of directors. They were respected businessmen and leaders in the Christian community and known to be honorable representatives of Christ. God could not have used more committed Christian businessmen or more spiritually mature servants of His to minister to my husband.

"How nice, honey. Go on!" I urged anxiously.

"Anyhow, we talked for a while, and then they asked if I would like them to pray with me. Naturally, I said yes. They laid hands on me again and began to pray ... Then everything got quiet and something happened, something real strange happened ... " His voice lowered to almost a whisper and his eyes glazed over with a faraway look. "The third man—the one I didn't know—began to speak words about me ... He told me things about myself he could never have known! Things no one knows—not even you. Only God. It had to be God. It was definitely God, honey. It was wonderful."

At once I felt impressed that Alex had received a word of knowledge ministered through that Christian man—one of the nine gifts of the Spirit that I had learned about in my study of 1 Corinthians.

I watched my husband now. His face had a sweet expression. He seemed at peace, happy. *Finally, after all these years of praying, God had His own time and way to woo my husband by His Spirit.*

His face fell slightly sullen.

282

"Alex ... honey, are you disappointed? Did you expect something else?" I asked softly, putting my arm around his shoulder.

"I don't know ...," he said quietly, even humbly. Then his eyes brightened. "I think it's pretty wonderful!"

Tears filled my eyes. "So do I, Alex. So do I."

Alex appeared at peace—content—in his work and in his life during the days following that meeting. He worked hard for the promised vice-president position, but I feared he was paying a high price for it. The long evening hours that he spent during the week entertaining customers along with his boss, I spent immersing myself in the Scriptures and in classic Christian books by Billy Graham, Oswald Chambers, and Catherine Marshall, to name a few. I was still on a quest for more truth, wisdom, and knowledge to really know how to live my life as Paul urged, "the more excellent way."

Some of the books I read were gifts to our family from Judge Stahl. Giving Christian books to others was almost a ministry for him. But by now his visits were more than giving us books. He was becoming a member of our family.

The judge loved our kids. In fact, they knew him as "Uncle Judge," and they dearly loved him as Alex and I did. When Michael told the judge about the time he prayed with Mommy and Jesus came into his heart to live, tears welled in the judge's eyes. He was as proud of Michael as a biological father, grandfather, or an uncle would be.

On one of those visits to the house, the judge was not only loaded down with books for all of us, but he also had a special gift for Michael. It was a wooden cross on a leather strap to hang around his neck. Michael was thrilled. He treasured that cross. From that day forward, Michael was never without it. He either wore the cross or carried it in his pocket; and when he became old enough to drive, it hung from his rearview mirror in whatever car he was driving, year after year.

When it came to books, Judge Stahl clearly was led of the Holy Spirit because he always brought just the right book exactly when I needed it! One was *The Cross and the Switchblade,* about the powerful ministry of the Holy Spirit guiding David Wilkerson and the glorious conversion of Nicky Cruz, a former gang member on the streets of New York City. It was another wonderful example of a Christian, David Wilkerson, hearing the voice of God and obeying His direction. That testimony of the divine appointment God created by sending David to Nicky to witness Jesus to him and other gang-bangers was absolutely thrilling, just as exciting as reading testimonies like the story of God sending Peter to Cornelius in the New Testament book of Acts.

I loved reading Christian books and great testimonies for Christ, but the Bible was paramount to my life. As I endeavored to live it to the best of my ability, I became an emotionally healthy wife and mother. God's Word was my guidance to help me parent and teach my three children His principles without being preachy. I was learning many of God's truths in His Word, and I wanted to remain open to more truth—and I wanted to remain teachable. Also, I retained the conscious knowing that not only were God and my family watching my life, but other people were watching too.

One day when I was picking up Steven after his morning preschool class, the pastor, who also was director of the school, stopped me. We had had a previous conversation in which I had shared some of my testimony with him and his wife. Now the two of them greeted me, and he asked, "Alisha, will you share your story with our church congregation?"

I was shocked.

"Me? Well … ah … thank you, Pastor, but I could never do that … I mean, speak before your congregation." My face started to feel flushed. "I don't know how to give a speech, and I would be too frightened to stand before a group."

"Alisha, I want you to consider something before you decline my invitation," he gently chided. "God has done great things for you. Don't you feel you should offer your thanks to Him by telling others?"

The pastor's words tugged at my heart. I knew he was right. But I had shared my testimony only one-on-one. I could not imagine telling it to a congregation. Of course, I also knew there would be no way I could ever repay God for all He had done for me; not even sharing my testimony could repay Him. I decided I should pray about it that evening.

When I did, instantly I remembered the day I was born again and how I had vowed to tell others about Jesus, just as Nora had told me.

I want to do that, Jesus. I can do that. I have done that. But, Lord … a congregation? That's altogether different! I don't think so.

I was scared. Then words of Scripture came to my mind: "But ye shall receive power, after that the Holy Ghost is come upon you; and ye shall be witnesses unto me" (Acts 1:8).

Wow, I mused, *I didn't expect that!*

I felt that Bible verse was meant to prompt me to obey. I was convinced I should accept Pastor's invitation. Alex agreed. The next day I did so, but not without fear and trembling.

I agonized for days over what I called then, "my speech." How could I possibly prepare for this in only a week? By the time the Sunday evening for me to speak arrived, I had a full written outline to guide me—practically my whole story written word for word!

A babysitter had been lined up, but at the last minute, Alex decided to stay home with the kids. Disappointed, I drove to the church alone. Arriving early, I went into the sanctuary to pray. I was worried that I would embarrass both the Lord and myself. I knelt there, going over and over my outline, praying silently: *God, please don't let me forget a word or lose my place in the outline … and please, Lord, don't let me make a fool of myself!* All of a sudden a quiet peace came over me. I stopped quivering inside and felt that familiar stillness around me. I knew God was with me, and knowing that gave me confidence.

Just then, the pastor came in to greet me.

"Alisha, you'll do fine. I know it!" he said, gently taking my arm and leading me to my front-row seat. I did not turn around, but I heard the church filling up, people chatting behind me; then Pastor appeared at the podium.

When he introduced me, I began trembling inside again. I did not think I could get up to walk, but then I felt myself moving to the podium. I stood silently, looking at all the people seated—watching me. I froze. I could not begin to speak. *I'm so embarrassed.*

Everyone's staring at me, waiting for me to say something. Help me, Lord! Suddenly, the word *pray* came into my mind. I bowed my head and began praying aloud for the Holy Spirit to help me honor Jesus with my words, and I felt God's peace settle over me, washing away my anxieties. I knew I was ready to begin.

Without looking at my notes or gathering my thoughts, I began telling how I had come to know Jesus Christ as my personal Savior and all He had done for me and my family. I could hear myself speaking, but the words I spoke were not being carefully chosen by me. When I stopped speaking, my outline lay on the podium untouched.

Afterward, people came up to me, shaking my hand and making comments like, "What a beautiful testimony ..." "You are an excellent speaker ..." "This is truly a miraculous working of the Lord Jesus in your life ..." "Please pray for my daughter; I now truly believe Christ can heal her too ..." "I knew the Holy Spirit was speaking through you ..."

I was puzzled and a little wary since I was not completely aware of exactly what words I had spoken.

Pastor and his wife made their way through the people standing around me.

"Alisha," Pastor said with a big smile, "you did just fine. Just fine! I knew you would, because God wants you to tell this story everywhere."

After that, I just had to understand exactly how I had managed without reading from my outline—and even more mysterious to me, not having chosen my words before speaking them. The Bible again solved that mystery, when I read the words of Jesus spoken to His disciples before He sent them out: "Take no thought how or what ye shall speak: for it shall be given you in that same hour what ye shall speak." (Matt. 10:19).

Because Jesus Himself had spoken those words, and I did realize that was what had happened to me, in my simple faith, I believed. I took Him at His Word.

One morning during my prayer time, the Lord impressed me to open my home to women for prayer and Bible study, and instantly three names of women came to my mind. I did not know anything about how to conduct such a group. However, the Lord gave me faith to believe that He would lead me as He did when I spoke before that church congregation. It was a little scary to me, but it was also exciting; and I hoped Alex would approve. He did.

To our nucleus of four, weekly the Lord added more women: Catholics and Protestants from various parishes and denominations as well as non-Christian women who attended no church at all. The Spirit of God used our personal testimonies, the Bible, and prayer to draw many women to Jesus. Some women, who were already born again, received the gift of the Holy Spirit. Many brought their friends, who also became converted to Christ and were filled with the Holy Spirit. The miracles happening among us each week were bringing honor to the Lord Jesus Christ, and the news was spreading by word of mouth.

Women came from all over the city and beyond—even from Chicago. I will never forget Diane of Chicago. She was a lady visiting in our city, and on the morning of our meeting, she read an article in the major newspaper about a Christian woman, who was my friend and part of our group. Diane was so impressed with the story that she tracked her down by phone to talk more about it with her. My friend told her she was going to her weekly prayer and Bible study group that morning and invited Diane to come along, and she did.

The two of them were total strangers. We were all strangers to her. But that day had been orchestrated by God. That day Jesus met Diane, and He blessed our group by letting us show her His love and minister to her with His gifts of the Spirit. She received Jesus Christ as her personal Savior, the gift of the Holy Spirit, her prayer language, and divine healing. It was glorious to witness! She came into my home a stranger and left as our precious sister and part of the family of God. Our group did nothing but pray, and Jesus ministered to her by His Spirit. She went back to her home in Chicago and joined a Bible-believing church; studied the Bible; testified about her loving, healing Jesus; and eventually, opened her own home to women for prayer and Bible study.

The second invitation to share my story publicly came from an acquaintance, the mother of a friend of mine. She had heard about my testimony from someone who had been part of that congregation with which I had shared. She led a group of student Christians who met in the mornings before classes in the high school from which I had graduated, and she invited me to share my testimony with them.

I remembered the words of Jesus in Matthew 10:9. I did believe them, but I found on the morning I was to speak, I obviously did not have enough faith to really trust in them yet; so I took my same already prepared outline with me.

Following my testimony, I realized again that I had not even looked at my outline. And once again, several young men and women expressed how I had said things that "helped" them; one said my words had "spoken to her heart," and another commented, "Your words of love for Jesus really touched me." In general, they liked what I said.

Also once again, I was not sure of all I had spoken, since I was conscious of the fact that my thoughts were not formed before the words came out of my mouth. My friend told me she had been so blessed to hear my story for herself. That afternoon she phoned to thank me again and to tell me she had shared my story with her pastor, and mentioned the name of her Protestant church.

God had proven the faithfulness of His Word to me a second time. I never prepared an outline again. After that, every time I was invited to witness for Jesus, although I did not know the doctrine of the particular church or group—and I could not presume to know the hearts of its people or what they needed to hear of my testimony—I just asked God to cleanse and prepare my own heart to receive the guidance of the Holy Spirit to speak the right words.

When I first started sharing publicly, I did not understand as I do now that every believer is led of God the way He chooses. Some use an outline when teaching the Bible or speaking of the things of God, and some do not. The way God led me is the only method I know.

On a warm day in May, I was sitting on the porch having my private Bible study when God spoke to me through the Scriptures about being immersed in water baptism. Scripture taught me that it was an outward witness to one's inward faith and commitment to Jesus Christ. However, having been baptized as an infant and growing up in the Roman Catholic Church, I knew I could not ask my priest to immerse me in water baptism, and I did not know the practices or doctrines of baptism in Protestant churches.

Momentarily I became concerned about offending my parents by being rebaptized. Almost simultaneously I felt directed to read the tenth chapter of Matthew, and I turned to it. When I read verse 37, the truth of it overcame my concern. I knew God was speaking to me: "He that loveth father and mother more than Me is not worthy of Me" (Matt. 10:37).

The conviction of those words of Jesus went into my spirit, and suddenly I remembered the words I had heard that night in my bedroom: "If you will obey My voice and keep My commandments, I will give you the desires of your heart." There was no question. I knew I would obey, although I did not know how in the world it could happen.

Instantly I remembered my friend who had invited me to speak to the student Christian group. I talked to Alex about attending her church the next Sunday. He responded with a quizzical look, but he agreed.

After that Sunday morning service, I phoned the pastor and mentioned my friend's name and how much my family and I had enjoyed the service and his message, and requested to be immersed in water baptism. Before agreeing, however, the pastor made it his business to visit our home to hear my born-again experience firsthand. Soon, in a Sunday evening service, before the congregation and with Alex and my children looking on, I was immersed in water baptism according to the leading of God the Holy Spirit and Scripture.

I believed God led us to that solid Bible-believing church not only to make the way for me to obey Him in water baptism, but also for an even greater plan. The children really liked Sunday school, where they learned more about the person of Jesus and how He desired to be their personal Savior and Lord, which built on the foundation of what I was teaching them at home. We all greatly enjoyed attending

Sunday morning services and, sometimes, Sunday evenings, but it was especially good for Alex. He was now hearing a strong message each Sunday about the love of Jesus and our need for a personal relationship with Him, and the command of Jesus, "You must be born again."

Alex continued attending the monthly FGBFI prayer breakfasts, and the two of us attended the monthly dinner meetings. I believed that with everything God had been doing, Alex was surely closer to salvation.

It was the first Sunday morning in December 1970, eight months after my water baptism in the church. It had become our family's Sunday morning routine before going to church to watch Christian television programs. Following Kathryn Kuhlman's program *I Believe in Miracles,* we began watching Rex Humbard from the Cathedral of Tomorrow church in Akron, Ohio.

At the beginning of the program before his sermon, he invited those in the congregation who wanted prayer for healing to approach the altar. Alex left the room. I immediately felt compelled to kneel and pray. I did not know why, so I prayed in my prayer language. I was experiencing a wonderful joy, and the longer I prayed, the greater my joy grew. Then my praying stopped as abruptly as it had started, and I got up from my knees. I felt my prayer had to do with Alex, but I could not pinpoint it. *He must be getting ready for church,* I thought, before returning my attention to the television program.

Near the end of the sermon, Alex entered the room, smiled at me, and sat down for the last gospel song. He was still in his robe.

"I thought you were getting dressed for church, honey," I said.

"No," he answered softly, "I've got plenty of time yet."

Alex was quiet—almost pensive.

As soon as the program ended, I scurried the children upstairs to dress for church.

This day was Communion Sunday, and it was the practice of this denomination to serve communion only to those who had been born again. For that reason, Alex had never taken communion in this church. As the elders began to pass the communion trays, the same joy that had filled me earlier returned. I watched as the trays of bread and juice were passed from one person to another, up and down each pew in front of us. I looked at Alex and smiled. He smiled back. Looking at him again, I leaned closer and whispered in his ear, "Honey, I don't know why, but I have so much joy inside, I feel like my heart could burst any minute."

He turned to face me, gazed long into my eyes, then leaned nearer and whispered, "I know why. I wanted to surprise you when I took communion today. I was born again this morning upstairs in our bedroom, during the Rex Humbard program."

"Oh, praise the Lord, honey!" I whispered excitedly. I wanted to shout it to the whole congregation! *All this joy inside of me, and I have to contain it! This is one of the happiest days of my life! Thank You, my Jesus.*

After church Alex wanted us to drive to his hometown to tell his aunt, his mother's only living sister, and her husband that he was born again. I had never seen Alex happier.

Looking back, before his conversion, Alex had purchased his first, then second, thoroughbred race horse. During racing season, he would sometimes finish his last sales call early and go directly to the track to catch the last races. On those days, he left the races and went to a bar where the track people gathered and came home late at night. I could always tell when he had lost a bundle of money, because he would get really ugly before finally going to bed. The days he did not go to the races, the first thing he did when he walked in the door was to change from his suit into casual clothes, read the newspaper before dinner, then go to the horse barns at the track to talk to his trainer and the groom who took care of his horses.

Now, since his conversion, the daily change I was seeing in Alex filled my heart with joy. His routine was totally different. He came straight home from work in a good mood every day. After changing his clothes, he picked up his Bible, the one I had bought for him, and read it until dinner time. Now he only occasionally went to the horse barn in the evenings, and often he took the children with him. They liked being around the horses, especially Laurie, who loved horses and had read *Black Beauty* and every other book she could find about horses.

Alex behaved like a totally different person. The kids and I were thrilled. Our prayers had been answered. And I prayed this was the beginning of Alex's healing from his manic-depression and his deliverance from alcohol and the compulsion to gamble.

Sure enough, before long we would see the miracle of his being totally set free. But first God began to heal our relationship. The Lord was tearing down the remaining emotional barriers that Alex had erected. Everything was improving. We had "cuddle nights" again. Alex and I would talk about how much the Lord had done for our family. Alex could now see how many times God had intervened in our lives before and after my conversion and, now, his. We were very happy with each other. Alex would often tell me how much he loved me and how grateful to God he was to have me for a wife, and how much he wanted to make up for the heartaches he knew he had caused me over the years.

One early morning soon after his conversion, we awoke to an ice-covered winter wonderland outside. As Alex was leaving for work, we stood at the open door, admiring the splendid scene before us. The trees in our yard looked like fine crystal sculptures, and the small bushes looked like hand-blown glass replicas of bonsai, delicate and lacy, against a background of sparkling snow.

"Isn't it beautiful, Alex?" I sighed, leaning against his shoulder.

"Beautiful," he said, smiling at me.

"Be careful driving," I said, putting my arms around his neck. We knew the roads were like glass too.

"I will, honey," he said, kissing me good-bye.

"Have a good day! And, honey ... God go with you," I smiled.

Alex stepped through the door, and I watched him back out of the garage and driveway; then I closed the door.

Moments later he walked back into the house.

"What's wrong, Alex? Are the roads too bad to drive?"

"No," he said, with his boyish grin and playfully moving closer to me. Slipping his arms around my waist, he pulled me closer and kissed me long. "I'll be okay; don't worry."

"Oh?" I mused. "Then ..." I began giggling, "why did you come back into the house?"

Alex's face lit up with a wide smile and he said, "I was just thinking about how much I love you ... how happy I am ... and what a wonderful life we have." He kissed me passionately again.

"Well, that's nice, sweetheart. I love you too. And I'm very happy with our life. I'm very happy with you!"

Alex kissed me again and held me a few moments before saying, "Gotta go. I'll see you tonight."

"Hey! Again, be careful ... and God go with you, honey!" I said as he opened the door.

He spun around and smiled. "See what I mean? That's why I love you so much. Don't we have a great life?" he said, stepping out the door.

I stood there a moment; the tears welled in my eyes and rolled down my cheeks. *I've said "Have a good day" to him before he left for work all the years of our marriage, and "God be with you" since my commitment to Christ, and now he finally hears me!* Alex's sweet act of coming back into the house just to tell me how much he loved me warmed my heart the rest of that beautiful, cold winter day.

One night it dawned on me that I had not seen Alex drink a beer for several nights. Not long after, he called the children and me into the kitchen. We saw bottle after bottle of liquor lined up on the kitchen counter, along with several bottles of beer. The children were more amazed than I, as they had never seen bottles of liquor before. Alex was not a liquor drinker—beer was his choice—these bottles were gifts from his customers that had collected over the years and had been stored away.

"Daddy's not going to drink anymore, kids," Alex declared. "I'm through with that!" he said, confidently picking up the closest bottle, unscrewing the cap, and pouring the alcohol down the drain. I looked calm, but my mind was racing. *The way Alex's been living all these years has surely been the hard way, Lord. I can see he's determined. Thank You, my Jesus.*

The children's eyes were as big as saucers as they looked on. Tears welled up in my eyes as we silently watched Alex pour bottle after bottle of beer and expensive liquor into the kitchen sink. *That's all in the past now. I have a new husband.*

That night in bed, he said, "I'm determined, honey. I know I'll never drink again!"

I caught my breath. This was what I had been hoping and praying for all these years! I desperately wanted Alex to be healed of his mental disorder and freed from his addictions to alcohol and gambling. His words were pure joy to my heart. I silently prayed: *Please, Lord, help him follow through with his decision. Don't let it be like all the other times—empty, forgotten promises.*

"I'm very proud of you, Alex," I whispered, and kissed him.

The positive changes in Alex were appearing day by day. He rarely went to the stables in the evenings after work to see his two thoroughbreds. But after one of those infrequent evening visits, he said, "Honey, I believe the Lord wants me to get rid of my horses, sell them, but ..." He paused.

My heart and my thoughts started racing: *He loves those horses ... always wanted to own them and be part of the "sport of kings." This is the height of obedience for Alex if he can now give them up. He worked hard to make one a winner ... and he entered the winner's circle several times. Those horses are his pride and joy ... his dream.*

"Who's going to buy a horse this time of the year?" he asked. "Maybe, closer to racing season, but not now ... But I know," he went on, "I just know God is asking me to do this. I know He doesn't want me to gamble anymore. I've been praying about that," he said softly.

I was speechless. Although it appeared God was answering my long-time prayer that Alex would stop gambling, still his words left me stunned. *How wonderful that Alex, too, had been praying about this, Lord.*

"What do you think?" Alex asked, breaking my silent reverie.

"Alex ... honey," I cheerfully declared, "there's no doubt in my mind that if God is telling you to sell your horses, winter or not, there's someone out there who's going to want your horses. I just know it!"

His winning horse sold quickly. Alex was so anxious to do what he believed the Lord had asked of him, that when the other one did not sell fast enough, he gave it away.

When they were gone, Alex said he felt an inexplicable freedom unlike anything he had ever felt before. Immediately a Scripture verse Jesus had spoken popped into my mind, but I did not speak it aloud: "I give My Spirit to those who obey Me." Alex continued changing in different areas, bringing him even more freedom.

By now Alex had not only assumed his role as husband and father, but also his role as the spiritual head of our home. He did not curse anymore—not even a slip. He was more patient with the children and took more of an interest in them again. I was most impressed that Alex desired to have family Bible study once a week. He would gather us around the kitchen table, and we would read Scripture together. We and the children took turns sharing what each of us thought God wanted us to learn from it to apply to our daily living. Alex was good at leading too!

Now when invited to speak to Christian women's groups that were attended primarily by wives, the teachings of the Word for wives was incorporated into my testimony. I was learning from many of them that they desired for their husbands to accept Christ as Savior. I encouraged them to obey all God's biblical principles, but I especially emphasized the traits of the wife written about in Proverbs 31:10–31. I knew experientially those Scriptures would inspire their faith for adjusting their behavior in the marriage relationship to line up with God's Word. Those Scriptures had proven true in my personal life, and God had blessed me with a Christian husband. I was confident those Scriptures would do the same for them. And I had the privilege of seeing our healing Jesus and His Word change many of their personal lives, and the power of the Holy Spirit transform their families.

A loving and meaningful Christmas 1971 topped off another unforgettable year. We "adopted" two orphans for Christmas: a boy and a girl. This did not mean they came to live with us, but we were able to buy them presents we hoped they could use all year. Our gifts clothed each of them from the inside out—everything from underwear to snowsuits and boots! The kids and I wrapped each item individually and we wrote on the tag, "Merry Christmas! Jesus loves you, and so do we!" Then we made a celebration out of delivering the gifts to the orphanage on Christmas Eve.

After the kids were in bed for the night, I baked a birthday cake for Jesus and put a candle in the middle of it. That had become a tradition for the last six years. Christmas morning we lit the candle on the cake and sang happy birthday to Jesus. Afterward I told the children that what they had done by giving up some of their own presents so we could buy for the little orphans got a lot of notice from Jesus. Their faces lit up with big smiles. Then it was their turn. They ran into the sunroom to see the big surprises that were under the Christmas tree for them! Since Alex's conversion, living for the Lance family was finally everything I had always hoped and prayed it would be.

* * *

The New Year 1972 began as joyfully as 1971 had ended. Now our social life was also a joy, because Alex and I were meeting new friends all the time, couples who regularly attended the same monthly dinner meetings we liked. They were Protestants, Catholics, and messianic Jews. Also, they were members of not only different Catholic parishes but also various Bible-believing Protestant churches in the city, and some of those friends extended invitations for us to visit their churches: Presbyterian, Nazarene, Methodist, Episcopal, Assembly of God, Baptist and nondenominational, to name a few.

Having attended the Roman Catholic Church most of my life, the styles of Sunday morning worship in these varied denominations were fascinating to me. Rather than focusing on the differences, we were now seeing the family of God sharing one significant belief: that Jesus Christ is Lord. We were also learning more about the way God sees His people, not lumped together denominationally, but individually. We were no longer distinguishing born-again believers we knew as Catholic or Protestant or messianic Jews, but simply as brothers and sisters in Christ.

Not only was our Christian family growing, but Alex's faith was also growing by leaps and bounds. His personality had been miraculously stable since his conversion. There was no doubt in my mind that the Lord was healing him of his manic depression, because there was no more moodiness and no more Mr. Hyde rearing his ugly dark side. His temper was definitely under control. That brought another benefit: his blood pressure stabilized at normal, and he no longer needed his medication. He felt wonderful and believed God had healed him. I finally had entered my *season of contentment.*

The next time Judge Stahl visited our home, he brought us the book *Run Baby Run,* Nicky Cruz's own story. It was a powerful testimony, and I shared the story with the children. I also bought them *The Cross and the Switchblade* comic book to read. They were deeply moved by Nicky's testimony. The children's faith in God was growing.

I learned Nicky's movie, *The Cross and the Switchblade,* was playing at a local theater, and Alex and I took the children to see it. Then, soon after that, I read in the newspaper that Nicky Cruz would be speaking in what was at that time the largest exhibition center in our city. I mentioned it to Alex and the kids, and they all wanted to go.

That Saturday night, the auditorium was packed out. We were all inspired by Nicky's testimony and message. Many people went forward to accept Christ. Laurie kept whispering that she wanted to go down front to see Nicky. It seemed so unusual to me. She had heard other evangelists but had never asked to talk to them.

She asked again, "Mommy, please can we go see Nicky?" So I whispered it to Alex, and he only raised his eyebrows. Nonetheless, he agreed after the service to stay to see if we could speak with Nicky. I thought to myself that it would be unusual for the guest speaker to remain in the auditorium after the audience cleared.

But sure enough, the people made a quick exit, and Nicky was still in the front of the auditorium, so all of us walked down together to greet him and express our appreciation for what God had done in his life. Michael was profoundly impressed, and I told Nicky our little Laura had begged to see him. He got a big grin on his face, sat down on the piano bench, and held his arms out to Laura. She went to him, and he sat her on his knee, put his hand on her head, and prayed, dedicating her to Jesus.

The following morning, Sunday, we were watching Rex Humbard on network television. At the end of his preaching, he gave an altar call as usual; then he extended an invitation to receive Christ to the viewing audience. Laura got up off the floor and came over to sit next to me. I put my arm around her, and she leaned into my chest.

"Laura ... honey, do you feel all right?" I asked, feeling her forehead.

"Mommy," she whispered, "I want Jesus to come into my heart."

I was so touched, hearing such sweet words from my little girl. I smiled at her and stood up. Without a word to anyone else, I took Laura by the hand, led her into the living room, and closed the French doors behind us. I knelt down first, and Laura quickly knelt and scooted close to me.

"Would you like to pray, honey?"

"Yes, Mommy."

"Laura, just repeat Mommy's words to Jesus ... okay?" She nodded and bowed her head.

As I started speaking the first words, Laura lifted her head and opened her eyes, looking up as though staring at someone standing before her. Her countenance was so convincing, I looked where she was looking, but I saw nothing. Laura kept staring up.

I thought my heart would swell right out of my chest as she repeated my words so sincerely: "Jesus, please forgive me of all my sins ... and please come live in my heart forever."

Tears were streaming down her face by now and mine too.

It was very still in the room. The presence of God was evident, and Laura's face was glowing as she still held it up as though it were being held in a pair of hands.

Not wanting to disturb her spiritual moment, I sat back and watched her, waiting for her. She was still looking up and held her gaze, still caught up in the wonderful peace that enveloped us. I was still watching, watching. Suddenly a thought came to me that I should lay my hands upon her and pray for Jesus to give her the gift of the Holy Spirit. But I knew she did not know anything about that experience, and I wondered how I should explain to her what it means. Instantly I felt impressed not to be concerned, but just to pray for her.

I whispered, "Laura, would you like Jesus to give you the gift of His Holy Spirit?"

"Oh yes, Mommy," she answered, without even turning to look at me.

I gently laid my hand on her head and prayed a simple prayer: "Jesus, my Laura belongs to You. Please fill my little girl with Your Holy Spirit."

Seconds later the biggest smile came over her face as she spoke, "Jesus!" Then flowing freely from her lips came another language, fluent, melodic.

My heart raced with joyous energy. I wanted to shout and praise God. However, the language was still coming from her lips, and she was so reverent, I did not want to disturb this miraculous encounter between her and her God. It was awe-inspiring. Her face was still aglow with the Spirit.

I do not know exactly how long she knelt there praying in her new language, but I, too, continued kneeling; and listening with such amazement and gratitude to my Lord, I felt my prayer language coming as well. I remembered the night before when Laura had begged us to take her to Nicky. Now I was certain she had the intention to go forward to accept Christ then but did not know quite how to express it. As our Lord has a way of doing, that missed opportunity did not prevent Laura from receiving all God had for her, and in the process, I got the added blessing of sharing her special moment.

The children's spring school vacation was nearing. I wanted to take them somewhere special. I thought Washington, D.C., would be a nice trip for them. I had pleasant childhood memories of vacation trips by train with my parents, and I wanted my children to also have that experience. Alex thought it was a good idea. The kids did too.

We boarded the train and arrived in the nation's capital. The kids were excited. My joy came from watching the expressions of wonder on their faces as they excitedly viewed the historical sites, voicing their impressions about the new facts they were learning about their country's history. They might have preferred Disneyland, but I thought this trip had inspired a new pride in their country, and I hoped they would always have that same pride and patriotic spirit.

After vacation the kids were excited to be back in school. And Alex and I had our own excitement. Judge Stahl, a widower, became engaged to marry a lovely widow named Anne. She was from the South. They had met on a travel tour for Christians. He kidded me that he fell in love with Anne when he spotted her in the airplane somewhere over Italy. When he brought her to dinner to meet us, she was not only one of the most elegant senior women I had ever seen, but also the most gracious, a true Southern lady.

I had an afternoon reception for her and invited many women who were Christian leaders in Aglow, the Christian radio station, and other ministries, as well as wives of the judge's friends, to welcome her to our city. Our friendship blossomed and grew strong. We loved each other. She was "Aunt Annie" to our children. She had no children of her own, and one day she told me she thought of me as her daughter. That was my special blessing.

School summer vacation arrived. One of the first things on my agenda was to buy a puppy for the kids. They picked him from a litter of six white furry American Eskimo babies and named him Sammy. He was sheer happiness for the kids, and everything each of them had wanted in a dog.

Although I had been sharing my testimony publicly, I declined invitations during the children's three-month school vacation because I wanted to give them my full attention. Alex was still traveling for his job and was occasionally gone overnight. Some of those evenings, the children and I would have the special treat of McDonald's for picnics in the park. The kids would play on the swings, slide, and jungle gym, while I enjoyed watching them and hearing their carefree laughter. Some nights when Alex was out of town, I would let them each invite a friend to stay overnight.

The public library was within walking distance from our house, and we spent many hours there. The kids would bring grocery bags and fill them with books to read. Occasionally I planned a special day with each child. For instance, I would have a babysitter in, and the two of us would enjoy a bus ride downtown, visit the toy area in a major department store, window shop, and have lunch in a restaurant that offered a smorgasbord where they would select their favorite foods; over ice cream sundaes, we would talk about anything that was on their mind. Because they loved horses, once in a while I took them to a riding stable in a nearby small town and they would ride for hours.

Alex talked about buying a pleasure boat for the family and one day surprised us with it. The kids were so excited when he pulled into the driveway with the large new white boat with red leather seats for six. All their neighborhood friends came running to the house to see it. Alex let all the kids climb inside it and showed them the water skis he had bought and where they would place their feet when we taught them how to water ski. That was the beginning of wonderful summer Saturdays and Sundays after church when we went boating, fishing, water skiing, and picnicking on the shores of rivers and lakes throughout the state.

Our summer was topped off with a family vacation. We rented a furnished cottage for the first two weeks in August on the lake at one of the state parks. Alex was relaxed and still at peace with himself, which made everything peaceful and pleasant for the rest of us too. The kids had fun swimming, fishing, trail hiking, and horse-back riding.

One afternoon, as a family, we were slowly riding our horses single file down a trail when suddenly Steven's horse bolted out of the line, charging toward the thickly wooded area.

Turning his horse on its haunches, Alex took off after Steven. We all yelled, "Hang on, Steven!"

I froze in fear. Steven's horse was so fast that I was petrified Alex would not catch up to him. I saw the horse heading full speed toward a huge tree with enormous low branches, and Alex saw it too. He yelled, "Duck, Steven!" just an instant before the horse reached the branch. In a split second, Steven jockeyed his body and ducked—and his head just slightly missed brushing the low-hanging branch. Alex caught up with Steven, grabbed the reins, and halted Steven's horse.

I sighed with relief and loosened the grip on my saddle horn, saying a silent, *Thank You, Lord.* Oh, how grateful to God we all were that Steven had heard us in time! If not, he would have surely been severely injured or killed.

Despite this frightening incident, our vacation was a wonderful way to end an enjoyable summer. And there would be many more such summers with weekend excursions and fun vacations throughout the years to come. Life was good; life was happy for the Lance family.

Chapter 14

Grace and Power Abound

Daily now my heart was full with thanksgiving to God for how He was leading my husband step by step. He also continued leading me. Invitations to speak were coming in from other local Protestant denominations and women's organizations, as well as from Christian radio, for interviews and/or guest spots for biblical teachings. I did not seek any of those invitations.

Often Alex and I were both invited, but while he was sharing his testimony one-on-one, he did not feel impressed to speak publicly. But he was adamant that I should continue doing so. Alex sensed, just as I believed, that God Himself was opening the doors for our story to be told. This was as amazing to me as everything else God had done thus far, and I always remembered Pastor's words: "God wants you to tell this story everywhere."

I have cherished memories of every place I shared my testimony over the years, but one of the doors that opened to me made a special impression on me about how God the Holy Spirit was confirming my words of testimony. A member of a Mennonite church in a small town had heard about my testimony and received permission from his pastor to invite me to share it with the congregation during an evening service. I did not know Mennonite doctrine, just as I did not know the doctrines of other Protestant denominations in which I shared. I even wondered if it might be a small miracle that I, a woman, was permitted to speak in that church.

I could feel the peace of God while I was sharing. When I finished, I was still standing at the front of the church when a woman stood and held up her shoes, one in each hand, and said, "This testimony glorifies Jesus, and the Holy Spirit is with us. I felt I had to take off my shoes because I believe I'm standing on holy ground."

I do not know what the parishioners felt, but I was truly humbled.

Another time I shared stands out in my memory. I received an invitation from Sister Dorothy, a nun from the same order in our city as Sister Miriam.

"I've heard all about your testimony of Christ and healing," she began, "and I have received permission from my Mother Superior to gather together a group of our nuns, some priests, and laypeople to hear your story, if you will consent to share it with us."

I was truly humbled at the prospect of speaking before these particular people. My mind raced: *What do I have to tell them that they don't already know? These are the people I looked to most of my life for spiritual teaching.* I felt inadequate, unworthy to do this, and could not bring myself to accept at that moment; so I told her I would pray about it and call her the next day. Despite my concerns, Alex encouraged me to believe God wanted me to accept this invitation too. So I did. Sister was delighted.

In the meantime, I spent time praying against my fear of sharing before priests and nuns. When I entered the meeting room, I felt prepared to trust Jesus again, for the Holy Spirit to bring words of Christ's love to these people. I also felt impressed to shake hands with each person I was introduced to. As I reached out to shake the hand of a lovely-looking woman, a Catholic layperson, the word *hostility* came into my mind, despite her warm smile as she introduced herself. I was curious, but there was not time to think about that, for I would be speaking soon.

When I finished, again I did not know what all I had spoken. To my shock and embarrassment, one priest abruptly left the room as though what I had said offended him. But my concern was short-lived as the priest sitting next to me immediately got down on his knees and began thanking God for what he had heard, proclaiming his belief in my testimony. I flushed with humility and shared the tears of everyone in the room as I watched and listened to this precious man of God pray that God would send me everywhere to share this testimony. Everyone else expressed their appreciation to God for my testimony of Jesus; then many of the nuns and laypersons asked me to pray for them.

Oh Lord, I'm not worthy to pray for these people—especially these pious nuns.

I asked if I could just stand next to the priest while he prayed for them, but the nuns insisted that I lay hands on them and pray. To me, this was the height of humility on their part.

Somehow God gave me not only the faith to do this, but also the courage.

Driving home, I did not know why, but I felt impressed to pray for the pleasant woman in whom I had sensed hostility. I was still curious about that unusual piece of knowledge and wondered if it had been my imagination. Even so, I knew I could do nothing about it. Then I remembered the Scripture I had studied in the apostle Paul's first letter to the Corinthians in which he had named the "discerning of spirits" as one of the nine gifts of the Holy Spirit. If God had imparted that discernment to me about that dear lady, I knew I should continue to pray for her but could safely leave the outcome to Him.

The following day, that precious nun who had invited me telephoned to thank me. She told me how blessed everyone had been with my sharing and the prayer time. God had answered prayer for several. She also told me she was going to request permission from her Mother Superior for the group to meet regularly on Sunday evenings for prayer and Bible study. Those people sincerely loved Jesus and obviously wanted to grow in the knowledge of the Scriptures and serve Him even more effectively. I felt impressed that God had His special intentions for that group of dear people.

Alex and I continued to attend the Full Gospel Businessmen's monthly dinner meetings. It was after one of those meetings that I encountered an unexpected blessing.

A woman came up to me, flung her arms around my neck, and kissed me on both cheeks, saying, "My Alisha ... my Alisha!" I was amazed to see that it was the woman in whom I had discerned hostility at the Catholic meeting. Now she was expressing her love for me, saying, "Oh Alisha, I thought sure you would be the first person God would send me to, to ask forgiveness from. Alisha, I've been born again, Jesus has filled my life, and I've received the baptism in the Holy Spirit!"

I was very happy for her.

Excitedly she explained what had happened to her after I spoke that night. She was so upset by my words that she tossed and turned all night, with those words going over and over in her mind. The next morning, she visited a friend, complaining about me and the words I had spoken. But she continued attending the prayer group at the Catholic facility. Now she was totally free from hostility toward me and totally devoted to Jesus, and serving Him.

I have learned that Jesus never minds an honest doubter, like Thomas, who could not believe until he saw with his own eyes the nail scars in His hands. What a patient, merciful, gracious, and loving Savior we have!

It was such good news for me to learn that God had miraculously worked among that same group of Catholic priests, nuns, and laypersons weekly, and He had added to their number. It became the first Catholic charismatic prayer fellowship in our city.

I realized that precious Catholic woman's hostility toward me had been one more testing for me: testing how I would react to being misunderstood or having my beliefs, motives, or my integrity misjudged while serving God. I could see where I needed God's tempering of my personality by His Word in order for me to get through other unpredictable incidents, should they occur in the future. I was finding that it was through testings that I learned for myself how much I really loved others, how much I believed the Bible, and how much I really knew, loved, and trusted God through everything—good or bad—that came into my life. By now I had learned God's Word is worked into a believer's life experientially through these testings. I would soon learn that the school of testing was not over.

Although invited, Alex and I had never taken membership in any church we had visited but were still registered members of the Catholic Church. However, we had really enjoyed fellowshipping not only with Catholics but also with Protestant believers of different Bible-believing churches, embracing the whole body of Christ.

Despite the fact that I was criticized by some Catholics for enjoying my fellowship with Protestant Christians and especially for being their guest at church services, I continued doing so. Those criticisms had come too late. I had already read in the Holy Scriptures that God is no respecter of persons and that He loves all His followers the same, that we were all bought with the same high price and made members of *His church;* and because of that, Jesus Christ alone is our mediator, as the Bible makes clear: "For there is one God and one mediator between God and men, the man Christ Jesus: who gave Himself a ransom for all, to be testified in due time" (1 Tim. 2:5–6).

Since His believers each know Him as the *only Savior* and the *only "mediator* between God and men," He commands us all the same: to love one another and to forsake not the assembling of ourselves together. That is the basis for pure fellowship—whether it is two believers or a whole church congregation—because that is when God is in the midst of us.

I could not listen to my critics, because those commandments leave no room for differentiating between believers based upon the name of the church they attend. Our sincere love for the true and living God, Jesus Christ, is our only criterion for fellowship.

Besides, I had already gleaned from God's inspired Holy Scriptures the understanding that when we get to heaven, it will not matter what church we attended; but rather, *only what we have done for Christ will matter.* I had a biblical but also ecumenical understanding of the unity of the brethren, the believers, the followers of Christ, which grew out of my experiences of fellowshipping in other Bible-believing churches. Embracing the whole body of Christ was paramount to my Christian living and fellowshipping with those who belong to Jesus Christ, *Who is the church,* and understanding that we are members of the *invisible* body of Christ, meaning Jesus alone knows who are the true members of His church.

* * *

One morning I was making the bed, tucking the bedspread under the pillows and smoothing the last wrinkle while simply praising the Lord in my mind and heart for all He had done for our family. Suddenly words pierced through my mind: *You will write your testimony, and it shall be a book.*

I was stunned for a moment. Numbly I sat down on the side of the bed. The words had been authoritative and I felt them profoundly within, like the night I had received the gift of the Holy Spirit.

"Me ... write a book?" I asked aloud. "That's impossible! I could never write a book. Please, Lord, don't ask this of me."

But I knew that I had heard God's voice and that it was a command from God, not simply a polite request. Even so, that did not stop me from arguing about it. I dropped to my knees at the side of the bed.

"I can't write a book, Lord," I pleaded aloud. "I've never even taken a writing course. I wouldn't know where or how to begin. And with three children and a husband to take care of, where would I find the time? Oh, please Lord, hear me ... Please don't ask me to do this!"

More words came to my mind: *You will record your testimony, and Cara will type it.*

Cara? I do know a Cara, but I don't know her well enough to even know if she types!

The Cara I knew was president of our children's school PTA, and I was a room mother for Laura's class, serving on one of Cara's committees. I still knew very little about her personally. Was she a Christian? Could she type? I did not have the foggiest notion!

As I was still on my knees, my mind was now prayerfully wondering when and how in the world I could approach Cara about this.

"Oh Lord, I don't know how I'm going to do any of this," I sighed aloud. Instantly words shot through my mind: *My saints will assist you.*

His saints? I knew the Bible referred to Christians as "saints" in some instances. Silently I asked, *Lord, what do You mean? Who?*

How will I know these people? Do I already know them as I do Cara? Then I thought, *I barely know Cara.* There were no more words, but I felt at peace for the time being.

I decided to write the words I believed were from God in my journal and also on a piece of paper that I tucked into the inside pocket of the protective carrier that held my Bible. I did not know when I would write a book; I did not know how I would write a book; but what I did know, deep within, was that someday, someway, God and I were going to write a book—against all odds!

I finished tidying our bedroom and told myself that I had no choice but to release all this to God and trust Him. I had learned by now that if the words were truly from God, one day they would come to pass. I would try to apply what He was teaching me: I would *rest in God and wait for His timing.* At that point, I went on with my housework that morning, but now instead of feeling trepidation over what I believed the Lord had said I would do, my heart was filled with joy!

I recall the unexpected way God brought Cara to the group in my home. It had been only a few weeks after my experience in the bedroom when I felt impressed that I would one day write a book and Cara would type it. A postcard from Cara had arrived by mail announcing the day of her regularly scheduled PTA committee meeting. Because the date was the same day of the week that the women met for prayer and Bible study, I knew I would have to decline.

The next morning, a Saturday, I telephoned Cara to tell her why I was unable to attend her meeting. As I had experienced in many other situations, somehow our conversation led to talking about the Lord, and I ended up briefly sharing what Jesus had done in my life.

Cara listened then asked, "May I come over sometime so we can talk more about this?"

"Sure. When would you like to get together?"

"Right now?"

Smiling to myself, I repeated, "Right now?"

"Yes, if it's convenient for you."

"Well, yes ... ah ... that's fine. Just give me a few minutes to get dressed. I'm still in my robe."

Fifteen minutes later, Cara was walking through my door. She told me she had been a Lutheran Sunday school teacher for several years, which impressed me. We had a wonderful talk about the Lord. She responded to my testimony as I had responded to Nora's testimony. I felt impressed that our get-together that day had been God's divine appointment for Cara and me.

Before she left, I invited her to attend the weekly prayer and Bible study in my home anytime she could. She promptly rearranged her PTA meeting schedule and attended the next fellowship! It continued to grow. God continued to do wonderful works among us. Cara attended weekly and became born again and received the gift of the Holy Spirit.

In our home gatherings, the Lord had already led me to share what I had learned from Scripture about the promise of the Father to all believers: the gift of the Holy Spirit and its value, benefit, and function in the lives of believers. We studied more about the purpose and operation of His nine gifts of the Holy Spirit. Our Lord was teaching all of us together, just as though we were enrolled in His school of the Holy Spirit.

I still thought of His nine spiritual gifts as God's power tools to be used for us to minister to one another. I prayed at the beginning of each meeting that the Holy Spirit would stir up His gifts in all present. And He did. In this atmosphere of love, trust, and encouragement that God had created, many women had the courage to step out in faith and be used of God—some experiencing His gifts operating through them for the first time.

We were all learning together to trust, depend, and rely upon the Holy Spirit's guidance even more. God continued to increase our number, and more women accepted Jesus Christ as their personal Savior. God did marvelous things with this group, which grew too large for my home. But He had His own plan to extend its outreach.

Some women were led to open their homes in another area of our city and in surrounding towns. From this original group, God reproduced this same kind of fellowship. It was glorious, and Jesus Christ alone received the honor and the glory.

It was over a year later when I felt a distinct impression to talk to Cara about my book. She had continued attending the weekly prayer group in my home, and we had become fast friends. When I approached her, Cara was solemn as she listened to the whole story, including God's directive *You will record your testimony, and Cara will type it.*

When I finished, I asked, "Cara, do you type?"

Through her husky laughter, she answered, "Yes, I type."

She stopped laughing but continued smiling as she explained: "At one time, I worked as a typist, sitting at a typewriter for eight hours a day, typing from recorded medical histories ... and I love to type!"

Of course, God already knew Cara could type. He had known that Cara would become born again and be filled with the Holy Spirit and that our friendship would blossom and grow as well. This was more than a "mini" act of the Holy Spirit to me. It was major! This was the first confirmation of His words to me.

"Cara, this is amazing!" I said. "But I'm not a writer. I don't know when or how to begin to write a book."

"You'll know when the time is right," she said, "and you'll be able to do it. You didn't think you could speak publicly either, when the Lord opened those doors for you to serve Him. But He gave you the ability and you became a speaker. Don't you think He's capable of making you a writer?"

"But a book, Cara ... Why do you suppose God has asked me to do such a thing?"

"That's easy!" she said quickly. "Your testimony is true and powerful. No one can poke holes in it because it's all the working of the Holy Spirit; and besides, Jesus uses it to draw people to Himself. It challenges Christians to get real and walk right."

She broke out in a hearty laugh again and said, "Me included!"

I could not help laughing with her.

"Will you pray about typing this book?" I asked.

"I don't have to," she answered. "I already know God would have me do it. Oh, this is exciting! I just feel so much joy!"

I was excited too, but my mind was moving way ahead of Cara's words. I was sure the book would be a huge undertaking and would require discipline and a great deal of time—neither of which I thought I had for such a demanding project. Besides, I had no knowledge of God's timing: when I would begin writing or when the book would be completed.

Afterward I silently prayed, *Lord, help me to do this work that You've asked me to do—and to be faithful to it*. I had no idea then what it would mean to trust, obey, and wait for God's time for the book.

God was trying to teach me about waiting for His time, but my finite mind was finding it all pretty hard to learn. How does one learn to wait on God and recognize when it is God's time? Human nature has never changed. We all want what we want, when we want it—or at least if we do have to wait, we want to know exactly how soon our answer is coming. Waiting is never easy. Waiting for God's time is no different.

In the meantime, Alex's company was putting more and more pressure on him to increase sales. He often discussed this with me and asked me to pray for him. It was becoming obvious to me that the promised position of vice president of the company would carry a greater demand on his time. I could see he was feeling the pressure his boss was putting on him to be out more nights entertaining customers, which always involved drinking. When the company had social gatherings, I observed his boss appeared to be a heavy drinker. But I said nothing. I only prayed Alex would be strong and not allow Satan to tempt him to compromise his faith and make a wrong choice to go back to his old life.

Alex had been so positive. But over the next two months, despite my constant prayers, I sensed his frustration was building. He was now a long way from the happy, enthusiastic man he had been. He often vented to me his irritations about his job. But there were other times when he seemed content with it. Then I would see him change again, becoming agitated about incidents involving the job. His behavior was not difficult to put up with, as it had been before his conversion, but he was getting more agitated every day. Soon he was becoming short-tempered with all of us again.

The children were witnessing the change in their father too. I did not want them to be affected by his behavior and become discouraged, so I prayed a lot about that—and for them.

One day I was praying as usual that God would protect my kids mentally, emotionally, and spiritually while their daddy was going through this rough time when he had lost his stability in Christ. Words instantly passed through my mind, which brought comfort to me and reassurance for God's care: *My daughter, have no fear for your children, for they are always within My watchful eye, and I hold them in the palm of My hand.*

Those words meant so much to me, and they were words of promise I knew I would never forget.

I continued to pray for Alex, believing with everything in me that the Holy Spirit would help him. Although we still attended the Christian businessmen's monthly dinner meetings, Alex's worries about his job seemed to accompany him wherever he went and stole his enjoyment, even at those times. I was becoming more troubled about what seemed to be a spiritual conflict within my husband. I did not know exactly how to pray about what was happening, so I prayed for him in my prayer language.

While there was evidence that Alex's inner battle was heating up, during the course of this difficult time, there was always evidence that the Spirit of God was working in other ways. New reports of testimonies of people being touched by God after my having publicly shared kept coming in. Jesus was receiving the glory, but I was receiving something too. The Lord was using those good reports to spiritually lift me above my concerns for Alex.

Also, I was still teaching the truths of Proverbs 31:10–31 and other Scriptures about the marriage relationship before women's organizations and over Christian radio. They had all been true for me. My husband had become a Christian. But now the truth was that while I was witnessing other women's husbands drawing closer to Christ and moving forward into service for Him, Alex appeared not to be moving forward, but rather seemed to be losing ground. I believed he would soon see the light and resume his enthusiasm for his God.

As the year drew to a close, something inside Alex snapped, and two weeks before Christmas, he left us. He just walked out! He did not say why or where he was going or where he would be staying. But there was a part of me that was not surprised, and the Lord gave me peace about it.

I discerned that the social activities surrounding his job had made it easier for him to yield to temptation. Perhaps his spiritual conflict ensued over drinking and whatever else was expected of him in the course of entertaining customers with his boss. Perhaps Alex had to compromise his conscience to do his job as the company demanded. I did not know.

But as time went on, Alex appeared to have built a thick barrier between himself and God. I knew my husband loved me and the children. I also knew his leaving had nothing to do with us. We had not done anything to provoke him to such action. Satan had him by the neck!

His leaving created only minor concerns for me, and I felt complete spiritual peace and kept praying for Alex to turn to the Lord for the help he needed. For the children's sakes, I told them Dad had to go away and might not be home for Christmas, but he would want us to do all the fun things we traditionally did to prepare for the holidays.

The children and I decorated the Christmas tree. The kids did their own Christmas shopping with the money they had each saved from their allowances for doing house chores. Spending the money they earned was always a great boost to their pride and self-confidence. We wrapped presents and baked cookies and managed to turn the season into a fun and happy time.

Snow was on the ground, and more snow flirted with us a little bit each day now. It was beginning to look like Christmas. The children romped and played in the snow with their neighborhood friends, making their traditional snowman in our front yard.

Two days before Christmas, I was sitting at the dining room table wrapping gifts when Alex walked in the back door. He walked up to me and dropped to his knees.

"Honey, I've gotta have Jesus again! Will you pray with me?"

Oh, how I wanted to! I had prayed and trusted God for this moment. But somehow I knew I was not to pray with Alex and merely said, "Alex, I think this is between you and Jesus." The battle he was in was not my battle.

"Okay, I understand," he answered. Getting up from his knees, he turned and walked up the stairs. I heard him crying. When he came downstairs, his eyes were red-rimmed and his face shiny from tears. But his countenance had changed from when he left us two weeks before. He had a sweet, peaceful expression. I could see he was back again in his own safe harbor with God.

"Honey, I'm forgiven … Jesus forgave me."

He put his hand behind my neck, running his fingers through my hair, and gently pulled my face close to his. "I've always loved you, Alisha—you and the kids. I didn't believe this would ever happen to us again. What went wrong with me?" he asked. "I'm so sorry I've been so messed up."

I closed my eyes and dropped my head.

"Look at me," he softly ordered. "I'm never going to let Satan deceive me again! Never!" he declared boldly. "He really had a stranglehold on me. I know that now."

Love for him flooded my heart, and I threw my arms around him, kissed him, and said, "Welcome home, honey!"

The next thing I knew, he had picked up the phone and dialed a number. I wondered who he was calling, until I heard, "Judge? This is Alex. I just want to tell you that I've come back and Jesus has forgiven me. Judge, Satan has really had a hold on me. He deceived me in every way. When's the next prayer breakfast or dinner meeting? I want to get to the fellowship real soon!"

Judge Stahl told Alex the local chapter dinner meeting would be held the next Friday, and Alex assured him we would be there. Next he called Cara to let her know that he was back where he belonged. She was thrilled! When he had left the house, Cara felt impressed to fast for Alex and join me in prayer.

Friday came, and I was expectant. We had invited Cara and her husband and another dear friend, Judy, and her husband to go to the fellowship dinner with us. The six of us drove to the hotel where that meeting was held, and I was still feeling expectant. Deep within me, I knew something very special was going to happen to Alex soon. Would it be tonight?

Well-known, successful industrialist, George Otis, was the speaker. When he finished sharing his exciting and powerful testimony of salvation in Christ, receiving the baptism in the Holy Spirit, and crediting God for his business success, he invited those who wanted to receive Christ to come forward. Then he asked for those who wanted Jesus to fill them with His Holy Spirit to raise their hands. My head was bowed and my eyes closed as he started to pray, but I felt Alex's arm shoot up. Mr. Otis finished praying, and I hoped my husband had received what he desired.

Before we left the banquet room, Alex learned that the chapter in his hometown would be meeting the next night, and he wanted us all to go. Our friends agreed.

The next evening, we all walked into the banquet room, and we were immediately greeted by Bob Landon and Bill Scofield, who were in leadership with the chapter. They were especially glad to see Alex. "My brother Alex, I believe God is going to do something great for you tonight," Bob confidently said, giving Alex a big bear hug. Bob and Bill were two of the three men who had prayed with Alex at Bill's home after that chapter's prayer breakfast when God had revealed words of knowledge to Alex about his life, before his conversion.

How perfect for Alex to meet these precious men again. This could get exciting!

The guest speaker at the meeting, a senior gentleman, began his testimony then abruptly stopped.

"You're going to have to hear my testimony another time. God has other plans for this evening. He's going to do miraculous things." He called for those who wanted prayer to come up to the front of the room, and Alex and I were among the first to fall in line. When it was our turn, we stepped up. The speaker had a big smile on his face as he looked at me and asked, "What have you come for?" I knew what I wanted most.

316

"Please pray for my husband and me to know God's will for our lives." I looked at Alex, waiting for him to make a request, but he said nothing.

The speaker stared into Alex's eyes for a few moments before he spoke.

"And you're the one who's been holding everything up, right?" he said with a grin.

"Right!" Alex answered, smiling back.

"Well, son, tell me. What do you want from God?"

"I want everything He has for me," Alex quickly answered.

The man put his hand on Alex's head and prayed.

Instantly Alex's arms shot straight up over his head and he started praising Jesus. Then I heard syllables that formed foreign words quietly flowing off his lips. He staggered back, falling against the speaker's table. Had the table not stopped him, he would have been flat on the floor! This was a scene Alex Lance never would have permitted in the natural, if he had been the one in control.

I stepped back from him and joined the crowd now standing on the sidelines, stunned by the dramatic experience I was witnessing. My spirit swelled with praise for Jesus as I watched and listened to my husband, still seemingly oblivious to the more than two hundred businessmen and their wives in the banquet room.

By now many people were standing in one of the four prayer lines. Bob, who held a microphone, called to me and asked if I would give a brief testimony. When I finished, more people joined the prayer lines, until almost every person in the room was standing in line for prayer.

Then Bob grabbed Alex by the arm, pulling him toward one of the lines, his microphone amplifying his words: "Brother, the power of God is all over you; you've got to help pray for some of these people." He planted Alex in front of the line I was standing closest to. He began the only way he knew how.

"What do you want from God?" I heard my husband ask the woman standing before him.

"I love Jesus, and I want what you just got!" she said with a smile.

I observed as Alex prayed for her. Instantly her arms went straight up in the air, and she began praising God with the word *hallelujah,* just as I remembered I had. Then almost immediately, syllables rolled off her tongue, forming into an unknown language. Just as she requested, she received what Alex had experienced.

Lord, I can hardly believe my eyes and ears! God using my husband to powerfully minister to others! One after another, people stepped up for prayer, and Alex asked the same question; and the same thing happened. People who already were born-again believers were receiving the gift of the Holy Spirit. It was glorious!

Alex was as happy as when he had been born again, maybe even happier, by the time we left the fellowship that night. On the drive home, tears spilled from his eyes as he spoke about the special way God had touched him. The next morning, he shared with me something else extraordinary that had happened to him that same night. He had a vision of himself standing before a group of Indians in Alaska, telling them about Jesus.

"Honey," he explained, "it was so real that I could actually feel the cold air as I saw myself speaking. I knew for certain I was in Alaska."

"Alex, you seem shaken by this vision," I said. "But, honey, I think it's wonderful!"

Alex laughed and said, "I'm not positive if the vision means that God is actually calling me to be a missionary in Alaska. But it was so real … ," he said in almost a whisper, "… that I know I have something to do for God in connection with Alaska."

The following Sunday, Alex and I decided to take the family to the evening service at one of our local Assembly of God churches. To our astonishment, the guest speaker, Jerry Johnson, was a missionary to Alaska. Immediately I felt this happenstance of attending this particular service was more than coincidence.

Jerry and his wife, Pamela, were speaking in area churches about the need for Christians to go to Alaska to minister to the native Eskimo Indians. I could see by the expression on Alex's face that he was spiritually moved.

After the meeting, Alex went to talk with Jerry while the kids and I waited in the pew. Jerry's wife was seated in the first pew on the other side of the church, patiently waiting too. The pastor began locking the doors. Still the missionary and my husband continued talking alone in front of the altar.

Alex was pensive driving home and related very little of his conversation with the missionary.

Unexpectedly, one evening that week, the Johnsons stopped by the house, saying they had felt led of God to visit. Alex and I were surprised, but delighted.

Jerry told us that he had first received his call to Alaska twelve years before the Lord opened the doors for him to go.

Twelve years! Hum, this is interesting. Lord, I know you have Your perfect time for the book too. Please help me to have the faith and patience to wait for Your time, as did the Johnsons.

Jerry said he had always been an avid hunter and fisherman and was good at those sports, and that God uses his abilities in his missionary work.

What a coincidence! Lord, You know Alex is good at fishing and hunting too. This is exciting!

He went on to talk about having gone into the most remote areas of Alaska where a white man had never been seen by the Indians living there. He said that when he preached to them, he held his hunting rifle at his side.

"The Indians respect a hunter. That way," he said with a smile, "I get them to listen to the gospel!"

Pamela and Jerry told us that they had been praying that God would call someone—a man—to help them. When they were leaving that night, I think they already believed Alex was that man, because as they stepped through the door, Jerry turned to Alex and said, "Well, Brother Lance, I'll see you in Alaska!"

As we stood at the door watching them walk to their car, I wondered if Alex was "that man." If so, would Alex accept God's call?

Closing the door, I silently concluded, *Only God knows that answer.* I had learned that God knows the end from the beginning of our lives. I knew I could trust in that.

There was no more discussion between us about Alex's going to Alaska, but he immediately began corresponding with Jerry Johnson and sending him money to support the ministry.

I continued to remember the book in my prayers. I had kept a journal for many years, but I knew journaling did not a writer make. Not only had I recorded my thoughts and observations and the events of my life, but also I could see through journaling how the Scripture, when applied, worked in my daily life. Also, my journals reflected my spiritual progress. No one else had read them.

But since the day after Cara confirmed God's words to me and she agreed to type the book, I began re-reading my "before Christ" and "after Christ" journals to see if they might give me at least a way to begin this project. But I would wait to see how God would lead and for His inspiration to begin.

When it came to my ministry, invitations continued to come in to give biblical teachings on Christian radio on topics related to women. After my teachings, I was told, the station received the largest audience response ever. So I could see God the Holy Spirit had led me comfortably into a ministry to women. I shared with women's Christian organizations and in seminars, retreats, conferences, home prayer and fellowship gatherings, and more local Bible-believing churches throughout the city, state, and beyond.

Ironically, that included Reverend Rex Humbard's Cathedral of Tomorrow church. Alex was happy when I received the invitation to be guest speaker at its women's luncheon to which women from other Bible-believing churches throughout that city were invited. He encouraged me to accept it, even though I would have to travel a long distance from our home. Cara and I made a day's road trip to share Christ with that large gathering, and I still hold special memories in my heart, as does Cara, about all the works of God done for many of the women present at that gathering.

Nothing gave me more joy than sharing Christ with others, but I found myself becoming overwhelmed trying to take care of my family, busy household, and ministry. My public sharing was always done within the hours my husband was working and the children were in school. Only rarely did I accept an evening invitation.

When I thought about the fact that the Lord wanted me to write a book too, I wondered when in the world I would ever find enough time to do that. *Years from now,* could be the only answer. I had already been approached by three Christian publishers who had heard about our story and wanted to publish it. I prayed about each of those three offers, and each time I felt impressed to decline.

I always struggled with declining requests for me to do something for God, because I never wanted to say no to anything God wanted me to do. So these times, too, I hoped I had heard the answer correctly when I felt impressed to decline. Looking back, it does seem that it would have been impractical for a book to be part of God's will for my family at that time. Besides, I was already becoming stressed as I pushed to maintain my daily schedule in my home, plus receive drop-by visitors and telephone calls for ministry that came about as a result of sharing Christ publicly.

One day I felt so frazzled, so tired, I cried out for God to show me how I could go on juggling everything. *Lord, my life is getting out of control. I try to be available to those who feel they must talk with me or want to pray about their problem. I'm afraid to say no to anyone, Lord, because I'm not sure if I would be saying no to You.*

God's still small voice answered with words passing ever so gently through my mind:

My daughter, you are overaccommodating to people. Attend to your husband, to your children, and to your house, doing even the most menial task as though it were the Great Commission. I will make time for My ministry to others through you.

I immediately wrote the words on a piece of paper and tucked it into my Bible, until I could record them in my journal. I never wanted to forget them. As I learned to obey those words, I found great joy in doing even the most menial task. With that came wisdom and better organizational skills that restored order to my life.

God gave me a holy boldness to speak directly, but in love, to people about my time. I learned how to discern whether a person's phone call was urgent or whether I could call back when my family and household schedule allowed me free time. I learned to tell drop-by visitors that though I was pleased to see them, I hoped they would understand that I had only a limited amount of time to spend with them. And when I sensed it was time to stop, I had the confidence to politely let them know without offending them that I must get on with my home responsibilities and family commitments.

I was cognizant of the fact that the way I cared for my family and home was as much a testimony to Christ as the way I conducted my personal life. I was learning to know even better my sovereign yet practical God, who knew every circumstance of my life. And I knew I could maintain balance in my life only if I kept my priorities in order. I was learning that obeying what I believed to be the guidance of the Holy Spirit in all these matters kept Alex and me in harmony with each other. And just as God had promised that if I obeyed Him, He would redeem the time for me to serve Him, He did.

Almost a year later, Alex made his decision to resign his position as vice president and start his own business. I knew starting our own business would mean a big financial sacrifice that would require us to not only give up Alex's salary and benefits in favor of self-employment but also to mortgage everything we owned. We had managed to save a sizeable chunk of money for the children's college education. I expected to put all our savings on the line for Alex's venture, but I was nervous upon learning we would also have to put up our home and virtually everything else we owned for collateral. During this precarious midlife time, that was an awfully big financial debt to take on.

We would be back to where we started when we were newly-weds, owning nothing. Everything would now belong to the bank. However, my faith was in God and in Alex. There was no doubt in my mind that Alex could run his own business, since he had years of experience in the industry.

Alex took God as his partner and began the business, relying on His help. We worked together. He handled the buying and selling. I handled the phones and secretarial tasks. It was rough those early months. Alex was determined to operate the business with his partner's wisdom, and God answered his prayers time and time again. Alex was also determined to live a Christian lifestyle, and his personality remained miraculously stable. And remarkably, the business was solvent within one year.

In the meantime, the president of the board of directors of the largest Christian radio broadcasting company in our state, which owned and governed three stations (two in our state and one in Brazil), telephoned me to ask if I would permit my name to be entered into nomination for the position of trustee. Alex felt I should accept, pointing out that the kids were all leading busy lives now. Michael had graduated with honors and was already a freshman in college, and Laura would graduate in May. Between sports, the school newspaper, and after-school jobs, Laura and Steven, as well as Michael, were gone a lot, leaving me with more free time than ever before.

I had to admit that I would have preferred to have Alex serving in that position, since he had not been involved in any Christian service or mentioned his Alaska vision again, although he did still faithfully financially support the Johnsons' missionary ministry there. I was elected trustee (the only woman on the board) and began my service to the Lord with fourteen accomplished, successful, professional, and honorable Christian businessmen. Alex knew some of the men from Christian fellowships. He seemed proud of me.

Sales had grown by leaps and bounds during the second year, and the business was progressing financially. In anticipation of our future with all three of the kids soon to be in college and our eventual retirement, we reinvested all our profits into the company and acquired greater assets—and always tithed to our church and gave offerings to several ministries besides the Johnsons' work in Alaska. We had worked hard, especially Alex. But we knew our partner, God, had blessed us and made the business a running success.

One fall day while Alex was returning from having called on a customer outside the city, he decided to exit the freeway to drive some country roads on his way home. Alex was always driving rural roads looking for "the home of his dreams" in a natural setting and, hopefully, on the water—a river or lake. That day he found it! Excited, he hurried right home to tell me about it. It was for sale by owner. He thought it was providential that he had driven those particular back roads.

The next Sunday, he took the children and me to see it. It was located exactly twenty miles outside the city. None of us were anxious to see it, because none of us wanted to move; but when your husband and father is saying it is the dream home he always wanted and had worked hard for, how can that be disregarded? What was I going to say: *You can't buy it?*

"It's beautiful!" Alex said as he turned onto the road, driving slowly as we viewed the area. "Wait till you see it!"

We arrived and drove in front and parked on the circle. He was right. The house and the trees in front were impressive but immediately Alex ushered all of us to the back of the property, and we gasped. It was absolutely magnificent.

The trees were beautiful with red, orange, and yellow leaves. The twenty-five-year-old house with its four levels was custom built into the hill and surrounded by trees high atop that hill, overlooking a sixteen-acre lake. The woods to the right and left and across the lake from the house offered the illusion of a private retreat, camouflaging the surrounding homes also built on large lots but angled for privacy. It was a gorgeous, serene setting.

The property had redwood steps leading down to a deck with a mounted diving board and a boat dock. The kids instantly changed their minds and wanted to live there, and all of us had to admit it was a dream home, just as Alex had described. We liked the inside as much as the outside.

"We're going to be happier than ever in this house!" Alex declared. He said again that he wanted this home for his family and had worked hard for it.

The kids happily looked on as Alex and I signed the contract that very day. I prayed this home was one we could enjoy for years to come. I longed to plant roots and to let our roots grow deep here.

As a family, we worked together to clean and paint the interior and had new carpet installed. As always, the kids pitched in to help Alex and me with the packing, moving, and unpacking. After we had settled into our new home, Alex encouraged the kids to invite their friends over to boat, fish, and swim, and for cookouts.

Alex ran the company from an office on the lowest level of our new home. I still handled the phones and secretarial responsibilities, but in all those years, I never took a salary. Even though the company's profits increased greatly, Alex did not increase his salary. I was still running the household on his same monthly salary as before starting the business. Our goal was the same, to save for college and retirement, so we continued to reinvest the profits into the company.

Those early weeks when Alex took a break during the day, we would walk over the property. Sometimes we talked about needing to pinch ourselves to remind us that we were actually living in this home with all of God's appointments of nature surrounding it.

Now I was back in the present again. How long had the past held my mind captive? I glanced at the clock and saw it was almost eleven. The kids would be walking in from work very soon. I picked up my journal to record my thoughts. They were sad thoughts.

It's still hard for me to believe Alex had such wonderful spiritual experiences with his God then departed from it all. After Alex's family background and coming from so little, he achieved so much. To think he worked so hard to meet all his goals ... rose to the vice president position ... Then God granted his dreams and helped him accomplish his own successful business ... and he finally had his dream home on the lake ... I have come to believe that though God wants us to work hard and succeed, He designed us in such a way that we cannot gain meaning for our lives by only our work and career, and acquiring possessions. He designed us to receive our meaning for life in Him.

When Alex was ready to take early retirement, why didn't his vision of Alaska call him again, instead of his old lifestyle and another woman? It's a mystery to all of us. With all he had and gave up, I feel as sad for Alex as I feel angry at him.

The memory of all this tonight still stirred me and questions bombarded my mind, which I recorded:

How could Alex have been so greatly blessed, worked so hard to gain all that he had, and then give it up? Not to mention he was a well-loved man by his wife and children. I can't imagine how he could have done that. It's mind-boggling. He says the Christian life is just too hard for him to live ... but I don't get it. What was too hard about it? Or was it that young woman with the young body? ...

After my sarcastic thought I wrote **More later** and signed off for the night.

Gratefully, I tuned in to *In Touch* and caught most of Dr. Stanley's encouraging message. It was a good thing. My emotions, thoughts, and attitude needed an adjustment. I prayed for the kids and their safe drive home, and I prayed that God would help me better adjust to my new single status and be able to move on with my life.

I heard the kids come in one by one, and I went downstairs to greet them. We sat and talked for a while; then we all went to our own bedrooms—the kids, to study for a few hours; I, to listen to John MacArthur's radio program *Grace to You*. Remembering the last words in his teaching—that God will never leave you—I knew that was true; and I knew I needed to stay on track if I wanted to completely recover from my shattered dreams of the last three years. I knew the Holy Spirit was not only my comforter but also my helper, and I knew it would take God's help and His grace for me to make a healthy transition into my single-again life.

Before I turned off the light, my heart felt so thankful for all God had done for me in the past and how He was daily encouraging me to believe I could *begin again*.

Part 4
The Unexpected Turning

Chapter 15

Choices

The morning has not yet dawned, but I am awake. I glimpse the sunburst pattern over the ivory carpet created by the low night-light on the wall. Lying in bed, I realize this is the third day since our divorce. For some odd reason, I am remembering Alex's telling us after we moved into this home that because the business had done so well, we were finally going to treat ourselves to that family vacation in Hawaii we had always talked about. We never did.

But there were other delightful vacations after Alex became a Christian. Road trips to the Smoky Mountains and the fun we all had in Gatlinburg, Tennessee, while staying in that fabulous chalet secluded deep in the mountains ... and Quebec, Ontario, Canada, where we stayed in a cabin on a magnificent lake, boating and fishing ... The kids were excited when they caught lots of northern pike and Alex grilled them outside, and we ate dinners by the lake and watched the sun go down ... the weekend getaways to state lodges and boating and water skiing on lakes and rivers.

Memories ... what do I do with all these memories?

Slipping into my robe, I felt a morning chill in the room as I walked to the window-wall. Keeping the drapery closed against the cold glass, I separated the panels and the sheer window liner just enough so I could peek at the lake below. Once again, the ice-covered lake and snow-covered lawn and trees glisten as though they had been dusted with glitter. The scene before me offered a momentary winter solace.

Now I mused over this house, with its own unique personality like a character in a book. *It simply gives me pleasure. I am truly grateful for this house. I never take it for granted. It is a blessing, with the natural terrain that always stirs my heart and arouses praises from my spirit. I think it's a privilege to live here and a privilege to tend to it. But how long can we afford its high maintenance without Alex here?*

I had never coveted such a house, but I truly enjoyed the mental, emotional, and spiritual restfulness it offered me.

Waiting for my morning coffee to brew, I drew open the kitchen drapery. Day was breaking. I thought about the years I had stood in this very spot, awed by the beauty surrounding the lake: the bravura of blooming springs, the splendor of vibrant summers, the breathtaking foliage of falls, and the spectacular snows of winters. I felt as though I were on vacation all year round.

Now I poured my coffee and carried the steaming mug to my special corner and set it on the coaster. As I opened the drapery and the white sheer window-liner, light filled the room. I read a couple of chapters in the Bible and then picked up my journal. I did not know what thoughts I would record, but I was ready just in case.

Leaning back to rest my head, I thought again about how hard Alex had worked to buy this, his dream home on the lake. He loved this house. When we moved here, he was still working hard, putting in long hours, but it was exhilarating for him. He could leave his desk to look out at the serene setting or walk the property.

He had to travel some days, but working for himself, he figured out ways he could work the sales territory without having to be out overnight. He had had years of that and was glad those days were behind him—a luxury only because of owning the business. I had never seen Alex so completely satisfied with his work. He derived a sense of pride from it and a great deal of pleasure. In fact, the business was doing better than even he had expected. We were enjoying our life.

Graduation day from high school came for Steven, and like his brother and sister, he graduated with honors, for which we were proud. Michael had not wanted a party when he graduated. But Laura had a big one with family and friends, and now we were planning the same for Steven. This house was built for outdoor entertainment. We rented tables and chairs and set them up all over the yard. That day we picnicked with good food, good conversation, and lots of laughing, and some of my older nieces and nephews took the boat out on the lake. I could tell Alex was very proud and happy that others were enjoying his dream home on the lake.

God continued to answer prayer and guide Alex with wise decision making. Our profits had consistently grown year after year. Instead of spending more because we now could afford to, with Michael and Laura already attending college and in preparation for Steven's following right behind them, plus early retirement not very far off, we continued to invest all our profits back into the company.

Also, we had neither changed our style of living nor had we missed tithing to God's work. After a while, it seemed to us that our business success was in direct proportion to our tithing. The more sales and profits increased, the more our tithe and offerings increased—then again, the more we gained financially. We learned experientially that we could not outgive God.

We were living a life that after those first seven years of marriage, I would never have believed possible with Alex. But Jesus Christ had begun rescuing us in 1966 when He first came into my life. God needs only one person in a marriage or family to give an open door to the other members of the family for household salvation. I had watched miracle after miracle.

At this point in our lives, Alex and I felt like the most blessed persons on earth—not because God had prospered us or because of the money, but because of the fact that God had kept us together through thick and thin all these years, and we had been enjoying a Christian family and social life. Alex and I expected the coming year also would be a good, healthy, and happy one for our family.

Now a scene flashed in my mind, startling me, and I stiffened in my chair. I let my mind wander back three years ago to a snowy February morning in 1982. I could see myself settled in my special corner in front of the wall of glass, for my Bible study and prayer time, and enjoying the breathtaking winter scene before me. It was a heavy snowfall that looked like cotton balls floating to the ground. After praying for everyone on my list, for some reason I found myself thinking about "the book," as I had from time to time, and wondering what I should write next. Then I was carried back to the first time I had heard the words *You will write your testimony, and it shall be a book.*

I vividly recalled my reaction to those words. Pleading my case back then that I could not write a book was not without validity. I was not a writer. Even though I had kept a personal journal for years, I knew one could take great liberties with that kind of writing. I knew that was not like writing a book worthy of being published.

And in addition, I had reasoned with God that there was a big difference between speaking thirty minutes to an hour to a group or a radio audience and writing a whole book with private details of my life. I knew what that would mean. I wrestled with my fears about that and other issues: knowing that my motive for writing this book could be misunderstood, knowing what I wrote could be critiqued on every level, knowing the strain it could put on my family and the criticism they might have to endure. I thought that would be just too high a price to pay.

Eventually my healthy, reverent fear of God overcame my fear of what He was asking me to do. So I was ready to start. I only dabbled at first. My writing was terrible, and my many starts filled the wastebasket under my desk. Obviously, I was not in sync with God's time to start. Doubts entered my mind again.

In the meantime, I tried something else. I called my close friend, Dottie, who was not a professional writer, but a very good writer, nonetheless. She got me started by tape recording me speaking a portion of my testimony. Cara typed my words from the tape.

The very day she brought her typed pages to the house, only minutes later a minister whom I had never met before showed up at my door, unannounced. He pastored a local Bible-believing church, and at that time, he also produced a small Christian publication called *En Suma,* meaning "the body of Christ." He had heard about me and had come for the purpose of asking permission to print my testimony in the next issue.

Cara and I looked at each other in astonishment. The minister was flabbergasted when I handed him the typed pages. Each of us marveled at God's timing. My faith grew a notch for sure when my testimony was published "as is."

Faith was on the rise again a few months later when I received an invitation to be a contributing writer for a series of issues for another Christian magazine, *The Vision*. Rather than my testimony, however, biblical teachings were requested. Although a frequent radio guest delivering scripturally based teachings on topics related to today's contemporary woman, I had never written a Bible teaching. My own writing surprised me, as did the positive responses from the *Vision* readers. I believed God was definitely preparing me.

The truth is, God had only let me get my feet wet. I knew writing a few pages of my story or writing text for biblical teachings and seeing them in print was a far cry from writing a manuscript. Nevertheless, after that I found myself seriously praying for the inspiration to write.

More time went by until, curiously, a desire came to read one of my old journals. That stimulated memories, taking me back in time, and to my amazement, I felt inspired to begin writing. Words flowed through me onto paper like liquid being poured from a bottle. I was reliving every detail of God's intervention in my life. As it turned out, it seems my habit of journaling, which chronicled my life year after year, was a beneficial source of reference. Over time as I felt inspired to write or record more of my testimony, Cara typed the pages.

I managed to go on writing parts of my story—the good times— that detailed the miraculous works of God in my life and in my family. However, I found those parts did not fit together as I had hoped, but rather left big gaps in my story.

When praying about this, I felt distinctly impressed that the gaps in my story were the bad times, the painful times. I had carefully avoided writing about them. I did not want to relive them as I had the good times. *Besides,* I reasoned, *everyone has a skeleton or two hiding in their closet, but who wants to take theirs out to display before the whole world? Not me!*

I found myself more than a little reluctant to expose for public scrutiny my imperfections, my innermost thoughts and feelings, my fears and weaknesses, my actions and reactions, and that of my family, in the midst of tragedy. Also, I did not want my story to be a tell-all book. I only wanted readers to see God's amazing grace, His faithfulness, and to encourage them. But the truth was that I still cared too much about the opinions of others. Nevertheless, I knew God was definitely calling for more exposure!

That confirmation came when my now grown daughter boldly spoke, "Mother, God wants you to write the whole truth. Knowing the painful things God has brought you through and His faithfulness to make you the healthy, happy, and whole person you are today is what will help the people who read your book. That's your testimony! That's your story!"

Her words penetrated my heart and spirit, breaking down my resistance. Then it was clear to me. Since perfection is not attainable by anyone on Earth, we believers and nonbelievers alike, with all our imperfections, are no different today from those written about in the Bible. The same sorrows, fears, failures, sufferings, and tragedies, in one form or another, come to every person, every marriage, and every family. Though some are more extreme than others, all are common to the human condition. God forgave and changed those early believers we read about in Scripture and turned their tragedies into triumphs, and God, being no respecter of persons, had done the same for me.

I realized more exposure was necessary since the whole purpose of this book was to share knowledge and present evidence that would encourage other Christian and non-Christian *walking wounded* women to believe God could do for them what He has done for me. With that fresh reminder, I was committed to writing the whole truth. It was then that fear of the opinions of others instantly left me.

Fully yielding to include the not-so-pleasant as well as the pleasant details of my story had been a big hurdle to get over, but crucial to the cause. The struggle of it strengthened me emotionally, gave me courage, and stretched me spiritually. Time passed. When I prayed, I received no further direction about the book. Then ...

On that snowy February morning in 1982, as I prayed about what I should write next, words came ever so gently: *Go forward with the book, for the last pages are being written even now. It shall be used for your sustenance and My glory.*

I was stunned. Although such times were rare, I was now awestruck yet again that the living God had actually spoken His direction to me. In the natural, it was hard for me to get my finite mind around those profound words. I believed they were from God, but I did not understand the part that said "for the last pages are being written even now."

What could this mean? Could the "last pages" be our retirement and trips to Alaska to help Jerry and Pamela Johnson in their missionary work? Maybe we'll even take that family vacation to Hawaii too.

The other words also were puzzling: "It shall be used for your sustenance and My glory."

That makes no sense to me. Why would I need sustenance in any form from the book? We're doing great. Alex and I even help to provide financial sustenance for others ... for ministries.

This all was baffling, to say the least. I did not even mention it to Alex. I promptly released to God my questions and vain imaginings, and those revealed words, knowing if the words were from Him, they would come to pass in His time.

Little did I know that February morning how soon I would begin living out those words and how dramatically my life would change. Those "last pages" would unfold for me in shocking, unexpected ways.

* * *

Alex and I continued to work hard in the business. He and our partner, God, made the business so successful that Alex decided we could cut back our work schedule to half days. That was the first week of April 1982, only two months after hearing the words *the last pages are being written even now.*

With this gift of extra time in our days, I anticipated spending more leisure hours with my husband, doing fun things, going places, or doing nothing special, just being together.

Ever since we had started the business years ago, my weekdays had been confined to home in order to handle my job for our company. Between the business and caring for the needs of my family and home, my days were always full. Nevertheless, daily I managed to fit in early morning private Bible study and journaling. Most importantly, God redeemed time for my public ministry for Him. However, rarely did a day offer time for me to enjoy my other personal interests or my friends.

Now having that extra time in the day was sheer delight for me. It allowed me to accomplish everything without the usual rushing. Besides the anticipation of spending more time with Alex, I had more time to attend daytime Christian women's meetings, to spend an occasional luncheon and afternoon with a girlfriend, to relax by the lake during the afternoon to read or to write in my journal, to take a long, pampering midday bath if I chose, to work in my flower garden, or to enjoy my art craft.

Alex worked on our property some days, but then he appeared to become restless with the extra time on his hands. He began disappearing in the afternoons. Despite my cautious, gentle probing into his mysterious whereabouts, he avoided disclosing where he had been or with whom. I observed a change in him. It came slowly, only subtly at first, with a change in his routine, his habits, and his attitude. On occasion he was irritable with me for no reason, criticizing me for little things. I wondered what was wrong. When I asked, he apologized and assured me nothing was wrong.

One day in late April, however, he came into the house and promptly confessed to Laurie and me that he thought, after all these years, Satan was trying to pull him back to the horse races, but he declared he was determined he would not give in to that temptation anymore. We told him how proud we were of him for taking this bold, resolute stand.

But something else—something unseen—was going on within Alex. Not long after that, he stopped going to church; then he no longer attended the men's prayer breakfasts he enjoyed, nor did he want to attend the Christian dinner meetings we enjoyed together.

It was not long until the children and I realized that Alex had given in, after all. He had been frequenting the afternoon thorough-bred horse races. After we reminded him of his determination to resist that temptation and how proud we had been of him for standing tough, he told us not to worry, that he believed he had enough self-control to place only small bets for entertainment. As far as Alex was concerned now, watching the "sport of kings" and placing small bets on the horse races was just for relaxation and fun. Also, he declared then that he was determined not to get hooked this time.

After committing his life to Christ, Alex had given up his horses to what he believed was obedience to God's guidance. The horses were God's innocent creatures; owning them had not been a sin and certainly not all of his problem back then. It had been gambling for high stakes.

However, despite Alex's resolve not to get hooked again, soon after taking that first step back into his old life, he took another, and another. It was heartbreaking for us to watch what was happening to him again. The kids and I prayed hard for God to rescue him before it was too late. I begged Alex to get spiritual counseling, to ask Judge Stahl, Bob and Bill, or one of the other Christian men he knew to pray for him, but he refused. When asking him to see Dr. Herald again, the kids and I committed ourselves to join him in professional counseling—whatever it took—pledging our love and support for as long as it took for him to recover. He refused again.

Alex's worldly lifestyle was glaringly open. Now his compul-sive gambling was taking him to the thoroughbred races afternoons, day after day, and the night harness races, night after night during the summer months—and always to the bars after the races.

Judge and Anne Stahl always called on Sunday evenings. Knowing how much they loved Alex, I asked them to pray for him because he was going to the race track again, gambling and drinking too. We were like family. During Alex's spiritual relapse, the judge often stated, "How could Alex backslide after the Lord has done so much for him? Why doesn't God do something? Anne and I feel bad for you and the kids. You shouldn't have to go through this." He always concluded with the same question, "How could he forget so easily what God has done? I just don't understand this." I would just respond, "Please keep praying for him, Judge."

By now Alex was out many nights until the wee hours of the morning, and I fought my suspicion of another woman. I never accused him though.

One warm afternoon in October, Laura decided to wash her car in the driveway in front of the garage. She had very little free time, because she was carrying a full schedule at the university, which was a long drive from home. Her first class started at eight o'clock in the morning. She also worked two part-time jobs: one was working retail evening hours through the week and the other was waitressing Friday and Saturday nights at a family steak house. So it was a rare opportunity when she could fit washing her car into her busy schedule.

After wiping the car dry, Laura hung the towel over the rolled up window on her car to dry and spread the car mats out over the shrubs along the side of the garage.

Alex arrived home from the track and burst through the garage door into the family room, in a fury. He spit a few choice curse words at Laurie for leaving her car mats and towel spread out for "the whole neighborhood to see what yard apes we are." I was in shock. I had not seen this kind of temper for years. Then he turned his foul mouth on me for permitting it. He called Laura a "slob" and a "stupid idiot." My heart ached for her. He was out of control.

Oh no, not again. That sounds like "someone" I know.

I told Alex he should be ashamed, that he had no right to say those awful things to his daughter, and that he should apologize to her, and me too, and demanded, "Right now!" He just laughed at me.

Nothing Laura or I could say quieted him. He grabbed a beer from the fridge, mumbling about the "idiots" he had to live with, saying, "You don't know how hard it is for me to live with you people. You're so far below my intelligence." I gasped at that remark. *He has really gone off the deep end this time.*

Leaving the room, I found Laurie and tried to comfort her. She said, "Dad will never change for good, Mom. He's getting worse. He probably lost a lot of money at the track today! Even God can't change Dad, if he won't let Him. Don't you know that?"

Alex was still complaining through dinner about how the neighbors were probably saying what yard apes we all were. He called us "ingrates" and "worthless." It was disgusting.

I was already showered and dressed for one of my rare evening speaking engagements at a Methodist church in a small town south of us. It was one I had committed to weeks before, but now I felt I was in no condition to speak for God. But the meeting was in an hour and a half. How could I cancel on such short notice? What reason would I give? But how could I speak about Jesus, when I was so angry at my husband and felt so defeated? I was frantic.

Laura assured, "Mom, you go. You can't let Dad keep you from doing this. God will be with you; don't worry, and I'll be praying for you. And don't worry about me."

Alex was still uptight after dinner. I heard him still mumbling that we were all ingrates and worthless.

It started raining just before I left for the church. As it poured while I drove, I cried and prayed: *Lord, please ... please, help me. I've tried everything. Please, Lord, You know I can't bear any more! Please comfort Laurie. Oh Jesus, I thought Alex was healed—that I'd never see this ugly other personality again. And after being so blessed by You, how could he go back to his old life? And Lord, You know we don't provoke him. No human being could be so cruel to others—especially to his daughter. Lord, please don't let that horrible dark side, Mr. Hyde, take over Alex again. Save him from that. I couldn't bear it for him—or us.*

You've said in Your Word that You won't give Your believers more than they have strength to bear. I know I can't ever live with his abuse again. And I know You don't want me to live with it. Either deliver my husband from Satan or deliver us from him!

I started praying in my prayer language and arrived at the church, with a tear-stained face, wondering how on earth God could use me to speak of "heavenly things" after the "hell" I had just experienced in my home. I was there to edify the body of Christ, inspire their faith, and encourage them to trust Jesus Christ with everything in their lives. But I was the one in need of ministry.

I went into the restroom.

Oh God, I can't do this. I feel like a hypocrite. How can I be honest before these people when my home life is a nightmare! Jesus, I can't do this ... but, Lord, how would I ever explain to other Christians why ... what I'm living with? Oh, my Jesus, whatever should I do? Lord, I don't even know if I can feel Your leading tonight. Please, help me, Jesus. Tell me what to do ... what to say. Oh Lord, lift me above my ugly existence tonight. Forgive me.

Peace came and with it the still small voice of God: *My daughter, I only require that you tell the Good News. Do you not have good news to tell? Only be faithful, and tell My Good News in your life.*

My pain was gone. What a precious blessing! God was so faithful.

With that I reached for a paper towel, wet it, and washed my face. I freshened my makeup, put on a smile, and trusted God for the rest. I walked into the sanctuary, ready to obey the Lord. A few minutes later, I was introduced, and from that moment, God lifted me far above my circumstances and blessed the "good news" I shared. Ministry of the Holy Spirit to the people followed, and Jesus was honored. I went home renewed mentally and spiritually, having released all to Jesus and knowing that I could trust Him with my life.

The next morning, I knew what I had to do. I remembered my friend who worked for a Christian attorney, and I phoned to make an appointment; but she suggested I talk to him right then. The kids had already told me they thought their dad was getting worse, and they worried that if he kept on drinking like he was, he might slip over the edge and do something more terrible. When I told the kids I had made the appointment, they were relieved. Alex would be home on Sunday, and I knew I had to tell him about it then.

Alex sat lamblike at the kitchen table that evening, just as though his terrible scene of carrying on and accusing his daughter of being a slob and our family appearing to the neighbors as yard apes had not even occurred.

"Alex," I began cautiously, "I've made an appointment to see an attorney next week to file for a legal separation." His face went ashen. He was shocked and speechless, so I went on. "He's a friend of Marilyn, and I've already had a phone conversation with him about our problems. I've told him I don't want a divorce, so this is the only step I knew I could take. We just can't live together like this anymore. I won't live like this!"

"Oh honey, no!" he finally spoke. His eyes filled with tears.

"Please don't leave me. I can't live without you. I love you so much, and I love the kids too. I'll do anything, anything! Give me one more chance to prove it. I'll stop going to the races and betting; I'll stop drinking. Honey, I don't know why I did what I did. I guess I was mad at myself for losing a bundle and took it out on Laura and you. I'm sorry. You have to believe me. I won't do it again. Please don't leave me! Please ... please ... " His voice trailed to a whisper, and he reached across the table and took my hands in his. "Don't do this, honey."

Without answering, I went upstairs to Laura's room to tell her what her father had said.

"Don't listen to him, Mom. He's promised so many times, and I don't believe him. He might want to stop living like he is, but he won't be able to. Don't cancel your appointment—please don't."

I left Laura's room and went to Steven's.

"Mother, Dad's not going to change for good," he responded when I repeated Alex's promises. "Don't listen to him."

I went to Michael's room. He opened his door to my knock, heard me out, and was quiet for a few moments. Then he spoke.

"Mom, if he's really afraid this time, knowing you're actually going to see an attorney and file, maybe he will get help. I don't know, but this is what we've been praying for. Maybe he should have one last chance."

Monday morning I called the attorney. After I related Alex's words and my children's responses, there was a long silence. Finally he said, "Mrs. Lance, knowing the Christian you are and knowing how you've prayed for your husband to reach the point where he will choose to get help, perhaps we should delay filing for now. If he gets help, maybe your marriage and family can be saved. If he doesn't, well, you'll know you've done everything possible. I'll be praying for you."

When I hung up the phone, suddenly I felt emotionally confused again. I was afraid to give Alex another chance, but I would have done anything reasonable to keep my family together; and I did want him to get help, so I prayed for God to show me what to do. All the rest of the day and evening, I prayed for God's direction. Silence was His only answer.

Now I realized God had renewed my faith, after my sharing at the Methodist church, to stand strong in Christ, obeying His Word and His voice, forgiving Alex. By that evening, I made my decision to give my husband that "one more chance" for which he had begged. I prayed God would conquer Alex and deliver us all from his horrible dark side that was trying to take hold of him again. With continued determination to live Christ's way before Alex, regardless of his behavior, I believed the Lord would walk me through whatever trials lay ahead.

That night getting ready for bed, I told Alex I had cancelled my appointment with the attorney on the condition that he keep his promise to get help. Gratefully, again he promised he would. Then Alex made an unsolicited declaration to me: "I know my drinking and gambling are wrong, and I shouldn't do it and I'm gonna stop; but at least I don't mess around with other women like many of the guys I know. I tell them, 'I don't need another woman,' " he said with his winning smile. "I've got the best wife around. And I tell the guys that too."

I heard what he said and I wanted to believe him, so at that time I put my suspicion of another woman on the back burner, so to speak; but still I felt something inside I could not shake. I did not know what Alex went on to think before he went to sleep, but my thoughts kept me awake long after he was snoring.

Alex's overt lifestyle is humiliating enough to bear—but another woman? I know I could not endure that too. I hoped we had at least one decent thing left between us throughout these horrible months of trying and hoping and praying for Alex and my marriage.

The next morning Alex announced, "I want to see a psychiatrist. I want to get help."

I looked at him and answered quizzically, "Okay?"

"I'm afraid I'm going to lose you. Am I gonna lose you, Alisha? I don't want to lose you."

I was silent.

"I don't want to go back to Dr. Herald. Will you call today and make an appointment for me with another doctor?"

I thought that was the answer to all of our prayers.

"Yes, Alex, I will. Will you see a psychiatrist who is also a Christian?"

"Yes," he agreed, "That's even better!"

Giving Alex one more chance was risky. I could not have done it except for the track record he had established over the past twelve years of walking with the Lord. I reminded myself that my faith had to be in God, not in Alex. Cara, the judge, and Anne would be so pleased to know he finally wanted help. They had faithfully prayed for Alex to come to his senses and return to God.

Later I learned Michael had tape-recorded his dad one night when he was ranting about something, and afterward Michael had played it for him. Alex had listened to it all and said, "No one in his right mind could carry on like that."

That morning I called the Christian radio station, knowing that Christian doctors were interviewed from time to time. I spoke with my long-time friend, Bobbie, co-founder of the station. I asked if she knew of a Christian psychiatrist or psychologist. She recommended a Dr. Martin and gave me his telephone number.

I had been so emotionally shattered and distraught before now that I had told no one but Cara, the judge, and Anne about Alex's return to his old lifestyle, and I had maintained self-control when speaking with anyone else. For some reason and without intending to, I blurted out a desperate plea for Bobbie to pray for Alex and the rest of us. I ended up briefly sharing the truth about our situation.

Bobbie expressed her shock and her compassion. Of course, before now, she had known nothing of Alex's problems. She felt impressed to pray right then, over the phone. She began to pray for each member of our family. Then she paused, and the stillness went on for several moments before she spoke again.

"Alisha," she said, hesitantly, "this doesn't have anything to do with Alex's problems we just prayed about, but I feel impressed that your husband has had other women in the past, and he has another woman now."

Although I was shaken from hearing her words, I was sure they were from God; and though hard to admit, I knew I had felt the same thing within. I did not doubt Bobbie; her ministry was proven of the Lord. But those words were crushing to me now.

I reminded myself of what I knew in my heart. God always reveals the truth to me — as to all believers — when we're looking to Him with our whole heart. He's our Father, and we are His children. He doesn't want us to be deceived. He loves His children just as we love our children. Parents never want their kids to be deceived and will use any proper means to make them see the truth. Our heavenly Father is no different.

I knew this was a truth I now had to face.

Worn down as I was by the months of struggle and the recent days of extraordinary stress, throwing myself on God's tender mercies and loving kindness was by now a habit.

I can't confront Alex about another woman now, God. Frankly, I can't handle one more ugly thing. The truth has not been hidden from You, Lord. Oh, my Jesus, even though I know the truth and it hurts, I don't deny it; and I do want to face the truth, but I can't deal with it now. I'm so tired. I'm tired of all the stress, of all the pain and heartache.

Immediately I phoned to make the appointment with Dr. Martin for the next week.

Alex stopped leaving the house now. Instead of going to the races, he worked on the property all week, and he seemed to be in a good mood and displayed self-control. Was he praying? Also, I wondered every day before his appointment, *Will he keep his promise to see the doctor? Will he be honest with the doctor, and with me?*

Suddenly I was back in the present again. *These memories are hard. Help, Lord.*

I opened my Amplified Bible and felt impressed to read Isaiah 43 again. I did not remember all that was written in that chapter, but the peace of God came over me as I began to read verse 2: "When you pass through the waters, I will be with you, and through the rivers, they will not overwhelm you. When you walk through the fire, you will not be burned *or* scorched, nor will the flame kindle upon you."

I knew God was encouraging me again, emphasizing His earlier promise to be with me in any trial I might have to walk through. Closing my Bible, I then opened my journal to write my last thoughts for the morning:

I can hardly believe Alex's choices. They not only changed his life, but they changed our lives. Oh, I know I've written that before. No, I've written it more than once. This morning his choices trigger fresh, painful feelings in me that remind me I have a long way to go to be emotionally healed and to fully recover. But reading God's Word makes me know He's still trying to keep me on track so nothing will overwhelm me. Oh yes, that's right! I just read that. Thank You, my Jesus! Here I go. The third day of my single life ...

I signed off this morning's entry with *More later!* and closed my journal. I was ready to begin another day, whispering a prayer, "Help me hold it together again today, Lord."

Chapter 16

Consequences

It was dark when I arrived home. It had drizzled most of the day, so by the time I stopped at the grocery after work and shopped, forty minutes later the already freezing temperature had dropped. When I started driving home, the freeway was fine, but I dreaded my exit onto the winding country roads to our house. They would be getting slippery. *Lord, please protect me and others driving on these roads tonight.* I always prayed the same for the kids when they worked until the shopping center closed and were driving home on these back roads at almost eleven o'clock. *Thank God, none of us have had an accident.*

I lugged the bags of groceries in from the garage and put them away. I felt the emptiness of the house more than usual tonight. *Strange. I didn't feel lonely today. Too busy, as usual. But I guess it's natural for loneliness to creep in at night. Lonely, but I don't want company ... None of my feelings have made sense for the last three days. I feel out of step with the world. Maybe this is normal; I don't know. It was a good day at work. I think I manage there. But home alone ... I don't know ... I seem to relapse. I'm an emotional mess!*

After dinner I read the newspaper, then made a cup of tea and took it with me to my special corner. Closing the drapery, I muttered, "I'm really tired tonight." I intended to finish my novel, those same last two chapters. But I only managed to finish one chapter, because I kept having flashes of Alex. Finally, I put my book on the table, stretched my legs out, propped my feet onto the ottoman, and leaned back, breathing a long sigh.

The thought about the *choices* we make and their *consequences* came to mind. *Alex did make a right choice after Michael played that tape back for him and he heard himself ranting, and also when he thought he was going to lose me.* I let the memory take me back there.

After Alex had gone through several sessions with Dr. Martin but still had not offered to discuss them with me, I scheduled a private session with the doctor, at which time he explained to me that he had prescribed Alex a medication called lithium, which would maintain the chemical balance in his brain. "And, he also needs in-depth therapy," Dr. Martin said. "By the way, I warned him not to mix alcohol with the lithium." Both Alex and I already knew that.

Alex seemed determined to comply with the doctor's orders, and he obviously took his medication. Over the next eight to ten weeks, he continued his therapy sessions with Dr. Martin, which Alex told me, to his delight, began and ended with prayer. He was acting like a normal human being again. He seemed to enjoy feeling better. He was not drinking beer at home, and as far as I knew, he was not visiting bars.

But something happened during Alex's third month of medication. He started acting restless and agitated again, and by the end of that month, his behavior and emotional state were once more disturbing. I still had not seen Alex drinking, and I knew there was still no beer in the house. But he was disappearing for a few hours each day, and I suddenly realized, my heart sinking, that it might not be due to business as he had told me.

Concerned, I decided to count the pills in his refill prescription of forty-five pills to see if he had been taking them every day. I counted thirty-six pills. He had taken only nine!

Alex is smart enough to know not to take them if he drinks at the same time. It can be lethal! Has he made a choice? Are his absences telling me he's made a choice for alcohol over medication for health? Over our marriage? Over our whole life together? Over Christ?

"Help me, Jesus!" I whispered as I put the pills back into the container and placed it on the shelf in the exact same spot.

That afternoon I kept busy in an effort to escape all the negative thoughts—the anger, resentment, and fears—bombarding my mind. Alex was now outside working on the dock.

Like Scarlett O'Hara, I decided, *I'll think about that tomorrow!* I could not face one more confrontation or ugly scene. I could not even pray.

Finally I allowed myself to again think about this newest shock: *Nine capsules—he's only taken nine! He's tried to deceive me into believing he was still taking his medication and trying to stay well. He said he loves me and the children more than anything in the world. Oh, sure! He told Dr. Martin he had been a Christian and wanted God to restore him. Yet he still refuses any spiritual counseling from the men friends he knows would be glad to help him. What's going to happen to him? I've had it, though! I shouldn't care what happens to him!*

I said nothing to the children that night, but I knew I would have to deal with all of this tomorrow.

The next morning I called Dr. Martin to tell him of my discovery.

"Alisha, I'm sorry to hear this. He's a nice guy who just happens to have a big problem, which is unfortunate, but it can be controlled. I thought he wanted to be well. I can't help him if he's going to neglect my medical advice," the doctor responded. "Not even God can help him unless he wants to be helped. And I can't tell you what to do either. You'll just have to do what you feel God wants you to do."

I hung up the phone and cried aloud, "What more can I do?"

Instantly I was stilled within and I heard, *Enough.*

Heartsick from too many problems, too many promises, too many disappointments, and too many shattered dreams, I continued to move through the rest of that day in frenzied busyness one minute and sitting zombie-like the next—not daring to think, not daring to feel.

I knew I had to face my predicament, and I had to call the attorney. Immediately I was struck with a paralyzing fear like the one other time, years ago, when I had told Alex we had to separate. Now I was afraid to leave my marriage, and I was afraid to stay. Then another kind of fear struck.

What would the Christian community say if I separated from my husband? I had been in the public eye for so many years. I had prayed with hundreds of women, encouraging them to obey biblical teachings for wives and to believe for their husbands' conversions to Christ, not to mention all those people with whom I had publicly shared my testimony at women's meetings and church services and over Christian radio. Now my husband and I were separating.

I can't do it, Lord. The Christian community will scorn me. I've never exposed my husband's abuse and addictions. Will people say I've failed as a wife? That I'm in disobedience to Your Word and out of Your will? But I can't stay with Alex either, Lord. Yet ... more than all that, I'm afraid that I'll shame Your name by breaking up my marriage.

My fear, my pride, and my shame were unbearable. On my knees, I begged Jesus to help me, but no words of guidance came this time. It seemed as though the heavens were brass, and my cries to God could not break through. I would have done anything to keep my family together, short of ever again being a victim of abuse. I would never again intentionally endure Mr. Hyde's cruel behavior.

The next day, new information came to me from a reliable source. Adding insult to injury, Alex had indeed crossed over the line into adultery. My discerning had been true, and Bobbie's words had been from God. Now all that ugly truth was confirmed. My husband had professed his love for me and the kids and had begged for that one more chance, but he had not only tried to deceive me by pretending to take his medication, but he had also entered a relationship with not just another woman, but a much younger woman.

I felt numb.

Calmly I went to the kitchen and put on a pot of coffee. After the coffee maker gave its last wheeze and sigh, I filled a mug and carried it into the living room. Sitting on the sofa, I took three deep breaths and exhaled slowly. I allowed myself to think about this new confirmation of Alex's deceptions. It was the height of insult to me, his wife—and insult to God.

Just at the time in his life when God has blessed him financially more abundantly than either of us would have imagined possible! Is this what all my prayers for him over the years have come down to? Instead of his God and his faithful wife, he has chosen another woman? What consequences await Alex—all of us—for his choices?

I felt a shudder. *You have to pray, Alisha. You have to hang on to God,* I told myself. But I was at the end of my strength—unable to pray, unable to even cry. *Now I know why I heard, "Enough."* God had seen it all. I would give Alex no more chances. Everything had been done that I knew to do. I would do no more.

Robot-like, I walked into the kitchen, picked up the phone, and dialed the attorney's office, ready to eat humble pie and tell him that "one more chance" had not worked. He agreed to see me on January 2.

That evening I knew what I had to do. I was quivering inside when I sat down with Alex and quietly told him I just could not do this anymore, that I had made the decision to file for a legal separation. I did not say anything about his deception with the medication or the other woman. I did not want to go there. I did not want to hear any of his excuses, declarations of love, or any begging for another chance.

He seemed to calmly listen and accept what I said, almost as though he expected it—as if it were inevitable.

"Okay," he said, and he got up from the table and went downstairs to his office. I sighed with relief. I could hardly believe he did not explode at my announcement. I went upstairs to my special corner and breathed easier because I had gotten through that without emotionally caving in. *How will we get through the holidays?*

The next day, we would all feel the fallout of Alex's true, unexpressed emotional reaction to my words the night before.

It was two days before Christmas. The children were on college break and were all home that particular evening. Steven was in his room studying, Laura and I were at the kitchen table icing gingerbread men, and Michael was in the den off the family room when Alex walked in the front door. We exchanged a pleasant enough hello. I wanted to keep everything as calm as possible, to get through the holidays.

I sighed with relief when he went directly down to his office on the lower level and closed the door.

Suddenly Alex burst through the door into the family room. He held a double-barreled shotgun in his hand—pointed directly at me.

Laura and I froze in fear. Michael walked out of the den at that exact moment. Alex yelled at me, "You're dead if you leave me!"

"What are you doing, Dad? Put that gun down!" Michael calmly demanded.

Alex did not move the gun; it was still pointed at me, and he yelled, "I mean it; I'm gonna kill you!"

"You don't mean that, Dad; give me the gun. Come on, Dad. I can tell you're drunk," Michael said. "Give me the gun, and go on downstairs and sleep it off."

Turning to look at Michael, he appeared almost afraid of him for a moment. Alex was not facing his little boy. He was facing a young adult man, larger and stronger than he.

Steven heard his dad and came running downstairs to the kitchen. Seeing the gun now pointing at Michael, he screamed, "Dad! What are you doing? Put that away!"

Speaking quietly but firmly, Michael, taking small steps toward his father, urged again, "Dad, give me the gun. You don't know what you're doing."

Alex had a fierce look in his eyes as he glared at Michael, not saying a word, but with the gun still pointed at him. Michael showed no fear, but I was so scared for him.

Then he turned again and pointed the gun at me and shouted, "I told you I'd kill you, if you leave me!" I was petrified. I thought he was ready to pull the trigger.

Steven was afraid for Michael and started to step down into the family room to help him, but Michael ordered, "No, Steven! Stop! Get Mom and Laura upstairs!"

Steven took a step toward me, saying, "Come on, Mom."

I started to get up from the table.

"Sit down!" Alex roared. "You can't get away from me!"

Steven halted in his steps. Submissively, I slowly lowered myself down in my chair. Terrified, Laurie had not moved.

"Go, Steven! ... Now!" Michael insisted.

Steven was torn. He wanted to get us out of there, but I could see he was worried about leaving his brother. I was torn too. I wanted to go, and the kids wanted to go; but we were so afraid for Michael.

Alex started cursing me. "I told you, I'm gonna kill you! I'm gonna kill all of you if you leave me! Then he screamed, "I hate you, and I hate everything you stand for!"

Michael got mad. "Stop talking to Mom like that! Give me the gun, Dad!" he shouted. "I mean it, Dad! Give it to me now, or you're going to jail! Which is it?"

Alex turned the gun on Michael again, and Steven started again to step down to help his brother.

"Don't come down, Steven!" Michael demanded. "Get out of here! Get Mom and Laura upstairs!"

"Come on, Dad ... you're out of it. You don't know what you're saying. I mean it; give me the gun, now!"

Alex was cursing and daring Michael to come closer.

Suddenly Michael moved like lightning and rushed his father, pinning him to the wall.

It scared us so badly that the three of us automatically reacted in fear and ran upstairs to Laura's bedroom and locked the door behind us. We huddled together, listening at the door to the rumbling below and simultaneously praying fervently for the safety of both Michael and Alex.

Instantly we heard Michael yell, "Go on, Dad; get downstairs and sleep it off!"

Alex continued mumbling threats to kill us, that he would hunt us down like animals and kill us one by one. It was unimaginable to be hearing these awful threats coming from Alex again. But by now I knew it was not really Alex, but rather that evil one I called Mr. Hyde, who could somehow overtake Alex at times like this.

"Don't make me hit you, Dad. Just get down there. I don't want to do this to you, Dad, but I'm warning you right now ... if you act up like this one more time, you're going to jail!" Michael was in control. With that we heard the door to the lower level close.

My brave son came upstairs and said, "It's okay now. He's in his office. I've got the gun. It was loaded. I took the shells out, and I took all the boxes of shells out of the cabinet and put them where he can't get to them. He can sleep it off in his office on the sofa. He's locked in for the night.

"Mom … you okay? Laura? Steven, Dad's not getting out of there until morning. He'll be sober then."

"Thank God," I said.

Michael had saved our lives by risking his own life to wrestle the gun from his father's hands. He handled the crisis so calmly, reasoning with his Dad and controlling the incident. Michael had never been disrespectful to his father; he had never raised his voice or talked back to him, much less had a physical confrontation with him. None of the kids ever had. They did not dare.

Before Michael closed the door behind him, he said, "Mom, God doesn't expect you to go on living with Dad. He's not a cruel God! If Dad won't let God help him anymore, you can't help him—none of us can. He's so far gone he doesn't know what he's doing, especially when he's drunk. You've got to get away from him."

Laura and Steven chimed in, "Yes, Mom. You've got to!"

"We'll go with you to see an attorney," Michael said, looking at Laura and Steven.

"Yes, we'll all go with you," Laura agreed.

"You're right. I've already made my appointment with the attorney. It is the day after New Year's. This is so terrible! We should all get out of here now," I urged.

"No, Mom," Michael went on, "Dad's afraid of me now. After tonight he knows he'd better stay away from all of us, or I'll call the sheriff and he'll go to jail. He's not going to hurt you when I'm around. You've gotta be careful when he's drinking, but you'll be okay."

"I hope you're right," I answered in a barely audible whisper.

Everything was calm and quiet now. We all left Laura's room and went to our own bedrooms, locking our doors.

After a sleepless night, I was out of bed very early in the morning but did not go downstairs until eight o'clock to make coffee. Drawing back the drapes in the kitchen eating area unveiled a magnificent Christmas Eve morning bathed in sunshine.

This should be a time of family peace and joy. Instead, today is the aftermath of a nightmare!

The house was quiet as I sat alone at the kitchen table, my mug of steaming black coffee resting there before me. Frightening flashes of the night before kept assaulting my mind.

The children never knew about the other time, years ago, when their father threatened to kill me if I left him, but last night was déjà vu for me. *Lord, it all happened so fast none of us could even get to the phone to dial 911. It was over in minutes. I know this … no one knows how they'll react when a gun is pointing at them. Laura and I were paralyzed with fear. We couldn't have run if we had wanted to. No one moves, no one breathes when they're staring down the barrel of a gun with someone's finger on the trigger. Mr. Hyde blatantly took his last and final stand. Oh, I shudder to think of what might have happened if Michael had not been home! But, I know better. There's no doubt in my mind God had him here to protect us.*

I was startled by pounding on the office door. My whole body tensed and my arm jerked, sending the mug flying from my hand into the air, where it came down and bounced on the table before crashing to the carpeted floor—not breaking, but spilling coffee. I sat frozen, not knowing what to do.

Michael also heard the pounding, louder now, and came from his bedroom. He unlocked the door and stepped back without opening it—and without speaking a word—waiting for his dad to open it.

I was nervous.

Alex opened the door and stepped into the family room, appearing calm. Then he turned and stared at me.

I quickly got up, grabbed a handful of paper towels, and immediately dropped to my knees by the table to blot up the coffee. Swiftly rising, I walked to the kitchen sink and stood with my back to Alex, praying he would not say anything to me. He did not. He said nothing but instantly left the house through the door to the garage.

His meek demeanor now made me wonder if he had been incensed and provoked last night because he was drunk and maybe did not even remember it, or if his act had been premeditated, intending to kill me because he knew I would be seeing the attorney next week.

Alex stayed away all day and all night. But still the children were concerned, and they made sure one of them was always with me.

Unbelievably, we managed to have our pre-planned traditional Christmas Eve exchange with my parents at our house, trying to rise above the horrible ordeal of the night before. Mother and Dad questioned Alex's absence. I made no excuse for my husband.

"I don't know where Alex is," I softly replied. They sensed my embarrassment. I could see the concern on their faces, but they asked no further questions.

The children and I spent Christmas Day at my parents' home. When my sister and brother and relatives questioned Alex's absence, I choked back my embarrassment and quietly gave them the same answer I had given my parents. All of them were kind enough not to ask more questions, but they had to know something was seriously wrong.

Alex stayed away from home day and night all that week, except for short periods on mornings when he quietly slipped in and out of his office through the garage door. Even so, the kids never left me alone. They worked it out so one of them was home with me.

The day of my appointment with the lawyer, all three of my young adult children accompanied me. They were courageous and thoughtfully interjected mature, reasoned comments as I told the lawyer the ugly truth about my need to immediately get a restraining order against my husband as well as file for a legal separation. The attorney assured me Alex would have to leave the house soon.

Leaving the office, I felt as though an enormous weight had lifted. The children and I would stand together through this, but we were sad about Alex's unwillingness to let the Lord and Dr. Martin continue to help him. What would happen to my loving Dr. Jekyll? What would happen to the Alex that Dr. Martin described as "a nice guy, who just happens to have a big problem"? My children had witnessed just how cruel and threatening Mr. Hyde, their father's dark side, could be, when Alex tried to kill them and me. I recall praying that God would spiritually shield them from possible negative emotional effects of that terrible night.

After that incident with the gun, I was too ashamed, too embarrassed, to seek help, even from my dear Christian friends. After seeing the attorney, I lived for the rest of the week in silent isolation and emotional pain. In the meantime, my parents were shocked when I told them I had filed for a legal separation. Strong Catholics, they did not believe in legal separation any more than divorce. But I could not let that bother me. Eventually I learned Michael told them about the terrible things his father had done.

Only a few days later, it was mid-morning when Alex stormed into the house, slamming the front door, startling me. I was in the kitchen. The kids were in their bedrooms. Music from their stereos could be heard. Staring and pacing around me like a lion ready to pounce and devour his prey, he finally roared, "What's this I got in the mail today?" I realized that he had picked up his piece of registered mail from the post office, with the filing notice for a legal separation and a restraining order.

Angrily he waved the envelope in the air. He was completely out of control. I backed myself away from him and leaned against the counter.

"No legal separation!" he screamed. "I want a divorce! I hate your guts! And I hate everything you stand for! I want to be rid of you once and for all! But you're going to ruin me and my business if my customers find out about this!"

I remembered again the Scripture *A soft answer turns away wrath* and softly requested, "Alex, please calm down."

Surprisingly he did. He leaned against the counter across from me, seemingly in control again, but still glaring at me.

"Alex, how can you think I would ruin you?" I said quietly. "I'd never do anything like that."

As though ignoring my words, he said in his most punishing tone, "I'll ruin you as a Christian! I'll call the Christian radio station, for starters!"

"Alex, why would you want to ruin me as a Christian? I've done nothing to harm you or your reputation," I answered softly. The fleshly and soulish parts of me were becoming afraid again, and I wanted only to quiet him and show some strength, to discourage him from carrying out his threats. "Besides," I added defensively, "my life is an open book for everyone to read. What could you say to ruin me?"

Alex glared at me again with hate in his eyes. "Don't worry; I'll say something," he promised. "I'll make it up if I have to. And they'll believe it too, and that will be the end of you!"

I did not answer him. I knew that in his emotional state he was completely capable of doing to me exactly what he had threatened.

"And you or no court is gonna get me out of my house! This is my house!"

Instantly, with bold confidence I dismissed his threats and walked upstairs to my bedroom and locked the door behind me. But inside I was terrified to the core at what he might do next. Fortunately, he quietly left the house.

Oh God, I prayed, *help me to endure what is ahead!* I had no idea how much "enduring" would be required of me. I said nothing to the children about this incident.

By the next morning, I was a basket case. The kids were still in their rooms, and I was alone in the kitchen. I dropped to my knees and pleaded for God's mercy. *God I'm afraid of Alex. He might really kill me, but I'm more afraid of sinning against You. I don't want to get a divorce and be out of Your will. Oh my Jesus, please tell me what to do. I can't stand this anymore!*

Instantly I was stilled within. And in that stillness, the command came: *Call Cara.* I got up and dialed her number. When she answered, I told her nothing of what I had been experiencing. I simply said, "Please pray for me, Cara."

She asked no questions but immediately began to pray in her prayer language. As she did, I began to cry. Deep, wrenching sobs shook my whole body. *I don't want to divorce, Lord. I don't want to sin against You.*

Suddenly Cara stopped praying, and I stopped crying simultaneously. Stillness hung like a thick fog. Neither of us spoke. I was conscious only of a sweet peace enveloping me. Out of the stillness, my spirit received bold, distinct words: *You are forgiven, daughter. I do not hold you accountable.*

I gasped. I could not speak. I could not move a muscle. I was caught up in the presence of God. Instantly *Isaiah 54* came in a whisper to my mind and spirit.

Thank you, dear Jesus, I sighed.

"Cara," I said, "if you have your Bible handy, will you please read Isaiah 54 to me?"

"I have my Amplified Bible," Cara answered softly. She began to read and my spirit leaped as I heard: "Fear not, for you shall not be ashamed; neither be confounded and depressed, for you shall not be put to shame. For you shall forget the shame of your youth, and you shall not (seriously) remember the reproach of your widowhood any more... For the Lord has called you like a woman forsaken, grieved in spirit, and heartsore—even a wife (wooed and won) in youth, when she is (later) refused and scorned, says your God. For a brief moment I forsook you, but with great compassion and mercy I will gather you (to Me) again."

Oh Jesus, my Jesus, I silently groaned. *Thank you.*

At once the evil, tormenting fear, the pride and the shame, lifted. I knew my God had sovereignly intervened to release me spiritually from my abusive husband.

Cara went on to read, "...and great shall be the peace and undisturbed composure of your children."

My heart leaped again. *Peace—peace!—for my children.*

I listened intently as Cara continued: "No weapon that is formed against you shall prosper, and every tongue that shall rise against you in judgment you shall show to be in the wrong."

Cara continued reading to the end of that chapter. My heart was full with gratitude for God's faithfulness. Then I knew what I should do.

"Cara, thank you. I have to hang up now."

Fearlessly and confidently, I dialed my attorney's number, forgetting that his office would be closed on a weekend. But he answered right away.

"Mr. Manning, this is Alisha. My husband wants a divorce. It's okay. Please file another restraining order against him and whatever other papers necessary," I said resolutely.

"Are you sure, Alisha?"

"Yes," I said, "I'm absolutely sure."

In the days that followed, I read Isaiah 54 over and over. Through His Word, and through Cara, God ministered to my grieving spirit.

Looking back, even before Alex demanded a divorce, which forced me to wrestle with myself in prayer, I struggled against that drastic step because I was solid in my faith in God's absolute truth of Scripture and knew God hates divorce. After all, as a believer I loved what the Bible said God loves and hated what the Bible said God hates. Cara, Judge and Anne Stahl, and everyone else with whom I was well acquainted knew I did not believe in divorce (and was not even comfortable with legal separation) and that no human opinion could have caused me to take this drastic step—not even my dear, devoted friend, Judge Stahl.

I remember a phone conversation I had with the judge when he wanted to plan some time to pray with Alex. I explained that Alex had previously ignored my pleas for him to seek spiritual counsel from him or Bob, Bill, Jerry Johnson, or some other minister.

"If Alex doesn't want help," the judge replied, "I know God doesn't want you and the kids to live with him the way he is. I don't know why you don't divorce him!"

I was shocked. I knew the judge was stringently against divorce. Had that statement come out of his painful emotions because of his fatherly love and caring for me and the kids?

"Judge, there's only two reasons I can see in the Bible for which God approves of the breakup of a marriage. You know what they are too."

I went on to paraphrase those Scriptures: "One reason is, if the unbelieving spouse wants to leave, or actually leaves, Scripture says to let him leave. The believing spouse is not morally bound because we are called to peace (1 Cor. 7:15). And the other is a reason Jesus Himself makes clear in the Gospel of Matthew; that is, a believer cannot divorce except on the grounds of adultery" (Matt. 5:32 AMP).

In frustration, he came back with, "Why, Alisha, don't you know the way Alex is living and treating you is *worse* in God's eyes than infidelity?"

That remark stunned me. However, it was thought-provoking. *Is Alex's backslidden condition and behavior toward me worse in God's eyes than the sin of adultery?*

One day in prayer after that distressing phone conversation with the judge, I know now that God tried to get my attention to minister comfort and deliverance to my grieving heart with His Word. I recall having felt impressed to read the Scripture Malachi 2. When I did, simultaneously the word *faithless* came to mind.

Although I had read the book of Malachi before, I could not remember what that particular chapter was about. Nevertheless, turning to it, I began reading from verse 1; and as I continued to read, I saw that chapter was all about unfaithfulness. When I got to verse 13 and started reading, the words almost took my breath away: "And this you do with double guilt; you cover the altar of the Lord with tears [shed by your unoffending wives, divorced by you that you might take heathen wives], and with [your own] weeping and crying out because the Lord does not regard your offering any more or accept it with favor at your hand. Yet you ask, Why does He reject it? Because the Lord was witness [to the covenant made at your marriage] between you and the wife of your youth, against whom you have dealt treacherously and to whom you were faithless. Yet she is your companion and the wife of your covenant [made by your marriage vows]" (Mal. 2:13–14 AMP).

Interestingly enough, I realized those Scriptures actually supported Judge Stahl's remark.

Was God telling me Judge Stahl had been right?

Then came the confirmation of Alex's adulterous affair with that young woman, and needless to say, I re-read those particular Scriptures that I had paraphrased to the judge, as well as those in Malachi 2:13–14. And I remembered that terrible evening of the gun incident, when Mr. Hyde reared his ugly head again and tried to kill me. Finally, all those Scriptures had come to the forefront of my mind.

Nonetheless, as a believer, I still could not bring myself to consider anything but a legal separation until the day Alex refused to go along with the legal separation I had filed and demanded a divorce instead. Although I had struggled against it, when Cara prayed with me and the Holy Spirit whispered into my spirit *I do not hold you accountable* and *Isaiah 54,* I got it! Then I knew that I knew that God had sovereignly intervened to rescue me from the dark, abusive side of Alex, Mr. Hyde. I knew I was in God's will to be divorced from him.

Cara was disappointed about Alex's choices and the consequences that had affected us all. She loved Alex and had prayed during this period of his being backslidden that he would return to the Lord. In fact, Cara had prayed and fasted again for Alex, just as the Lord had led me at times to pray and fast for her and her family's needs.

Now during this most difficult time of waiting for our first court hearing, the memory of Alex's fierce, chilling words and actions assaulted my mind over and over. I knew believing Isaiah 54 was my assurance and comfort. Walking it out and allowing God's Word to control my emotions, my motives, my behavior, and my decisions might be quite another thing.

A few days after Alex's demand for a divorce and his threats of ruining my Christian reputation, I was served with divorce papers. I was having a bad time of it as I thought about the reality of our divorce again. I could not imagine ever having the courage to identify myself as a divorcée. Pained beyond belief one day, I called Cara.

"Cara, why didn't God answer all my prayers for Alex's healing and deliverance? Why hasn't God conquered Alex like He did Saul of Tarsus? God can do anything, and it breaks my heart that He hasn't changed Alex after I've believed and prayed so long and hard."

Cara said nothing for a few moments and then answered, "Alisha, I don't have to tell you that God won't go against a person's will. You know that. Alex had a choice, just like you did and just like I did. And he chose his own will and way, not God's.

"And don't say that God didn't answer your prayers for Alex. He did. Alex was born again. Even after he backslid, God was merciful and restored him to Christ. Remember the Word says in Mark 13, "… he that endures to the end shall be saved" (vs. 13). If Alex can't overcome and endure to the end, that's not your fault, and it's not God's fault either."

But life's not over for Alex, I thought. *I'll leave him to Jesus.*

"Besides," Cara went on, "Alisha, look what God has done in your life because *you* chose to give up your own will and follow God's. Look at the strong Christian woman you are. And your children are all born again. God has answered all your prayers, Alisha. He's been faithful to you. Don't grieve Him by saying He hasn't."

"But Cara, how can my life ever again honor the Lord?" I persisted.

"Why do you say that, Alisha? Are you questioning God after He has released you?" Cara's tone was mildly chiding. "Yes," she went on, "God does hate divorce. But you're the one who has reminded me that God knows the end from the beginning of our lives—and that goes for Alex's life too."

"But divorce, Cara …"

"Stop!" she interrupted. "How can we question God? How can any Christian judge what God chooses to do? He asked Hosea, one of His prophets, to marry a harlot as a sign to the people of Israel because of their backslidden condition. Listen to this: "When the Lord first spoke with and through Hosea, the Lord said to him, Go, take to yourself a wife of harlotry and have children of her harlotry, for the land commits great whoredom by departing from the Lord" (Hos. 1:2 AMP).

"Read the book of Hosea again, Alisha."

I did not answer.

"Even Proverbs … all through the Proverbs," Cara went on, "God warns men not to go near prostitutes. But here, God tells Hosea—one of His prophets!—to marry a *harlot* and even have children with her. How many Christians today would understand if God told one of His well-known, dedicated servants to do that? God is sovereign, Alisha. Who can counsel God?"

Over the next days and weeks, God used Cara's words and His own Word (especially Isaiah 54) to lift, touch, and console my fragile emotions. I took comfort in knowing God had seen my marriage from beginning to end and that He was the only one capable of judging fairly. I would need His constant nurturing from the Word to stand in the face of Alex's unknown actions yet to come.

Although the court's restraining order confined Alex to his lower-level office only to conduct business, he was still coming and going from the house. I did not know how they arranged their schedules, but the kids were still making sure one of them was with me. Michael urged his dad to do what the court ordered and leave altogether, telling him it was for the best. His answer was the same: "Nobody's getting me out of here!"

More than once, although I had said nothing to him about leaving, out of the blue he would scream at me. "You're never getting me out of this house! I'm going to stay here and make you more miserable than you ever dreamed," he taunted, "even though it's hard to be around you. Without me, you'll probably starve. You're too stupid to take care of yourself!"

In the days that followed, Alex did his best to keep his promise. He would yell at me from his office, saying despicable things to me, tormenting me with false accusations and threats. Another restraining order was issued. This time it required him to completely leave the premises, but Alex defiantly insisted he was not leaving. When I complained to my attorney, he disclosed that even Alex's attorney had urged him to comply with the court order. Still Alex did not budge.

After that there were days when I could sense an atmosphere of evil when Alex was in the house. He meant it when he said, "Nobody's getting me out of here!" because without provocation, he shouted those words repeatedly during the next couple of weeks. Remembering the Old Testament account of Passover, when the Lord literally protected His people, the Israelites from evil, I prayed each day that God would also keep His hedge of protection over and around me, the children, and our home, so that none of Mr. Hyde's evil intentions could possibly touch us.

It was early one evening in July when I went to the kitchen to dial Cara's phone number to ask for prayer. Holding the phone to my ear, waiting to hear her voice, a sudden flashback, a sting of recollection of Alex's threats, sent shivers down my spine, and I silently declared to myself: *We still need bold prayer to hold back the next onslaught of Alex's evil words and actions.* I knew, given Alex's state of mind, he could try to strike again at any moment.

Cara came on the line, and I simply asked her to pray hard for me. She did not ask for details. The two of us often asked each other for prayer, but neither of us needed details; we just started praying and let the Holy Spirit lead us. My eyes closed as Cara began praying. Suddenly I heard Alex open the door from his office. I looked over only to see him glaring at me.

Quietly I interrupted Cara's praying and said, "Please keep praying, but I have to hang up."

Thank God, there was no further incident. Alex went back downstairs.

Early the next morning, Alex left the house as usual, and immediately it seemed as though the atmosphere changed for the better.

Later that morning, Alex returned with a truck, packed up his clothes, his office—everything—and left the house without a word. I wondered what had happened to change his mind. His last threat, his promise, was, "You're never getting me out of this house!"

Cara called that evening. I told her that, curiously, this morning Alex had abruptly moved everything out.

That is when she told me she was sitting at her computer at work that morning and suddenly felt compelled to stop keying and pray for me. She said the swiftness, boldness, and assurance with which her prayer came astounded her as she pleaded: "God, honor her integrity. Get him out of that house today!"

Part 5
New Beginnings

Chapter 17

God Has Seen It All

Along sigh escaped me. I was back in the present again. My memories left me sad for my Dr. Jekyll, because he could not stay on track with Jesus to fight Mr. Hyde for his freedom in Christ, for me and our children, for our family life.

A verse of Scripture came to mind, and I reached for my Bible and read it: "Love bears up under anything and everything that comes, is ever ready to believe the best of every person, its hopes are fadeless under all circumstances and it endures everything [without weakening]" (1 Cor. 13:7 AMP).

Now opening my journal, I began writing the thoughts that were coming:

That verse 7 in 1 Corinthians is a hard teaching. I sure haven't lived up to that kind of love because I have definitely weakened …

I paused, examining my love for Alex. *God knows Alex has been a well-loved man by me and his children. But I don't think the issue was whether or not we loved him enough.*

Gripping my pen again, I went on to write:

I tried to believe the best of Alex; I tried to have hope under all those terrible circumstances the last three years. Being the proverbial optimist, I gave him that one more chance he had begged for, and I tried to stand by him when he went for professional help, until he gave up, himself, on getting well and until the other woman entered our relationship and I found myself staring down the barrel of a loaded double-barreled shotgun. I don't understand his mental disorder and that dual personality. He was free of Mr. Hyde while he was living by God's biblical principles for twelve years. There are definitely conditions to walking through this Christian life. It seems to me it all gets down to our choices. I'll never understand why Alex chose to go back to his old life, but Jesus says in the Bible, that after one is saved, then if he chooses to return to his sin, it's like a dog returning to his vomit ...

The thought of that instantly halted my writing again.

I realized that while I felt sad for Alex this evening, at the same time, I felt resentment toward him for allowing himself to be drawn back, returning to his sin and departing from Christ and making his selfish *choices* that brought sad *consequences* not only for him but for our entire family. Maybe he was not strong enough to do it himself, but he also *chose* to refuse all the help available to him.

My next thoughts went down on the page:

God knows I need His forgiveness. These bouts of resenting Alex come and go. He is fortunate that he's still loved by Jesus. His love doesn't come and go. Forgiveness is always available for Alex. And thank God I know it's always available for me ...

A flashback interrupted my writing, beckoning me back to that morning Alex abruptly moved out. I stopped writing and rested my pen on the page to keep my place, and instantly I was back there in July 1984 again.

The children stayed with me even after Alex moved out, just in case Mr. Hyde came back to kill me as he had promised he would. But he stayed away, and peace was ours. The tension was gone. We could now express our feelings freely and be ourselves. Living without the constant tension we had experienced for so long was liberating for the kids and me—liberating to our minds and emotions, and to our spirits.

The four of us were a team, keeping our sense of family and taking care of this high-maintenance home. Laura and I kept up with the inside of the house. Michael and Steven continued to take care of the outside. That was a real chore! I have the greatest respect for my children for the responsibility they showed during those hard times, both to take care of our home and for individually doing their part to make our days pleasant. We took care of one another.

For now, it was as though my children and I emotionally huddled like sheep for warmth and protection and inner healing. It was sheer delight for me to know that my children were now at peace in their home. And I sighed, remembering God's promise to me for them: "And great shall be the peace and undisturbed composure of your children" (Isa. 54:13 AMP).

During the last six months before Alex moved out, it seemed he was bent on trying to make the Lord's Day the most miserable day of the week for us. Now our Sundays were peaceful and restful once again. I knew these first weeks of rest were a luxury for me before I would have to get a job. Plus, I anticipated there would be many hard days ahead with court hearings. I knew God needed to heal deep wounds within my woman's heart, hidden from the eyes of everyone but God, my journal, and my closest friends. I never knew what Alex would do next or what grief and heartache might lie ahead for me. So I wanted to take advantage of this time. I desperately needed rest.

For me, rest came on those lazy afternoons when I spent quiet times sitting alone on the edge of the boat dock, dangling my bare feet in the water, making the only ripples I could see on the sixteen-acre span of lake. One day the tranquility I felt around me opened my mind to beautiful new thoughts about how I wanted to live my life. With those thoughts of my new future came longings for old innocent joys of girl-times and unfulfilled dreams. Now those images loomed in my mind: *I will design and sew again. I will paint in oils again. I will read the rest of the books on my bookshelf on quiet nights alone. I will play the piano more. And I want to find new interests to enjoy along with my old ones. I want to bring new beauty into my life.*

Somewhere deep in my heart and spirit, I could hear the words from Isaiah 54: "For though the mountains should depart and the hills be shaken or removed, yet My love and kindness shall not depart from you, nor shall My covenant of peace and completeness be removed, says the Lord, who has compassion on you" (v. 10).

The day the announcement of our petition for divorce was in the newspaper, I prayed God would not permit any Christians to call me whom He knew to be only curious. Not that I felt any obligation to discuss the details with anyone—I did not—but I prayed that only my true friends would contact me because they cared, really cared, about my children and me.

Dottie, my Christian friend for many years, was the first to call that morning after reading the newspaper. She had been shocked to learn the news, but she did not pry. She only said, "Alisha, I know you would permit this divorce only with good reason." I praised God for her faithful friendship and her faith in my walk with the Lord.

Besides Cara, Judge and Anne Stahl, who regularly stayed in touch and supported me, and other good friends, all dear sisters in Christ, telephoned. Phyllis, Glyn, Bobbie, and Judy, who was living out of state, called to pledge their love and support. I received no negative phone calls or comments from anyone. I received only love. For that reason, I believed my God was proving His promise to me in Isaiah 54: "Fear not, for you shall not be ashamed; neither be confounded and depressed, for you shall not be put to shame" (v.4 AMP).

I was fortunate to land a good position as director of sales for a company. Learning and working my new job required long hours and filled the days of waiting for our first court date. I walked into the house from work one evening, got as far as the kitchen, and heard, "Surprise!" coming from the voices of my kids, relatives, and friends gathered in the family room. Laura had planned a party for me, complete with banner and balloons and lots of good food. I felt very loved. That love and the peace of God would sustain me throughout the difficult times ahead.

Just as I suspected, given Alex's personality, the divorce hearings were not without heartache and pain. The oath I took before cross-examination by our attorneys, promising to tell the truth, had been serious to me, but not to Alex. In each of those early hearings, Alex ignored the fact that he was not just speaking to the court, but he was speaking before God.

Listening to his answers to questions and his statements of false accusations against me to support his reasons for wanting to divorce me was shocking. I was emotionally ravaged and angry. I wanted to stand up and scream right out loud, "It's not true! Alex, you know it's not true!" Instead, I screamed in my mind, *God, You know it's not true. This isn't fair!*

Alex's persecuting lies felt like daggers jabbing at my heart again and again, and I wanted to retaliate in kind. And I would have, except for having already been leaning hard on the Lord in prayer and Bible study. All those Scriptures I had learned and walked in before Alex became a Christian were the same basic ones I needed to cling to now. I was dealing with Mr. Hyde's behavior again, although from a distance. I was in the same kind of battle, and I had to remember to stand behind the Word and to obey it to the best of my ability.

I had learned that God the Holy Spirit always knows when we are really trying, but struggling, to obey His Word, and He helps us overcome.

I felt prompted to read chapter 5 in the book of Galatians, which I had read many times before. I knew well the verses that reveal the personality and character of Jesus Christ, which governed His behavior: "Love, joy, peace, patience, kindness, goodness, faithfulness, gentleness and self-control. Against such things there is no law [that can bring a charge]" (Gal. 5:22–23 AMP).

I sensed the Holy Spirit wanted me to see something specific about those verses to apply right now. I remembered it was the power of those Scriptures along with others that had protected me when I was up against Mr. Hyde before Alex accepted Christ, and the same Scriptures would protect me now as I dealt with Alex's dark side again. I needed that Word to be reactive in me.

It was also clear that I needed an attitude adjustment. If I wanted to stand up against Alex's false accusations now without reacting in kind, then I had to allow those same Scripture verses to govern *my* behavior. It seemed Alex was always saying something false against me to our kids or saying something really cruel to me that triggered my anger, and I would want to retaliate. Keeping my mouth shut and guarding my emotional reactions were a challenge.

I readily recognized when my attitude, words, and specially my thoughts, were out of Christ's character. When I knew I had stepped into my carnal, fleshly reactions, I made the choice, although often through gritted teeth, to get my mind in gear again and step back into those attributes outlined in Galatians and behave God's way. It dawned on me that this had become my daily practice.

I clearly saw that obeying these Scriptures empowered me to use self-control. Just as in the past, in His gentle ways as my heavenly Father, God was showing me this exercise of obeying these Scriptures would give me the power that would eventually bring me into healing for my emotional wounds and move me into complete recovery so I could *begin again.*

Obviously, the issue of money and dividing the assets comes into play for every divorce trial, and ours was no exception. When I prayed for God's wisdom regarding a fair settlement, I felt distinctly impressed that I should not argue with Alex over a money settlement. And at the same time, I felt directed to turn in my Amplified Bible and read Hebrews 13. When I read verse 5, I knew it was guidance for me: "Let your character or moral disposition be free from love of money [including greed, avarice, lust, and craving for earthly possessions] and be satisfied with your present [circumstances and with what you have]. For He [God] Himself has said, I will not in any way fail you *nor* give you up, *nor* leave you without support. [I will] not, [I will] not, [I will] not in any degree leave you helpless *nor* forsake *nor* let [you] down (relax my hold on you)! [Assuredly not!]."

I knew if I obeyed the first part of that verse, 5a, then the last part, 5b, was a guarantee to me of God's promise. From that time on, I kept those words in my consciousness whenever the issue of money was discussed. I knew my very personal God was coaching me, and I knew I could trust His Word. When there was an occasion for me to speak with my attorney or when Alex called me to talk about our financial settlement, God gave me the grace to obey His Word. I said only, "I just want everything to be fair for both of us. We've both worked very hard for what we have."

My not arguing or making any financial demands was disarming to my husband, and he softened his attitude, actions, and reactions toward me. He was being very kind to me now, calling once in a while just to see how I was doing. I was curious—and cautious—knowing his track record for deception.

In mid-September Alex asked me to have dinner with him to discuss our finances. He had been civil, so I agreed for two reasons: first, I wanted to keep things cordial to get through these court hearings; and second, he was still the father of my children, and for their sakes, I would do my part to make things amicable.

I met him at the restaurant, and he greeted me and behaved with the same gentlemanly manners and finesse that was normal for my Dr. Jekyll. At dinner I expected Alex to begin conversation about our finances, but instead, he started by telling me he still loved me and wanted me back. He went on to tell me that he had asked Jesus to forgive him of everything he had done to the kids and me, and he had asked God to come into his life again. However, I noted, interestingly, that he did not specifically ask *me* to forgive him for the past or the recent lies he had told about me in court.

Then, with the dichotomy that is his personality, he immediately switched the conversation to money. He talked about the fact that the attorneys were the only ones who stood to gain monetarily from these ongoing proceedings to determine a settlement and that he wished the two of us could agree on a settlement and end it all. I did not trust Alex, and although I respectfully listened to his suggestion, I made only one comment: "Alex, we should work all this out through our attorneys and the court."

Two days later, I received a letter from Alex, dated the evening after we were together:

September 16, 1984

Dear Alisha,

Thank you so much for having dinner with me last night. It was very painful to say good-bye; however, I believe a lot of good came from it. I am finally becoming grateful to you for taking the course of action you have because I can now admit my emotional problems, coupled with the alcoholism I suffer from, have caused all of our problems. I am deeply sorry for doing the things I have done to you and causing you to take the desperate action you had no alternative but to take. It has caused me to realize I do need help and lots of it to return to a normal life. I can now at least take the blame for whatever financial and emotional costs come from the divorce. The road will not be easy for me and will require a lengthy period of time for me to once again be a mentally and physically healthy person. Whatever I have certainly was accomplished with your help, and you have always been a good and loving wife. I cannot fault you for this mess, and I will always love only you.
– Alex

Even so, not surprisingly, as the final hearings for a settlement began, I saw that Mr. Hyde's greed influenced Alex and when it got right down to the nitty-gritty of dividing our money and assets, he clearly wanted to keep all of it for himself. After one hearing, he called me at work and screamed into the receiver, "You're not getting any of my business or my money! I'm the one who worked hard to earn that money!"

It was nearing Thanksgiving, and by now it had been a grueling eleven months of court hearings. During those hard months, choosing to yield my thoughts, actions, and reactions to God and His Word kept me standing spiritually strong. However, my emotions and my body were worn down.

Alex brought gifts to the house for us on Christmas Day. The children and I got through that uncomfortable time as well as the rest of the holidays. Then I received notice that the final court date was set for January 15, 1985, when our financial settlement and divorce would be finalized.

At that time, troubling information came to light about Alex's financial deceptions carried out during 1983, when I had given him that *one more chance* for which he had *begged*. Unbeknown to me at that time, he had been using that period to plot and carry out his schemes: influencing our company's board of directors' votes to replace me with his brother as an officer and trustee, and selling some of our assets and hiding others—all of which were in our company's name. That information was shocking and grievous to learn after the fact.

To top it off, my position as director of sales, which earned me a decent salary, was used against me. With my employment background prior to marriage, working in our business, and now with this new job, Alex's lawyer, who was widely acclaimed to be the best divorce attorney in our state, argued and proved to the court's satisfaction that I made enough money to support myself. Unexpectedly, everything took a twist of facts, making our final hearing a fiasco.

Alex had agreed to continue paying the children's college tuition, while they would maintain their jobs to support themselves. Now I doubted whether Alex would keep that promise for his children. Only time would reveal how right I was.

Surely that exposure of more of Alex's deception would have stirred in me more desire for strong retaliation if God had not been my constant influence and if I had not hung on to God's promises in Hebrews 13:5. Because I believed that Scripture instead of trying to retaliate, I had a calm assurance within that despite Alex's deception, the Lord would keep His promises to me.

The settlement was not fair to me, said my attorney, my children, and my parents. I understood how they felt, but God's scriptural promises were deep in my heart. It was true that Alex now was left with a lot of money and assets to hang on to, because everything we owned, except for our home, was in the company's name—and he was the company! Never mind that I, too, had sacrificed for the company, and unlike Alex, I had worked without a salary all those years. But I do not blame Alex for that, and I do not regret having done that. I believed I was doing it for the right reason at that time.

Nonetheless, in place of money, I had something more valuable to me: continual peace. No amount of money could buy that for me. And I had been given more faith to believe my very personal God. I knew He had His own ways of righting the wrongs done to His children.

Before the divorce was final, Alex was already living with the other woman, many years my junior. I had to remember, God had seen it all.

Now back in the present again, I realized my emotions had been stirred tonight, just as they had over these last three days. And there was still a battle going on in my mind. My conflicting emotions were hard to deal with. They disturbed my peace from time to time, triggered by memories of all that had brought us to divorce and to this, my third day as a divorcée looking back.

But even though I battled my sins of the flesh and mixed emotions over this time, God was showing me that I indeed had been in His will. I learned one of my hardest reality lessons: that I was not exempt from the heartache of shattered dreams just because I was a faithful Christian.

God had brought my husband into salvation and into a wonderful life, making him successful in his business and financially blessing him more abundantly than either of us would have imagined possible. Yes, God had spread my husband's table with an abundance of blessings. But in the end, Alex chose not to follow his God who had shown Himself loving, forgiving, faithful, patient, and merciful. I hoped this was not a final decision.

I had continued to read Isaiah 54 every day. It felt to me as though those Scripture verses were being permanently written on my heart and spirit so that I could instantly recall them as needed to free me. With those Scriptures, I believed the Holy Spirit was leading me on my path to emotional healing, recovery, and wholeness.

At the close of this third day after my divorce, I realized my memories and my journaling had been cathartic—therapeutic, healing, liberating—helping me to look squarely at my emotionally devastating past with Alex and at the reality that *God had seen it all* and Jesus had been with me through it all. It was emotionally and spiritually energizing to know that God was with me now and would be with me in the future. At this moment, I also knew that it was now time to move forward and *begin again.*

.

Chapter 18

Remember Not

"Remember ye not the former things, neither consider the things of old. Behold I will do a new thing; now it shall spring forth: shall ye not know it?" (Isa. 43:18).

Only God knew what it would take to move me forward. His amazing grace brought healing, deliverance, and complete recovery. It was not instant, but it came gradually as the Holy Spirit led me to walk through experiences that tested my level of trust in Him and His Word as a single-again woman. I thought for the rest of my life, I would see in my mind the loaded double-barreled shotgun Alex had held on me, invoking the same paralyzing fear I had felt at that moment. And I was sure that at least emotionally, I would always be connected to Alex.

But my faithful God did for me, once again, the impossible. In His mercy, God ministered to me through the love and prayers of my friends, Judy and Cara. In what seemed almost like a surgical procedure, the Holy Spirit led Judy in a powerful prayer that felt, spiritually, as though my mind and soul were completely severed from the tormenting fear of Alex's demonic acts and threatening words. I felt as if I was cut free from every negative aspect of my twenty-six years with Alex, as though the Lord was reassuring me that He was in that extraordinary prayer to deliver and heal me from the pain of the past: "For the Lord has called you like a woman forsaken, grieved in spirit, and heartsore—even a wife [wooed and won] in youth, when she is [later] refused and scorned, says your God. For a brief moment I forsook you, but with great compassion *and* mercy I will gather you [to Me] again" (Isa. 54:6 and 7 AMP).

I had trusted in God's promises to me in Isaiah 54, and He had not disappointed me. In that unexpected, astonishingly mysterious, out of the ordinary prayer ministry, God had faithfully performed what He had promised. This ministry was more liberating for me than I could have ever anticipated, and I now felt freed to move on with my life. I continued taking one step at a time on my path to recovery.

The notice of our divorce was published in the newspaper among the other vital statistics, yet I still did not receive a single negative phone call from anyone—Christian or not. I was never questioned in church or in any fellowship I attended. Given my high profile, all the Christian leaders and nearly everyone else who knew me personally had time to learn of my divorce. If anyone responded to the news with negative comments, they or no one else related them to me.

And, on the other hand, not one Christian called to pray with me for the restoration of my marriage or the state of my soul, which they might have done if they had believed me to be out of God's will. Some Christians may have scorned me, but if so, I never heard about it. Isaiah 54 was definitely working in my life, and I felt as though its words of promise provided a hedge of God's protection around me: "Fear not, for you shall not be ashamed; neither be confounded and depressed, for you shall not be put to shame. For you shall forget the shame of your youth, and you shall not [seriously] remember the reproach" (v. 4 AMP).

Now more than ever, I counted on God to give me His complete victory over this devastating trial. There was still one more battle going on in my mind. Defeating thoughts kept attacking my psyche with the accusation that my being a divorcée now disqualified me from serving God. Based on that thought, because of my new marital status, I did not feel I should continue to serve as a trustee on the Christian radio broadcasting board of directors; so I wrote a letter of resignation, explaining my reason.

The president of the board telephoned me to say that my resignation had not been accepted. "We have all known your Christian walk for many years," he said, "and we believe you would not submit to divorce without good reason and in accordance with Scripture. You have nothing to be ashamed of, Alisha, and it was unanimous with the board: we all want you to remain as a trustee."

That was a great encouragement to me, and I knew it was another confirmation of God's promises. However, the battle in my mind was fierce and continued to beat me with humiliation for being a Christian leader who was divorced. I felt my testimony of Jesus had been tainted, and, therefore, my public ministry destroyed. I tried to fight my thoughts, but the accusations kept coming.

One day when I was in the midst of this battle, I knew I needed prayer and called Cara to tell her about it. I concluded in this weak moment that as a divorcée, I was, no doubt, a blight on the body of Christ and thought of as a fallen leader; so I was sure that my public ministry was over. Her first reaction was to declare, "Alisha, the devil's a liar! He's the accuser of the brethren; put those thoughts out of your mind!" Of course, I knew all that. But even after she prayed for me, as hard as I tried, I could not shake those accusing thoughts. They haunted me.

Soon after, Cara and I were attending a Christian fellowship dinner meeting, which was led by a man of God whom Alex and I had known for many years and who knew Alex and I were no longer together. He, as others, did not know why we were divorced because I had never exposed my husband's sin.

After dinner I saw him walk to the microphone, cueing the audience that the evening's program was ready to begin.

"I just got word that our scheduled speaker is unable to be with us tonight," he announced, "but we're fortunate to have a very special guest with us. I know her, and I know she has a tremendous testimony."

I was waiting, along with the rest of the crowd, for him to introduce the speaker when he asked, "Alisha Lance, will you come up and speak to us whatever the Lord puts on your heart?"

Stunned, I looked at Cara, who was looking at me—and grinning. Leaning closer, she whispered, "So you thought God wouldn't use you to speak for Him anymore, huh? The devil's a liar, Alisha!"

My heart filled with joy as I spoke to this group about my faithful Jesus and the works He had done in my life, encouraging the group to put all the weight of their troubles on Christ and His Word, to seek His holy will, and to trust Him with their lives.

Only a month later, once again God shed His grace on me in a special way to confirm His ministry in me. It was during another Christian fellowship dinner meeting. I enjoyed the powerful testimony of the guest speaker, who was from England. He extended an invitation for prayer to the audience for personal salvation. Those of us who did not go for prayer left our tables to greet one another and to fellowship.

I was just ready to say my good-byes when I felt a tap on my shoulder. Turning around, I was surprised to see the guest speaker, whom I did not know personally, smiling at me. I looked at him quizzically, thinking he had mistaken me for someone else. Before I could say anything, he handed me a small, folded piece of paper and, without a word, turned and walked back to continue praying for people. I was confused. He had not even asked my name. Still puzzled, I opened the folded paper and read: "The Lord is using you, but He's only just started. Receive everything He has for you and be a blessing to many."

My heart swelled with joy. I took a deep breath and placed the paper in my Bible, where it remains to this day. I had never seen or met that man of God before that night, nor have I seen him since that night. God's encouraging promises to me that I should not fear or be confounded and depressed, because I would not be put to shame had proven true, and I had been greatly blessed. Now there was no doubt in my mind He was encouraging me with another of His promises in Isaiah 54: "You shall establish yourself in righteousness (rightness, in conformity with God's will and order)" (v. 14 AMP).

The Holy Spirit used those two experiences to confirm to me, once and for all, that God alone had appointed my ministry for Him to others. And no one person, not Alex's threats to ruin me as a Christian, not even Satan's accusations to my own mind in a weak moment, would change that. Those accusing thoughts stopped completely. God was continuing to show me the unique relevance of His promised words to me in Isaiah 54, which would help me overcome anything negative—even *my own mind.*

The winter and spring months seemed to fly by. My job was rewarding but demanding. Nevertheless, I got caught up on my reading in the evenings and kept filling the pages of my 1985 journal as well as recording in my "Spiritual Lessons for Daily Living" book. I was getting emotionally and spiritually stronger every day. In fact, I was accepting invitations again to share my testimony or biblical teachings in various public forums and over Christian radio.

One of those invitations was to speak at the annual Catholic Women's Conference on the Holy Spirit. At first and only momentarily, my imaginings plagued me regarding that particular invitation, because of my new marital status. Then on reflection, I could only thank God for His promise, *You will not be ashamed, nor will you be put to shame,* because in my mind it was a miracle that although my divorce was, presumably, known to the leadership of that group, still I had been invited to address Catholics. I was grateful because I have a deep love for my Catholic sisters.

My twenty-three-year-old daughter, Laura, was free the day of the conference, and she decided to come with me for support. When I was introduced, I walked up onto the stage and to the podium. After praying for God the Holy Spirit to lead me to glorify Jesus, as I always pray, I paused.

Looking out over that full auditorium of women, who were looking back at me and waiting for me to begin, I realized something unusual was happening. Obviously the Spirit was holding back my words. In a split second, unexpectedly, the thought came that I should invite Laura to share a few words. I knew that had not been my thought, so in faith, I acted on it. I told the audience my daughter had accompanied me, and I proceeded to invite her to the podium.

Laura, who was seated in the front row, had a look of pure shock on her face. Nonetheless, she walked to the microphone and greeted the audience and began speaking with all the poise and confidence of a seasoned orator. Then she acknowledged the large number of young women, some of whom were young mothers. Although Laura obviously had no prior idea she would be addressing these women, to my amazement her words flowed as though they had been preplanned. It was obvious that the Holy Spirit was leading her.

Listening intently to her brief but encouraging words, I was glad they were being taped. She concluded: "And to those of you who have young children, I want to say ... your children are or they will be facing temptations and difficult decisions and choices every day during school and when they are with their friends. Be sure to give them a foundational teaching in the principles of God, so when they are faced with those temptations and need to make a decision or choice—especially when they are teenagers—they will make the right ones. I remember when I was growing up and throughout my school years, I had a good reminder each day after school, because when I walked into my home *I always saw Jesus*—by my mom's example."

She paused before closing with, "Mothers, when your children come home from school each day, let them see Jesus in you."

Instantly the audience burst into applause. I was stunned. Laura had never made such a comment to me. My mother's heart swelled and I was blessed beyond words—not only for what Laurie spoke but also by the fact that we were being so warmly embraced by this particular group.

* * *

Throughout the year, I was feeling the financial burden of maintaining our large home. I did not want to disrupt our lives again so soon after the divorce and all we had been through, but I had to be practical. My young adult children would, no doubt, soon want to live on their own, or they might even want to marry in the not-too-distant future. I knew I could not physically or financially maintain this property alone. However, I did not know when I should sell it, so I released my concerns to the Lord and prayed that He would cause me to know.

As summer was coming to a close, once again I began anticipating the winter expenses for the house, especially the high cost of fuel oil. One Sunday morning in late August, I picked up the newspaper and began reading the front page, when I felt impressed to turn to the classified real estate section. My eyes fell on a small ad under condominiums for sale, headed "Summit Place High-Rise." As I read, I felt compelled to see that condo, and without reading one other ad, I put down the newspaper and telephoned the real estate agent to make an afternoon appointment.

I liked the building and the condo; but it was only a one-bedroom unit, and I knew it would be too small for Laurie and me. The boys had already let me know that whenever the time came for selling the house, they were planning to get their own place.

Why didn't I see in the ad that it was only a one bedroom? This was a waste of the agent's time and mine. I thought sure the Holy Spirit had directed me to come here.

"Your ad impressed me," I said to the agent, "but somehow I missed the fact that it was a one bedroom. I apologize for taking your time. I really need two bedrooms."

"That's no problem," she kindly responded and quickly offered to show me two-bedroom units in the building.

But I declined, confessing, "Thank you, but on second thought, I need to sell my home before buying another; so perhaps I should wait, because I'm not sure when I will be ready to do that." I felt so dumb. This was embarrassing.

There was a moment's lull, so I quickly added, "Again, I'm really sorry for taking your time."

The agent responded, "That's okay. I've enjoyed meeting you." She paused. "By the way, what style home do you own, and where is it located?"

After describing the house and mentioning that it was on a lake, the agent's eyes brightened. She asked if I would consider allowing her to show it to a particular client who was open only to purchasing a home on the water. "There's no obligation on your part," she urged. "I'd just like my client to see it."

I hesitated because I thought I had already failed to correctly interpret that "nudge" to see this condo, so I did not know if this was the time to sell my house either; and besides, where would we move to?

As though reading my thoughts, she said, "Really, don't worry; you are under no obligation to sell just because I show it to my clients."

So I agreed to a showing, without even a discussion about a purchase price. Her clients came to view the house, and I was immediately presented with a written offer for a purchase price that took my breath away. It was far greater than the appraisal price considered in our divorce settlement!

Amazed, I realized that the Holy Spirit had indeed been leading me, if only to make contact with this realtor. But I knew nothing would have happened unless I had followed that nudge and taken a step of faith to phone that particular realtor for an appointment. And as a result, I felt a strong conviction that because God had seen Alex's deception in hiding our assets, the Lord intended to make it up to me, at least in part, with the profit on this sale. I was right in trusting that God had His own way of bringing about financial justice for me.

The next day, the real estate agent brought the buyer's signed purchase contract to the office where I worked for my signature of acceptance. After she left, I was on the telephone calling about a condominium advertised for sale in the newspaper. I had to move fast, because I had only thirty days to find a place to live! One of my customers was using the copy machine in front of my desk. When I hung up the phone, she said, "I wasn't eavesdropping, but I could not help but overhear your phone conversation. Alisha, are you wanting to buy a condo?"

"Yes. Well, buy or rent. My home has sold and I have to be out in a month, so I need to find a place to live ASAP!"

"Well, dear, my husband and I have a condo we need to sell soon. We just closed on it last Thursday, but afterward we were standing in the condo living room and he said, 'You know, I just don't think I feel well enough to make this move.' We still have our house, so if you're interested and can buy the condo immediately, we'll sell it to you for exactly what we paid for it.

"And, Alisha, you should know I bought it from a friend, who just had it completely redecorated, but he did not include the thirteen thousand dollars in the purchase price. He just needed his money out of it in a hurry. So you will be getting the same blessing we were getting—a like-new interior included in the already below market price."

"That's very generous of you!"

"Would you like to see it," she asked and quickly added, "and can you make it today, after work while it's still light? It's located in Summit Place, the high-rise, and I want you to see the views of the city. They are just spectacular day and night!"

Summit Place. Hmm ... I feel this is no coincidence.

"Yes, I would!" I excitedly answered.

The children and I went to see it, and we all loved it! It was a two-bedroom, two-bath unit, with entire glass walls with sliders to each of the two balconies, one off the living room and one off the master bedroom. All these new things happening reminded me of God's promises to me in the verses in Isaiah 54: "O you afflicted, storm tossed and not comforted, behold, I will set your stones in fair colors and lay your foundations with sapphires ... and all your walls of precious stones" (vv. 11, 12 AMP).

This condo did not have a foundation, floors, and walls inlayed with precious jewels, but it was beautiful—and far more than I had dreamed I would live in. Because my sons would be moving elsewhere, they were especially pleased that the high-rise had twenty-four-hour manned security for the safety of their mom and sister, two single ladies.

I began preparing for our move, which meant scaling down a great deal. The boys took some furniture pieces, and I planned to run an ad to sell other furnishings and also planned to have a garage sale. It was then we learned of a family in a small town south of us whose home, sadly, had burned to the ground. Instead of selling anything, we gave them furniture and everything from beds and bedding to tables and chairs, lamps, accessories, garden equipment, and clothing. The parents appreciated everything, and their teenagers were thrilled to have all the clothes my kids gave them.

The four of us tried to spend what little leisure time we had outside enjoying the lake before we had to move. On those early crisp Saturday mornings in September, before I started packing, no one was on the lake. I took my coffee out and sat on the bench by the water. The still waters were calming. With God's appointments of nature surrounding me, I could almost feel its pulse beating with mine. The thick woods on all sides wrapped me in solitude and utter beauty. It always made me think of God's majesty and aroused praises in my heart and spirit.

I would miss this house, Alex's dream home on the lake. It would always hold both happy and sad memories for me. I would never forget it, but now it was time for me to *begin again*—and God had made the way. Without any effort on my part—no advertising of our home to sell nor house hunting for another—the transition had been made, and we had moved. There was no doubt in our minds that the Holy Spirit had orchestrated it all. With His miraculous intervention, my confidence in my heavenly Father for all future major decisions grew solid in my mind and heart. My *winter of discontent* was behind me.

* * *

God's Words of promise in Hebrews 13, Isaiah 54, and Isaiah 43 given to me by the leading of the Holy Spirit for guidance, encouragement, and assurance to go through the unique circumstances in my life continued to help me *begin again*. I knew God wanted me to be as happy in my new marital status and my natural daily life as I continued to be in my spiritual life. Just as I had done in our lake home, I created a special corner for myself in my new bedroom in front of its wall of glass, with my same comfy pale gold brocade Chippendale chair with the same ottoman, and the same table beside it on which sat the same oriental lamp. That is where I now would spend my very early mornings and late evenings. And this beautiful October, I would be spending some of my downtime on either the balcony off the living room, where I viewed the spectacular city lights to the south, or the balcony off my bedroom, where I had a different but equally beautiful view beyond the magnificent treetops and overlooking the north part of the city as far as the eye could see.

Each day of my new life was peaceful and became even more restful and enjoyable in this condo. I was on an exciting love journey to complete recovery with the One who never disappoints but stays faithful to His promises: "… I will not in any way fail you *nor* give you up, *nor* leave you without support. [I will] not, [I will] not, [I will] not in any degree leave you helpless *nor* forsake *nor* let [you] down (relax my hold on you)! [Assuredly not!]" (Heb. 13:5b AMP).

One Sunday months later when my sons came for dinner, I asked Michael how his part-time business was doing. Sadly and regretfully, he told me that he would have to close the All-American Muscle Company, for which he was a high-performance car designer. After he designed the special features and ordered the parts, his service contacts did the mechanical installations. Because Michael received such satisfaction from this work, the news broke my heart. It seemed that though it was great for him to have more clients, it was also difficult, since it created an operation that was becoming too high volume with his having to go to school and work a full-time job as well—and too expensive, without a large enough cash flow.

Immediately I thought perhaps his father would want to help him with a loan or invest in the company since it had such promise. But I did not tell Michael what I was thinking. I hoped by now, with so much water under the bridge between Alex and me, that he would be receptive to my request. Perhaps he now would want to help our son achieve in his own business just as he himself had achieved, and to feel the same satisfaction and to reap some of the same rewards he himself had enjoyed.

The next evening after work, I changed clothes and sat on my balcony to read my mail; then I settled in my special corner with my novel to relax a little before Laura arrived home and we would cook dinner together. I thought again about Michael's having to close his business, and without consulting with him first, I picked up the telephone and dialed Alex's number.

When he answered, I got right to the point, explaining my reason for calling. Instead of responding the way I had hoped, he immediately screamed into my ear: "No! I won't help him. I won't help any of you … I hate your guts! I hate the sound of your voice … I hate everything you stand for, and I won't be happy until you're dead!"

He slammed the receiver in my ear.

By now, having lived in constant and complete peace, the shock of his hateful, cruel tone of voice and threatening words shook me to the core. It felt like a curse had been pronounced upon me. Now I was especially grateful to be in this twenty-four-hour manned security building.

For the next couple of days, Alex's words kept resonating in my mind. I would shudder with cold chills and pray in my prayer language until the fear left. If not for the Lord's totally delivering me from my ex-husband's tormenting words and assuring me with *His Word* that I had *His protection,* I would have been afraid to leave my condo. Isaiah 54 was still gloriously working in my behalf: "You shall be far from even the thought of oppression or destruction, for you shall not fear, and from terror, for it shall not come near you. Behold, they may gather together and stir up strife, but it is not from Me. Whoever stirs up strife against you shall fall and surrender to you… No weapon formed against you shall prosper. And every tongue that shall rise against you in judgment you shall show to be in the wrong" (Isa. 54:14b–15, 17a AMP.)

Alex clearly had not improved, nor was he any more sensitive or generous with all the money he now had. In spite of his own company's financial success, he was not willing to share the blessings, even with his son, to help him possibly achieve that same level of success.

Unhappily, Michael had to close what had the potential to be a financially successful full-time business. However, although no longer working his business, he still got pleasure from displaying his own prized 1986 Turbo Buick T-Type at car shows. He had purchased it new and with his high-performance design knowledge had taken it beyond factory performance to legal and off-road high performance Stage 4, which is what his license plate read. He was proud of it and maintained its pristine condition.

I never told Michael I had made a request of his father to invest in his company and that he had rejected that request. Having gone to school and completed a four-year program, Michael was now reaping the rewards of his hard work as a journeyman union industrial electrician. Yes, Michael was doing just fine—it was Alex's loss!

It was hard to believe after my phone call when Alex, or I should say Mr. Hyde, spewed out his hatred on me that he would ever have the nerve to talk to me again. Nevertheless, with Alex's dual nature, he would call me from time to time about one thing or another, just as though he had never spoken those terrible words, and always got around to expressing his regrets for his choices. Because of the children, I wanted to remain amicable. But I was uncomfortable with his innuendos about reconciliation. I never responded or continued that line of conversation.

Alex was still living with his girlfriend, so when he called one day to ask me to go to Florida with him and suggested we buy a home somewhere on the water, which had been our retirement plan, and proposed that we start our life over again, I was stunned. Nonetheless, I knew that was not God's will for me. I declined his offer.

Only a couple of weeks later—in fact, the very day of what would have been our wedding anniversary—a thought came to mind that it was all quite sad because Alex, or rather Dr. Jekyll, obviously still loved me; and it was a shame for our family because the two of us one day in the not-too-distant future would be sharing grandchildren. Instantly words passed through my mind: *Daughter, do not look back. I have released you. He is married to another woman.*

I was taken aback, because of his recent request for reconciliation. But I quickly came to my senses and realized that with those words, God was helping me get my mind and emotions back on track with reality—and revealing new truth.

Because the children had not mentioned their father's having remarried, the next time I spoke with Laura, I asked her. She said, "No, Mother. If Dad was married, I would know about it."

Soon Laura phoned in a huff. "Mother, you can't believe it! I was in the dentist's office today, and the assistant told me she was surprised to learn about Dad's remarriage! I said, 'No, he's not married.' She said, 'Yes he is; I met his wife.' Can you believe it,

Mom? He didn't even have the courtesy to tell us first! I had to learn it from a dental assistant!"

I was sorry she had to learn such news in our family dentist's office. It had been not only shocking for her but also embarrassing. But I was not shocked. I learned that immediately after the day I had turned down Alex's proposal, he secretly married his paramour. Now God's words played over in my mind: *Daughter, do not look back. I have released you. He is married to another woman.* Nothing is hidden from God.

As for me, now with the confirmation of Alex's remarriage, I felt even freer that evening while sitting in my special corner thinking about the whole bizarre thing. My thoughts centered again on Laura's disappointment and embarrassment over getting the news of her dad's marriage the way she did. But I had to admit I was glad Alex was remarried.

It might have appeared to others that Alex's life was going better than mine now that he had remarried and I was still alone. But those people could not have known that after our divorce, although Alex had been living with his girlfriend, he had also been trying to get me back up until the time he remarried.

But I did not care what other people thought. I knew the life I had was a successful and a fulfilling life. My confidence in God was solid. I thought with Alex's remarriage, that chapter of my life was now closed. I believed God had a plan and purpose for me and that I would go on to live out my unique destiny.

After Alex remarried, I had only two occasions to see him. Alex and I did have necessary phone conversations about the children from time to time. Once with the upside of his split personality, he even phoned me to discuss the new will and trust he had had his attorney draw up. I refused to listen and reminded him that he had a wife to discuss it with. He responded with some unkind, derogatory remarks about her, and I retorted with, "Alex, you should be ashamed of yourself, saying that about your wife."

He just laughed and said, "Well, it's true. I can't talk to her about these things."

I could not help but silently consider some sarcastic remarks I wanted to throw back at him. But I controlled that urge—and my tongue. Like so many other times, that phone conversation ended with Alex's innuendos about regrets for his choices.

When I think of one specific time his telephone conversation ended with words of regret, I once again realize the power that our choices—and consequences—have. Laura was speaking with her father on the phone.

When I was aware they were ending their conversation, I whispered for Laurie to ask her dad for me if he knew of a car dealership and salesman from whom I could feel safe to buy a used car. Ten minutes after their conversation ended, Alex phoned me. I was surprised to learn he had already spoken with the car salesman he deals with and told me the gentleman would be calling. I thanked him for acting so quickly.

Surprisingly, he went on to say, "Alisha, I'm so grieved inside."

"What do you mean, Alex? Are you ill?"

"No. I'm grieved over us. You could have been driving a Cadillac … and we could have had our home on the water in Florida now … the way we always planned."

His words were stunning. He had expressed his regrets before, and that was uncomfortable. But now I realized he was still living with those same regrets even after being married to that younger woman he just had to have. His statement was very sad to hear.

"Alex, don't look back. Neither of us can look back. You made life choices that changed our lives forever."

"I know … I know," he softly answered.

It was an awkward silence.

"We can't undo what has been done," I finally said, "We can only go forward … but, Alex, I do appreciate your having contacted your salesman for me. Thanks again. Take care of yourself. Good-bye."

"Yes, okay." He paused then said, "You too," ending with a tone of sadness in his voice.

It made me ponder yet again how important our life choices are. Sometimes, once made, they are hard to change. Oh yes, Jesus is always ready to forgive us if we repent, and He will put us back on course to live a Christian life. But sadly, the regrets for the consequences of our choices might be felt for the rest of our lives. I hoped Alex's regrets would not be permanent.

Chapter 19

New Things

The Holy Spirit began gently leading me into the new things He had promised, which turned out to be more than leading me to my high-rise condo. After God Himself had made the way for me to move into Summit Place, I never gave a thought to its prestigious address or the affluent people who might live in the building. It was just the condo I knew God had led me to live in.

But then I became acquainted with my neighbor in the building, the wife of a United States senator. Over time I met the senator and other residents who were notables. I was also meeting more affluent people outside my residential building. I knew I was out of their league; they were in a social and economic realm altogether different from mine.

After all, I was from a simple upbringing, and during my twenty-six years of marriage, I had been a full-time wife, mother, and home-maker. From the age of thirty when I was born again, outside of socializing within the circles of family, close friends, and Christian gatherings where I fellowshipped or was invited to speak, and with the exception of my husband's work-related social events throughout the years, I had not stepped into any other social circles.

Nonetheless, these new prominent people I was meeting were befriending *me*. Curiously enough, I did not feel intimidated by them; in fact, I felt impressed to share my testimony of Jesus with some of them. There was no doubt in my mind that the Holy Spirit was at work and that God had created these divine appointments.

One night I was wondering about all of this and what God was doing with my life. Instantly I had a flashback of the time my girlfriend and I, as naïve eighteen-year-olds, had vacationed on Miami Beach and spent time people-watching at the world-famous Fountain Blue Hotel—only observing the affluent, who were guests. Although we had known we were out of our class, at the same time, curiously, we felt comfortable among those people and were not intimidated.

Then I had flashes of other times before marriage when I had worked for the association and in my position interacted with public figures in my job and its related social gatherings, mixing with the higher echelon. Then followed a flash of my former director and members of her association's board of trustees, and Judge and Anne Stahl—all of whom had sought me out and become my life-long friends. I was not in their social and economic classes either.

But what exactly was God showing me? I wondered. Then instantly I realized God wanted me to see that He had allowed me to be in those past circumstances and experience those acquaintances and relationships in preparation for this time in my life. I felt impressed with the thought that without my having a clue, God had been molding me for such a time as this in my life—that of sharing Christ with these precious, prominent people whom He loves. I understood what had been happening for me was an awesome revelation of the truth of God's Word: "Your eyes saw my unformed substance, and in Your book all the days [of my life] were written before ever they took shape, when as yet there was none of them" (Ps. 139:16 AMP).

More exciting "new things" began happening for me. Sometimes they were scary, because they took me out of my mental, emotional, and spiritual comfort zone. But at the same time, these new things would be the very things that would continue to stretch and mature me spiritually—and they would always bless me. God was definitely orchestrating my life.

Now God was opening the doors and leading me into other new venues to share Christ. I received an invitation to speak at a Business and Professional Women's Club banquet. I knew there had been press releases about the event, because some friends told me they had read in the newspaper that I would be the guest speaker. Personally, I knew very little about the club and nothing about the program for the evening, and just showed up at the time I was expected. The large banquet room was filled to capacity. As I sat at the speaker's table, during dinner I looked out over that audience of lovely, well-dressed, and well-educated career women, and suddenly I was struck with fear.

Oh God, what am I going to say tonight to women like these? They are probably all college graduates, accomplished and successful. I don't know how I was selected to be their speaker. Who am I to be speaking to them?

I got really nervous. I started perspiring. I was aware that I was in full view of everyone in the room, and they could easily detect my facial expressions and see every move of my body. I forced myself to regain my composure and tried to display some poise and self-control — while in truth, I was ready to fall apart.

As usual I had nothing prepared. I had nothing to speak about except Jesus. At this moment, I doubted if these women were expecting to hear the gospel from their speaker. The longer I stared at those faces, the more fearful I became.

I always prayed about my invitations, and I had felt impressed God wanted me to accept this one. But now looking at the faces of these women, I realized I was definitely out of my comfort zone. Always when I shared with groups of women, they came expecting to hear my testimony or biblical teachings.

Shamefully, I started trying to think of some reason I could politely excuse myself and leave before the program started. I quickly knew I could not lie. So that was out. But the nearer to the end of the dinner it got, the more fearful I became. *Please, Lord, give me Your confidence and Your strength to do this. Please fill my mouth with Your words. You've never failed me yet, but, oh, I hope I don't make a fool of myself!*

Instantly I felt God's peace within and ever so gently words came: *Have no fear, My daughter, for when I open a door for you to speak, it is because Jesus is going in after some of His sheep.*

The fear left instantly.

From the time I was introduced and stood at the microphone before that sophisticated group with their eyes focused on me, I cannot remember one word I spoke for the next thirty minutes. But afterward there was a crowd around me thanking me for my "beautiful words," and a line formed of women who either wanted my prayers or wanted to tell me about their own experiences with God. There was no doubt in my mind: that night, in that place, while I spoke, *Jesus had gone in after some of His sheep.*

When I arrived home, I was still feeling the excitement of the evening. I knew that was an experience I would not soon forget. I slipped into my robe, made myself a cup of green tea, and took it to my special corner. Turning on the light with one hand and simultaneously setting the cup and saucer on the table, I slid back into my chair. Stretching my legs out, I put my feet on the ottoman to completely relax. With my head back, I went over every detail about the evening in my mind.

It was such an unusual experience, but oh, how God the Holy Spirit had ministered to me, without anyone in the whole room knowing my trepidation, overcoming it with those precious words! Repeating those words in my mind, I was awestruck by them all over again and reached for my journal to record the whole event, including those powerful words, and closed with:

Although I don't know where God will send me next or what type group I will be standing before, I do know I will not be afraid of their faces. I will remember God's words to me this night for as long as I live. More later …

* * *

I was perfectly happy in my job as director of sales, when unexpectedly I was offered a different job, which was selecting, organizing, and hosting group tours for a financial investor group. The only hitch was that I had to take a very large cut in salary, because the tours would be all-expenses-paid trips for me. Although I knew neither how to plan group tour destinations and accommodations nor how to host them, I was assured I would be thoroughly trained and would not only learn the tour business but also would love it. Because of the Lord and that profit on my home, my monthly income could be supplemented. I reasoned that in lieu of a large enough salary, I would have travel opportunities that might never be opened to me again. With that, I accepted the job.

I worked for a wonderful woman who I would later learn was a born-again Christian. She hosted the overseas tours, which I desired to do one day as well. While learning the tour business, I traveled to fascinating places. It was hard work but offered me exciting life experiences. I enjoyed the people who joined the tours, the educational experience, and the historical and other beautiful sites offered by cities in America.

As the months went by, my life was busy. In addition to my full-time job, I was working part-time, doing occasional design jobs for an interior decorating firm. Nevertheless, God continued opening doors to extraordinary experiences, exciting *new things* of which I would never have dreamed. The pleasant memory of one of those experiences comes to mind.

I received an invitation to be the chairperson for the 1988 American Lung Association's corporate fund-raising event, a black-tie gala to be held in the ballroom of the Hyatt Regency Hotel. One of my cherished friends, Glyn, believed in me, and she believed I could do it. Actually, she was the one responsible for my receiving this invitation.

Laura also was enthusiastic about the fact that her mother had been invited to fill, what she considered to be, a prestigious position. She told me she was certain I could handle it, even though she knew I had no experience in this area.

However, I was not so sure I could plan and carry off such a big event. Nonetheless, because Laurie agreed with Glyn, I knew I needed to earnestly pray about it, not only because it was a type project I had never attempted, but also because it would require a big commitment of my time and energy. Then I remembered the retirement dinner-dance party I had planned for my former boss lady and friend, which turned out to be a success. Afterward, I felt impressed that I should accept the invitation.

Fortunately, I knew business professionals with varied talents and abilities, who kindly accepted my invitations to chair committees, and others who were willing to serve on committees. Planning the event proved to be fun and a satisfying diversion for me.

The gala plans were completed, and the day arrived when I was scheduled to address the corporate fund-raising committee. That morning I was feeling anxious about it as I sat in my special corner drinking my second cup of coffee. I wanted to deliver a good presentation. While dressing, I got a case of the jitters. I told myself I should not feel intimidated at the prospect of doing this, because I was certain I was in God's will. Nevertheless, my nervousness persisted. The meeting was only two hours away.

Then the memory came of that time when I was frightened to my toes to speak before the Business and Professional Women's Club. I remembered the paralyzing fear and God's words that overcame that fear right before I was introduced to speak, and how I had promised myself and God that in the future I would try never again to fear the faces of people.

Also, I recalled that lesson had not been learned too soon, as it had prepared me for an event that had followed. I was invited to be the keynote speaker for the World Day of Prayer observance in which twenty-six different Christian churches were participating. And near the altar of the largest church in our city sat church dignitaries—Roman Catholic monsignors and priests as well as Protestant bishops and ministers of those various denominations—listening to me! Not fearing the faces of people was important for me to remember that day speaking before those church luminaries.

Today, again, it was important for me not to fear the faces of those who made up the corporate fund-raising committee to which I would report. Then a Scripture came to mind, and I silently repeated it; and as I did, my confidence was reinforced: "I can do all things through Christ which strengtheneth me" (Phil. 4:13). Later that morning, in the boardroom of one of our city's most prestigious law firms, I stood without fear before chief executive officers and presidents of some of the largest corporations in the city and state to present our gala plans and my matrix for accomplishing them within budget.

The gala was a social and financial success, bringing in thousands of dollars for the American Lung Association's pulmonary research, and drew an impressive audience of corporate executives and notables in our city and state. The success of the event did something for me too. A special blessing was finding that I had put together and led an impressive team of professionals who had worked hard, made a great contribution, and had a lot of fun doing it. The experience spiritually conditioned me to believe I could succeed in whatever ventures might challenge me in the future. I found that the Amplified Bible gives emphasis to God's promise of Christ strengthening me to do all things as it is written, "… I am ready for anything and equal to anything through Him Who infuses inner strength into me: I am self-sufficient in Christ's sufficiency" (Phil. 4:13). These *new things* were a dramatic reminder of the healing and restoration in my life.

* * *

At that time, Laura and I were still enjoying living together. We both worked hectic schedules, and Laura's job as a stockbroker for a large national securities company was especially demanding; but we spent precious times together some evenings and on Saturdays. On Sundays, oftentimes the boys came for dinner. Laurie would soon be moving to her own place. I had mixed emotions: I was happy for her, but at the same time, I would miss her terribly. And I would be completely alone for the first time in my life.

Afterward, the condo felt too big, too empty. Once the usual cleaning and other household responsibilities were done, I found I spent most of my weekdays after work on one of my two balconies, weather permitting, or in my special corner. One evening I decided I did not need all this space. I would be perfectly happy in a small one-bedroom unit.

I had learned experientially over the years that God is interested in everything in and about a believer's life, so one night I was praying about when to sell my place and a fair price to ask. A figure popped into my mind. I gasped. *That's so much more than I paid for it, Lord. Am I hearing You correctly?* During the time I had lived in this condo, I had not even put a paintbrush to it.

Because I have never believed that my every thought is from God—on the contrary, it could be my own thought or vain imagining—I released that price from my mind. By now I knew from Scripture that if it were from God, it would come to pass.

I listed my condo with a real estate agent who, interestingly, priced it higher. However, my listing contract ran out without my condo being sold. Obviously, my timing to sell was not God's time. I had missed the mark.

That was okay, though; I did not crumble over it. I had already learned that God is gentle with His children, and when I do misinterpret His lead, He gets me back on course somehow. I simply reminded myself that all things work together for good for those who love God, and opened my Amplified Bible to read that Scripture verse: "We are assured *and* know that [God being a partner in their labor] all things work together *and* are [fitting into a plan] for good to *and* for those who love God and are called according to [His] design *and* purpose" (Rom. 8:28). Then I released the sale of my condo to God's will and time.

One evening soon after, I entered my building, stepped into the elevator, and greeted a resident who was new to the building. She knew my place was for sale and mentioned she had overheard a conversation between two residents, one of whom was looking to buy a different condo; but she did not know them. Immediately, James, a recent widower, flashed into my mind.

Two weeks later on a Saturday morning, I was sitting on my balcony reading my Bible when James popped into my mind again. His wife and I had attended a Christian women's fellowship meeting together a few months before she passed away. She and her husband had lived in the building several years in one of the largest three-bedroom units. A thought came to mind: *I wonder if James would want to scale down to less space, since he's alone.*

The thought did not leave me, so on faith I telephoned James and asked him that question, explaining that my condo was for sale.

"As a matter of fact, Alisha, yes, I have been thinking about scaling down to a smaller unit. May I see yours this morning?"

Thirty minutes later, he was knocking on my door. After James took a walk through the unit, he joined me in the living room.

"Alisha, I like your condo," James said. "I want to buy it."

"You do?" I answered with surprise. "That's wonderful. I'm glad it meets your needs."

"Just give me a fair price, and I'll pay it," he said. "No haggling." He grinned at me and leaned back in his chair, waiting for my answer.

He took me by surprise, and suddenly I could not think straight. *A fair price, Lord? What should I say?* Immediately the price that had popped into my mind months before came to mind again. I took a deep breath and in faith spoke it.

"That's a fair price," James said. "You've just sold a condo!"

James left, and I praised God for his faithfulness. I quickly worked the sale figures on paper, and after my seller expenses, I would still gain quite a profit.

Again, in thirty days I needed to vacate. I learned that a real estate agent who lived in the building had a one-bedroom unit listed, so I requested a showing. When the agent unlocked the door and we walked in, I gasped. It was the same unit the Holy Spirit had led me to view two years before. I knew instantly that it was perfect and signed the contract right then.

That evening the owner telephoned me saying, "Alisha, I was thrilled to see your name on the contract. I had been praying that God would make my unit desirable to a Christian."

I was amazed. In this high-rise with its 178 condos on twenty-two floors, I had purchased the unit owned by the Christian woman who had befriended me when I first moved into the building. Interestingly, she had introduced me to the wife of James, who bought my unit.

The three of us had attended a Christian women's fellowship together a few months before. She had not known I was planning to sell my condo, nor had I known she had put hers on the market. In fact, she and I had not been to each other's homes, since we met in the lobby when we went to the meeting; so I did not realize the one-bedroom condo was hers.

She marveled when I told her that the Holy Spirit had led me to view her unit two years before, and as a result of that leading, her real estate agent at that time had sold my home on the lake. She told me when her listing ran out back then, she had not put it back on the market until recently. Between the sale of my condo to James and my purchase of hers, God met the needs of three of His believers.

The principles of God's Word were working in my behalf. I had faithfully tithed 10 percent of my monthly net income and had given offerings for the Lord's work since my divorce; however, I never gave to receive money. God was blessing me in many other ways too. I knew God was righting the wrong done to me with Alex's financial deceptions.

Also, I knew God's promise to people who tithe was true and sure: "Bring all the tithes (the whole tenth of your income) into the storehouse, that there may be food in My house, and prove Me now by it, says the Lord of hosts, if I will not pour you out a blessing, that there shall not be room enough to receive it" (Mal. 3:10 AMP).

"Give, and it shall be given unto you; good measure, pressed down, and shaken together, and running over, shall men give into your bosom. For with the same measure that ye mete withal it shall be measured to you again" (Luke 6:38).

With God the Holy Spirit's direction, He was causing me to make good financial decisions that were blessing me. And I was being blessed in other ways as well, because I was really enjoying my tour travel. During that time while hosting a lovely land and cruise tour to Alaska, on one of those relaxing July early mornings on the ship, I was sitting on the deck reading my Bible when I had the distinct impression that soon I would be leaving this tour travel position for yet another *new thing*. I did not know if that thought was from God or my imagination, so I did what I always do. I released it to God.

Then in October, my tour group was at the elegant and lavish Greenbrier Inn, set in the mountains above White Sulphur Springs, West Virginia. It was the third time I had been to this historical inn.

It boasted of being a favorite place for rest and relaxation for several U. S. presidents.

On this tour, as on other visits, during the early morning before the activities for the day started, I was sitting alone on the portico, praying, reading my Bible, and writing in my journal, inspired by the magnificent fall scenery of nature surrounding me. Unexpectedly the thought popped into my mind again that God was preparing me to move into a *new thing*. I wondered what exactly that would be. No answer came.

My time was at a premium with my tour job, plus doing occasional interior design work; and now added to my schedule on the weekends was driving my aging parents to the many places they needed to go; including, banks and grocery shopping.

One day I had a thought about operating my own design business. But I was not sure the thought was from God. Nonetheless, the more I considered it, the more I realized the advantages of owning my own business and having the freedom to work my own hours. As an independent designer, I could work from home with catalogs and samples and have the freedom to take care of Mom and Dad's needs, should they increase over time.

Because of working part-time for the design firm, I knew how the interior design process worked. Once my design plan was approved by the customer and the items were ordered, I had free time before delivery and installation. For that reason, the notion of owning my own design company made perfect sense to me.

A couple of weeks later, I was on tour when I knew in my heart and spirit that this tour was my last one. It was a knowing I could not explain to anyone else. Nevertheless, I was confident that the knowing was from God. Since He leads one step at a time, I would wait for God to show me when to take the next step.

Soon I felt impressed to resign from both my full-time and part-time jobs. I finished my design work in progress for clients and told them that I was resigning.

Three days later, I awakened and felt compelled to go downtown to the government administration offices to purchase a vendor's license and register the name of my own design company. And so that morning, I took a step of faith, and The Art of Living Interiors was born, a complete commercial and residential decorating service. I believed God had gently guided me toward this full-time career that would provide for me financially, and I could also manage my own time to be available, should my parents need me.

My sister, Mary, and her family lived out of town, and my brother, CJ, was still working full-time. Now it was comforting to know that when Mom and Dad needed more help, I was already positioned with the freedom to give it because of God's plan for me.

I did not advertise for work, but almost immediately I began receiving referrals from former clients at my part-time design job. From then on, all my work came by referral from satisfied customers. The Holy Spirit directed my thoughts to begin this business, but I had to use my intelligence, common sense, and hard work to operate it successfully, to make a living.

Once I read a piece by Mac Hammond, who wrote in his Winners Minute newsletter: "Some people think faith and reason are incompatible. They believe you must check your intellect at the church house door. But they're wrong. The truth of God's Word will stand up to the most rigorous scrutiny. You don't have to lay aside your questions to begin a relationship with God. In fact, He extends to us an open invitation to explore His truth. In Isaiah 1:18, He says, 'Come now, and let us reason together.' The great author C. S. Lewis once wrote: 'Anyone who endeavors to be a Christian will soon find his intelligence being sharpened. You are embarking on something that is going to take the whole of you, brains and all.' "

The Lord was faithful to the promises He had made me when our divorce settlement was being negotiated, and He directed me to read Hebrews 13 again: "For He [God] Himself has said, I will not in any way fail you *nor* give you up *nor* leave you without support. [I will] not. [I will] not. [I will] not in any degree leave you helpless *nor* forsake *nor* let [you] down (relax My hold on you)! Assuredly not!" (v. 5b AMP).

I was still alone as a divorcée in my middle years, but *God had not left me nor relaxed His hold on me.* Now I knew God as my provider. I planned my own time. Between placing design orders and waiting for delivery and installation, when I felt inspired to write the next pages of the book, Cara typed them. Also, God was still opening doors for my public ministry. I could see with my owning my own business, the Lord had designed a perfect plan for me to make a living, to benefit my parents, and to serve Him. I continued to enjoy working The Art of Living Interiors from home. It was a lovely period in my life, and although there were stressful times with my mother in and out of hospitals and my own challenging circumstances, God continued to show me His keeping power.

It has been said, "Life happens while we are living it." I was working hard at my business six days a week, and although doing no more than lending a hand and driving my parents to doctors, banks, and to the grocery or for other type shopping—and then squeezing in my own home and personal responsibilities—trying to do it all took a lot out of me. And when I was overly tired, it was a struggle to make myself keep going.

Many times as I prayed for more strength, I would feel my level of energy increase to lug my heavy catalogs and sample books of carpet, fabric, and wallpaper in and out of my car and into clients' homes. Some days I would begin my day without first praying for strength and would find myself wearing out. Then I would have what I call a "duh moment," when it would suddenly dawn on me to just stop—and pray.

Each time I wondered why in the world I waited until I was almost completely drained before I just asked for God's help. I knew it was written in Scripture, "You have not because you ask not." That is plain and simple. God wants us to *ask*. Always, when I finally got around to *asking*, God would answer and give me more than the physical strength to just *survive* that moment in time; He gave me *more than enough* and *over and above* what I *asked*—just as He promises in His Word.

With that remembrance, I found myself recalling a powerful example of that absolute truth in God's Word about simply asking and in faith believing. This time it involved my son Steven. The pages of Steven's life up to now had read like pages of Scripture, ever since Jesus had blessed him with a miraculous, medically confirmed healing as a young boy. Although at the time his story touched many people, now as an adult the full story is his to tell. The powerful example about simply asking God in faith believing to which I refer now took place in my home one early winter evening when Steven was a college student. His faith would be greatly tested.

After Steven turned on the gas starter in the fireplace and put a lighted match to the kindling, fire exploded in his face, blowing him across the room and catching his hair, face, and neck on fire. Steven put the fire out with his hands. When the paramedics arrived, they immediately checked him over. Then one of them quickly wrapped his head, face, and neck in yards of gauze, remarking with amazement that his hands showed no sign of burning. We were all grateful his clothing had not caught fire, which might have caused even more of a catastrophe.

I rode to the emergency room with Steven. I felt helpless as I witnessed his misery. In all of the excitement, I did not say much, but I was praying. In just a few minutes, we would arrive at the hospital.

Up to now, Steven had not spoken a word, but he had displayed a strength that marveled me because I knew his pain had to be unbearable. Then I heard a forced whisper from the open breathing space in the mass of gauze: "Ohhhh … the pain … I … can't … stand it!"

I ached for him. At that moment, I suggested that we join our faith and *ask* the Lord to work a miracle. We clasped hands to pray. I *asked* Jesus to take the pain from Steven, completely, and cause him to heal quickly. Steven managed to agree with a whispered, "Amen."

Only moments later, we arrived at the emergency room. The doctor removed the gauze, took one look at Steven's burns, and ordered the nurse to give him a shot for pain. I heard Steven tell the doctor that he did not have any pain.

My heart leaped and filled with praise. The doctor and nurse looked at each other, their eyes and faces expressing unbelief, because Steven had second-degree burns around and under his right eye and down the whole right side of his face and neck. Nevertheless, he sat there with no pain and in complete peace. The doctor looked even more closely at the burned areas. I heard him tell Steven that he was a fortunate young man, because he did not know how the eye itself had not been burned.

When the doctor finished his examination and treatment, he told Steven that it would take about six weeks for him to heal and warned that he might have scarring in the worst places. He directed Steven to see his family physician for an examination and release before going back to school and work.

The nurse removed big burned clumps from Steven's hair. Then the doctor took out a pad and wrote two prescriptions, telling Steven that one was for the pain medication he would need. Before he could tell him what the other one was for, I heard Steven say, "I won't need the pain medication." The doctor stared at him for a few moments and then shook his head in disbelief. He handed Steven the other prescription for an ointment medication and released him.

God was so good. Just as Steven and I had joined our faith together and *asked* Jesus to take the pain away completely and cause him to heal quickly, God honored Steven's own faith. He continued to feel *no pain* and was indeed *healing quickly.* He felt well enough to go back to school and work in two days, without seeing a physician first. By the end of five days, his burns were completely healed — leaving no scars. If not for his hair, almost burned to his scalp and looking like stubby wires, no one would have believed that Steven had ever been touched by fire. Neighbors, relatives, and friends who saw him after he was burned were totally amazed with his complete and rapid recovery.

Although Steven had received minor injuries in baseball and football over the years and had the usual cold or flu bugs from time to time, God had not intervened with divine healing for those conditions. However, when we *asked* our *ultimate* source, Jesus, to help Steven, He miraculously worked in my son's behalf a second time to do what would have been impossible for man, just as it is written in Scripture: "And He (*Jesus*) said, 'What is impossible with men is possible with God'" (Luke 18:27 AMP).

I had learned to depend on God's faithfulness to His Word — that "all things work together for good for those who love God and are called according to His purpose." So there were always lessons to learn, not only from bad times, but also from good times.

The Art of Living Interiors was providing me with a good living. In fact, the business was doing so well, I came to the place where more and more clients were requesting my services. I knew I could no longer handle the workload alone. By the end of that third year, I was facing another decision: to either move the operation from my home to a rented building or shop and hire one or more designers to handle the increase and expand the business, or to close it.

It was amazing that before that decision was even made, the Lord went before me by opening to me another door of employment with the local ABC television network affiliate. I was offered a position, but with an apology from the general manager, who was interviewing me, that it paid less than he knew my experience would demand. He was right. The salary was much less than I had been earning. Silently, I reasoned, *That will not be an issue if the company can meet my needs.* I knew the only way to test whether this was indeed the door God had opened for me was to be honest and tell the GM the terms by which I would accept the job at that lower salary.

When I explained that I would, only occasionally, need time off during working hours to take my elderly parents to doctor appointments, for medical tests, or to be with them should they be hospitalized, the GM readily agreed, as did the man who would be my immediate supervisor. This was unheard of in business. At least I had never heard of it. But my God knew I had to support myself, and He knew the heart of my employer and the very job that would benefit not only me but also my parents. Within two weeks I had closed my business — relieving me of the responsibilities of expanding — and started my new and very interesting position.

This extraordinary job offered me new, exciting experiences as well. Our station sponsored and promoted various events that I was able to attend with VIP tickets for myself and one guest — everything from Broadway theater to the opera and symphony, jazz concerts, and other musical extravaganzas like that of Tony Bennett, Bette Midler, and Cher, to name a few. And just in the course of doing my job, I met some of the theatrical and musical stars at cast parties or at our station when they were interviewed. My job was one of the most enjoyable in memory, and these perks that came with it were such fun. It was a great time in my life. I was given much favor during my tenure at the television station. And my GM and supervisor kept their word to me regarding my parents, as my father was hospitalized twice and I was given time off to be with him.

Again, after I had dealt with a hard situation with my parents, it seemed an opportunity for another new thing, a beautiful experience, would open to me.

My daughter and son-in-law, Robert, live out of state, and Laurie and I decided to meet in New York City during my vacation. We stayed at the Waldorf Astoria. It was nostalgic for me to experience some of the places I had visited in my youth. We had a wonderful time browsing book stores, antique shops, and Tiffany's, and shopping at Bergdorf Goodman, Bloomingdale's, and the other stores I had enjoyed.

Because I was an employee of ABC, our station's promotions director arranged for us to have tickets to network shows and to tour ABC and meet some of the personnel, and then to watch Peter Jennings in the studio delivering the evening news. My daughter and I had a delightful time experiencing the New York City I remembered, as well as the New York City we discovered together.

Another time God granted me a long-time desire when my sister, her husband, and son, and my daughter, Laura, and I vacationed in Italy, visiting cities from Milan to Florence, Venice, Pompeii, Rome, and Vatican City and traveling the Amalfi Coast to Sorrento and the Isle of Capri. They all offered simply breathtaking sites. I felt so blessed to have such an opportunity. What pleasures! Just as God had promised me in His Word, He was favoring me more abundantly than I ever could have thought, imagined, or dreamed.

Soon one of my greatest blessings came when my father was hospitalized for a serious colon surgery, leaving him with a colostomy. At that time, I was both humbled and blessed when Dad privately asked me to pray for him and he accepted Jesus Christ as his personal Savior, entrusting his remaining years to Him. This was one more precious testimony to God's ongoing faithfulness to the power of His redemption and His generous supply of grace upon grace.

Now the days became more precarious for my parents. However, they stubbornly chose to remain in their home. My siblings and I respected their determination to hold onto their independence, but that presented more concern for us. My sister, Mary, still lived in another city, so our parents' needs continued to be the shared responsibility of CJ and me. We spent a great deal of time running back and forth between our homes and our parents' home to do whatever they needed. Whenever possible, Mary pitched in to help them, as did some of the grandchildren.

Though I was doing no more than sharing our parents' caregiving, without enough free time to even take care of chores in my own home, I had to push myself to accomplish it all. That took a lot out of me. However, I would not have had it any other way because I wanted to be there for my aged parents. No matter how difficult, I knew I would never regret that.

But possibly it did not occur to others just how hard that was on me. Unlike my brother, who was retired by now, I worked every day because I had to work. I did not have a choice, if I wanted to eat and pay my bills. Whenever I was at my parents' home to take care of their needs, again, unlike CJ, I did not have a spouse at my own home taking care of my responsibilities. No one was picking up the slack for me. That was a rough time.

I found at middle age, my energy was tapped out by the time my workweek was over and Saturday and Sunday rolled around to be with my parents. Nevertheless, I had to keep going on my weekends, whether or not I needed rest. Back then when things became especially stressful, I believe I existed on prayer—asking Jesus for a big dose of physical strength to do everything I needed to do—and with God's help, I managed. I found during those difficult times, relief always came in one form or another; and I would find myself favored with another promised new thing.

Laura called me at work one day and asked, "Mother, can you get your vacation next month? I'm taking you to Paris for your birthday!" I gasped. My brother said he could handle things with Mom and Dad.

Laurie and I traveled on our own for ten days around Paris, the city of light. We drank in Paris, with all its historic and beautiful sites, including the Eiffel Tower, Notre Dame Cathedral, the Louvre Museum, the Ritz Hotel, and many other places synonymous with Paris. We also toured Versailles, which is the walled town outside Paris, with its magnificent royal chateau built by King Louis XIV. It was a fabulous vacation, and I thanked my daughter profusely for my lovely birthday gift. I was blessed beyond words.

During this period of time, Laura had been urging me to retire and visit her more, or to at least spend my winters with her in the South. I always missed my daughter. We missed each other. Giving up time visiting with my own daughter over the years in order to remain partial caregiver to my parents had been hard on both of us.

After many exciting and rewarding years with the television station, I did finally retire in September 2001. When I told my brother I now desired to spend time with Laura, I think he was sensitive to that because he had a married daughter who had lived out of state. Now CJ assured me he could handle things for Mom and Dad if I wanted to spend the winter with my daughter and son-in-law. Our plan was that when I came home in the spring, I would take over with my parents, and he and his wife would be free to travel or use that spring and summer whatever way they chose.

Winter 2001 with Laurie and Robert was such a pleasure. I always enjoyed my son-in-law as much as I enjoyed my daughter. They have a very peaceful household. They are both great hosts and very accommodating. Knowing my commitment of time to my parents and the stress and concern for their aging and medical problems, my daughter insisted that I take time to completely rest. She made sure I had no obligations to be anywhere or to do anything I did not feel like doing. What generosity of heart!

It was the only time since I was twenty-three and married that I was not taking care of the needs of someone else in some way. And I realized it was the only period when I had time to just concentrate on what I wanted to do. At first it was not easy to slip into that mode of self-caring, but once I did, it felt comforting. I realized I needed that time to give myself.

From the time I was born again, I had lived with inner joy and peace, but I had been under severe stress for many years, and that could not have been good for my body. I felt this was an important time for me to completely de-stress.

It was not only a winter of complete R & R, but also great fun. My daughter and I traveled to Palm Beach, Florida, to enjoy a delightful week together at the Breakers Hotel & Resort, an extraordinary oceanfront hotel with a luxurious spa. We included shopping on Worth Avenue.

And Laurie planned something more as part of my treat: we toured the internationally renowned Edna Hibel Museum in which her own work is exhibited. Laura knew Edna Hibel was not only my favorite living American artist, but my all-time favorite American artist whose work is in demand by collectors internationally and is exhibited in prestigious museums, galleries, universities, and palaces throughout the world. I had purchased her fine art years ago, before she became world-famous as she is now.

Laura and Robert together entertained me royally, taking me to new and interesting sites. And of course, during my stay, Laura and I did all our other favorite mother-daughter activities. Happily, my visit with them was the most restful period I had known in years. It was one of the most pleasurable winters of my entire life. Also, that particular winter with Laura caused me to know beyond a shadow of a doubt that God not only wants to give His children their hearts' desires, but He also wants them to do more than merely *survive* their trials of life. Rather, He wants them to *thrive!*

Chapter 20

Favor: God Keeps His Promises

Returning home from Laurie's, it became clear that the R & R I had enjoyed was not a coincidence, but once again it had been God's faithful preparation for what was ahead.

The events that unfolded during the following months ushered me into a new and painful season of my life. The trials of health issues and unbearable grief and loss are more than I am ready to write about here, but suffice it to say I eventually knew victory in each situation because of the unfailing love of Jesus who helped me to *begin again*...and *again*...and *again*.

By God's grace I was back on my feet and ready to meet a new challenge by 2004, when my aged parents agreed to move into my home. I had the privilege of caring for my father 24/7, with the help of hospice and my sister, when she could be there. Mom helped me as much as she could at age ninety-seven to take care of Dad's daily colostomy needs. We kept him bathed and clean-shaven and resting on fresh bed linens every day. Those were the most gratifying and simultaneously the hardest times I think I have ever lived.

My strength was completely sapped by the end of each day. And because Dad was awake off and on throughout the night, I slept fitfully, always listening for his call. Each morning I would think I could not get out of bed and put one foot in front of the other. But I would pray for God to give me strength, and as I began my routine, doing the next thing I had to do, I could feel strength come to my body. I have learned God does not just give us strength, but *God is our strength.*

It was just after New Year's Day 2005 when I awakened one morning with a start, and immediately, without any forethought, "the book" was in my mind. The shocking thought came that I should begin writing a new draft of my story. Some time before, the word *restructure* had come to me about the book. I did not have a clue what that meant or how to restructure it, but I was sure that word was from God. When I had prayed about the book from time to time, I had always felt impressed to wait. Now the timing for writing a new draft simply made no sense to me. I did not want to grieve God by arguing, but I found myself doing just that: *How can this be possible, Lord? This has to be the very worst time for You to ask this of me.*

It would be a difficult task to tackle in the midst of such a tough, complicated time of daily caregiving. I went on to silently reason with God: *Surely, Lord, You know I don't have enough hours in the day to squeeze in one extra household task, much less taking on the enormous project of restructuring the material I have already written and writing a new draft of my manuscript.*

I did not know how in the world I would do this, but I did know from past experiences that every time God called me to do something for Him, the Holy Spirit always provided everything I needed to do it. So I released it all to the Lord.

Even though I had done no serious writing for the book in a long time, only adding a new page here and there to my first draft, I had never stopped writing in my personal journals.

Remarkably, God inspired me to begin reading some of those journals, which got me started writing again. Using them as reference, I began to write in the evenings after my father and mother were settled for the night.

Although I wrote late in the evenings and sometimes into the wee hours of the morning, all the time I worked at restructuring my first draft and wrote new pages, I felt as though a covering of peace rested over me and I was being revived. While caring for my dad, the Lord continued to bless me by redeeming the time to write as I walked through the difficult months with the strength, patience, and peace that can come only from God. The fact that with the Lord's help I worked on this book while nursing my father amazes me still.

Then one July evening in 2005, my Dad passed on to be with the Lord as peacefully as he had lived his 99½ years, while holding the hand of my mother, his wife of seventy-eight years. My mother remains with me.

During this time devoted to the care of my parents, except for brief phone conversations, I had little time to be with my friends, I was unable to attend my special fellowships, and I was no longer able to accept invitations to share publicly. I was definitely out of the loop, so to speak.

In April 2006, I invited some of my closest Christian friends to gather at my home for lunch and fellowship: Dottie, Cara, Glyn, Judy, and Susie. It was wonderful. Both Cara and Judy lived out of town, so they stayed overnight. The next morning I was telling them about previously hearing from God to restructure my manuscript, and more recently feeling impressed to begin writing a new draft, which I had been working on ever since.

Judy listened and responded, "Alisha, I feel impressed to help you." Then unexpectedly she went on to say, "I know a computer guy. I'm going to have him build a computer for you. It will be so much faster and easier for you to write your new material."

I was flabbergasted—and grateful. Within the month, that computer expert had transferred everything from my old computer to the new one he built for me. It was exactly what I needed. Just as she promised, Judy took me from the dark ages of using a 1983 PC into the twenty-first century of computer hi-tech! Judy also volunteered to help in any other way she could, and her assistance and encouragement was invaluable to me.

Six months later, God even fulfilled my desire of over twenty years when Judy and I were able to visit Israel. The timing was perfect, since Mother was staying with my sister. Not only was it a dream come true to tour the Holy Land, but as often happens, God had more in mind than just the trip itself.

It was November 12, 2006, when we arrived in Israel—but our luggage did not. Immediately we made a claim with El Al Airlines and hoped our luggage would come in on a later flight. That first night after dinner, Judy and I met three lovely ladies from Trinidad, the West Indies, who were also with our tour. I invited them to join us. One of them, a beautiful young gal named Phyllis, overheard me remark to Judy that I was not sure how I was going to walk the tour the next day without my walking shoes, which were packed in my lost suitcase.

"What size shoe do you wear?" Phyllis asked. When I told her, she said, "I have an extra pair of shoes you can wear," and she went on to explain that she had bought them on a whim and slipped them into her suitcase even though she had already packed a couple of pairs of walking shoes. She smiled, "Now I know why I bought them. They are *your* shoes!"

I was delighted and grateful when, in her room, she handed me the spanking brand-new Easy Spirit tennis shoes. Minutes later when we arrived in our own room, almost immediately the telephone rang. It was Phyllis. She said, "God knows exactly where your luggage is, Alisha, but it is lost, I believe, because God is going to use it as a testimony." I did not have a clue how that could be, but I thanked her again.

As it turned out, although we were told each day that our luggage would be there the next day, we never did get our luggage. That meant no change of clothes and no makeup. Unwilling to forego a day of touring to shop for clothing, we spent our evenings washing out the same clothes and wearing them each day. Fortunately, Judy and I had both dressed in layers for the flight, so we could vary our outfits a bit each day. We were just grateful for hot showers, soap, a hair dryer, and a room with a balcony on which to hang our wet clothing overnight.

Each morning at eight o'clock, we happily boarded our Bus 6, feeling a little damp—and sometimes very damp—but always looking forward to the inspiring agenda for the day. Although it was not always easy to put on damp clothes, we found many reasons to laugh over our situation and to laugh at ourselves. We found out we could live just fine without our "war paint" and a different outfit every day. We never lost our joy! In fact, we had lots of laughs with our fellow travelers on Bus 6 as well.

After the last dinner of our tour, we boarded our bus for the drive to the airport to depart Israel, and on the way, our escort announced that his microphone was open for anyone who wanted to tell what the highlight of the tour had been for them. Several took the microphone. Then a lovely woman named Patricia walked to the front of the bus and spoke into the mike:

"What has impressed me on this tour has been Alisha and Judy …"

What? Judy and I looked at each other, puzzled. Both of us wondered, *What on earth does she mean, and what is she going to say?*

"Their luggage was lost," she went on, "but I never heard them complain. I can't imagine what it would be like to be without my clothes and everything else I need for this entire trip! They've been happy and laughing throughout this tour. They've been a testimony to all of us. In fact, none of us could grumble about anything, with them on our bus!" The whole group applauded. Phyllis's words had indeed been fulfilled.

Oh, but God had an even greater plan for all of this! Judy's luggage was found and delivered to her home the day after we returned from Israel, but I never did receive mine. Immediately I mailed claim forms to El Al and Continental Airlines, but to no avail. My claims and numerous phone calls were never addressed. Finally, after a few months, I stopped calling altogether, and I just accepted the notion that my luggage was gone forever. I rationalized that my suitcase contained only things—nothing of value compared to what is eternal.

But God is so good. Ten months later, while working on this book, I had a major decision to make regarding publication. When praying about it, I felt impressed of what I thought was my answer, but then I began to question if perhaps this was my own thought or imagining. The word *sign* came to my mind, but I dismissed it because I had never asked God for a sign for any reason and did not plan to do that now.

The next morning I awakened early and began praying about the decision I needed to make soon, saying, *Lord, I have to know what to do.* Then the word *sign* was suddenly in the forefront of my mind again.

Jesus, I began praying, *I don't want to seem unbelieving by asking You for a sign now after I have believed and trusted You all this time, but I really want to be certain I'm in Your will ...* I paused for a moment, wondering what exactly I should ask the sign to be. At once and totally unexpectedly, my lost luggage, which I had not thought about for months, came to mind, and in faith I asked: *Lord, let my long-gone, lost luggage be found and returned to me soon as a sign that the thought I received in prayer was my answer from You and I am on the right track to make it my decision.* Then I released it to God.

Amazingly, two weeks later on a Sunday morning, I received a phone call from an employee of British Airways. She announced that my luggage had been sitting in London, England, for months with no ID. Obviously, the leather strap that held my ID had broken free.

She went on to tell me that just the day before, one of the employees had finally decided to open my suitcase and look inside, where my name and address were clearly displayed on a paper right on top, as I had left it. When I shared these details with those I had kept in touch with from the Israel trip, we praised the Lord as this, too, seemed part of the *testimony* Phyllis had spoken of originally and which God had brought about in His time.

Given the whole story, I am astounded that my luggage was sitting in London, England, for ten months, since London was not even in our flight pattern. I cannot get over the fact that God obviously kept my luggage safe in London before orchestrating its return—having used particular people and airplanes in His time frame to get my sign to me regarding the very book you are holding.

You have already read on previous pages about my desire to know God and His ways, and perhaps your spirit is inspired to know His ways too. This story about my lost and found luggage is another clear demonstration by the Holy Spirit of God's ways. I have learned that God has no limits. His miraculous works come in a million different ways—even through a simple piece of lost luggage! God can do anything, as Luke writes in his gospel: "The things which are impossible with man *are* possible with God" (Luke 18:27).

* * *

God has continued to fill the pages of my life with His love, His presence, and His guidance. There have been new and different testings for me as a single woman. I have stood on my own feet and walked out my new life, but never alone. Because of God's unfailing love, I have been able to walk on in joy—and in a great state of mind as I make my way with dignity.

I never forget that even in the midst of so many blessings, I continue to live in a fallen world where anything can happen to change life in an instant. But regardless of what might come along to challenge the mental, physical, emotional, or spiritual soundness I am enjoying right now in this season of my life, I can count on God's unfailing love and His promises to see me through to victory.

I have learned that while the Bible does not guarantee us a smooth, untroubled, crisis-free walk, each of us who calls Jesus Lord is guaranteed that victory if our faith is solid in Him. I have also learned that with God's unique plan for my life lived out thus far, His Word and the power of the Holy Spirit will not only take me through to the other side of any suffering in the human experience, but it will also give me my best life to live each and every day. With that assurance, I will never be afraid of what tomorrow might bring. And with that same assurance, I have let go of yesterday.

In comparison to my former life, I feel I am standing on the mountaintop. But there is nothing super spiritual about me or where I am in my Christian life. I know I am still on the "potter's wheel," being molded by God's hands. I am still a work in progress.

In the molding process, I will undoubtedly struggle from time to time, but with the Holy Spirit's help, I will stay on that divine wheel where I am being designed to be more than my mind tells me I am capable of being. I have confidence that God knows what He is doing. And so I will yield to God's conforming process, because I know with His molding, I will be a little more changed—not perfect, but a little closer to being the complete woman God created me to be.

I know now how God molds and shapes me. It is with acquiring more knowledge of His Word and allowing the Holy Spirit to experientially work a little more of God's character into my life through more testing of my faith. We never have to fear God's conforming process. God desires to make His changes at the deepest level, in our inward parts—our heart, mind, soul, and spirit—to develop our character, to renew our mind, to build healthy emotions, and to grow our faith, so that no matter what we face personally or whatever is going on in the world around us, we will be established in Christ and will not be shaken.

We never know how much faith we have in God, His principles, and promises in the Bible until we are tested. Many of us falter at times, and emotional wounds that have healed still cause us an occasional limp; but none of us ever really walks alone through our testing and spiritual growth.

Knowing that I am a long way from perfection, I desire to remain teachable. I understand that it is not how we start walking God's path for our life, but it is how we finish walking it that counts.

The kind of hard circumstances I have endured are not unique to me. *Walking wounded* women all over the world are going through the same kinds of things, maybe worse. They are wives, mothers, daughters, sisters, grandmothers, neighbors, and friends, who are suffering behind closed doors as I did. During my thirty-plus years of public ministry, over and over I have heard the heartbreaking stories of emotionally wounded women, too embarrassed to expose their problems to anyone—not even to their pastors or Christian friends—too ashamed to ask for any help at all. And I have known their pain and shame.

In my ministry of the Word to these women, I also can promise them that they are not alone. And I can promise them that if they will place the full weight of their hard circumstances, their very lives, on Jesus Christ and His Word, the Holy Spirit will lead them through to the other side of their pain, shame, and hard circumstances, just as He did for me. I can assure them God has designed a good plan and purpose for them, as He has for all His children.

However, none of God's children can make choices for others, not for a spouse or even a child, because each of us is responsible to make our own choice whether to trust God and His Word for our lives. We each have a destiny to live out. No one can live out my destiny, and I cannot live out another's. We must each choose to trust our heavenly Father.

Some of the women to whom I minister have not had a loving biological father they could trust; therefore, I have found it is sometimes harder for them to get their minds around the unconditional love God has for them. Always I can promise them that God is the ultimate, perfect Father. He does not give empty promises. He gives His children promises in the Bible that are unique to their circumstances—promises He intends to make good on, if they will trust Him to do so.

My faith in Christ and His Word remains simple and uncomplicated. I feel I am a blessed woman for merely having taken God at His Word. I am just an ordinary woman who chooses to place her faith in an extraordinary God. But I do not take lightly the price Jesus Christ paid for my salvation, my life here on Earth, and my eternal life.

I could cry when I see a painting of a white-skinned Jesus hanging on the cross, with a crown of thorns on His head, spikes in His hands and feet, a spear-punctured wound to His side, and only a few streaks of blood coming from those ruptures in His body. Then I want to shout, "No! That's not a true picture of my Jesus!" In that rendering of Him, His wounds and the blood coming from them look like a finger looks when it is pricked, with a small trickle of blood running from it.

One who calls himself or herself a believer must see the truth of Jesus Christ's crucifixion on the cross—what He really suffered for our sins, for our salvation, and healing—beginning with that crown of thorns shoved onto His head that dug into His scalp, and those thirty-nine stripes that slashed deep into His flesh, ripping open the skin on His back. He had to have been a mass of blood before He was ever laid on that cross and spikes were hammered into His hands and feet to hold Him there. Even so, none of His bones were broken.

The truth is, Jesus was not clean like that painting depicts. Common sense would tell us His blood had to have been gushing from every rupture, gash, rip, and puncture throughout His body, including the wound in His side. Christ's blood had to have poured from the top of His head down to His nailed feet, covering His entire body, spilling and running from the base of that cross. None of us should be ignorant. We were bought with a high price.

I cannot forget the words in the Gospel of Luke between Jesus and one of the two thieves crucified on either side of Him. The thief recognized Jesus for who He is and said, "Lord, remember me when thou comest into thy kingdom. And Jesus said unto him, 'Verily I say unto thee, today shalt thou be with Me in paradise'" (Luke 23:42–43).

What mercy Jesus has! It reminds us all that it is never too late. No one is beyond forgiveness. Hearts that ache in silence are heard in heaven. Whether we acknowledge love from others or even accept and love ourselves, always, always, always, we are loved from above.

Truly we live in the greatest, most exciting hour in history to pursue happiness, success, and prosperity; but even so, for some of us, our souls are not prospering and peace eludes us because we are also living in our most dangerous hour, with the threat of terrorism. It is an hour when it appears that the enemy of God and of everything good and decent is spewing out the vilest of every evil imaginable against us. Widespread serious social ills such as abuse of all kinds, domestic violence, infidelity, addictions and perversions of all kinds, crimes against women and children, and other insidious ills are rampant in our society and contributing to the breakdown of the traditional family.

From my own experience, I urge you, if you or any member of your family is subject to spousal abuse and domestic violence or any form of abuse or violence, to believe God does not want you to stay in your abusive circumstances. I know beyond a shadow of doubt that God does not want one of His children to be a victim of abuse and violence, nor does He want one of His children to be the perpetrator of abuse and violence toward another. No one deserves to be abused for any reason. The good news is, however, that the love, healing, and deliverance of Jesus Christ are not only offered to the victim of abuse, but they are offered to the abuser as well.

Even those who are not victims of these social ills live with other difficult issues, since this is an hour in which anxiety and pressures are moment-by-moment realities for most people. In his book on stress, author, Dr. Richard Swenson, wrote, "No people in the history of humankind has ever had to live with the stressors we have acting upon us today."

If there was ever an hour in which we needed peace and a power greater than ourselves as individuals and as a society, it is now. A minister of the gospel once said, "With God's peace you can live in the eye of the hurricane of life." He was not speaking of the world's peace that is dependent on everything going well. Rather, he was speaking of the Prince of Peace, the very presence of peace Himself, who remains with us in the worst of times and the best of times.

If you do not yet know this Prince of Peace, Jesus Christ, as your personal Savior and Lord, I hope that by reading my story, you now are convinced that He *does know you*, just as He knew me when I was yet unaware. Also I hope that you now believe He loves you as His precious child, just as He loves me, and He wants to help you, just as He did me.

Before you began reading the first page of this book, I revealed my reason for writing it on an introductory page entitled "A Word from the Author," and I reiterate that reason here: I wrote this book to offer you not an alternative source of help for your problems, but what I have come to know as the *ultimate* source of help—Jesus Christ. While I know many helps are available and I would encourage you to take advantage of those helps as I once did, nonetheless, in writing this book, I am compelled to ask you to go one step further and try the *ultimate* source of help of Whom I speak. Because of my source of help, Jesus Christ, I was permanently freed from the pain of my past so I could *begin again*. That was years ago, and I am still free and living in God's peace. And the same freedom can be yours.

Looking back, I do not know if it was God who tried to get through to me before my wedding, with that frightening dream of my *faceless groom*, to warn me that Alex was not the man I thought he was and that I should not marry him. What I do know is that but for this union, my three beautiful children would not have been born. The other thing I clearly know is that Alex's unexpected turning from my loving Dr. Jekyll to cruel, abusive Mr. Hyde pressed me hard into the Lord until I searched for Him with all my heart and found Him.

Because of my choices, God has delivered me from every negative circumstance, and in the process, He has revealed Himself to me in miraculous ways. What I lost was only temporary anyway, but what I have gained will be mine for all eternity. So I do not look back on my life with regret. Yes, the pages of my life have been filled with many kinds of pain, but I now call them "spiritual growing pains," the kind that made me lean into my Lord for answers and guidance that no one else could give me to walk through those trials and on to where I am now. I do not despise my painful trials, for it was in those trials that I learned my most valuable emotional and spiritual growth lessons.

I believe the Bible: that it is not only the power unto salvation, but also the power to live my best life. Had I taken any other turn in my life, I might not have found the treasure of my heart, the *pearl of high price*, Jesus Christ, who daily gives me peace that surpasses all understanding—no matter what turmoil is going on around me or throughout the world. Once again, I am reminded of the psalmist's words about God's perfect knowledge of men before they are born: "Your eyes saw my unformed substance, and in Your book all the days [of my life] were written before ever they took shape, when as yet there was none of them" (Ps. 139:16 AMP).

My life continues to be satisfying and very rewarding, in spite of the fact that I remain alone on this path with no companion at my side. I do not know if God will choose to bring a husband into my life with whom to live out the rest of my years. If He does, I believe I am bound to run into him somewhere along the same path I am on. I will have to compromise neither who I am nor my faith in Christ, because God's man for me will appreciate my faith, and value and cherish me for the woman I am.

I believe the love of a man and woman in marriage is a beautiful thing, especially beautiful when the two of them are equally yoked in their Christian faith. God has given me a great capacity to love. But I believe that I, as all of us who desire to know and live God's destined purpose for our lives, must find out how to spend my love. Fortunately, I can peacefully leave this, too, in God's hands alone.

God has been faithful to His promises to me for my children. I am cognizant of the fact that had it not been for Jesus Christ, our lives might have turned out quite differently. My relationship with my children has quietly made a transition from "mother and child" to "friends." However, they show me great love and respect as their mother, for which I feel blessed.

They still make me feel they need me too. They request my prayers for their needs from time to time, and sometimes they only need me to lend a listening ear. But always they honor me by sharing their interesting lives with me. I treasure the closeness I have with each of them.

As for Alex, because of him, I have learned the most valuable spiritual growth lesson in my Christian walk. I will never take for granted, in the most humble sense, what I think I now know about God and His Word—particularly about forgiveness. I thought I did know how to *truly forgive*. I thought I had forgiven as God's Word makes clear we must do as Christians. But I, as well as my children, had to learn *true forgiveness* on a deeper level than I personally, biblically had comprehended before.

Christmas was nearing, and I was wrapping gifts the day Alex telephoned me.

"Hi, it's me." With the sound of his voice, as usual, instinctively, every muscle in my body tensed. "Alisha," he began, with gentleness in his tone, easing my posture, "you're the one person I know for certain whose prayers God hears and answers."

I was puzzled.

He nervously continued: "I am scheduled for surgery on December 28, and I'm scared to death I have cancer. The doctor has told me there's a fifty-fifty chance. I haven't told the kids. Will you please pray for me?"

"Yes, of course, Alex."

Then, after listening to the details of his physical problem, I told him that our children would want to know, emphasizing that they loved him and would want to support him with prayer too.

There was a long silence before Alex spoke again.

"Alisha, the devil broke up our family ... and he used me to do it," he said, with what I perceived to be great sadness and regret in his voice. Although it was now years after our divorce and his remarriage, I felt that confession was good for Alex.

"Please be assured, Alex, all is forgiven, and I hold no bitterness or resentment toward you." Then I quickly added, "Alex, I'm glad you felt you could turn to me to ask for prayer, but I hope you will turn to Jesus again and put your trust wholly in Him."

When I shared the news with Laura and Steven, they each expressed their concern. Michael expressed his concern too, when I told him, but afterward he was pensive. I wondered what he was thinking. Michael, whom his father had verbally assaulted during his terrible gun threat, also had, I believed, carried the deepest wounds. He detested what his father had done, but he also hated his necessary confrontation with his father, even though it had saved our lives. That had created a breach between Michael and his dad.

On Christmas evening following the festivities at my parents' home, my children and I met at Laura's place to pray for their father. We knelt in the living room around the cocktail table, held hands, and began to pray aloud, one by one.

I sensed the Holy Spirit's presence as Laura opened the prayer. I was next, and I began praying aloud for Alex's healing. Then without forethought, I heard myself praying, "Oh my Jesus, I plead for Alex ... please ... please do not hold this charge against him." Instantly I knew the Holy Spirit had pleaded forgiveness for Alex through me for the treacherous way he had treated us.

We each reacted emotionally and spiritually to those words. We also watched a miracle of healing unfold before our eyes. Michael, always stoic, began to tremble, just slightly. Then, although completely out of character for him, he broke emotionally—with tears. Immediately I had a mental picture of him as a little boy and a flashback of him as a young adult rushing his father to the wall and wrestling the gun from his hands. His father had caused Michael deep pain in more ways than one. I had the distinct impression that the Lord was sovereignly freeing and healing that part of Michael's life.

Michael's tears stopped. We were each silent as we knelt, experiencing the presence of God with us. Out of the silence, Michael began praising God, with lifted arms. It felt as though time was standing still, as the Lord ministered to him — to each of us — ministering to our hidden, painful emotional wounds inflicted upon us by Alex. God's redemption was taking place within each of us on a deeper emotional level — down to the roots!

Before now, I, as did each of the children, had believed we were fully recovered, emotionally, because we had forgiven Alex and had been living with peace regarding him. But something more was needed, something that God alone knew and only He could do for us.

Afterward we spoke of what had taken place the moment we went to our knees. I explained that I had been surprised by the words that had seemed to bypass my mind and come from my spirit. I had never been impressed to pray that way for Alex, because I thought I had forgiven him long ago. And Michael confirmed that as I prayed, he felt the pain he had felt for years leaving him.

Laura spoke. "Mother, Jesus is our example. Didn't the Holy Spirit lead you to do what Jesus did when He hung on the cross? Jesus said, 'Father, forgive them, for they know not what they do.'"

Instantly our minds felt the full impact of my prayer and now God's Word. We were grateful that Christ had worked in our hearts and spirits, because we knew that we would not want Alex to reap the same treachery that he had sown in our lives. I silently rejoiced that the faithfulness of God to my children and me had taken place just as His Word declares: "Now to Him Who, by (in consequence of) the [action of His] power that is at work within us, is able to [carry out His purpose and] do super-abundantly, far over and above all that we [dare] ask or think [infinitely beyond our highest prayers, desires, thoughts, hopes, or dreams]" (Eph. 3:20 AMP).

That late Christmas evening as I sat in my special corner with my cup of tea, I relived in my mind the details of our experience. Reaching for my journal, I wanted to record this spiritually blessed night for me and my children—and for Alex. I began by writing the words, *Merry Christmas to all and to all a good night!* After recording the whole event, I concluded with the following:

Yes, God the Holy Spirit breathed on us tonight. With His breath of the Spirit, Jesus led me to plead for Alex that God would hold no charge against him. With that, God freed Alex, thereby, freeing us too—once and for all. God taught us a deep spiritual truth tonight that I believe we could not have learned any other way—the true meaning of forgiveness: "...If you forgive the sins of anyone, they are forgiven; if you retain the sins of anyone, they are retained" (John 20:23 AMP.) Most importantly, we honestly and sincerely did not want Alex to pay for his treachery.

I can't help but think again about Alex's surprising telephone call to me the morning of our divorce, for the express purpose of thanking me for sparing his company from being legally dissolved for the division of assets, followed by his declaration of love for me, and then his sad confession: "I just can't live the Christian life ... it's too hard. You're stronger than I am, Alisha." I remember my response: "Alex, you're wrong about me. I'm not stronger than you. I couldn't make it through a day without Christ. He'll be there for you too, whenever you feel you need Him." God knows I don't rejoice in Alex's regrets for his choices and the consequences they have brought. I genuinely pray that all his future choices will bring him peace.

On this Christmas evening, the children and I prayed not only for Alex's physical healing but also for his spiritual healing—that he will make a right and permanent life choice to return to Christ. Although I still don't understand how he could turn back ... I don't question You anymore, Lord. Just as so many times over our twenty-six years of marriage when I released Alex to You, I release him to You this one last time. Tonight I am confident that the last pages of this book You spoke of were written when you led the children and me into total forgiveness for Alex. With this closure, I am free to continue moving forward, physically, emotionally, and spiritually. Now, once again, I give myself completely to You, my

Jesus, and ask You to direct the next small step You want me to take on this love journey of fulfilling my purpose—and my destiny.

We were happy to receive the good news that Alex came through his surgery just fine, and no cancer was found in his body. And the children were there for him during his convalescence. Although we still did not know how God was spiritually working in Alex's life, what we did know was that God was surely taking care of us as we yielded ourselves to Him. It had been a long, hard journey with Alex; but life was good, and God was more than faithful.

Upon reflection of the vital necessity God's Word has been to my life, I vividly recall that morning in 1984 when I was emotionally and spiritually struggling against divorce and how desperate I was for spiritual guidance and to know God's will for my life. I will never forget the Holy Spirit's *powerful* but *gentle* whisper into my spirit: *Isaiah 54.* Now I recognize that its truths of promise have brought me into complete recovery and have all been proven: "No weapon that is formed against you shall prosper, and every tongue that shall rise against you in judgment you shall show to be in the wrong. This [peace, righteousness, security, triumph over opposition] is the heritage of the servants of the Lord ... this is the righteousness or the vindication which they obtain from Me [this is that which I impart to them as their justification] says the Lord" (v. 17 AMP).

* * *

It is a beautiful early fall evening in 2007, as I sit in my special corner, sipping my piping hot green tea, enjoying the private oasis I have created for myself. I now know that I have indeed not only lived out, but have written the "last pages" of my life with Alex. You have also seen that God continues to write new and different challenges and testings as well as exciting new experiences on the pages of my life. By His amazing grace and His unfailing love, I will walk on in joy to live my best life with dignity.

Before laying down my pen, I want to leave you with these closing words of hope: God has not promised any of us an easy life.

On the contrary, all our lives will undoubtedly be filled with trials, testings and challenges on every side. But never forget that God is faithful! He not only keeps His promises to us and takes us through to the other side of each problem, but also He gives us favor with *joy unspeakable and full of glory.* When we allow Him to lead us, He rewards us with blessings beyond compare.

God is also no respecter of persons. Recovery and wholeness have not been worked into my life because I am someone special, nor has Christ done miraculous works in my life and used me to tell others about them because I am exceptional in any way. I am absolutely no different from you. It is simply the result of believing God's Word and trusting His promise to perform it in my life according to His will.

The Holy Spirit has led me step by step in completing the book you are holding. As you have read the miraculous pages God has written in my life, I pray you have not seen me on these pages, but Jesus Christ. I hope you recognize by your own inner conscience that you have been reading truth on these pages, and I pray you will invite Jesus into your heart and trust Him to write the miraculous pages of your own life.

I feel blessed beyond words with God's grace as I fulfill what I believe to be my God-driven purpose: to write my story for you. Whether you are among the *walking wounded* women longing for much-needed hope, healing and wholeness or living an ideal but empty life and longing for purpose, I encourage you to learn to know the living God intimately and to believe His promises in the Bible are true. I pray that each of these pages has glorified Jesus Christ and has blessed you and that they have inspired you to believe that with God's help, *you can begin again.*

Breinigsville, PA USA
10 June 2010
239638BV00002B/15/P